Starving on a Full Stomach

To David + Gina,
to strong winds
and
stout hearts

from a new friend
for, I hope, all time

Diana

29 Sept. 2001

RECONSIDERATIONS IN
SOUTHERN AFRICAN HISTORY

Richard Elphick and Jeffrey Butler, editors

Starving on a Full Stomach

Hunger and the Triumph

of Cultural Racism in

Modern South Africa

Diana Wylie

University Press of Virginia

Charlottesville and London

The University Press of Virginia
© 2001 by the Rector and Visitors of the University of Virginia
All rights reserved
Printed in the United States of America
First published in 2001

∞ The paper used in this publication meets the minimum requirements of the American National Standard for Information Sciences—Permanence of Paper for Printed Library Materials, ANSI Z39.48-1984.

Library of Congress Cataloging-in-Publication Data

Wylie, Diana [date]
   Starving on a full stomach : hunger and the triumph of cultural racism in modern South Africa / Diana Wylie.
      p. cm. — (Reconsiderations in southern African history)
   Includes bibliographical references and index.
      ISBN 0-8139-2047-7 — ISBN 0-8139-2068-X (pbk.)
      1. Malnutrition—South Africa—History—20th century. 2. Famines—South Africa—History—20th century. 3. Nutrition policy—South Africa—History—20th century. 4. South Africa—Race relations—History—20th century. 5. Racism—South Africa—History—20th century. I. Title. II. Series.
   RA645.N87 W95 2001
   363.8'0968—dc21   00-012981

In memory of RER (1920–1999) and THM (1948–1985)
and
In celebration of Xenia and Duncan

Contents

Part Three
People without Science: A Modern Rationale for White Supremacy

Part Four
The Triumph of Scientism and Cultural Essentialism

Illustrations

Preface

I STARTED TO WORK on this book before Nelson Mandela was released from prison, and I completed it nine years afterward. The book bears the mark of that great transition in South African history: because the project began when the apartheid state had lost a good deal of legitimacy, but not power, I wanted in the 1980s to expose its damages; after 1990, it became easier to ask how apartheid had managed to survive for so long. The history of racism could be more readily examined, instead of dismissed as loathsome.

The genesis of the book lies in stories that had been piling up in my memory from the beginning of my seven years in Africa. They remained simply memories until 1986. Then I began to research the history of food in South Africa because I believed the subject would allow me to understand better the human consequences of an industrial revolution that took place in a colonial setting. Since I was completing a detailed case study of one chiefdom, I now wanted a large canvas; I admired one painted richly by Jack Goody when he depicted cooking, cuisine, and class throughout the world as well as another, equally rich, by Sidney Mintz when he took on sugar in his epic, *Sweetness and Power.* Once I made my decision for these abstract reasons, the stories flooded back to consciousness, infusing me with energy and curiosity.

The germ of the project was probably planted in my imagination as I sat in Heathrow airport in 1979 waiting for the flight that would take me to southern Africa for the first time. Perhaps to display her benevolence, an elderly Anglo–South African lady began to address me on the subject of the food black South Africans eat. "We are trying to teach them to eat brown bread," she said, "but they insist on white." During the months and years that followed, I heard this tone of weary paternalism again and again. Usually it was repudiated by younger white South Africans who remembered with distaste the signs on butcher shops that in their youth had jointly advertised Dogs' Meat, Boys' Meat. They also remembered the jokes their parents had told about African diet and manners. (How much sugar did Hastings Banda ask P. W. Botha to put in his tea? Two spoons in a cup, five spoons when he drank from a jam tin.) Nearly any discussion among whites about African food seemed burdened with either guilt or condescension. The subject was bringing home to me in an appropriately visceral way what it meant to be dominant or subordinate in a rigidly hierarchical society.

Since my destination in 1979 was actually Botswana rather than white South Africa, I was soon challenged by African assumptions about my own diet and manners. Staying with a Tswana family in a small village in the Kweneng, I was admonished by my hostess when I assumed that the porridge I couldn't eat would be thrown away; food was not to be wasted, and it was to be respected. I had been guilty of bad manners. One evening her daughter cautioned me that I would not want to eat their supper because it was, she stressed, "an OLD cock." When she lifted the lid off the three-legged iron pot, I discovered that age mattered less to me than the sight of the entirety of the old bird simmering—head, beak, eyes, feet. Avoiding waste was easy, but paying respect involved forcing myself to jump over great divides of custom and habit. Sometimes those leaps required faith that I would not fall ill. Once, at a Tswana cattle post near the Limpopo River, I was offered milk still warm from the cow. Struggling to convey my rudimentary medical knowledge in English and Setswana, I tried to explain to my hosts my fears of the microorganisms in unpasteurized milk. Perhaps they were immune, I said, but coming from another country, I wasn't sure I was. "So, you say you are different from us," their son summed up, articulating exactly the impression I had not wanted to give. Later, in Pondoland, when I was explicitly researching diet and nutrition, I found myself instead having to insist that I did indeed want to eat Pondo food rather than sit at the table with my host and dine on Western dishes prepared especially for me. Most encounters over food seemed freighted with either heavy or amusing social significance.

These stories lay imbedded in my memory until uprooted by my decision to write a history of the past century in South Africa focusing on food as an index of the changing quality of life. That century unavoidably tells the story of the evolution of African poverty. While many new European and American books about food bear titles like "tastes of paradise," my choice of place and population ensured that paradise would hardly ever appear and that even taste would be subordinate to survival. The subject matter allowed me to gain insights into colonialism and racism that were far more intimate than research on wages or political parties usually affords. I was struck, for example, by missionaries' boldness in presuming to tell African mothers when to nurse their infants, and by industrialists' discussions of how to increase worker efficiency by improving rations, as if raising wages would not do the trick. Whenever I typed words related to "food" into computers at the South African government's archival depots, files concerning malnutrition and shortage would appear on the screen. Reading them, I learned how the justifications for white supremacy were changing in South Africa during its first industrial century. Quite unexpectedly, I was discovering that apartheid had nutritional roots as well as consequences.

The subject of food is virtually limitless, and so the writing of this book has demanded major exclusions. I have not written a history of manners or of food symbolism. (The meaning of neither the raw nor the cooked is discussed here.) Nineteenth-century Africans would be put out to discover that beer, considered to be liquid food, is for the most part omitted, largely because the topic is too big. Further, given the constraints of time and space, I had to decide whether to stress the social history of food, on the one hand, or the politics of hunger, on the other, and decided on the latter largely because the bulk of my data happened to tip the scale in that direction. Since *Starving on a Full Stomach* is a foray into a rather fresh field, it leaves a great deal of unexplored ground for future researchers. I hope that this book will provoke them to investigate further the southern African complexities of that coy dictum "we are what we eat."

Because I did not want to be limited by the state's views of its problems, I selected three research sites where I would be able to consult medical records and speak with Western and African doctors and their patients, as well as with local families. Each site represented one type of settlement from which African people have migrated: urban townships, periurban plots, and the rural reserves. I chose Alexandra township in Johannesburg because it has had a clinic since 1929. KwaZulu's Valley of a Thousand Hills—or more precisely the clan areas of Nyuswa and Qadi near Botha's Hill, Natal—qualifies as periurban because for several decades buses and taxis have enabled its people to commute to work in nearby Durban and Pietermaritzburg; most important, it has been home since 1951 to a health center, the Valley Trust, committed to monitoring and improving local nutritional standards. I chose the third site because it lay far from wage employment, in the roughest and most remote part of the largest African "reserve" (later "homeland"), the Transkei; a hospital named Holy Cross was founded between Lusikisiki and Flagstaff in 1920 and so I worked from there. I hope these local case studies will reveal more of what was actually occurring than policy-based discussions customarily do; despite the best intentions of their authors, official records tend mainly to reflect what the state thought ought to have been happening.

In these sites as well as in the provincial capitals where the archives are located, I was treated during my sabbatical leave from Yale University's history department in 1988–1989 to the kind hospitality for which South Africans are rightly known. I list the names of my hosts and benefactors by region in inadequate recognition of their generosity to someone they did not allow to remain a stranger for long. In the Transvaal, I was particularly helped by Mark Gevisser and his family, Horace and Eunice Mpanza, Henning van Aswegen, Susan Booysen, Tim Couzens, Johann and Jeannette Groenewald, J. D. L. Hansen, and Bruce Murray. In Natal the following people gave various kinds of aid: Adelaide Magwaza, Ruth Edgecomb, Heather Hughes and David Brown, Bill Freund, Chris and Julia Mann, Dr. Halley and Joyce Stott, Kovin Naidoo, Drs. Bruce Buchan and Margaret Barlow, and Irina Filatova. My Transkeian helpmeets included Nona Goso, Dumisa Ntsebesa, Solly Solinjani, Mr. and Mrs. Francis M. Magazi, Drs. Lizo and Nomsa Mazwai, Prue Bolus, Jeff Peires, Noma Mda, and Dr. Gerrit ter Haar. In the Cape, Sandra Klopper and Michael Godby became my family; I was also helped by Jean Le May, Rodney and Betty Davenport, Colin Murray, Diane Nash, Elizabeth van Heyningen, Patricia Davison, and Michelle van der Merwe.

While writing, I benefited from the critical advice given by members of the Southern African Research Program, the Agrarian Studies Program, the Beaumont Club, and the History of Medicine Workshop, all at Yale University; the Rodney Seminars at the African Studies Center of Boston University; seminars organized by the nutrition and history departments at Tufts University; the CRCSA-NEWSA annual conference, the Medical University of South Africa, the University of Durban-Westville, the University of the Western Cape, the University of Cape Town (anthropology seminar), the Society for the Social History of Medicine Conference on Medicine and the Colonies, and the Science and Society in Southern Africa Conference at the University of Sussex. I am especially grateful for the intellectual stimulation provided by teaching in Brian Jorgensen's core curriculum program at Boston University. I am grateful, too, for support in the form of a publishing subvention from Boston University Dean of Arts and Sciences Dennis D. Berkey. When the process of writing seemed to take far too long, Isaac Schapera helped me take the words of missionary Robert Moffat to heart, "Have patience." I want particularly to thank Colin Bundy, Jeffrey Butler, Brenda Danilowitz, Saul Dubow, Richard Elphick, Derick Fay, Susan Grace Galassi, Robert Harms, Angelique Haugerud, Peter Hawkins, Simon Heck, Russell Helms, Eugenia Herbert, Emily Honig, Jeannette Hopkins, Elizabeth Kaufman, Anne Laurence, Yusufu Lawi, Chris Lowe, Shula Marks, Colin Murray, Dana Robert, Patricia Rosenblatt, Amalia Sa'ar, Hilary Sapire, Martha Saxton, Ian Shapiro, Mugsy Spiegel, Molly Sutphen, Andrew Taylor, Howard Venable, and Heinrich von Staden. Their critical and personal help infused me with the energy to bring my memories to life in this academic form. Their friendship was my sustenance.

Starving on a Full Stomach

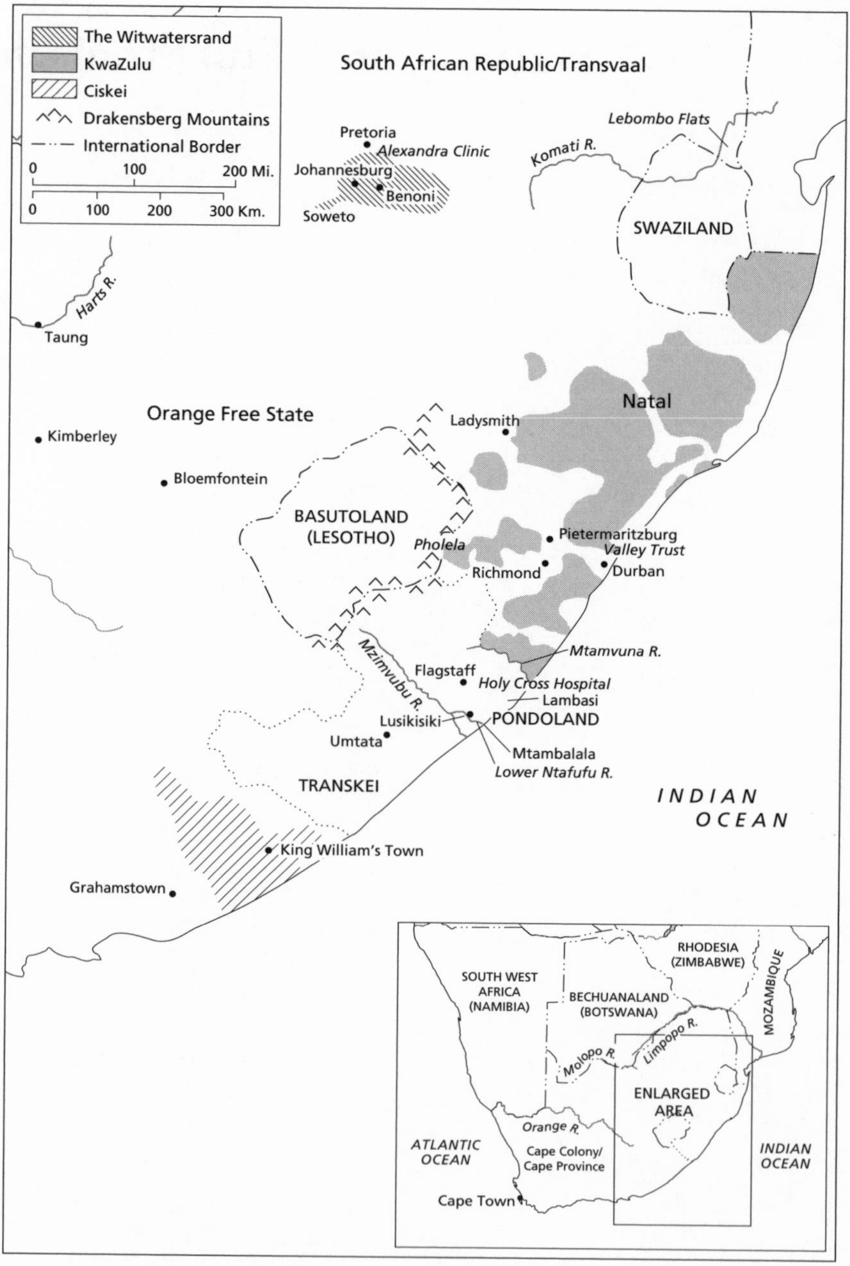
The Witwatersrand
KwaZulu
Ciskei
Drakensberg Mountains
International Border
0 100 200 Mi.
0 100 200 300 Km.
South African Republic/Transvaal
Pretoria
Alexandra Clinic
Johannesburg
Benoni
Soweto
Lebombo Flats
Komati R.
SWAZILAND
Harts R.
Taung
Natal
Orange Free State
Ladysmith
Kimberley
Bloemfontein
BASUTOLAND
(LESOTHO)
Pholela
Pietermaritzburg
Valley Trust
Richmond
Durban
Mtamvuna R.
Mzimvubu R.
Flagstaff
Holy Cross Hospital
Lambasi
Lusikisiki
PONDOLAND
Umtata
Mtambalala
Lower Ntafufu R.
TRANSKEI
INDIAN
OCEAN
King William's Town
Grahamstown
RHODESIA
(ZIMBABWE)
SOUTH WEST
AFRICA
(NAMIBIA)
BECHUANALAND
(BOTSWANA)
MOZAMBIQUE
Limpopo R.
Molopo R.
ENLARGED
AREA
Orange R.
ATLANTIC
OCEAN
Cape Colony/
Cape Province
INDIAN
OCEAN
Cape Town

South Africa

Introduction

Starving on a Full Stomach: Hunger and Ideologies of Exclusion

The Native is starving on a full stomach.

Anonymous, 1938

From the moment it became a united and independent country in 1910, South Africa was caught in a contradiction. It inherited from Great Britain the inclusive language and universal doctrines of the Enlightenment, and yet it excluded the majority of the population from participation in its political institutions. At the time, and for decades thereafter, most white South Africans lived easily with the dichotomy, partly because the racial hierarchy was hardly peculiar to the new Union, situated as it was in an imperial world and on a continent recently partitioned among the great powers of Europe.

When the twentieth century opened, many Europeans had justified their belief that the races were essentially different and unequal by citing biology. They looked at physical types and found them necessarily connected to particular cultures and languages. They delineated the boundaries of these racial categories by measuring bodies, and they fixed the resulting human typologies in time by declaring them impervious to historical change. Joined to evolutionary paradigms, these thoughts could result in the following version of South African history: "the transition from sheer savagery through various stages of barbarism to civilisation is represented . . . by the Bushmen, all hunters; the Hottentots, mainly herdsmen; the Bantus, mainly husbandmen; and the Britons, who constitute the higher cultural element."[1] The rising popularity of this scientific form of racism in Europe had coincided with the imperial partition of the tropical world beginning in the 1880s.

Scholars commonly explain the demise of the theory's popularity by citing the devastation it caused when implemented by Nazi Germany in the 1930s and 1940s.[2] After World War II many Europeans continued to feel the need to explain racial difference, and they devised new justifications for racial hierarchies. Drawing invidious distinctions among the races on the basis of their cultures became a more respectable form of racism than ranking them on the basis of their bodies and biological makeup.

In South Africa official attempts to make race domination intellectually respectable took the form of apartheid in the wake of the postwar retreat from scientific racism. The Afrikaner nationalists who gained power in 1948 used ethnos theory and the Bible to justify their programs for "separate development." Ethnos theorists argued that it is "the will of a people . . . to remain immortal as a people," meaning that each ethnic group had fixed traits that the state should help them preserve.[3] Similarly, many Dutch Reformed Church members believed that the biblical story of Ham justified their domination of Africans, though not all supporters of apartheid believed the tale was true.

Given their limited appeal, ethnos theory and conservative biblical interpretations do not explain why many ordinary whites accommodated themselves intellectually to apartheid for so long. Cultural racism, the use of racially ascribed cultural attributes to explain differences in wealth and power, appealed broadly to people who felt pride in what they believed was white achievement and virtues. It won tacit support for apartheid programs like homelands — labor reserves where Africans were required to exercise their sole political rights — even from people who otherwise considered themselves democrats.

Further, many whites must have noted reassuring similarities between apartheid-era social engineering and policies adopted by other modernizing regimes in the postwar world. Apartheid was not exactly an international aberration, though it was the last defender of a colonial racial order in Africa. It was a mutant of the modernism then sweeping the Western world. South Africa's solutions to postwar challenges — decaying cities, agricultural development, overpopulation — shared more traits with those proposed and implemented in Europe and the United States than has been commonly acknowledged. The pariah status South Africa earned by clinging to state-mandated racial privilege in a decolonizing world has tended to camouflage these similarities. The hubris of South African modernism had close kin in development plans devised in Washington and London and Paris, and after decolonization in national capitals like Dar es Salaam and Addis Ababa. In all those places, especially starting in the 1950s, bureaucrats drew up large-scale solutions to complicated social problems; they promised a rational administration that would produce wealth and leisure and a future free of conflict. James Scott has recently called the South African variant of this system "high modernist utopianism of the right," as illustrated by the state undertaking massive social engineering in the form of forced removals and homeland schemes. While the South African regime was unusually preoccupied with military security, it did share with less militarized governments a modern drive to improve "the human condition with the authority of scientific knowledge and . . . to disallow other competing sources of judgement."[4]

It might be argued that most white South Africans did not need to fashion elaborate ideological justifications for a social order from which they richly benefited. And yet, while apartheid was obviously intended to maintain white supremacy through the ancient logic of divide and rule, it constantly posed racial and cultural purity as an ideal to be preserved. Grand apartheid, or the setting up of homelands for each African "tribe," was a response to political demands, both domestic and foreign, that Africans be included as citizens within the Union of South Africa. Uprooting unemployed Africans from cities and dispatching them forcibly to rural areas where they would have their sole citizenship rights was a response to the massive urban influx of Africans that accelerated in the 1940s, and the cheapest possible means of providing some form of state welfare to the very poor. Apartheid was also a pragmatic means of serving the material interests of poor whites, Afrikaners who needed sheltered employment. The laws of the apartheid regime helped employers to keep their wage bills low, though they wreaked havoc on the health of black workers and their families.

It is not enough to enjoy these riches; people must be seen to deserve them. Conversely, social suffering must be satisfactorily explained to give credibility to the pride that, along with fear, lies at the heart of race domination.

Hunger

"The Native is starving on a full stomach," an African man replied one day in 1938 when a committee of three white men asked him to comment on the health of his fellow Africans.[5] This perplexing oxymoron offers a glimpse of people struggling to understand a world of profound social change that was impinging upon them in the most intimate ways. Modern times were affecting how their bodies felt. Working in industry, buying food, and consulting physicians were also affecting how people understood their own and each other's cultures.

Why were the white men bothering to ask about Africans' health at all? The South African government had sent them to rural areas to investigate whether many African children were "starving or undernourished." Their visit occurred at a time of mounting international alarm and publicity about nutritional well-being. In South Africa this concern was made even more pressing because its industrial revolution, begun only fifty years earlier, had suddenly disrupted people's traditional diets. Many people were concerned that Africans, in particular, were growing too weak to till the soil or to man the new mines and factories. This diffuse insecurity afflicted both blacks and whites.

What did the African man convey by his cryptic reply? He was living at a time when famine had become a danger of the past and the pangs of hunger were pinching less, at least when he had access to cash, than at times earlier in his life. And yet, he had reason to think, he was "starving" though his stomach was "full." He was probably not indulging in nostalgia for a romanticized past, though the sour milk that he had once assumed essential to his daily meals was now meager in quantity or altogether lacking. His formerly diverse diet had become monotonous. Too often he was eating his cornmeal porridge ungarnished by wild greens or meat or milk. Having lost his ancestral standards for a good life, he was living in a state of longing for new commodities and old staples. He was "starving on a full stomach."

The man was expressing one view of what it means to be poor in modern times: to have enough to survive but too little to feel secure. His precise meaning remains opaque because we do not know his identity and he did not elaborate as far as we can tell. We do know that this sensation was unique neither to him nor to his time and place. What at first sight seems to be an idiosyncratic statement is actually a vivid, nonscientific expression for what some scholars would call endemic and class-based malnutrition. Formerly, starvation was likely to lead to widespread death, but fifty years into South Africa's industrial revolution it resulted in the survival of the poor in a compromised or diminished state. Both the nameless man and southern Africa were passing through a historical transition that much of Europe had already undergone. Preindustrial forms of poverty were giving way to ones unique to industrial life: poverty used to afflict households with too few laborers to provide a decent subsistence, but now it struck those with too little cash or land.[6] The African man was reflecting on the consequences of living through this historical process.

The way some experts interpreted this process was bound up with the growth of cultural racism, the idea that Africans could be excluded from institutions because their cultures were inferior to those of whites. Many whites saw African hunger as evidence of basic cultural incompetence. If black people resisted the lessons of modern science and failed to manage their land successfully or to eat intelligently, they were making themselves outcasts from modernity.

If the poor are those who have their reality officially defined for them by others, it should come as no surprise that the experts were never the hungry themselves. The voices of authority belonged to medical doctors and researchers, social scientists, and the men responsible for administering African areas. They framed their understanding of African hunger in isolation from, and often in opposition to, African belief systems. Through their writings and their meetings with one another as well as with state officials, they helped to mold public understanding of African hunger in their times, building an image of African poverty with which the state would one day have to contend. As their professions suggest, their knowledge proved powerful because it had the weight of scientific authority behind it.

Many of the authorities on African hunger in the following chapters would probably have described themselves as political liberals. It is true that, because they were not political theorists, they did not have to answer directly the question: "[H]ow [did] liberal principles with their attending universal constituency get undermined in such a manner as to politically disenfranchise various people[?]"[7] They did, however, have to address the question of what caused hunger, and their answers had bearing on who deserved to be a citizen.

The chapters that follow investigate the thought of people who dealt with the twentieth-century South African face of this problem: how to explain the existence of poverty and, more particularly, hunger in such a way that the problem would be addressed and perhaps even solved. Most of the experts in this book struggled to frame a powerful and coherent argument linking popular nutrition, national well-being, and ethics. They were using science to make moral claims that in an earlier age would have been the work of religion. Well-intentioned people, they did sometimes endorse ideas that had damaging effects on African welfare, even while they provided the service of documenting social suffering. This book is an attempt to understand their vision and their blinders.

Paul Slack has observed that in Tudor and Stuart England the precise nature of policies toward the poor was determined by which observers gained public attention. When the clergy spoke loudest, the poor tended to be regarded as objects of charity, "targets for the pity, sympathy, generosity and sometimes admiration of their betters." When magistrates caught public and private imaginations, the poor were seen more as a threat, to be "excluded from sympathy and aid, if not eliminated altogether, in order to preserve public order, public morality and public health." When economic writers gained popularity, the poor would be viewed "as a potentially productive resource: needing only proper training in labour to yield profits for the general good."[8] What is interesting about Slack's formulation, and germane to this study, is the autonomy he gives to public opinion. He does not present it as the creature of the state, pure and simple. To understand cultural racism in South Africa we must look not only at state functionaries or apartheid ideologues, but also at the authorities they quoted, proving the defects of African culture so flagrantly apparent in African hunger.

Authorities on African hunger in twentieth-century South Africa were speaking to fellow Europeans who had long ago left behind preindustrial food values. They no longer prized quantity above the quality of food, or distributed it to advertise age and gender distinctions, as Africans still did. Rather, food—and the knowledge associated with it—had become a way of publicizing class distinctions. Africa's failure to generate its own industrial revolution, one that could have helped to end hunger on the continent, came to be seen not as the result of the conjuncture of demographic, climatic, and institutional factors, but as the result of a lack of moral traits like "enterprise" and of cultural ones like "science." As Daniel Headrick has observed, during the era of high imperialism Europeans were confusing levels of technology with levels of culture. "Easy conquests," he went on to say, "had warped the judgment of even the scientific elites."[9]

Historical Debates over Cultural Chauvinism and Scientific Hubris

During the apartheid era liberals and Marxists wrote histories of South Africa with the goal of stripping the state of legitimacy. They did so by stressing African resistance and initiative. Scholars also devoted their craft to showing how a state whose wealth was based on cheap African labor had facilitated plans devised by captains of industry to maximize their profits. Before 1990 these worthy perspectives were crucially important to discredit a regime that seemed unlikely to give up power, but the release of Nelson Mandela from prison made the effort to see how the regime managed to last so long an intriguing, as opposed to a retrograde, endeavor.

In the 1980s, white racial ideas and ideologies began to be studied as historians explored how apartheid and its segregationist antecedents had actually worked. Saul Dubow's *Racial Segregation and the Origins of Apartheid in South Africa, 1919–1936* (1989) effectively set the stage for these studies by analyzing the power of segregation as an ideology: its strength lay in ambiguity and flexibility, that is, in its power to conceal "the level of oppression which underwrote it" and its ability to define "the range of feasible political alternatives."[10] In *The Making of Apartheid, 1948–1961, Conflict and Compromise* (1991), Deborah Posel studied the making of the apartheid state between 1948 and 1961, concluding that it derived not from a grand plan, but from a process of compromise between the state and employers, whose interests were often in conflict. Ivan Evans in *Bureaucracy and Race* (1997) extended this kind of inquiry to the Native Affairs Department, arguing that its rural wing, a "vacillating liberal outpost," was overshadowed from the 1950s onward by urban planners who made the department and, most notably, the entire country into an "arrogant apartheid fortress."[11]

This book follows the path marked out by some of the above-named scholars. The final chapter investigates how the scientific and scientistic perspectives on African hunger, in particular, and poverty, in general, were articulated by the apartheid state in terms of policy. However, as Dubow cautions against in his *Scientific Racism in Modern South Africa* (1995), I do not propose that apartheid derived simply and directly from theories asserting white racial or cultural superiority. To imply baldly that European hubris produced apartheid would be to omit the whole world of material interests and political machinations. Such a teleological approach would assert that ideas bear the lion's share of responsibility for policies like segregation and apartheid. Rather,

I examine the emergence of a form of cultural racism that contributed to the ideological context within which those policies developed. I explore one way by which "whites came to persuade themselves of their innate superiority and God-given 'right to govern.'"[12]

Dubow argues that scientific racism in South Africa began to fragment and collapse in the 1930s for two reasons. He endorses the commonly accepted view that Nazism deprived the theory of biologically ordained racial difference of all respectability. He adds that the presence of poor whites made it hard for racial ideologues to claim that only nonwhites had a hereditary propensity to degenerate. Afrikaner nationalists in particular were loath to argue that poor whites were flawed biological matter; rather, they had been damaged by their deprived environments and the government's task was to "uplift" this mainly Afrikaner population.

The ascendant power of cultural racism, on the other hand, is reflected in the protracted debate over whether African poverty existed at all. The history of South African poverty began to be written in the early twentieth century with reference to both whites and blacks. In his 1919 pamphlet *The South African Agrarian Problem,* W. M. Macmillan showed that both races were victims of the way wealth was being accumulated in rural areas, but little more than a decade later a five-volume inquiry into South African poverty, funded by the Carnegie Corporation of New York, singled out poor whites. Until the 1989 publication of its sequel, *Uprooting Poverty,* also funded by Carnegie, a covert struggle was waged between those who sought to address African poverty and those who sought to deny that it existed, arguing instead that African material culture was by nature primitive.[13] This slowly dawning acceptance of African poverty as a national problem was helped along by the work of some of the researchers in this book.

Apart from South African historiography, there are two bodies of literature relevant to the issues raised by this book. They are the histories of health and food. Both literatures reflect authors struggling with cultural chauvinism and scientific hubris. Sometimes they write to praise a national cuisine or a medical discovery. They may focus, though, so narrowly on the technical causes and cures of disease that the very scope of their inquiry is in itself an advertisement of the power of science. Conversely, they may react against what they see as a retrograde orthodoxy and write primarily to debunk imperial medicine. Authors writing from the perspectives of both praise and attack seem to be embroiled in a love-hate affair with Western culture and its pretensions. Neither perspective demonstrates much curiosity in scientific and cultural pride as having force in its own right.

The hunger experts in this book, for the most part, regarded the imperial health legacy as a source of pride. They revered the dramatic medical breakthroughs of their times. It was certainly true that surgery was becoming more hygienic and drugs more powerful. There was demonstrable progress in the realm of health. The threat of famine was ending; new crops were grown locally; imported foods were available for purchase by those with access to cash.

Many writers on the history of health in twentieth-century Africa took these victories as proof that the imperial legacy stimulated progress. From the 1950s to the 1980s, Michael Gelfand, for example, published more than twenty-five volumes, many celebrating the discoveries of hero-doctors like David Livingstone. Similarly, in the 1960s, Lewis Gann and Peter Duignan drew up a balance sheet of empire whose credit columns listed prominent medical contributions.[14]

In reaction against such accounting and lionizing, a new breed of historians has exposed the metropolitan interests lying behind imperial efforts and the damage they inflicted on the health of the colonized. John Farley has shown capitalist nations expanding irrigation schemes and hence diseases caused by parasitic worms throughout the third world in the twentieth century, while Meredeth Turshen has argued that malnutrition and tropical diseases, both "products of specific historical stages of colonialism and underdevelopment," increased in colonial Tanganyika. Similarly, Andrew Mushingeh's work presents the history of health in the Bechuanaland Protectorate as the story of immiserization by noting that rates of venereal disease, for example, went up under British rule from early in the twentieth century. On the other hand, a more optimistic demographic historian, Bruce Fetter, is seeking to show that life expectancy increased throughout southern and central Africa in the 1900s. One major problem dogs all such efforts: the absence of a body of precolonial medical data to serve as a baseline for comparison with the colonial period. Thus, assessments of the imperial impact, whether indictment or praise, have the distinct air of being preconceptions or speculations.[15]

It is hard to share imperial pride or pessimism today partly because evidence about health in African history is weak. One of the attributes of the poor is that they are not counted. This commonplace is nowhere more true than in South Africa, where nearly all numerical indices that allow detailed analyses of European demographic history are missing. No one computed the national rates of infant and adult mortality, fertility, nuptiality, or causes of death for black South Africans; nor are there statistics for height indicating whether the black population has been stunted. The South African government recorded African birth and mortality statistics for virtually no rural black area. In the late 1960s it stopped registering cases of kwashiorkor after collecting them for only six years. The absence of these figures does not, for the most part, set it apart from the rest of the continent, where numbers are similarly scarce, but the numbers do exist for South Africa's three other "population groups" (whites, Coloureds [people of mixed ancestry], and Asians).

Malnutrition is difficult to measure because it is hard to define. In the late twentieth century, nutritionists conventionally identify three kinds of malnutrition with reference to the tropical world. Famine is easy to identify. It describes what happens to people when they have absolutely too little to eat: they cannot resist infection, they have to stop working, and their children no longer grow. The condition is newsworthy and forms part of the contemporary image of suffering Africa. Newspapers carry photographs of skeletal children in Somalia, Liberia, or Sierra Leone, victims of civil war in countries that have nearly ceased to exist, scratching for kernels of grain at the bottom of empty barrels. Since most residents of affluent countries experience undernutrition so little, they tend to associate the word only with such visible suffering.

A second category of malnutrition is seen in the stigmata that it leaves on the skins of the hungry. Scurvy is vitamin C deficiency, usually caused by low consumption of fresh fruits and vegetables over the course of several months. Vitamin C forms cementing substances like collagen that strengthen blood vessels and increase resistance to disease. Symptoms of the deficiency include bleeding gums, slow healing of wounds, and bleeding in the gastrointestinal tract. Pellagra or niacin deficiency appears on the skin in the form of a "butterfly mask," in rough and sore, reddened patches, often accompanied by diarrhea and depression. The deficiency commonly arises from excessive consumption of maize without significant amounts of meat, vegetables, or fish. *Vitamin A deficiency* results from a diet low in fruits and vegetables as well as low in the fat needed to absorb the vitamin. Its symptoms are persistent diarrhea and night blindness or, at worst, destruction of the eye by scarring and desiccation. Because the liver stores vitamin A, a seasonal lack of milk and meat damages health less than a persistent absence does. Protein energy malnutrition or PEM describes mainly undernourished children under the age of five and primarily between the ages of one and three years; the child fails to grow or gain weight and develops symptoms of gastroenteritis and fevers. If the child survives, there is not necessarily any long-term handicap, except possibly short stature. Two types of PEM are commonly distinguished, marasmus and kwashiorkor. In both cases, a child weighs significantly less than the expected standard for her age, has coarse, reddish hair, and has wasted muscles. Only marasmus derives from an insufficiency of food; kwashiorkor, it is now believed, afflicts infants who are trying to fight an infection while on a diet high in bulk but low in calories or protein.[16]

A third, less dramatic but more pervasive experience could be called debility or "starving on a full stomach." Due to low intake of food or a poorly balanced diet, a person is unable adequately to grow, lactate, work, bear a child, or recover from disease. Because individual needs and social expectations vary considerably, what is "adequate" cannot be defined with any precision. Good nutrition is an elusive and culturally bound concept.

Some scholars have recently tried to replace the false specificity of quantitative physiological requirements with a more embracing concept of "capacity to adapt to environmental changes without unacceptable loss of function." This scholarship focuses on "nutritional status," that is, the entire complex of the disease environment as well as public health measures, and not just the food that is actually eaten. This broad definition is justified because disease may both cause and result from malnutrition. People may consume enough nutrients but their living conditions may be so poor that they suffer from parasites or, overworked and debilitated, they are unable to stimulate their children's appetites. An emaciated child may be well fed but, after drinking unclean water, suffer from diarrhea (the most significant cause of child mortality and sickness in the third world); if she cannot retain nutrients, she may fall victim to a viral disease like measles. Unclean water is only one environmental attribute affecting nutritional status; also relevant are the number of persons living in a small space, the dust flying about in the workplace, a mother's habit of sterilizing her baby's bottle, the medical advice she has readily available, and whether her household's real income is rising or falling. As one scholar has recently argued, "[I]mproved nutritional status is not . . . evidence of improved nutrition." The converse is equally true: simply increasing the food supply will not cure malnutrition if poor housing, unemployment or low wages, and infectious diseases persist.[17] One may consume an excellent diet and still be malnourished, and the symptoms of malnutrition may be produced by more general causes than a poor diet. The diffuse and nonspecific nature of most states of malnutrition allow the concept to exercise rhetorical force often greater than it actually merits.

Despite this emerging doubt about the precise accuracy of scientific claims, including those made within a less prestigious medical subdiscipline like nutrition, they remain in many ways protected from full critical scrutiny. The dangers of scientism are still alive, even in the hands of historians who repeat the findings of the clinic, the laboratory, and the statistician as if they were necessarily true. Historians researching the human impact of apartheid and its predecessor, segregation, face an impressive array of documents, often generated by the experts who are the focus of this book. They can quote studies measuring the height and weight of schoolchildren in the 1930s. They can cite the caloric intake of Indian families in Durban in the 1950s.[18] The numbers are easy to use. They readily confirm the process of immiserization visible in the most overcrowded homelands. They support the attempts of many liberal and

Marxist historians to deny any legitimacy to state claims, especially before the early 1990s when free elections were first held. But are the statistics correct? As the following chapters will suggest, medical evidence should be approached with caution. Nutritional data often reveal more about the researchers and their social context than they reveal about the hungry themselves.

Medical pride is apparent in the way some commentators privilege medical over environmental causes of disease. Medical causes are, after all, more susceptible to a physician's intervention than political ones. Randall Packard drew attention to the conservative political implications of the failure to understand "structural contradictions in the development of racial capitalism in South Africa" in *White Plague, Black Labor,* his study of tuberculosis in South African history.[19] The experts in this book, like Packard's TB doctors, were caught up in a long-standing dilemma: How much social context needs to be known in order for a particular health problem to be understood? Can we stop at investigating food supplies, should we research agricultural systems, and what must we know about the political and economic context of those systems?

Tension between environmental and technical explanations of what ails the body has persisted throughout the intellectual tradition of Western medicine. At least as early as pre-Christian Alexandria some doctors believed that air, wind, water, work, and food should be studied, not the diseased body alone. This tension over causes has grown, especially since the seventeenth century when European doctors began to apply the laws of the basic sciences—first, chemistry and what became known as biology, then botany and physics—to their understanding of the body. In the nineteenth century, certain forms of therapy like homeopathy were devised in reaction against clinicians' tendencies to localize organically the cause and cure of disease. Some analysts feared that the environment would be forgotten as a cause of good and bad health, and holistic responses to the clinic grew as doctors investigated cells in their laboratories, gaining knowledge that their patients did not have about their own bodies. In 1848, the year that Karl Marx and Friedrich Engels published *The Communist Manifesto,* the German pathologist Rudolf Virchow (1821–1902) began trying to reorient the study of sickness away from an exclusive focus on the laboratory and toward the social conditions that produced the diseased cells; Virchow, a radical liberal, insisted that "medicine is a social science, and politics nothing else but medicine on a large scale."[20] Adoption of his perspective was limited, in part, by the rise of bacteriology in the late nineteenth century, turning attention away from individual and social behavior and toward invisible infection as the cause of sickness. Ever since, a tension has persisted between social and biological analyses of what causes ill health. Such analyses may be found in every chapter of this book, as concerned observers ranging from African doctors to apartheid planners grappled with the question of where the first cause of African weakness or sickness really lay: Was it in African ignorance of science, or was it in poverty?

Historians of medicine, social historians, and demographers have similarly debated the relative importance of medical versus environmental causes of disease. On nutrition, they have focused attention on the following question: How large a contribution did improved quality and quantity of food make to the high rate of growth of the world's population since about 1700? The scholarly tendency since the 1990s is to repudiate or at least to modify the tight causal link drawn in the 1950s by Thomas McKeown, a British medical doctor, between increased food supply and a decline in mortality from infectious diseases. McKeown was reacting against an overvaluation of the role medical doctors played in reducing mortality in the modern West and specifically against the way wonder drugs had narrowed thinking about what causes and cures disease. Physicians who adopted sulpha drugs and antibiotics in the 1940s were prone to identify and treat a single necessary cause. McKeown, in shifting perspective from this myopic fixation, retained a monocausal perspective of his own. He argued, by process of elimination rather than by explicit proof, that because more food was grown in Europe between the seventeenth and mid-nineteenth centuries than earlier, people's health must have improved and, therefore, people lived longer from the second half of the nineteenth century on.[21]

The Italian demographer Massimo Livi-Bacci recently replied to McKeown's 1976 book with a brief and trenchant counterargument, maintaining that, in the long term, mortality figures demonstrate no necessary relation between nutrition and demographic developments. Throughout history, he writes, people have generally adapted to food shortages by changing their habits. They cultivated more land, and their body sizes adjusted to the limits imposed by the environment.[22] Livi-Bacci's perspective is more appropriate to this study than McKeown's for two reasons: it takes the burden of proof off weak data about past patterns of health and food supply, and it accommodates the fact that concepts of good and bad nutrition have varied widely over time. Probably because of the pressing nature of South Africa's crisis of legitimacy during the apartheid era, its historians and social critics have tended not to acknowledge this debate and have, rather, treated malnutrition as a given.

Contemporary historical scholarship on hunger has generally emphasized unfair or damaged social structure, rather than poor food supply, as the primary killer of people. John Post, discussing the last great European subsistence crisis in the mid-eighteenth century, pointed out that neither "ignorance" of people nor shortage of food can alone explain its causes and effects. That epidemic of death resulted, Post wrote, from "social disarray and dysfunctional behavior." Diseases were spread in jails and workhouses crowded with criminals driven there by joblessness and high food prices. Infections spread during the long cold winter of 1739–1740 when people lived in close quarters, sharing their bacteria and lice. The resulting sickness appeared to result from food shortages, but it was cured only when states worked to improve the general environment of the people they governed. When public administrations set out to restrain unemployment, vagrancy, begging, and migration, and also provided food, fuel, shelter, and health care to the needy, most mortality epidemics ended. The same point has been made with reference to starvation in more recent times. During famines in the two world wars, people died in Warsaw, Holland, and Venice because of the "increased 'transmissibility' of infections resulting from upsets in the social order, overcrowding and a worsening of hygienic and environmental conditions."[23] Narrow medical history is being supplanted by a broader, environmental perspective. People engage in intense debates over how to define a "damaged" social structure and how to locate its causes.

Most popular writing on food and nutrition today exudes reverence not only for a particular bodily aesthetic standard but also for a certain kind of science: clinical, technical, quantifiable. People who write about food come from societies that enjoy plenty. They are themselves well fed. While the historical flux in ideas about proper diet and nutrition sped up with dizzying effect in the late twentieth-century West, these rapidly changing orthodoxies do not appear to have weakened popular faith in the scientifically calibrated diet. At the time of writing, margarine has been accused of contributing to high rates of cholesterol and therefore heart disease, overturning the previous orthodoxy that butter was to blame. Perhaps this fixation on the numerical values of food is a sign that those people who feel adrift in an age of waning religious faith are groping for some sense of control over their destinies. Billboards and advertising today depict fashions in food with alluring vividness and a frequency that could be called obsessional; this trait is also apparent in contemporary conversation. I imagine that never before in history have so many people spent such a large proportion of their waking hours confronting seductive images of food. Newspapers daily publicize new and contradictory insights into the meaning of the European aphorism "you are what you eat."[24] Whatever the origin of this widespread malaise, when people become fixated on such numbers as calories and cholesterol levels, they can seem grotesquely oblivious of the nonmeasurable factors, spiritual, political, economic, and environmental, that contribute to a decent or to a wretched life. I would agree with Roland Barthes that modern culture has both trivialized the issue of food and inappropriately invested it with guilt.[25]

Histories of food tend to reflect the cultural stereotypes of their authors' place of origin. Italian food histories manifest greater interest in the culture of food; British authors focus on demographics and agricultural change rather than on the evolution of taste. Histories of American food have tended to focus on the puritanical guilt with which Americans are said to invest the act of eating. It should come as no surprise that writing on food in Africa has primarily concerned famine. The only book I have come across that actually celebrates African cuisine in South Africa was published in 1982; *Funa, Food from Africa* is filled with color photographs and recipes that would mark it, in any other context, as an ordinary coffee-table book. In the African context, so pervasive is the stereotype of hunger that the book is virtually unique and now out of print.

The history of food in Africa began to be written with a social rather than a clinical bias. Audrey Richards gave it an enthusiastic curtain-raiser in 1932 when she published *Hunger and Work in a Savage Tribe,* based on her preliminary research on the Bemba of Northern Rhodesia. A preface by her teacher, Bronislaw Malinowski, said that his own work had slighted the fundamental importance of food in social organization by overemphasizing the lesser world of sex. Richards was especially concerned that male labor migration, in particular, and the cash economy, in general, were breaking down the cohesion of the extended family and effectively robbing people of their once robust diet. Richards seemed to be opening many significant avenues for sociological and historical inquiry.

One new direction was taken by Henrietta Moore and Megan Vaughan in *Cutting Down Trees* (1994), intended originally to restudy Richards's material in the light of subsequent changes in productive relations in northern Zambia.[26] The authors discovered that many of the crises perceived by Richards had not really come to pass. Rather than finding that the cash economy had caused the breakdown of productive and kinship relations, Vaughan and Moore were impressed by the flexible and innovative strategies the Bemba had devised to work the land and share resources. Quite simply, Bemba society had not broken down. The idea that it would do so, and its people would become malnourished, had been so powerful that colonial officials constructed agricultural policies on that presumption. Instead, there had been no decline in slash-and-burn agriculture; even in the 1980s people still cut down trees.

Moore and Vaughan's study is related to my own in several ways. Their book focuses on how knowledge about African social problems was constructed and changed over time, and they recognize that this knowledge intervened in the functioning of Zambian social systems. (They credit Michel Foucault with pointing the way to recognizing the indeterminacy of their sources, or, rather, the coexistence of "a multiplicity of interpretations.") Like many other scholars investigating the colonial encounter, they see Richards and other experts mutually engaged with the Bemba in a struggle over material and symbolic resources. They go on to argue that knowledge was created by both parties to the colonial encounter.[27]

Ann Stoler and Frederick Cooper have elaborated this point of view in their edited volume *Tensions of Empire* (1997), examining the exclusionary practices and inclusionary claims of colonial cultures. They argue against the Manichean dichotomies between colonizer and colonized, as popularized by Frantz Fanon, for example, by noting that the colonial world was made by both vigorous parties rather than by white domination alone. And yet, within this joint colonial endeavor, they noted that imperial condemnation of African cultural backwardness became increasingly harsh in the 1940s, a conclusion that the present study endorses. They go on to note that these new "principles of 'cultural racism' were honed as part of the intimate workings of empire in debates over domestic arrangements, the upbringing of small children, early pedagogy," and so on.[28]

I did not, however, discover a symbiotic relationship between African and imperial systems of knowledge. The experts framed their understanding of African poverty and hunger in relative isolation from what the poor and hungry thought about the origins of their plight. Except in cases of famine, there is little evidence of experts comprehending and responding to local paradigms of knowledge. The power of the laboratory and of international modes of scientific thinking was too great. On the contrary, the following chapters will reveal occasional glimpses of educated Africans being swayed by the force and authority of scientific inquiry to the point of criticizing local diet and habits of mothering and of agriculture. There are surely dangers in romanticizing folk knowledge, as if modern times had produced no tools of value for improving the quality of life. It is also dangerous to denigrate or ignore folk knowledge, tendencies that continue to characterize the new, nonracial South Africa. This aspect of cultural racism is one legacy of white supremacy that will long outlast the apartheid regime.

Racism is a protean beast, changing its shape to fit the moment, always seeking to make the elite seem dominant by natural right. At the time of conquest the urge to rationalize dominance is often at its weakest. The ancient Athenians, for example, justified their plans to subjugate the Melians by stating simply, "[We do it] because we can."[29] When the actual work of overrule begins, the dominant engage in a more elaborate intellectual exercise to justify their privileges.

This book begins by telling a version of southern African history quite different from the one associated with the rise of cultural racism. Since pride in the accomplishments of European history lay at the heart of white people's sense of their superiority, the first chapter compares European and African history with special reference to diet in order to see where their significant similarities and differences lay. The second historical chapter assesses the actual strengths and weaknesses of African food culture—the way food was produced and the values associated with it—by scrutinizing the nineteenth-century historical record.

Because white people often justified their dominance in terms of the benevolence of white rule, the second section looks at paternalism in practice. A rural chapter examines the way government officials treated people suffering from famine in order to discover how this relationship changed over time. An urban chapter looks at how social scientists tried to update paternalism, collecting more scientific information about the social order on which a welfare state might be built. Both chapters reveal paternalism being outmoded by urbanization and associated political developments of the 1940s; partly in reaction against the rising cost of providing welfare services to growing numbers of poor Africans, a new tone of impatience was infecting official interaction with all Africans, and it was expressed in cultural terms. Paternalism was becoming bankrupt as a justification for white domination.

Because the glories of modern science constituted another pillar in the ideological architecture of white supremacy, the third section examines the growing image of Africans as a people without science. Some scientific researchers and medical doctors contributed to cultural racism the idea of the malnutrition syndrome, that is, that Africans were to blame for their hunger and disease because of poor agricultural habits. The scientists' research and work nevertheless documented the damage that South Africa's particular form of industrial development had inflicted on African bodies.

Faced with evidence of this physical damage and the daunting expense of paying for its redress, the South African government after 1948 divested itself rhetorically of most claims to paternalism. It stopped using the father-son or trustee-ward language that carried promises of a shared future, and instead framed Africans' political and cultural destinies as irrevocably separate. The last chapter shows the state throwing its ideological weight behind culture as the justification for minority rule. Trying to implement the political corollary of cultural racism, it set up homelands where experts would force Africans to become, by their lights, more efficient and, therefore, self-sufficient farmers. The ferocity of its response to peasant resistance helped to kill the image of the benevolent state, but the denigrated image of African culture lived on.

When the British sociologist Paul Gilroy wrote that racism "rests on the ability to contain blacks in the present, to repress and to deny the past," he was implying that dispassionate historical inquiry could act as a potent weapon against it.[30] He was suggesting that nonpartisan study of the past can reveal not only the causes of social suffering, but also the complex reasons why cultures have produced different material and technological achievements. I try in this book to view events occurring during South Africa's first fifty years from a perspective less clouded by the social pressures afflicting those who lived through them. History can indeed be an antiracist weapon attacking the tendency that is with us always to draw invidious distinctions. And yet, I am aware that all knowledge is filtered through ideology. Like science, history is a powerful form of knowledge that can both collude with authority and undermine it. And so, I must conclude this introduction with a similarly two-faced statement of what I have tried to do: to write a correct history, fully aware that writing any history is to participate in a power game.

Part One

Cultural Racism's Fertile Ground

CHAPTER ONE

European Cultural Pride

An Evaluation

> The fortunate is seldom satisfied with the fact of being fortunate.
> Beyond this, he needs to know that he has a *right* to his good fortune.
> He wants to be convinced that he "deserves" it, and above all, that he
> deserves it in comparison with others.
>
> *Max Weber, "The Social Psychology of World Religions," 1915*

SOUTH AFRICAN CULTURAL RACISM at the dawn of the twentieth century was made up of a jumble of inherited ideas and contemporary impressions: low esteem for African material culture, intense pride in European progress since the age of the skin-clad Celts, contempt for work habits that seemed unschooled in "the dignity and the necessity of labour," as well as a strain of scientific racism expressed in disparagement of "native mental capacity."[1] This mix often emerged in statements that Africans had "a certain constitutional incapacity for continuous and sustained effort."[2]

By the 1940s new kinds of judgments were coming to dominate European attitudes toward African culture. African visitors to Fort Cox Agricultural School in the Ciskei, for example, listened to the acting principal, A. L. Vanderplanck, address them one spring day in 1941 in words as condescending and full of furious judgment as if he were an Old Testament prophet. "Today the people are reaping the harvest of all those seeds of sin sown by many of you for generations past," he said. He drew their attention to the wages of those sins: "Your stock are dying; you have to buy most of your food; your children are suffering from the effects of malnutrition." Switching his metaphor from the Bible to local techniques for identifying witches, he named the culprits, "I smell out the men and blame them for most of these sins. The men have had all the opportunities to put things right but have failed."[3] By observing that they had overstocked their land, planted their crops badly, failed to engage in

1. Proud butchers display their wares in the Pinelands Cooperative Butchery, Cape Town, 1953. (National Library, Cape Town)

cooperatives, and persisted in paying bridewealth, Vanderplanck clearly had in mind a more general menace than the men in his Ciskeian audience. The problem was African culture itself.

Vanderplanck was speaking from a pinnacle of pride in modern science. He was implying that agronomists and nutritionists had created knowledge about how to make the earth produce riches and how to keep people healthy. If African people turned away from these lessons, then they were benighted. Some of his contemporaries even called Africans "ignorant in regard to how to live."[4] By the 1940s white South African judgments of African culture had become peculiarly harsh, focusing on the twin assumptions that Africans were unhealthy and did not know how to make the land productive.

These invidious comparisons between European and African cultures were so widely and commonly drawn that few contemporary observers bothered to investigate possible reasons for their historical differences and similarities. That silence allowed for the creation of potent historical myths. All the more powerful for being unexamined, these stories tended to lie at the back of researchers' minds, providing an unconscious starting point for their inquiries.

The popular white vision of African material culture derived from the natural tendency to make invidious distinctions. It was shaped by a heritage of idealizing certain kinds of luxury, and it was enhanced by European cultural pride in industrial-era science and technology. The following two chapters attempt to deconstruct cultural racism by investigating the food histories of Europe and Africa with the express intention of avoiding an idealized view of either African or European history. Perhaps the historian's craft can unmask the process by which the South African white elite justified its racial dominance.

The Drawing of Invidious Distinctions

Food lies at the heart of group identity, as Leviticus knew. Social groups throughout time have used diet to differentiate themselves from one another. The following sample of dietary boundaries suggests how pervasive this trait is. In medieval Europe rural folk ate black bread that city dwellers would never touch, believing it made the peasants stupid. Feudal lords ate white bread baked from refined wheat flour. They ate fresh game, while peasants—people living in households deriving a large part of their subsistence from their own labor on the land—had to make do with dried or salted meat when they were lucky enough to have any at all, and the lords said it was in the peasants' nature to eat inferior old meat. Judgments about food also reflected regional and religious identities: Mediterraneans scorned the meaty diet of northern Europeans, believing that fighting and feasting reinforced one another; Protestants distinguished themselves from Catholics by rejecting Lenten abstinence and the church's war on meat. Similar stories may be found in Africa. Africans in Natal found Amatonga migrants from Delagoa Bay disgusting because they ate fish, poultry, pork, and monkey. Shangaans looked down on anyone who ground maize between stones rather than soaking it in water before pounding it, as they did. Some Zulu people today remember being told as children to be suspicious of the Sotho because they ate cats.[5]

Such distinctions grew not only from the imperatives of group solidarity but also from the need to justify the distribution of scarce commodities. These needs and the stories waxed and waned with changes occurring in a given social order. While feudal lords attributed peasants' diets to their crude natures, members of the industrial bourgeoisie blamed the poor morals and ignorance of working men and women for their physical weakness. When these time-honored attitudes were exported to the colonies, their judgments came to be expressed in racial terms. In the twentieth century modernizers used diet to prove the backwardness of peasants, especially ones who were resisting their scientific reforms.

Before the ninth century in Europe quantity rather than quality was the mark of status, the rich eating more, rather than significantly different, polentas, soups, and porridges. From about the twelfth century court life encouraged the upper classes to define themselves according to the refinement of their manners and their cuisine, rather than its quantity. When population growth drove individuals to appropriate forests and cut them down for pastures, the eating of wild food decreased; roots, bulbs, and berries came to be thought of as marginal food or, as Hildegard of Bingen wrote, "contrary to human consumption."[6] As the rich claimed the forests and the game within them for their exclusive use, they explained that they alone could eat fresh meat, while peasants would become ill if they tried.

Historians argue that these cultural boundaries sharpened in the early 1500s when rural poverty drove unprecedented numbers of peasants into town. Townsfolk were so frightened by the migrants' need that they responded with what Fernand Braudel has called "bourgeois ferocity," repressing them with new severity—shipping them into exile, closing the city gates—and treating them as parasites.[7] One example of this denigration of peasants comes from a Bolognese storyteller who expressed a common incredulity that intelligence could ever, short of a miracle, be found in the countryside; he cautioned that it would prove futile to "introduce some noble medicine through the mouth of a peasant . . . because by his nature he is accustomed to coarse and rustic foods, according to his boorish nature." Others agreed that "among men of the countryside it would be a miracle if one turned out to be of acute intelligence and prone to study, especially where such coarse foods are eaten."[8]

In the late eighteenth century more egalitarian sentiments were overriding these feudal judgments even in the realm of diet. Jean-Jacques Rousseau lambasted the "extreme inequality in our lifestyle," which had led rich and poor to degenerate from the simple and regular ways of nature; indigestion seized the rich who indulged in "overly refined foods" and the poor who stuffed their stomachs greedily.[9] Dietary ideas of the Enlightenment were expressed most famously by the French gastronome Jean Brillat-Savarin. His book *The Physiology of Taste* became a classic not only because it reflected engagingly his love of taste and the social pleasures of dining, but also because it suited the sensibilities of a new age. Brillat-Savarin depicted the senses as springing from the soul and, because all humans have souls, everyone needed to derive pleasure and health from food: "The pleasures of the table are for every man, of every land, and no matter of what place in history or society."[10] Traces of such egalitarian attitudes can be found in contemporary writings from England, too, even though the "science of gastronomy," to use Brillat-Savarin's phrase, remained less central to English culture and identity. A. F. M. Willich, lecturing in London in 1799 on the connections between diet and health, drew no distinction between the needs of rich and poor. The farmer as well as the lord, he said, would suffer alike from trying to digest "all incongruous mixtures and compositions, for instance milk and vinegar," which produce "an acid and acrid whey in the stomach, . . . an indigestible coagulated mass."[11] The human body and not its class would determine what a stomach could bear.

The new class distinctions generated by the industrial revolution modified such Enlightenment emphasis on traits held in common by all mankind. Middle-class Britons in the nineteenth century, for example, included diet among the characteristics distinguishing the deserving from the undeserving poor. The undeserving had been debauched by their appetites, wasting their money on unhealthy food and, mainly, drink. Thomas Mayhew's study of London's "street-folk" in 1849 depicted the profligate as so degraded in their "moral physiognomy" that he led his fellow countrymen to think of them as members of an alien tribe living in the heart of civilization. They had brought this degradation upon themselves by allowing their appetites to run away with them, unfettered by reason and morals. Street-folk were popularly seen, according to Gertrude Himmelfarb, as "some vestige of primeval nature . . . mocking the proud presumptions of modernity." In Mayhew's era the deserving were defined as the more virtuous "laboring poor," people who would spend their hard-earned wages on tea and bread rather than beer and chips. Forty years later Charles Booth, in *Life and Labour of the People in London,* helped refashion the image of those who deserved society's attention, making it more inclusive and less harsh. He included among the deserving poor anyone whose problems—sickness, unemployment, old age—were not of their own making. Among other remedies, middle-class social reformers proposed that these deserving poor should be fed school meals and taught to eat properly so they would not be dragged down to join the lowest of the ill-fed, drunken, and poorly clad poor.[12] Sometimes this late Victorian and Edwardian meliorist spirit was manifest in cooking classes that would teach the proletariat to avoid too many sweets.

These class attitudes slowly filtered through to the colonies over the course of the nineteenth century, though they seem initially to have been muted by admiration for natural man. Early in the century European travelers and missionaries had expressed mainly curiosity and appreciation of the food they were served in Africa. Ludwig Alberti praised the health of the AmaXhosa in 1807, perhaps even idealizing their apparent resistance to disease, and described their laudably "simple," though diverse, diet in detail. In 1856, Dr. W. H. I. Bleek found Zulu beer "when fresh is the most refreshing and pleasant beer I know" and seemed grateful for any food he was served by African families when traveling beyond Cape Town. Writing from the eastern Cape in the 1850s, John Ayliff described Xhosa cuisine fully and passed no negative comment on it. When John Mackenzie wrote about living on the Kalahari fringes in the same decade, he noted that during years of plenty, "the food of the Bechuana was such as Europeans could enjoy, and some of it would be regarded as a delicacy."[13]

There was no universally accepted and scientifically defined orthodoxy of correct diet until the twentieth century. When nutritional science was born early in the century from health crises occurring among sailors, army recruits, and factory workers, its lessons spread quickly around the globe. Modernizers of many different political stripes grabbed on to Brillat-Savarin's aphorism "Tell me what you eat, and I shall tell you what you are" and used diet as an index of progress. In places as far flung as Mexico and Mozambique, people defined modernity in terms of diet. Mexican revolutionaries in the 1930s, for example, instructed peasants to avoid "bad preparation of food, the lack of inspection of foodstuffs, and overuse of frying, of greasy, dry, and irritating foods." During the same period, the new African elite in Mozambique, the *assimilados,* were defined as those who slept in beds and did not eat maize porridge. They were modern, and peasants who subsisted on maize were not.[14] These invidious distinctions are essentially tales people tell about others' folkways, but there were indeed differences, as well as unacknowledged similarities, between African and European cuisine in preindustrial times: What were they, and why did they exist?

The Historical Foundation of Food Snobbery

Civilization is popularly defined with reference to luxury, that is to say, the monuments and pursuits of the upper classes.[15] The absence in most parts of Africa of a distinct upper-class culture has made it hard to include Africa within this popular definition of the civilized. A luxurious diet, quite different from the food eaten by the vast majority of the populace, evolved only in those areas of the continent where there was an elaborately hierarchical social structure; in Ethiopia, for example, peasants drank barley beer, while Amhara nobles sipped honey wine and flavored their stews with cloves, cinnamon, and black pepper from Zanzibar and the Far East.[16] European cuisine had borne such elaborate markers of rank and class since at least the fifteenth century when the spice trade, begun during the Crusades, had thoroughly permeated urban cooking. One index of the growing importance of cuisine may be found in European cookery books: the oldest extant ones are manuscript collections of recipes prepared in the homes of monarchs in the fourteenth century; the first printed one appeared in Latin in 1479. Only in the late seventeenth century were cookbooks available for purchase at low prices; then people of more moderate means and not only monarchs, aristocrats, and a few rich merchants could consume feasts like this one from northern Italy: red and white wine, "cakes and curds and whey with sugar confections on top," "gelatined hen," "lasagne with cheese, saffron, raisins and spices," and "fish with a pepper sauce."[17]

In none of the chiefdoms of southern Africa at any era did rulers dine so luxuriously on such diverse, imported foods. In the court of the Zulu king Shaka (1823–1828) and his successors, luxury was largeness. Shaka's mother's cooking pot for fermenting beer was said to hold sixty gallons. An important Sotho man's ox-hide calabash for holding sour milk was so heavy when full that it took six men to lift it. Luxury was also plenty. Regiments of beaded and brass-ringed girls living near Shaka's residence were kept busy carrying pitchers of beer and milk, and baskets of boiled blood and beef, to feed the king's visitors.[18] The abundance derived from tribute. The rich had to send annually to the chief's court either a cow or a part of each slaughtered beast, while ordinary people sent tribute of maize. Luxury, finally, meant the exotic. A regiment occasionally was dispatched to the coast to bring back wild bananas to the king's court.

The food cultures of ordinary people on both continents in preindustrial times were markedly similar. While southern Africans probably ate more protein in the form of milk and meat than did most preindustrial Europeans, the majority in both places had similar attitudes toward food. Most people talked about what they ate, not in the minutely calibrated way nutrition is discussed today, but with lust for feasts and fear of famine. Food meant celebration and survival.

Especially before the nineteenth century, the core of the diet of ordinary people was starch, though it could be laced about with tastes derived from meat or simple carbohydrates such as sugar or honey. Scholars estimate that until the late 1800s, and even into the twentieth century in southern Europe, people obtained at least two-thirds of their total calories from starches.[19] Except for the wealthy, the excitement of taste must have been of secondary importance. Food ranked relatively low on preindustrial scales of aesthetics, as suggested by the pragmatic tone of many African proverbs: "God made food for men to eat, not that they might worship him."[20] And it was the amount rather than the quality of food in the fabled Land of Cockaigne that rendered people delirious in medieval and early modern Europe.[21] For the vast majority who were not wealthy in preindustial times, taste was a luxury, and sufficiency was central. To be well fed was to have a stomach so full of food that hunger was kept at bay. To be hungry was to be reduced to the level of an animal, at least in the eyes of the well-off. As one southern Italian doctor described the hungry, "so haggard and thin were they, and, furthermore, they stank so badly that when approaching citizens or wandering through the streets or churches or public spaces, they caused instantaneous giddiness and dizziness."[22]

On both continents peasants knew cycles of hunger and plenty. Sometimes dearth occurred in the lean months after the last harvest had been consumed and the next one not yet reaped; in Europe these months of deprivation could drag on from April to July, after the period of indulgence between harvest and Christmas had burned itself out with feasting and merriment. At other times, a drought or blight destroyed the crops of one or more seasons, or a panzootic of cattle disease made the taste of milk only a memory. These "acts of God" were what gave annual feasts their joy and even their fervor.

Sometimes after a run of good harvests the European population grew too large for the land to support during subsequent leaner years. Later, markets and new agricultural technology—the use of plows rather than hoes, or reaping machines rather than sickles—would prevent this shortfall. But, in preindustrial Europe, population could rise and fall with increases and decreases in the level of production or trade.[23]

Hunger was often a consequence of warfare, and some wars, as in the case of the Thirty Years' War, were strategically based on crop destruction. Zulu military expansion, in early nineteenth-century South Africa, created havoc over a vast expanse of land because the soldiers carried few provisions and ate the harvests of those whose cattle they were plundering. Hunger drove people into mountain refuges, forests, or newly dense settlements where they managed to survive by finding wild food, hunting, or even committing acts of cannibalism.[24] Such stories have parallels in European history from Carthage to Stalingrad.

During these crises of subsistence, households on both continents stayed alive by devising ingenious and sometimes horrible strategies. They scattered to forage for food such as bark, seeds, or roots to grind into flour and bake into bread or boil into porridge. Zulu people threshed and ground certain famine foods—black roots, *ngoni* grass—before cooking them. During drought, the stomach of a dead buffalo might be squeezed for moisture. The hand of man was also apparent in determining who was entitled to survive. Privilege could determine survival. The patriarch of a large African household was as unlikely to starve as was the lord of a demesne.

Famines lasted in southern England until 1650, in northwestern England until later in the century, throughout the Continent in the eighteenth century, and in Ireland and the Scottish highlands until the middle of the nineteenth. They forced people to eat cooked nettles, moldy cereals, and even the entrails of animals discarded by slaughterhouses.[25] In seventeenth-century Burgundy the hungry became black and thin from eating grass; they were also said to have indulged in cannibalism, an act of extremity today's popular imagination has reserved for Africans.[26] Infanticide was said to be widespread in Europe until the late nineteenth century, "hardly less prevalent in England," Disraeli wrote, perhaps exaggerating, "than on the banks of the Ganges."[27] Letting the weak die allowed the stronger to survive, and so families on both continents sometimes had to fragment by jettisoning hungry dependents. From at least the thirteenth century in England, some tried to counter this tendency by writing maintenance agreements into their wills, marriage contracts, and transfers of property so that the strong would be obliged to provide a decent ration— a set number of bushels of wheat and barley each year, for example—to the old and weak.[28] Africans sometimes "divorced" less productive family members like old women, leaving them to struggle alone in the veld. People also begged and sought patrons who might feed them. All these acts born of ingenuity or despair helped peasants stay alive and families avoid extinction.

What are the possible reasons for the relatively greater culinary diversity and refinement among preindustrial European elites? The answers are institutional and demographic. In parts of Europe during the early modern period wealthy farmers possessed greater or more efficient means than their African counterparts for extracting surplus in rent and taxes from those who worked the soil. They benefited from a land tenure system in which communally held land played a decreasing role or none at all. Despite disasters like the Black Death of 1345–1348, when one in three or four Europeans died, the population density was higher in Europe than in Africa. The growth of population in Europe— tripling between the beginning of the Common Era and 1700—had occurred in spurts punctuated by demographic crises, but it had provoked people to expand their areas of cultivation even into the mountains and to increase the size of their fields at the expense of their grazing.[29] Agricultural historians tell us that when grain supplies failed to meet the demand of newly large populations, farmers worked harder and cleared new land in order to take advantage of rising grain prices. The key engine here that was lacking in Africa was the commercialization of agriculture: European towns, markets, and money had been developing in tandem since the 1000s and 1100s.

African rulers wielded weaker powers of expropriation than landlords in Europe, because peasants could escape from overbearing chiefs to abundant land elsewhere. The low density of population in southern Africa led to a low level of agricultural productivity. No impetus was given to an "agricultural revolution" by the pressure of population. No legal regime at the level of the state allowed a shift to proprietary title in land, and consequently to increased production encouraged by relative security of tenure. Access to land within chiefdoms depended on relationships that could be ruptured by the mere appearance of disloyalty. For political as well as ecological reasons, African households and even whole villages frequently decamped to resettle elsewhere on the sparsely populated landscape.

Black farmers had little incentive to make investments in more efficient and abundant agricultural production. (The same story is generally true of South African whites until the twentieth century.) With few regional exceptions, agricultural productivity and transport networks remained so poor that, when mining began in the late nineteenth century, employers were compelled to import grain to feed the miners from as far afield as the Americas and, for a time, from the African grain farmers of nearby Basutoland, an exceptional case. While famines that killed were rare in a land endowed with open veld for grazing and foraging, so were marketable surpluses. Where surpluses were produced, as in Basutoland, the catalysts were peasants' desire to increase food security as well as the material rewards derived from serving regional markets during the colonial period.[30]

Centers of population like London stimulated production on the farms in their own vicinity, but such centers were few in southern Africa. In precolonial Africa, commodity production did not flourish in the absence of cities, markets, reliable transportation networks, and coin-based currencies. Markets were almost nonexistent in precolonial southern Africa, but in Europe they provided to those with cash a diversity of foodstuffs, including spices such as cinnamon and mace imported from the East Indies for the very rich. Those Europeans without specie were drawn to market towns to beg, though in times of extremity they might find the doors of medieval towns locked against them, or those beggars who were fit might be chained and made to clean the city's drains. European cities could present popular health in preindustrial times with more of a blight than a boon. The press of humanity within them provided fertile ground for the spread of infections, often via polluted water supplies, and it was these epidemics, more than famines, that caused demographic crises.

Southern African settlements, without the population density of European cities, offer no evidence of similar epidemiological crises. South Africa had the additional advantage of space for foraging and for relocation near more reliable water supplies or fresher fields and pastures. Africans resisted such infections partly, too, because their housing was relatively more sanitary—the bush provided a cleaner lavatory than the fetid public places and latrines of preindustrial European cities—but also because they lived in a less harsh climate. Southern African winters are relatively mild, and the veld provided important vegetable supplements to the local cereal-based diets, that is, wild food like melons, tubers, and spinaches, which could be dried for use throughout the year.

State structures, more elaborate in Europe than in Africa, could provide more extensive charity. The phrase "poor relief" occurs only in post-Reformation Europe, and especially in the context of the expanding French, Dutch, and British states.[31] During food shortages in Tudor and Stuart England, local magistrates sought to ensure that their parishes had adequate grain supplies by prohibiting exports, importing grain from the Baltics, and searching barns and granaries to survey accurately the local corn supply.[32] Parish taxes were collected for distribution to the deserving poor, while in parts of Europe larger institutions such as *hôpitals,* usually associated with the Roman Catholic church, provided emergency relief.[33] These institutions were only as effective as their powers of administration were strong. When, for example, the French government adopted laissez-faire economic policies during the grain shortages of the late eighteenth century, it provoked revolts and food riots by failing to ensure that the grain would be distributed widely and at what was perceived to be a just price.[34]

In southern Africa, on the other hand, poor relief had to be less extensive because chiefs generally had limited powers to extract wealth from their subjects. They did exact annual grain payments or labor for their wives' fields, they stored the sorghum or maize, and their wives would cook it for visitors and the poor. This patronage could make the difference between life and death for solitary people. European paternalism, although institutionally more elaborate, did share some traits with this image of the chief as beneficent patriarch.

Mainly, though, southern Africans survived by fragmenting their households and moving, rather than looking to the state or ruler as patron. Lacking markets, African agropastoralists had to adapt to the vagaries of climate and politics, changing the density of their settlements or shifting the burden of their diets from sorghum to maize.[35]

Other systems for coping with hunger belong to longer spans of time. In response to demographic, climatic, or economic changes, European farmers altered the balance between pastoralism and cultivation, and consequently the proportions of meat and grain in their diets. People in Germany, England, and Holland did eat a good deal of meat during the later Middle Ages, from about 1350 to 1550, because the plague had reduced the population and allowed arable fields to be converted to pasture.[36] In some remote and agriculturally backward areas, such as the northwest of England, the conversion was premature: it encouraged the population to rise before transportation networks grew reliable enough to guarantee sufficient grain when local harvests failed; and so, when food prices rose at the end of the sixteenth century, people died.[37] One response was to change crops. During the lean years of the late eighteenth century, the Dutch, like others in northwestern Europe, shifted their diet from cereals to the cheaper, higher-yielding potato.[38] In nineteenth-century Britain food stocks rose with crops of turnips and clover in formerly fallow fields; those fields, fertilized by grazing cattle and sheep, then provided unprecedented amounts of cattle feed, and more meat and dairy products.[39] These strategies may have been the cumulative result of a number of smaller decisions taken at the community level, often in reaction to changing prices.

All these strategies devised by western Europeans and southern Africans to survive the preindustrial constraints, catastrophic and systemic, on production of food were transcended by the massively greater productivity of industry, called conveniently, if not entirely accurately, the "industrial revolution."

The Industrial Revolution Removes Hunger from Nature

In Europe the agricultural and industrial revolutions took place over half a millennium; in South Africa these same processes occurred within a single lifetime. Mindful that most Europeans remained farmers and domestic servants until well into the nineteenth century, and in some places into the twentieth, I am using the word *revolution* more for conventional convenience than for strict accuracy. In this context, *revolution* means the dramatically increased productivity that occurred as fossil fuels, like coal, replaced organic sources of heat energy, like wood. Machines released production from dependence on the land: they freed fields from having to grow fodder for farm animals; coal, in time, added millions of acres to forests and arable land. And so, in the words of E. A. Wrigley, "Real income per head . . . could, for the first time in human history, rise substantially and progressively in all classes of society."[40] Production eventually became vastly more efficient as machinery such as spinning jennies and steam drills replaced muscle power.

South Africa's revolutions in production occurred at breakneck speed partly because the technology used to mine its diamonds and gold did not have to be invented on the spot, and was imported from Europe and America in the late nineteenth century. A proletariat available to work on the mines was produced partly by legislation restricting movement, imposing taxes, and limiting African access to land. Within only a few years of the mineral discoveries, modern institutions and classes capable of servicing an industrial society were functioning in South Africa. The mining industry served as the conduit for rapid change, though it was a force creating not only extreme modernity but also extreme poverty in southern Africa.

During their respective industrial revolutions both continents proved Thomas Malthus wrong, or at least correct only for the preindustrial era. The eighteenth-century economist had predicted that every rise in population would be followed by a regression when food stocks fell below the minimum needed to keep the newly large population alive; a famine would ensue, weakening popular resistance to infection so it became difficult to determine what had killed the surplus people. Instead, around the time of the industrial revolution, food production rose. The European population grew—in part because it was not decimated by epidemics and because people were starting families at an earlier age—and escaped famine because more were surviving to work the land more efficiently. In the eighteenth century people put more land under the plow, and they introduced more and better crops, partly in response to the demographic boom and the related rise in cereal prices.[41] In Europe as in Africa later, people began to suffer from hunger not because the aggregate supplies of grain fell short of their numbers, as Malthus had predicted, but because they lacked cash or land.

The sequence of the agricultural and industrial revolutions varied from place to place. In England increased agricultural productivity—new crops of maize and potatoes, cultivation of new land, new techniques and implements—preceded the "mineral-based energy" revolution so that a larger and healthier workforce arose even before the jennies began to spin.[42] The end of famine in England resulted not only from agricultural innovations but also from the development of national produce markets by the late seventeenth century when river traffic transported grain. In South Africa, a modern agricultural revolution—the commercial production of large-scale surpluses—did not occur until the twentieth century, and the order of the two agricultural and industrial revolutions was reversed; in addition, national transport networks lagged far behind.

The histories of South Africa and western Europe are linked by the fact that their industrial revolutions allowed them to defeat famine. To paraphrase Gertrude Himmelfarb, the industrial revolution was removing hunger from nature and bringing attributes of poverty, including malnutrition, to the forefront of history, which is to say that men could create and influence these states of being by political action.[43] Economic factors like wages and prices, which people could try to control through the state, increasingly determined their health as they lost their hold on the land. Concepts of poverty were changing. In Europe the growing numbers of the poor were increasingly seen as involuntary victims of rapid social change, whose plight should be addressed by the state and society rather than by the church and the manor.

Popular strategies for survival were expanding but they were also narrowing because of increased dependence on access to cash. Many have agreed with Engels, who wrote in *The Condition of the Working Class* that workers lived more comfortably before the industrial revolution, but it is difficult to assess so simply the consequences of the first peasants' decision to move to town. They suffered, but so, too, they were saved in their new lives: famine did end; their diet was sometimes better than in the countryside; they remained vulnerable, though more to the vagaries of the economy than of nature.[44] Their motives for moving were similarly complex. They were both lured and driven to towns. Enclosures in Britain and taxes in South Africa propelled toward the new industries people who might well have preferred to stay at home; for others farm life appeared less alluring than life in the city or mine compound.

Wages may have defeated famine, but they did not defeat hunger. In both settings, these early industrial workers found that they had to spend a large percentage of their incomes on food—between 50 and 80 percent in nineteenth-century Germany.[45] Most of that large proportion was spent on cereals, especially on bread. A fall in wages or a rise in food prices led to less bread on the table. In late eighteenth-century Rouen, a weaver who missed a day's work would make his family hungry.[46] Nor would his employer have felt responsible: early modern wages, like those of South Africa's black miners and factory workers, were often intended to feed only individuals, not their families.[47] With subsistence plots around their homes, the fortunate among these early workers would add vegetables, meat from poultry or pigs, and even milk to their meals. Many living in compounds or tenements had no such luxury. As a substitute, their employers helped them still their pangs of hunger, and at the same time become addicted to the workplace, by providing brandy or beer as part of their pay. Later, sugar replaced liquor as the most commonly prized and immediately gratifying gustatory reward for hard labor.[48] A similar pattern emerged in the United States, as in western Europe and South Africa during the early stages of industrialization. Manual laborers' former diet of porridge and milk was replaced by tea, bread, and sugar.[49]

When hard continuous labor, disciplined by a relentless clock, was fueled by cheap rations, workers' health suffered. South Africa's first black miners had to drill underground for twelve hours at a time with little more than porridge, coffee, and a biscuit to sustain them. Employers, driven callous by the lure of profit, might have anticipated some physical damage; after all, awareness of a link between diet and health had existed for centuries.[50] This vague sensibility was first pushed toward a more robust concept of nutrition by the health problems men suffered when they were living within all-encompassing institutions where they worked, slept, and were fed. These unintended laboratories were prisons, the military, and mine compounds. In each case, men were literally captive to the meals served them by their keepers—one pound of biscuit and one gallon of beer daily without fruit in the eighteenth-century British navy, porridge without beer in the first South African gold mines. John McManners has written evocatively of the dietary advantages of living outside institutions in eighteenth-century Europe: "no doubt [people] supplemented their food supplies by tilling odd corners, keeping animals in hutches, gleaning in hedgerow and common, begging, poaching, and pilfering. That was why it was so dangerous to become institutionalized. . . . Survival became difficult when there was no scope for enterprise."[51]

Institutional diets led to scurvy, among the first nutritional "diseases" to be identified.[52] The disease was not contagious, but sick workers, soldiers, or prisoners were costly ciphers, dependent on the support of their employer or jailer. Poor diets were false economies for employers. From such pragmatic roots, modern nutritional science was born.

This new science of healthy eating would instruct future generations on how to overcome ignorant dietary habits of their forebears. And yet it was clear that "ignorance," "improvidence," or "immoderation," all common terms for judging the hungry, were insufficient causes. Malnutrition could be brought about by high food prices and by individual or group behavior as much as by dearth of food or lack of knowledge about it. A working mother who left her children alone for most of the day was not necessarily ignorant of what to feed them. If she fed them too poorly to resist tuberculosis or gastroenteritis, the cause may have been her own obligation to work. Her absence and the wages she was paid, along with the price of food, were determining the health of her family.

The way experts framed these problems in the first half of the twentieth century in South Africa tended to focus attention on how much food was available nationally and how to educate Africans to eat a cheap, balanced diet, rather than on their poverty. Ignoring "entitlement" meant ignoring explosive issues like wages and land loss. The economist Amartya Sen has tried to shift the explanation of hunger and famine away from a focus on how much food is available—the Malthusian obsession with the ratio of food to population—toward the question "Who can command what resources?" He called attention to two kinds of "entitlement" relations, one based on ownership, the other on exchanges. Ownership is acquired by inheritance, trade, or production, whereas "exchange entitlement" has a more complicated genesis. One may acquire a bundle of commodities in exchange for selling labor, assets, or produce, and for paying the taxes that subsidize social security benefits.[53] During their industrial revolution, black South Africans obtained only the most restricted "exchange entitlement" rights.

In order to keep wages down and avoid unrest the South African state prohibited the organization of black workers. It alienated land on a racial basis, decreeing in 1913 that Africans could acquire rights to land only within the reserves, a law that helped choke off Africans' own agricultural revolution.[54] Further, the state narrowly defined who was to receive welfare provisions such as free education and health care. Black workers, many of them forced off the land in the nineteenth and early twentieth centuries by military defeat or

legislation, entered a state of poverty from which neither humanitarian policies nor their own political and economic organizations were allowed to rescue them. Unlike Europe's first workers, they were intended by those in power
to be labor migrants oscillating between urban workplaces and rural homes.
At the same time most families left at home in rural areas suffered a declining
quality of life for the same reasons: wages were kept artificially low, and the
state provided very little welfare. Political structures with their roots in the
colonial era, most notably a racially defined franchise, prevented most Africans
from bargaining up their wages until the 1940s and, thereafter, not until 1973
when Durban workers successfully initiated a labor movement. They took to
the streets waving University of Natal research pamphlets proving that their
real wages were falling. Until then, as a result of their "exchange entitlement"
rights, real wages of workers had risen in Europe and principally among the
enfranchised white workers of South Africa.

In rural South Africa the state constricted African "entitlement" by allo-
cating capital only to the enfranchised. South Africa's agricultural revolution,
when it finally began at the beginning of the twentieth century, was a racially
biased one. Mining capital was used to fuel white agriculture alone. Investment of tax revenues in irrigation schemes, mechanized farm equipment, and
fertilizers made agriculture on white farms more productive. Like much else
in the South African economy, agribusiness remained dependent on mining.
Especially in the twentieth century, black South Africans could participate in
this revolution only as wage laborers.

One heritage of industrialization within a colonial setting was the consistently high proportion of food purchases in black household budgets, especially in contrast to those from other industrialized countries. Workers who
could organize and vote spent a decreasing percentage of their incomes on
food; by the mid-1970s, South African whites spent 18 percent of their personal consumption budgets on food. And so, South Africa parted from the
rest of that world in the following crucially important way: while elsewhere
the percentage of household budgets spent on food was declining, only in
South Africa did that percentage stay static. Between 1948 and at least 1983, it
stagnated at 34 percent.[55] Because this percentage applies to all "population
groups" and white personal consumption expenditures on food were low and
falling, it reflects the decline of subsistence agriculture, the increased urbanization of Africans, and their consistently high food costs.

So, too, South African demographic patterns differed from those of other
industrialized nations. The black birthrate did not fall as in late nineteenth-
century Europe where people chose, through birth control and deferred marriage, to have fewer children and thereby improve their material standing.
South African families, many hit by generally hopeless poverty and labor

migration, tended to fragment so that customary constraints on population growth fell away. Families were no longer decimated by famine as had sometimes happened in preindustrial times, but fell victim to the stresses of labor migration and modern poverty; also, parental control of engagement and marriage was waning in the same period, and communities heaped less opprobrium on unwed mothers.

Ironically, the South African state was contriving to undo its own prosperity. By suppressing or banning social and political movements that could raise the general standard of living, the state set limits to the growth of its own wealth. Local markets for manufactured goods remained small. State planners and employers only slowly learned that per capita worker productivity was inhibited by an increasingly large workforce that was debilitated and disaffected. At the end of the twentieth century the large demographic bulge of unemployed and undereducated black youth faced a late industrial world in which unskilled labor was needed less and less. The weakness that afflicted many as a result of their impoverished diets, and that was compounded by their disaffection and lack of education, made them even less likely to be the skilled and productive workers needed by a shrinking and more specialized labor market. The population growth that might have fueled an agricultural revolution in another era was occurring in the wrong context. South African race legislation thwarted the nation's movement toward the kind of industrial prosperity its European model had achieved.

Conclusion

Many white South Africans justified their privileges by imagining themselves the inheritors of a long tradition of luxury derived from their ancestors' command over nature. Sustaining this image entailed failing to see similarities between African and European history. Acknowledging them would perhaps have led to greater empathy with the people they dominated and a less keen sense of cultural difference, or it could have made empire impossible altogether. Idealizing the European past also involved failing to comprehend or acknowledge where and why European historical experiences diverged from Africa's.

Failure to investigate historical origins does not, of course, mean timidity about making historical claims. Those who were party to public discussions on African hunger and poverty in the industrial era were in a sense amateur or unwitting historians. Most used European history as a model for South Africa's development, deriving agricultural development policies for southern Africa from European success stories, even though they bore no necessary relation to Africa's social or agronomic conditions. Europe's successful strategies for defeating famine within its own borders became the template for saving dying Africa from itself. Physicians, research scientists, Native Affairs Department officials, and social scientists saw their mission as instructing and lending a hand. They based their faith in the superiority of Western culture on the demonstrable powers of modern science and technology to conquer hunger, and their pride influenced their understanding of their own history.

There is nothing unusual or blameworthy about groups disrespecting each other's food cultures as a means of expressing their identity and pride. And, as the epigram from Weber suggests, people appreciate stories justifying why their tables and bellies are full, while others' are not. It is significant that Weber's words come from his reflections on the psychological needs served by religion, because, in some respects, food also addresses those needs. On the one hand, food, like religion, signifies group membership; it is a particularly potent index of group identity because we incorporate it into our bodies. On the other hand, food, again like religion, addresses private needs; as William James observed with reference to the failure of science to address the "interest of the individual in his private personal destiny," religion has the capacity to affect one's sense of security at the most basic and individual level, and food shares that ultimately reassuring power. James went on to note that "as soon as we deal with private and personal phenomena as such, we deal with realities in the completest sense of the term."[56] People experience feelings as facts, and feelings associated with food cannot help but enter the realm of thought.

When these feelings are systematized into an ideology, they can wield enormous power. Regular and public depictions of the ill-fed as responsible for their hunger may lead them to be ignored or even punished. Especially in an era of mass communications and intrusive state structures, such ideologies, derived from popular impulses, can easily gain the force of self-fulfilling prophecies.

CHAPTER TWO

Before the Land Was Lost

African Food Culture in the
Nineteenth Century

Kudliwa okukhona kuyekwe okungekho. (We eat what is there and
don't eat what is not there.)

Zulu proverb

INDUSTRIAL-ERA EUROPEANS commonly found African diet monotonous
and unhealthy. Especially in the early twentieth century many believed these
traits derived from the more general African flaws of laziness and improvidence. In the pages of a 1909 medical journal, for example, a medical officer
named George Albert Turner accused African women of "trading away mealies
for small showy articles which are of no use to them." Like many of his contemporaries, Turner believed these poor consumer habits were "combined
with a constitutional inability to commence work except under compulsion,"
and thus "the natives in many parts at certain seasons of the year . . . deterio-
rate physically."[1] Living in the modern world where produce had become relatively bountiful year-round, people like Turner looked upon seasonal food
shortages, and the values and technology giving rise to them, as unnecessary
vestiges of the preindustrial past. They lamented that Africans tolerated seasonal hunger because they lacked an enterprising spirit. As the twentieth century wore on, these judgments evolved into more general depictions of African
ignorance and incompetence.

Many Africans reacted to these negative images by painting an idealized
picture of the precolonial past. Nelson Mandela, for example, when on trial
for treason in 1964 spoke admiringly of a time when there had been no rich
and no poor in South Africa. Less politically engaged figures lamented the loss
of a golden age that had existed as recently as the late nineteenth century when
"very few young persons died; all lived to old age." Rural Africans commonly
believed that rainfall declined after white settlement began in the seventeenth
century, but rainfall is notoriously erratic and hard to measure; one field can

2. In the heart of the Zulu kingdom women share a laugh around iron and clay cooking pots, circa 1930. (*Cape Times* Collection, National Library, Cape Town)

be inexplicably favored with more rain than its neighbor.[2] Europeans traveling through rural areas in the nineteenth century sometimes contributed to such romantic images, whether because they wanted to encourage investors to exploit the apparently rich land and its labor, or because they genuinely believed, like Rousseau, that men living in a state of nature enjoyed robust health.

These conflicting portraits of preindustrial African life—one utilitarian and the other romantic—demand an inquiry into the nature of African food culture in the nineteenth century. What traits led it to be disparaged? What technology and values lay behind seasonal food shortages? Does the historical record allow us to discover how healthy Africans were in the preindustrial past? Answers to these questions will emerge from an investigation of South Africa's land and how people adapted to its constraints in preindustrial times.

A Difficult Land

A visitor to South Africa today could easily mistake that country for a land blessed with plenty from the beginning of time. Deep green vineyards in the southwestern Cape produce abundant good wine. Orchards bear peaches, apples, pears, and citrus; and such tropical fruits as papaya and pineapple grow along the coast. In autumn vast fields of maize yield more grain than South Africa itself can buy up, and then turn golden in the Orange Free State and parts of the Transvaal. Beef and dairy stock are able to grow fat on the sweet grasses.

That South Africa has been a primeval cornucopia is a misapprehension. Two cardinal characteristics of South Africa's land are that, in most places, it is dry and the soil is poor. The bounty greeting the modern visitor was created only in the twentieth century by the expenditure, especially between the depression and the 1960s, of large sums of state funds on irrigation schemes. Before the technological innovations of the 1900s, the land showed little promise of producing vast quantities of surplus crops or of supporting large, concentrated herds of stock. The development of sizable urban markets beginning with World War II, as well as the availability of capital and the shortage of African labor, justified the mechanization of South African agriculture.

Today's bounty, created so recently, may not last. Intensive irrigation may dry up the underground streams used to water the fields and lead to the salinization of the land. Commercial ranching hinders the full recovery of drought-stricken grasses and soils.[3] The future is fraught with risk of failure or at least limited productivity, as was the past.

Most of South Africa is so dry that the first farmers to inhabit the region, during the first millennium of the Common Era, settled entirely within the zone of high summer rainfall. When Bantu-speaking agriculturalists crossed the Limpopo River, moving slowly southward from their supposed place of origin in what is now Cameroon, people settled only in the eastern third of the country where twenty to forty inches of rain fall yearly, usually between the months of December and February. There they could both grow crops and graze cattle. The wettest region within this eastern third is the narrow coastal plain lying beside the Indian Ocean. In the summer, trade winds moving westward toward the Atlantic Ocean drop rain there and on the west side of the Drakensberg mountain escarpment, but by the time winds reach the great central plateau, they are prone to absorb the little moisture the earth affords rather than deposit any rain. Freshwater lakes or rivers are too few to remedy this aridity. Only three great rivers—the Zambesi, Limpopo, and Orange—exist in southern Africa, but the latter two tend to lack water during most of the year. Neither can the short rivers be navigated or used for irrigation; they run too swiftly down the steep hilly escarpment toward the Indian Ocean.

Because the southern tip of the continent rose slowly and continuously in prehistoric times, ancient rocks lie near its surface. Therefore, the soils are generally shallow and immature, though the soil regimes do support good grasslands at high altitudes. While the greatest natural boon to the region's agriculture is the vegetation on which stock and game can feed, they cannot congregate in large numbers throughout the year because the winters are long and dry. Thus, the soil and the seasons required canny seasonal adaptations.

Another problem curtailing agricultural productivity was disease. Epidemics more commonly struck cattle than humans. Cattle could readily be infected with nagana (trypanosomiasis) in low-lying river valleys, and so people have preferred to develop their pastures in the high grasslands where there is no tsetse fly. East Coast fever can be contained by dipping, isolation, and judicious slaughter, but its cure remains to be discovered.[4]

Even though such basic attributes of the past as the amount of rainfall and extent of forestation are still in doubt, this characteristic of preindustrial times remains beyond dispute: survival has often been precarious. Grain could be stored for only a couple of years before growing moldy and indigestible.[5] Periods of hardship might afflict a settlement during a drought or an epidemic of cattle disease or a plague of locusts, and, even in the best of times, hardship was likely to visit small households, with too few people to produce subsistence. A household might be small because it had been visited by illness crippling its adults and killing its infants, or because its stock holdings were insufficient to pay bridewealth to the fathers of several young women. Too few workers was as fearsome a prospect as a drought; both forms of disaster reduced people to begging and desperate foraging. People anticipated seasonal food shortages and, to some extent, provided for them by the judicious storage of grain, seeds, and dried leaves, but misfortune could strike even the provident unawares.

The following Zulu case study of southern African food culture was located on the fringes of conquest, in an area that could be called a "deep reserve" because it remained relatively intact up to the late nineteenth century. It had not lost large tracts of land through conquest or purchase. Its people would have known about the frontier wars of the eastern Cape (1779 to the 1860s), the displacement of mainly Sotho-Tswana people by the migration northward of Afrikaners (1836–1854), the British annexation of Natal in 1843, and the sporadic attacks on African chiefdoms north of the Vaal River by the new Afrikaner republics—the Orange Free State (1854) and the South African Republic (1852). Upon hearing these stories, people living in the Zulu chiefdom are likely to have felt increasingly insecure, but they were not profoundly affected until the eve of the twentieth century.

Adaptability and Risk Aversion: A Zulu Case Study

Famed for their beauty, Natal and KwaZulu comprise a dramatic and richly diverse landscape. Their climate varies with altitude and topography. The land sweeps from a tropical coastal plain, up through a temperate benchland, to the northern foothills of the great Drakensberg escarpment, bitterly cold in winter. The story below concerns the hinterland of Durban, especially along the route northwest to Pietermaritzburg.

We enter this landscape in the mid-nineteenth century through the eyes of an outsider, a trader named Richard Harwin, who had returned to England after spending 1850 to 1861 in the Durban area. His tone, both lyrical and pragmatic, appears at once sincere and designed to beguile possible investors. He described the Durban hinterland as a promising site for commercial agriculture, listing its resources in detail. Wild and domesticated tropical fruit—Cape gooseberries, African "plums," grenadillas, guavas, loquats, and peaches—thrived along the coastal belt. Fertile fields lay sixty miles inland for oats, beans, and maize, and were also good grazing for cattle. Sheep and wheat would flourish, he said, at the higher altitudes. Game—springbok, "wild turkey" (probably bald ibis), quail, buffalo, leopards—abounded, much of it good to eat. Predators, with only a few exceptions like the bold hyena, stayed far away from the open districts where farmers had burned the sheltering cover. Harwin knew enough about farming not to wax lyrical about the "broken" land of Inanda, one of the African reserves (land set aside for African occupation) closest to Durban. Arrestingly beautiful to the eye as its hills roll on apparently forever, it is nevertheless so steep that it could support, in Harwin's words, no more than "a few goats and cattle, or a few natives."[6]

Harwin's description of the African inhabitants of this natural paradise revealed views characteristic of many settlers of the mid-nineteenth century. He opened his reminiscences by announcing that Natal had "strictly speaking . . . no aboriginal population" because only a few hundred people had escaped the ravages of "the destroying Zulus" and their chief, "the murderous Chaka." The 150,000 or more black people who had moved to Natal by midcentury had been drawn there, so he said, by the "guide and protection of the white man's rule." Now refugees, they owed no common allegiance to anyone but the British government. They had owned huge herds of cattle until lungsickness had killed thousands, filling the air with carrion vultures and the stench of rotting flesh. This disaster would have created a gustatory windfall because, he wrote, "of animal food they will also gorge immense quantities but of the flesh of the pig, and of domestic fowls or of eggs they will not eat." In normal times, their food consisted chiefly of "milk turned artificially thick and sour and of mealies (maize), pumpkins, sweet potatoes, the produce of their gardens, cultivated by the women." Harwin did not refer to the health of these refugees and their descendants, suggesting simply that old people tended to be abandoned when they were "used up."

Harwin was wrong in saying that only a few hundred Africans in Natal had survived the *mfecane* (the wars that led to the making of the kingdom) or had moved south to gain white protection, but it is true that many of the family groups living there had come from the north to escape political conflict and warfare after the Zulu clan began to expand its control over other Nguni clans in the late eighteenth century. The clans currently in the valley—Qadi, Nyuswa, Embo, Ngcolosi—first arrived there in the 1830s as refugees from the wars of Zulu imperialism to the north and stayed because the land was teeming with game and relatively uninhabited.[7] Their lives continued to be disrupted; a roll call of disasters includes drought, rinderpest, locusts, East Coast fever, lungsickness, and war. Harwin did refer to food and raised the important question of how the sick and old were regarded and treated. He ignored African medical treatment and was probably unaware of how Zulu people thought of the causes of disease, or what remedies they tried, and whether nutrition was a concept of any meaning. What did the people of the Durban hinterland actually eat, and how had their diets changed over time?

The staples of an ordinary nineteenth-century Zulu diet were fermented milk, cereals boiled as porridge, and cultivated vegetables, eaten twice daily, first after milking and then before sunset. Zulus spoke of solid and watery foods. People stored their food by fermenting in the form of thick sour milk *(amasi)* and sorghum beer. Sour milk—extraordinarily rich in cream where the cattle grazed on long grass, but low in yield after calves sucked—was ideally the basis of each of the two meals eaten daily. Only children drank fresh milk. Beer was a seasonal delight, the postharvest reward for a good season's crops. People ate boiled or roasted maize every day, supplemented by pumpkin, beans, taro root, and sweet potatoes. The consistency of the porridges depended mainly on how coarsely the grain was ground and how long it was boiled. When the grain and vegetable supply ran short in late winter and early spring, that is, between June and August, people scoured the bush for wild spinaches *(imifino),* gathering greens perhaps three or four times a week in the spring, drying some leaves for winter meals when they might have to ration themselves to one daily meal. While looking for *imifino,* they could also hunt for bitter herbs to help their stomachs accommodate the radical shifts in diet brought by the changing seasons. Meat was rarely served. Even if one of the six or so annual hunts bagged a buck, some people at home, such as a low-ranking dependent, might not receive a share in the spoils. People ate beef—roasted on embers or boiled—after a beast died of natural causes or had been sacrificed for a particular ritual purpose, but they rarely slaughtered cattle for food.[8] (The meat of a beast dead of natural causes would be disinfected by boiling with a germicidal plant.) Sacrifices served a defined social purpose such as a marriage feast or a sickness that demanded a dying beast to cry out to the ancestors for a cure. By-products of a slaughtered beast produced highly prized dishes of fatty dumplings and sausages and congealed blood. Only at such times and few others did nondairy animal fat enter Zulu diet. There were, of course, regional anomalies; people living on the coast, for example, ate mussels.[9]

The dishes and culinary practices of all strata of Zulu society were fundamentally the same. The well-being of different social strata probably did not differ greatly during times of plenty, while the benefits of high rank were felt most keenly during times of dearth. Status was mainly evident in the quantity of food that a senior wife or mother-in-law in a large household could serve to dependents and visitors, though servants tended to do the cooking in a rich man's household. Those who had surplus were also likely to receive it, as when meat was sent to households one intended to impress, such as those of district *izinduna* (leaders). As a proverb said, "Meat baskets usually exchange." That the production, preparation, and storage of food was women's work does not set Zululand apart from most areas of the globe at most times. What is unusual, compared to Europe, is the relative lack of privilege enjoyed by high-ranking women, that is, women related to a chief or the king. As one early adventurer, Henry Fynn, put it, "Queens and princesses labour [carrying water and wood, digging fields] with as much pains as the poorest women." Fynn was overstating his case. Privilege did exist. It was apparent, for example, in the longer period of rest and isolation—five to ten days—enjoyed by a new mother who had someone to work for her.[10]

Within households, privileged access to food did exist, especially when meat was distributed. Each category of household member—men and women, boys and girls, older and younger—customarily received a designated cut. Men ate the head, women ate the breast. Groups did not eat together; women came into the cattle kraal to eat after the men had finished and left. The nutritional consequences of apportionments were probably insignificant both because such feasts were rare and because children, to whom less was distributed, made up for skimpier portions by hunting their own small prey in the pastures while they herded. Boys and girls, too, trapped rodents and birds, insects, caterpillars, locusts, and termites while they herded, and herd boys drank fresh milk, often sucking it straight from the udder.[11]

Since a newborn was not allowed to nurse until its umbilical cord had dried and fallen off, its first food was *amasi,* blown into its mouth from an adult's cupped hands. (Zulu mothers withheld their colostrum from infants, believing it was poisonous.) Thereafter, for the first two or three years of its life, the child nursed, supplementing mother's milk with *incumbe,* a watery mealie porridge, and then with increasing amounts of solid food as desired; a baby, however, was never given greens or vegetables. After her few days of postpartum rest, the mother would carry her infant to the fields on her back, laying it on a goatskin in the shade while she worked, and nursing it during breaks from sunrise to sunset in the peak season. As children grew older they assumed more responsibilities for feeding themselves and their younger siblings.

The burden of work falling on an individual woman's shoulders depended on how many other women lived within her household and on her own status among them. In the nineteenth century, households ranged in size from two to a hundred houses. A polygamous man would provide each wife with a house, all arranged in a semicircle in order of rank on both sides of his own dwelling. In principle, each wife grew food and cooked for her immediate family, sending a dish to the house where her husband was sleeping that week.[12] There was a considerable amount of voluntary sharing of labor and food among the wives, while senior wives or the mother-in-law extracted obligatory and sometimes onerous labor from the brides. Their role upon marriage was one of servitude. Their offspring—four or five on average—could be deprived of a fair share of milk if the relationships between the women of the household were strained. Women in large households could have less hard labor; women from small households were more likely to complain, "When can I find time to look for food, if I am harassed?" They had to cope, for example, with the rats or doves scavenging among ripe crops, with the stalk borer infesting the sorghum, or with the small boys bewitching pumpkins. One can imagine the husband of one of these women seeking the aid of a local doctor whose specialty was scaring away corn-eating birds. Husbands were said to grow thin if their wives were too busy scaring away birds to cook, and their children were so busy with chores that they had no time to milk the cows. Alone, or with a few sisters-in-law if she were lucky, a wife would have to heap the ears of corn on raised wicker platforms and, when winter approached in May, beat them with four-foot-long flails and then winnow the grain by pouring from one basket into another. With little help, she would then pour the grain for winter storage in a "great underground bottle" in the cattle kraal, its location hidden by a flat stone and earth. As senior woman in the household she alone would ordinarily be allowed the honor of removing the stone to fetch the grain.[13] Those who had helped her expected a gift or reward of food, and they begged for it.

Though the lion's share of the work of providing subsistence fell on women, men traveled through the countryside searching for homestead sites whose ground was not so moist that the corn would rot, preferably firm soil in a warm, wooded country where there were rivers.[14] They cut brush in new fields; guarded the crops against wild pigs, monkeys, and baboons; and hunted, herded, and milked the cows. Milking was the only male activity crucial to daily functioning, and boys were allowed to do it (their job was already to keep calves away from the milking cows). Therefore, households could tolerate the absence of their adult men for long periods when they served as *impis* or soldiers for the Zulu king.

The drought-prone environment and the difficulties of storage shaped what people ate and the risk-averse habits some would call peasant conservatism: for example, planting crops resistant to drought, even if they took longer to ripen; or scattering various seeds in a field rather than only one type of crop. Harwin and others would have regarded the diet as monotonous. In fact, its outstanding characteristic, although the staples came principally from three types of plants (cereals, root vegetables, and herbs), was its variety. People grew at least five kinds of maize, seven types of sorghum, and more than fifty-five vegetable types and gathered more than twenty-five kinds of wild spinaches. They intended to enjoy varieties of flavor in their beer by brewing ten distinct ways. In the veld many kinds of wild fruit and honey were found by women as they collected firewood or by children while herding. Taste was associated more explicitly with beer than with solid food; if they had enough of this pleasant and refreshing brew, they did not "touch any other dish." Many prized the sweetness in sweet potatoes and sugarcane and sometimes added honey to sour milk to counter its sour taste, but ate mainly to feel full, a sensation that could be joyful as the following paean of praise reveals: "We love the Almighty; for (it is his doing that) we eat corn, and mix thick milk, and slaughter our meat, and eat our meat, and eat our mealies, and eat our wild sugarcane." The proverb "We eat what is there and we don't eat what is not there" clearly expresses a hardheaded sense that one should feel grateful to have any food at all.[15]

Famines, caused notoriously by the *mfecane* but more often by drought, cattle disease, and pests, taxed the ingenuity of ordinary folk when their energies were at their lowest ebb. Survival depended on the ability to identify and prepare the wild plants of the veld. To be palatable, some plants—sweet potato, black roots, *ngoni* grass—had to be threshed or dried and ground before being cooked. Certain roots needed to be boiled continuously for twenty-four hours to be rendered nontoxic, so they did not cause insanity. Sometimes famines were named after the plant food that had allowed victims to survive; thus, the famine in Zululand of around 1861 was called *"Ilanga li ka Mbete"* (literally, "the sun of the dew," though Mbethe was also the name of a famous rainmaker) after the marks people left in the dewy grass when searching for figs. The hungry sometimes broke their taboo against eating dogs, and fish or shellfish if they had moved near the coast.[16]

One strategy for survival that strained the social fabric was the shrinking of the sharing network for food and labor. A visitor was likely to return home empty-handed only during a famine. The poor who received gifts of food as charity or as reward for weeding or reaping would beg and receive nothing in times of want. Even bridewealth payments fell off; this kind of contraction was undoubtedly the least socially damaging of all, but fathers continued converting their payments of cattle into promises of future cattle transfers, or into iron or money, especially after the 1896 rinderpest epidemic wiped out nearly all the region's herds. Switching the form of *lobola* (bridewealth) caused no long-term social damage but probably did reduce the bride's household supply of milk. By the end of the century, when trading stores were beginning to be established in remote areas of Zululand, the money substituting for *lobola* allowed fathers of the brides to purchase food to meet the shortfall in their household supply.[17] In time, money would provide a better buffer against natural disasters than the Zulu king had ever been able to give.

The Zulu king used food to advertise his power, rather than to provide popular welfare. Luxury in largeness, plenty, and the exotic characterized his court. So, too, did many food rituals and forms of etiquette. The king drank from a calabash without using his hands, and his guests in the *isigodhlo* (the king's private enclosure) lay on eating mats to be fed by servants. (Not having to use one's hands to eat was a clear mark of status; Shaka, the king, illegitimate son of a chief, was insulted as a young man by having to eat milk curds from his hands as if he were a person of no rank.) Kings and queens would chew, but not swallow, their first mouthfuls of meat, and were said to prefer old meat and watery, not thick, curds that were seen as the food of menials. Boys carried water to Shaka with arms extended over their heads. One young mat bearer who spied on a meal his father was fed in the court of Dingane in the 1830s saw him lying on his stomach, not using his hands, as he was fed meat and helped to drink from baskets of beer. Dingane had given directions on how and when the father was to be fed, and presumably also decreed that the man would have to crawl away afterward on all fours. Some visitors to this court wrapped animal fat around their heads like bandages, and many ate it raw.[18]

Extraordinary sanctions reputedly were meted out to those who flouted royal ritual. Those who ate the first fruits of the harvest before the king had formally and ritually decreed that the time for feasting had begun were said to have been killed or to have had all their cattle taken away. The cuts of meat one received at a feast advertised his political importance, while to miss a meat and beer feast was both an occasion and a metaphor for losing power.[19] With the ceremonies orchestrated as a means of protecting the king, anyone breaking their rules could be interpreted as a wizard or thief intending to make him sick.

The Zulu king's regiments ate a great deal of meat. In time of war, soldiers on duty received captured cattle to slaughter, though those off duty usually drank milk from a small herd of captured cattle, "the milk being the only remuneration for their services during their lives." They could feast on the herds and *amasi* of their foes. A man who had been in close combat was rewarded with many gifts of cattle, and the folk who begged him for meat would call him a great man. A coward's meat would be put in water, the hot roasted prime pieces going to heroes alone. Stored grain found in deserted kraals was requisitioned and sent back to fellow troops who may have eaten nothing but bad meat for days. The difficulty of provisioning the Zulu army was a major reason why its wars of expansion were so devastating to the region. Robbed of domestic animals and grain, their victims sought refuge in secluded places where they could find buffalo, elephant, and hippo and, at the worst, resort to cannibalism. Some people swore such acts of desperation never occurred before the rule of Shaka. The epithet of *cannibal* was a convenient accusation for fear-stricken people to throw at their enemies, but diverse sources suggest that cannibalism did indeed occur. Undoubtedly, hungry people often hunted for melons, locusts, and wild plants, or stole others' green mealies to eat raw. Hungry soldiers were known to soak their shields of hides to eat.[20] In more ordinary times, they would carry meat spitted on a stick to eat as they traveled.

Despite his remarkable authority the Zulu monarch was not obliged to, or capable of, providing extensive welfare. That a government should supply food to "women, children and weak and decrepit individuals" was a concept of social welfare unknown except to states wealthier and stronger than the Zulu kingdom.[21] The Zulu king, like any other precolonial southern African chief, could not cope with problems of large-scale transport and storage. His inability to provision his own army indicates that his bounty was sufficient only to provide for his court, not for his people at large. The best he could do was to store enough grain from his tribute fields to entertain visitors at court and feed destitute individuals there; in these ways alone he could be a patriarch, that is, a father figure who protected his "children" or subjects from hardship. Some proved stingy, and their greed is memorialized in songs. "[W]hen he eats, [he] never looks around," his people sang of Cetshwayo, "he has no time for anyone else." He may have inherited this trait from his mother, who was famous for never offering anyone a drink of beer, and he himself was known to serve stored food—*amadumbe* (taro), sweet potatoes, potatoes, bananas, and pineapples—only when he learned it was rotting or that people were hungry.[22]

Zulu food culture reflected another ranked system than the one growing in the Zulu court from the beginning of the nineteenth century. Beliefs about health, and how food affected it, also revealed the power held by the dead over the living.

Diseases that were not simply diseases were believed to be caused by the ancestors, interceding in earthly life because they were hungry. From beyond the grave, they would reenter the lives of the living when they needed to be fed. A cow or goat would be stabbed so that its dying cry would reach the ears of the ancestors—for this reason, a silent sheep would not do—and its meat would be left for one night on a special hearth so that the ancestors might come and lick it. Feeding was a way of encouraging ancestors to grant an abundant harvest or a rapid recovery. A man who had been in pain discovered that he was afflicted because his dead brother wanted meat; the man's wives were relieved because they feared he had been suffering from a disease rather than from an ancestor's hunger. A chief, in his dreams, might hear a dead man say, "Do you already forget me? I thought I would come and ask for food," and the chief might fall ill if he refused it. Similarly, a man told by the ancestors in a dream to abstain from a certain food would get sick if he disobeyed. The dead were not above being chastised when their hunger caused trouble for the living. Because they embodied the spirits of former chiefs, lizards, for example, could be told upon infesting a village and giving rise to illness, "Here is [a slaughtered bullock] for you. Eat and depart." Occasionally, a man who loved his stock would rebel against such demands, saying, "This disease longs for meat; but I will not kill cattle," and, fearing that the spirits of the dead would impoverish him, he sought other means of placating them. Because sacrifice ate into wealth, a decision to kill a beast was made principally by heads of villages or households. A woman's dreams could not cause a bullock to be slaughtered until the ancestors' wishes were confirmed by a diviner.[23] Not all claims heard from the ancestors were regarded with reverence and belief. People sometimes gossiped about greedy liars who said they had dreamed about the ancestors simply in order to occasion a sacrifice and satisfy their own craving for meat.[24]

If a person died, it was because the ancestors wanted him or her to join them and so refused to take away the poison. These beliefs may have been to some extent metaphorical, yet the chain of causation was no doubt deeply felt and sincerely believed. The centrality of food and hunger to peasant concerns is also apparent in the ritual form of Zulu burials: a man was buried with seeds in his hand, and food was placed for him behind his home.

In the realm of the practical, people acknowledged that some diseases were simply diseases, with no ancestor held responsible. Mundane afflictions were spoken of in terms of what persons had ingested. Enemies could cause harm by putting poison in their rivals' food. In such cases, as well as in dysentery and fevers, a *nyanga* or curer might prescribe an emetic and a tonic or sedative derived from the hundreds of medicinal plants. Some families handed down their special knowledge of roots and herbs from one generation to another. They knew, for example, how to prepare a mixture to consume just prior to the First Fruits ceremony so that they would be able to digest the green food available to them after a winter of dried grain. Medicines might be prepared as cold or hot infusions, as essences or powders, vapor baths or emetics. The intent was to dispel impurities of the blood, an excess of bile or "filth," or intestinal parasites. The herbs may have ameliorated the symptoms; for example, an extract made from the boiled roots of the *iHlinzanyoka* tree relieved chest pain.[25] The principle of homeopathy was deeply imbedded in many of these practices, and sometimes the same word described both the medicine and the disease.

The power of ingested substances to effect well-being extended even to ideas about character and destiny. This belief was reflected in dietary preferences and taboos, including, in all likelihood, the practice of washing hands before meals. A. T. Bryant, an ardent compiler of Zulu plants and foods, described the Zulu belief that food built up bodies and qualities of the mind as well. Drinking the contents of a beast's stomach was believed to cure barrenness. A pregnant woman could influence the shape of her unborn child's head by eating chicken. Praise singers were said to have powerful memories because they ate tripe. Old persons were properly the only ones who should eat the small lobe of a beast's liver because it caused forgetfulness. (This practice was surely a self-fulfilling prophecy!) The roster of food taboos—predicting, for example, that a man eating entrails would be stabbed in the bowels by his enemy—included blanket prohibitions, albeit with temporal and regional variations, against fish, hartebeest, fowls, and pigs. To eat these was considered a sign of antisocial intent, as a man eating sour milk at another's home would reveal that he wanted to return for evil purposes.[26]

Survival was perilous in a landscape visited by warfare, locusts, cattle disease, and unreliable rainfall, where people had limited ability to generate and store an abundant surplus to tide them over their troubles. It is not surprising that food played so central a role in the cosmology by which the living explained their destinies to themselves. The precariousness of survival in the nineteenth century was reflected in the central importance given to safeguarding fertility: a woman could not eat the meat of a cow that had died while calving; sour milk, forbidden to strangers, was often associated with semen and was said to produce virility.[27] Zulu-speaking people in the nineteenth century had no concept of nutrition equivalent to that of the late twentieth century, but their cosmology and herbal practices were not inherently hostile to such an idea. They did not exclude the possibility that one day a concept of nutrition based on the balance of energy-giving food components (carbohydrates, fat, protein) could be harmoniously incorporated into their daily lives and beliefs.

Throughout the nineteenth century there is no evidence that the nutritional welfare of Zulu-speaking people was consistently poor or inexorably deteriorating, even though such practices as denying milk to a nursing mother were probably harmful. Despite the intrusion of white settlers in Natal there was still enough land available to peasants for the old strategies of survival to succeed. Economic doldrums kept boundaries and control over land use in Natal ill defined. Even Africans who lived there as rent-paying tenants enjoyed diverse opportunities to earn money by trading in ivory, cattle, or maize; by hunting on shares with Europeans; and even by acting as agents for absentee European landlords. In the 1870s whites were vacating the land while Africans in Richmond, for example, were selling large quantities of maize even to the British army from 1879 to 1882 while it was fighting its last Zulu war.[28] Before white farmers began, at the end of that century, to demand and acquire more African labor to produce food for the Rand gold and Natal coal mines, their African neighbors' and tenants' inherited strategies for leading healthy lives remained relatively unassailed.

These inherited strategies were enriched by innovations and by selective adoption from Europeans and other Africans of new dietary and farming techniques. During Shaka's rule people adopted new culinary practices like carrying their milk in gourds rather than in skin sacks, frying meat and green corn pancakes in soup fat, and, later, cooking in three-legged metal, rather than simply clay, pots.[29] Beliefs about the connection between food and health changed slowly, but converts to Christianity were known to throw over old taboos rapidly; thus, Protestants were said to refuse to eat the meat of a beast dead from sickness, and Christian women generally were permitted to milk cows. Their openness to innovation allowed pagans and Christians both to survive and prosper as long as land and labor were abundant.

Conclusion

Nineteenth-century travelers wrote vividly about the new world of southern Africa, but they did not provide a reliable basis for comparison with the later medical history of the region. As Harwin's reflections indicate, their visions were often idealized, designed to foster colonial intervention. In any case, their medical knowledge differed so profoundly from today's that their analyses are hard to correlate with what is now known. They considered sickness to be caused by foul air rather than by bacteria or viruses; Henry Fynn, for example, believed in the early nineteenth century that the Portuguese in Delagoa Bay suffered from fevers and ague because they breathed noxious vapors from swamps.[30] The European folk knowledge of the time blamed diseases among westernized Africans on such perceived habits as not changing into dry clothes after being caught in the rain. Another example of European preconceptions bodes particularly ill for the accuracy of early medical statistics. Europeans found a good deal of syphilis in nineteenth-century South Africa, because they had come expecting to find it and because they often confused its symptoms with those of leprosy. Though nineteenth-century perceptions can be misleading, they do at least reveal the following facts of life.

South Africa is a poor country, and life was hard in precolonial times. As Turner observed in 1909, people were indeed subject to debility and disease on a seasonal basis. When spring approached and people found their winter stores low while the cold, dry weather continued, they were prone to suffer from lack of vegetables and milk. Particularly debilitating was scurvy (vitamin C deficiency), which could afflict people after months without vegetables and fruit; their gums and gastrointestinal tracts would bleed, and their wounds healed slowly. The rainy season brought its own maladies when rain washed excrement into streams and wells so that people were likely to contract diarrhea and dysentery that, in turn, prevented their food from nourishing them. The result would be immobility or lethargy and greater susceptibility to infections such as pneumonia. Some diseases were caused by conjunctural misfortunes like the coincidence of drought with a plague of locusts and an epidemic of measles.

People survived in the difficult environment of southern Africa by adapting frequently and creatively to the challenges posed by the land. They moved and changed the shape and density of their settlements as required by security and by shortages of water, fuel, and fertile soil. They embraced, and even sought out, new cultivating and culinary techniques. Their circumstances did, of course, constrain their choices and make them averse to risk. Without elaborate state structures, long-distance transport, or long-term food storage, they remained shrewdly cautious, though hardly lazy or improvident.

Accusations of improvidence and laziness missed the point that the survival and prosperity of individual African households depended upon an abundance of hard-working people. More cattle meant more wives, and more women laboring in the fields brought in bigger harvests and more beer to entertain and to pay work parties. Household size and social standing were one: a monogamist had to bear taunts because he would have little or no beer to serve visitors. He would be called "a poor fellow who has nothing," and no one would sing his praises. A Zulu prayer aptly draws attention to the interdependence of wealth and numbers of people: "I pray for cattle, that they may fill this pen . . . for corn, . . . that many people may come to this village of yours and make a noise and glorify you. . . .[and] for children, that this village may have a large population."[31] Small households worked harder and produced less, and their children were more likely to be sickly. They would find it difficult to experience the good life—*ukunumuza,* that is, to pass *amasi* around with a spoon. This truism of precolonial life—that household size meant prosperity—characterized the entire region. The next century would see this ideal turned upside down.

In the nineteenth century, group strategies for health and survival in this difficult landscape were predicated on an abundance of land, allowing people to move to escape war, to find fresh fields and leave old ones fallow, to locate more plentiful water supplies, fields of *veldkos* (wild food), and game. The land supported life because it was so thinly populated that people could easily shift across it, hunting and herding, foraging and cropping. These flexible strategies were one day bound to become constricted when sheer demographic growth necessitated the adoption of new strategies, including the introduction of private land tenure, a process dramatically hastened by European colonization. The problems plaguing Africans' health grew as their ways of life changed, living in closer and less sanitary quarters, working with greater exertion on the mines and in factories, and as low wages prevented them from adapting to these changes in a manner likely to foster healthy lives.[32]

Modern Europeans disparaged African food culture not only because it seemed monotonous, but also because it reflected what they would have called magical values. Much southern African medical, including nutritional, lore was charged with sexuality or reproductive power. Safeguarding fertility was one of the goals of local medical as well as of ritual practice. Dietary taboos were often linked to procreation, and milk was treated with care because it carried energy that should properly circulate only among people who formally shared a household. As Jack Goody has argued, it is not illogical that "the two activities central to the domestic domain, cooking and copulation, should be closely entwined, each one subject to specific prohibitions and preferences that in their turn define those important aspects of the socio-cultural system, marriage and eating."[33]

Many of the following nutritional practices derived from beliefs about the paramount necessity of safeguarding fertility, and they were not necessarily healthy. Mothers may have been weakened when prevented from consuming milk products while pregnant and nursing. Nguni men missed valuable sources of vitamins and protein by spurning greens and eggs. While the diseases of affluence like obesity and heart disease probably afflicted few people, considering their hard labor and the rarity with which they consumed sugar and meat, *amasi* did contain a good deal of animal fat, and so some of the more idle rich were rather rotund, as may be seen in early drawings of Nguni chiefs. Zulu royal brides were deliberately fattened on a diet of meat, sugar, salt, and millet beer, so that by the time of the wedding they could no longer walk.[34] When Rousseau celebrated the moderate consumption of "natural man," he was seriously wide of the mark.

While European societies closely associated cuisine with class, agrarian societies linked food with fertility. These beliefs belong to the category of thought that Weber labeled "enchanted." People see "mysterious incalculable forces" emanating from the ancestors, whose spirits must be implored or placated in order for people to survive. A worldview that treated nutrition as a "technical means" of governing survival was part of the "process of disenchantment, which has continued to exist in Occidental culture for millennia" and to which "science belongs as a link and motive force."[35]

At the same time as preindustrial people tried to control nature through spiritual means, by feeding the ancestors, for example, they possessed more scientific knowledge than industrial people commonly do. They knew more about the properties of the natural world than the people who came to teach them modern science. Weber recognized that "the savage knows incomparably more about his tools" and knows perfectly well "what he does in order to get his daily food and which institutions serve him in this pursuit."[36] George Albert Turner, the medical officer whose thoughts began this chapter, knew less about South African nature than did the "South African natives in their kraals." He made grave mistakes about what constituted a healthy diet; thinking that fresh vegetables, for example, consisted mostly of water, he wrote that they supplied limited nourishment to the body. One crowning irony of imperial cultural chauvinism is that people who themselves possessed less local scientific knowledge disparaged those who knew more.

The hubris of conquest would ensure that Turner's science would reign dominant, little affected by local knowledge. In most cases when syncretism and imitation occurred, it would take place on the African side. This chapter suggests that cultural racism was not actually a response to African improvidence, lack of enterprise, or conservatism, because these traits did not really exist. It arose from the gap between preindustrial people's vulnerability to hunger, on the one hand, and the industrial societies' apparent freedom from hunger, on the other. It grew from European pride in their "disenchanted," scientific belief system as opposed to African ones that still used spiritual means, in addition to their own local scientific practice, to try to ensure group survival. European faith in the idea of scientific progress proved to be one of the principal popular wellsprings of twentieth-century cultural racism.

Part Two

The Benevolent Father
An Embattled Rationale for White Supremacy

CHAPTER THREE

The Politics of Famine

State Paternalism in Rural
South Africa, 1910–1948

I am distressed at the sufferings of my children. . . . But while I
sympathise . . . I cannot but remember that it is partly their own lack
of foresight that has brought them to their present extremity.

A. H. Stanford, chief magistrate of the Transkei, 1912

EUROPEAN TRAVELERS WHO ventured far beyond Cape Town in the early
nineteenth century sometimes encountered victims of famine wandering in
the dry hinterland. These hungry Africans, leaves or grass hanging from their
mouths, excited pity and wonder. One missionary observed "walking skeletons," looking worse than victims of famine he had seen in India. If they
crossed into the Cape Colony, how was government going to provide for
them?[1] Well over a century later, in 1946, one angry member of the South
African parliament used similar terms when he lambasted his colleagues for
ignoring the hunger prevalent among Africans: "I know it is easy for the Sena-
tors in this House to keep cool. . . . They do not see their children eating
grass."[2] Both the missionary, John Philip, and the senator, Hyman Basner,
were expressing a common image of famine, an extreme deprivation no decent
government could ignore.

From time immemorial famine has been one of the most potent emblems
of social suffering, unambiguous and irreducible. Demanding charity from the
better-off, it can evoke fear or political exploitation. It is conventionally
defined as a critical shortage of food that leads through hunger to starvation
and that substantially increases mortality in a community or region. But like
hunger and *poverty* its meaning is imprecise. How many people have to die,
and of what causes, before widespread hunger is considered a famine? Because
of silences in the historical record, we cannot be certain how often famine, of
whatever definition, occurred in precolonial southern African history.

3. Margaret Ballinger, member of parliament representing African interests (1937–1960), played a major role in politicizing the 1946 eastern Cape famine. She is shown here opening the first African day care center in Cape Town, circa 1949. (*Cape Times* Collection, National Library, Cape Town)

During South Africa's first four decades as a united and independent country, from 1910 to 1950, only about half a dozen famines occurred, following the state archives' use of the term. "Famines" reveal much about changing South African attitudes toward African rural poverty, especially among those officially responsible for administering African areas and safeguarding African welfare, employees of the Native Affairs Department (NAD).

The three famines considered below occurred over a thirty-four-year time span—1912 to 1946—broad enough to reveal two processes, at first sight, contradictory. They show famine itself being eliminated in modern South Africa. They indicate official sympathy for the victims of food crises demonstrably waning. International and domestic trade allowed food to be shipped into areas suffering from dearth and, at the same time, the NAD was growing more expansive and efficient in providing relief; this department was the most paternalistic of all the South African government agencies, dedicated to "uplifting" black people. And yet, especially in the 1940s, the NAD records show a marked increase in administrators' impatience with the needy, and the enhanced intent and effort to discipline them.

State Paternalism

In 1910, when the four parts of modern South Africa were fashioned into one country, the new government was weak, but it did possess a bureau, the NAD, charged with overseeing the African reserves and, therefore, with intervening in rural crises like famine. As employees of the NAD, magistrates bore direct responsibility for the government and welfare of Africans, but until 1924, when the NAD gained a full-time ministerial head, they enforced no articulated and coherent native policy. Instead, individual local officials—magistrates or native commissioners, in principle enforcing NAD proclamations and abiding by precedent—determined what happened on the ground. Each of the principal African reserves (the Transkei and Ciskei, Zululand, the northern Transvaal) was overseen by a chief magistrate or chief native commissioner, who reported to the secretary for native affairs in Pretoria.

A hierarchical skeleton underlay the sometimes benevolent skin of NAD overrule. In September 1910, a delegation from Chief Marelane of eastern Pondoland proposed going to Cape Town to welcome the duke of Connaught as he opened the first Union parliament and to interview the minister for native affairs. NAD officials were of two minds about this trip. A. H. Stanford, the chief magistrate of the Transkeian territories, where Pondoland was located, thought that officials had justified past encounters between chiefs and representatives of the British king as occasions that expanded African "ideas of the power and greatness of their rulers and strengthens their loyalty." But, personally, he worried that the visits would lead to "an exaggerated sense of their own importance and a consequent unruliness." The chiefs would show their pride and indiscipline by trying to bypass their "immediate superior," the resident magistrate, and communicate directly with the government in Cape Town or Pretoria. "[W]hile of course access is not to be hindered it is necessary at such times to emphasise the fact that it must be through the proper channels," Stanford wrote. The minister for native affairs wired back that though the Pondo delegation should not be discouraged, it ought to travel to Cape Town at its own expense. Undeterred, the Pondo still wished to meet the minister, "especially if [he] would be prepared to explain fully to the Pondos what government by Proclamation means." He was not prepared, and nine years later Marelane's secretary was still trying to get NAD officials to define how laws affecting the Pondo were made and how they might influence them.[3] NAD paternalists infrequently referred to the possibility that one day the children would be grown and able to govern themselves.

If the "proper channels" were followed, the NAD was likely to respond to African needs with sympathy, so chiefs and their delegates regularly framed their requests for help in terms that acknowledged the "power and greatness of their rulers." The idiom was patriarchal, an appropriate form of address for the patron-client relations within preindustrial societies. Officials admired their own idealized image. One magistrate contrasted himself to self-interested white traders by noting, "The Pondos think the speculators have no eye and no mercy—the only mercy they can expect is from the Government under whose protection they are." Such NAD employees opposed absorption into the justice department in 1923 on the grounds that they would then be placed "before the native no longer as fathers, but as correctors pure and simple."[4] Particularly during the early years of Union the chief's men habitually addressed the magistrates as their "fathers," and, in return, the "fathers" tried to safeguard their "children" from disasters like famine.

State paternalism shared many rhetorical traits with the patriarchy of the chiefs. They both used the language of fatherhood, labeling subordinates as "children" whose welfare would be looked after by a benign father. The father figure would sometimes have to discipline his juniors. Saving them from their errant ways might even entail a degree of violence, as when a Tswana chief forced reluctant subjects to contribute their labor to a communal project like building a dam or when a magistrate arrested a tax defaulter.[5] The relative importance of the three core values shared by paternalists and patriarchs alike—discipline, benevolence, and the exaltation of seniority—changed over the course of the Union of South Africa's first four decades.

While the shared language of political fatherhood surely facilitated the interaction of chiefs and magistrates, the chiefs undoubtedly felt stifled by their designated role as underlings. They all knew the fate of recalcitrant nineteenth-century leaders, like Hintsa, who refused to surrender to the British in the eastern Cape in 1835 and was shot trying to escape. The chiefs' sense of resentment and their manipulative counterstrategies are not always easy to read from the historical record. The above case of the Pondo chief's attempt to visit the British high commissioner, minister for native affairs, and prime minister in Cape Town was simply the latest episode in that chief's efforts to bypass local magistrates and communicate directly with more powerful men. The sentiment of deference cannot be assumed simply because the language was there.

Magistrates were caught in a contradictory relationship with their wards, one they seem not to have acknowledged and perhaps never to have perceived. On the one hand, they saw themselves as benevolent father figures who sought not only to ease social suffering such as famine but to educate Africans toward the day when they would assume more modern political rights. On the other hand, they frequently blocked African initiatives. Certainly, the promise of political adulthood had always been vague: there was no detailed plan for governing in the present or the future and certainly no timetable for self-government. Political changes were intended to be gradual and minimal.[6]

The Native Administration Act of 1927 aimed to centralize African administration and to make it more modern, that is, nationally consistent and efficient. From then on, the minister for native affairs could rule over all Africans simply by proclaiming a law, the extension of "government by proclamation" the Pondo chief had inquired about insistently and fruitlessly in 1912. The 1927 act also set up native commissioners' courts to adjudicate cases between all Africans, according to "traditional law," thereby "retribalizing" educated people who wished to be free of "tribal" strictures.[7] In addition, the act entrusted magistrates with the task of identifying and acquiring new land to increase the size of the reserves. While the act signaled the intention to govern more closely, it did not create immediate change, apart, no doubt, from increasing the paperwork magistrates had to submit to the head office.

The NAD skeleton was ossifying for several reasons. In the late nineteenth century its British colonial heritage began to be modified by the labor needs of the mining industry. In the early twentieth century it had to serve the segregationist program formulated by the South African parliament and cabinet. As Saul Dubow has argued, the functioning of the NAD was increasingly informed by an ideology of national efficiency that had been growing in England since the turn of the century. By the 1930s, the NAD was displaying a "technocratic approach to government" that celebrated scientific solutions to social problems as if "objectively valid solutions" could be discovered and imposed without reference to the majority's wishes.[8]

The NAD's increasing desire for tighter social control was provoked by its changing relationship to local people and often associated with highly unpopular legislation. The 1913 Land Act had not granted sufficient land to Africans; the NAD and its wards agreed upon that fact. Where they differed was in their analysis of the consequences: Africans argued that the finite size of the reserves caused their poverty; beginning in the 1920s some NAD officials countered that they misused the land by overstocking and farming it inefficiently, and that was why they were poor. In the course of defending this interpretation of the causes of African rural poverty, NAD officials demonstrated their greatest rigidity, formulating "betterment" schemes in the 1930s and mandating the culling of excessive stock. They went on in the 1940s and 1950s to require Africans to terrace their land and to rotate their stock through different paddocks rather than allow them to range free. By the late 1950s these agrarian reforms had evolved, through the Tomlinson Commission report of 1955 on the future of the homelands, into a mandate that people should live in villages, not beside their fields and pastures. This development program came to be backed by force. Ivan Evans, another historian of the NAD, has suggested that "betterment" was symptomatic of magisterial "blindness" to the inherently coercive nature of their rule and to the complex social changes over which they were presiding. Whatever its inconsistencies and its destiny, the NAD hierarchy embodied and exemplified state paternalism toward Africans. Along with, to a more limited extent, the Department of Public Health and, after 1944, the Department of Social Welfare, it provided social welfare to Africans. It played the legitimizing role that "citizenship" and "social service" played in democratic and democratizing countries.[9]

Magistrates and Africans often disagreed about what constituted a famine. Many Africans tended to use the word *starvation* as a metaphor for degrees of hunger and even more generally for "poverty," obliging magistrates to try to measure the need precisely in order to justify their requests for relief grain to the head office in Pretoria. They also had to divine who deserved to receive it. A dead weight of unproductive dependents was to be avoided at all costs; the country, they believed, simply could not afford it. One important trait distinguished the articulated values of paternalists from those of patriarchs: the NAD officials said that they believed in the free market and so were wary of being perceived as philanthropists, while the chief as patriarch knew that he won political support by being perceived as the giver of gifts.

Feeding the Hungry and Vetoing African Initiative: Pondoland, 1912

NAD officials were at their most benevolent in energetically dedicating themselves to rescuing their wards from threatened famine as in the 1912 crisis in Pondoland caused, as always, by many factors, including one that was new: food was available but the transport system was temporarily out of order. Africans and white administrators at all levels of government focused their resentment not on each other but on profiteering traders. Even the Chamber of Mines, which used these traders as labor recruiters, saw them as potential threats to the mutual trust essential for the survival of the labor migration system. During this crisis, NAD officials rarely displayed impatience with Africans or African culture, only occasionally criticizing younger men who drank beer rather than work for wages. (Some older African men agreed.) The NAD indicated that while wedded to free-market principles it was willing to loosen those commitments when necessary and step in to guarantee some social security. What it was unwilling to do was allow African initiatives to flourish independently of their control.

At first sight eastern Pondoland seems an unlikely place for a famine. Dramatically hilly country extending fifty miles inland from the shores of the

Indian Ocean, it received such plentiful rain that its black soil roads became slippery and impassable far more frequently than its fields were parched.[10] And yet people did know the hardship of food shortage in precolonial times. The causes had tended to be the result of different kinds of bad luck intersecting. An epidemic of influenza coinciding with a summer of low rainfall followed by a hailstorm could reduce people to hunger just as remorselessly as a consistently parching drought.[11] A succession of years with only fair crops would make people unusually vulnerable to a visitation of pests such as grub worms or locusts. Sometimes the shortages had one clear cause, as most famously in 1828 when the repercussions of Zulu empire-building to the north hit the Amampondo. They lost most of their herds to marauding *impis* then, just as they would lose them again to cattle disease when the animals were afflicted by lungsickness in the 1860s, red water fever in the 1880s, and rinderpest in the 1890s. From the late nineteenth-century the chief, as before, might have a few buckets of grain to give to his people when famine struck, but now he had a new layer of government to appeal to.

The "sky was adamant" in eastern Pondoland in the spring of 1912. For the second year in a row the rains had failed, causing a drought that, in the words of the chief magistrate, was "unprecedented in the memory of all" mature adults. Because the crops failed to grow, one missionary saw "starving Pondo children, who seemed to be all ribs and knees." Both the cattle kraals and the grain pits at these children's homes were empty since drought was not the only scourge in eastern Pondoland; an epizootic of a tick-borne disease called East Coast fever was wiping out cattle herds, depriving people of the beasts that drew their plows and carts; perhaps less than a third of Pondoland's cattle survived. As the missionary wrote, "The sun smote on us fiercely and the stench from the carcasses of the oxen that have died in plague and have been left to rot on the veld, was almost insupportable."[12]

Watching the skies in November 1912 for rain that never came, and staring at traders' shelves either bare or with only exorbitantly priced goods, the Amapondo were living in a state of rising panic. "We are starving here," one headman wrote to the chief magistrate, adding that he was looking to him for help because the magistrate was "our father."[13] Rumors circulated that some traders had been murdered and their stores robbed. What the chiefdom could not grow during this dry time it was having trouble importing. The problem had nothing to do with money; through selling their cattle hides and labor, the Amampondo had amassed enough cash to buy food. Rather, the shelves of traders' shops were virtually bare. Disease had stopped transport dead in its tracks. In an effort to block the spread of East Coast fever, the government had forbidden wagons pulled by possibly diseased oxen to travel along any major routes. Further contributing to the lack of transport, people were likely to withdraw their "salted" or immune oxen for use in their fields as soon as enough rain fell to allow plowing. No railway tracks extended into the chiefdom; a train ran south from Durban through Paddock to Harding in southern Natal and another route was being constructed north from the eastern Cape to Umtata, but eastern Pondoland lay between the two terminals. In these circumstances, "even Croesus may starve," one magistrate wrote.[14]

How many Amapondo would become "walking skeletons" or die? Only fifteen people were reported to have died in Lusikisiki district from the "moderate epidemic of fever" that followed, "caused by the presence of numerous unburied carcases about native kraals and the falling of unseasonable rains."[15] Hunger was probably apparent mainly in children suffering from edema and adults from scurvy. No images of people eating grass and leaves appeared in the sympathetic and concerned memos that magistrates sent through the NAD bureaucracy as they argued for, and obtained, higher advances of mine wages and added transport, two boons of modernity that helped to hold the front against famine. The market for produce and labor was also pulling the curtain down on the nineteenth-century scenario of suffering: grain could be imported from overseas and from commercial farms elsewhere in South Africa, and men could sell their labor on the mines.

While the rains and disease vectors had failed the Amampondo, their local government did not. The ethic of service among magistrates, seven in Pondoland, varied with individual character. At best, some officials meticulously monitored rations and relief work and were aware of the need to protect Africans against employers, the elements, and traders. They were benevolent men but they did not, of course, challenge the existing distribution of power. By presenting Africans as children in need of protection, they did prime the fledgling bureaucracies of the new Union to respond sympathetically to requests for help from the paramount chief, Marelane, who ruled eastern Pondoland in council and through local chiefs and headmen.

From October into December 1912, the resident magistrates threw themselves into energetic and imaginative attempts to meet the shortfall of grain. One suggested opening a shallow local port, Port Grosvenor, by ordering lighters from Durban to be hauled into the bay by hand. He also mentioned Port St. Johns, situated on the western boundary at the mouth of the Mzimvubu River, as a possible, though difficult, means of access to eastern Pondoland. Another magistrate wired the chief magistrate in Umtata that government had to supply transport—by which he probably meant mules—in order to "prevent [a] holocaus [sic]."[16] Yet another magistrate thought that the government should import a shipload of American mealies; Argentina was also considered a likely place to buy corn. Most of the seven district magistrates in Pondoland agreed at least tacitly with the request put to them by their "wards": that the Chamber of Mines should be persuaded to increase the amount of money it paid in advance to each mine recruit. The going rate was two pounds, but the magistrates thought five pounds might reassure men that their families would be able to buy food in their absence; the men themselves, supported by a few extraordinarily generous magistrates, lobbied for ten pounds. Magistrates tried, in vain, to estimate how much food their districts required.

These schemes reached the desk of A. H. Stanford, the chief magistrate in Umtata. His standard response was to restrain the activist sympathies of men in the field while passing their requests up to the next tier of desks in the NAD bureaucracy in Pretoria. The chief magistrate's main rhetorical tool against his local supplicants was to accuse them of "improvidence," meaning that they apparently preferred brewing beer to thriftily saving their grain for days without rain. In 1912, Stanford admonished a Libode headman, Qangiso Ndamase, for asking for protection against price gouging; Stanford's tone vividly captures the father-son role that lay at the heart of their relationship. "I am distressed at the sufferings of my children. . . . But while I sympathise with your people in their trouble I cannot but remember that it is partly their own lack of foresight that has brought them to their present extremity and I trust that they will learn a lesson from the hardships of this year and in future waste less grain in Kafir beer [sorghum beer] but instead store or sell it after storing sufficient for their needs."[17] The magistrate was ignoring not only the practical fact that beer parties mobilized and rewarded communal work but also that drinking together has historically had "potent social significance" in the political and social life of chiefdoms.[18] It was an uncomprehending refrain that echos again and again through magisterial correspondence: beer brewing drew the line between the deserving and the undeserving poor. One magistrate worried in January, even while watching people resow their fields due to drought, "The Natives must be fully aware that the agricultural prospects are poor and in the face of this knowledge considerable stores of grain are used for beer brewing. If, later on, the shortage of grain becomes serious they do not deserve to receive aid."[19]

The stern father was also a benevolent one. Stanford argued in a wire to Pretoria that government should provide transport either by its own mule wagons or by hiring transport riders. In addition, he recommended raising the mine recruits' advance from two to five pounds, because, given the price inflation of the time, the normal two pound advance would buy only one bag of grain.[20] Receiving these recommendations, the NAD in Pretoria arranged a Saturday meeting for members of the cabinet and, significantly, the Chamber of Mines to discuss the "threatened famine." Some of the most powerful men in South Africa—its government ministers and mining officials—were worried that the famine would cause the labor supply to shrink, drawing this conclusion from their knowledge of the sometimes "unscrupulous" men who served them as labor recruiters. These agents were white traders, generally residing in magisterial towns, who sold food and commodities to Africans at the same time as they recruited men to work underground in the gold mines of the Rand. Trading in the Transkei was known as a "safe and fairly profitable form of business," perhaps because local traders tended to charge double the price that grain sold for in Johannesburg.[21]

In the words of E. Barrett, an NAD official reporting to Stanford on the high-level meeting in Pretoria, the mines were "particularly anxious that the money [for higher advances] shall not pass through the hands of their agents the more unscrupulous of whom would not hesitate to juggle with figures to the disadvantage of the Native who in many instances is already in the debt of the trader"; if the traders received the advances, they might insist on paying them out in goods worth far less than the cash they received from the Chamber of Mines. Africans would have to be protected against such behavior for their own sakes and for the sake of the mining industry. Barrett feared that "the more suspicious Natives" would be deterred from signing up to work on the mines if they did not trust the recruiters to pay them fairly.[22]

Even General J. B. M. Hertzog—serving as minister for native affairs from June to December 1912, and a proponent of segregation rarely remembered for his paternalism—suggested that the director of native labor, Colonel S. M. Pritchard, should be sent to Umtata to discuss with the chief magistrate ways of preventing the "evil plight [of the residents of the famine-stricken districts] being turned by unscrupulous persons to private account. Pritchard discovered that traders were "generally not charging inordinate prices but on the contrary [were] fully alive to [the] seriousness to themselves of Native famine." He also found a situation so dire that the African population might "in [the] immediate future [be] reduce[d] . . . to a state of starvation," and he backed the increased advance: two pounds would be paid on recruitment, and the remaining three pounds once the recruit actually arrived on the mines, so that the chamber would be protected from absconders.[23]

The specter of having to provide famine relief at great expense, it must be added, did frighten the government, although it was, of course, cheaper to be proactive than reactive. Pritchard wired from the field that the NAD should "insist [on] self effort on part of Natives to protect themselves against distress and thereby prevent the imminent possibility of its being forced to undertake relief measures at enormous cost."[24] Stanford obligingly asked resident magistrates to tell their headmen that government would not distribute gifts of seed or grain "as long as people are able to earn money by working for their living."[25]

The men from the Chamber of Mines and the NAD had not been wrong in placing part of the blame for the food shortage on traders. A few were indeed profiteering. Some traders within the Transkei itself were using the shortage of grain to charge unprecedentedly high prices; the price of a bag of mealies had more than doubled to as high as fifty shillings, and they maintained these high prices even after improved transport had eased the shortage.[26] Many traders refused to answer magistrates' inquiries about the extent of their business because they feared the government would interfere.[27] At least one resident magistrate believed that any numbers they produced would have been incorrect, as "in every case their opinions appeared to be influenced by their personal motives or trade considerations."[28]

Africans who were in debt to them were unlikely to have regarded the traders' profits as fully legitimate. Nor does it seem that they won the magistrates' respect, perhaps simply because they were in trade. Scattered about five miles apart across the Transkeian landscape, they rented land (about four and a half acres each) from which they ran so many different operations that one observer in the 1930s said they "represent Western civilization in the Territory." They and their family members acted as bankers, dressmakers, pharmacists, undertakers as well as the conduit through whom new commodities—cloth, plows, sugar, tea—entered the reserve, and local produce—wool, hides, grain, African tobacco, cattle—left it. Their activities provoked some local Africans to resent their virtual monopoly of the trades. They and their commodities were said to be "the most important direct cause of the Native 'drift' to the mines and to the towns."[29]

Debts to traders were the household equivalent of drought. Whenever the Bunga, the council voicing the concerns of the whole Transkei, including Pondoland, discussed family budgets and the subsistence of the very poor, the vexed issue of traders arose. They dried up a family's resources. Although the councillors never used the expression "a just price," they clearly believed that one existed and that traders seldom offered it. Traders not only combined to pay uniformly low prices for peasants' grain and cattle, but they also charged high prices for grain and lanterns. Often, cash never entered the transactions at all; traders either extended credit indiscriminately, driving their customers into helpless debt, or paid for peasant produce with slips of paper "good for" the purchase of goods at highly inflated prices. In the councillors' verbal scenarios, a widow usually appeared as an exemplar of hardship. What if a widow, they asked, sold her green mealies to a trader and received a slip of paper only "good for" the purchase of sugar, which she did not want?[30]

Older African men, while blaming their "hunger" on the "flesh and blood merchants" who recruited labor for the mines, targeted their own errant sons as well, complaining that they spent their advances on clothes rather than on food for their families. Enoch Mamba protested in 1914, for example, that dandified young men were spending money on "girls instead of giving it to their fathers." Mamba, an Idutywa headman and one of the more educated and progressive members of the Bunga, as well as a former labor recruiter himself, regaled his audience with a colorful tale of a son squandering money on finery for a girlfriend and himself—"a high collar that would stand up until sunset, tanned boots as if he were a theatrical artist about to do a stage turn." The son would not have revealed that the garb was bought on credit. Soon his father would look up from the hard work of plowing and find that a stranger on horseback had arrived, a labor recruiter to tell him that his son would now have to work to pay off his advance. The father would be left to finish his plowing alone.[31] In this case famine was not only a metaphor for social suffering or poverty, but it also allowed people to discuss other issues that troubled them. Mamba's tale reveals that improvidence and loss of control galled African fathers as much as it bothered European magistrates.

Moved by Mamba's forceful oratory, the other Bunga councillors argued strongly against paying out advances in Johannesburg where the money could be easily squandered, and maintained that they should be paid at home. While the government and the mines feared that recruits would never reach the Rand if paid an advance in the reserve, Councillor Lehana argued that unless the advance was paid at home, "many families . . . would die of sheer starvation." Perhaps ruefully, one councillor remarked that in these "enlightened" days, sons were not content to live together in the homestead neighboring their father's; now each son "wanted to have his own kraal and wood for his own fire."[32] In other frayed families, sons living apart from their fathers were said to be waiting for them to die so they could claim their property. Undoubtedly these sons had complaints to level against their fathers' attempts to control their hard-earned money, but the Bunga, a forum for seniors, never expressed them, and we are left with an image of subsistence being threatened by selfish sons rather than by indolent fathers, although both types of behavior surely inhibited the women's work of providing large healthy meals to their families each day and of helping them to survive famine.

Labor-hungry white farmers were also suspected by NAD officials of trying to profit from the famine. They differed from the traders in writing to the NAD about their needs and interests. Farmers from as far afield as the Transvaal and the Orange Free State wrote to magistrates stating their needs for families of farm hands and the rates they would pay. One Free State farmer asked the chief magistrate for ten Pondo families used to farm life to work as herders for fifteen shillings a month and food or, since "all natives here prefer working for stock," for eight good sheep for six months' work.[33] The official reply was cool: the offer would not help the aged, infirm, or large families with small children, and most able-bodied men preferred mine labor because it paid better.[34] The farmers' lobby was not yet organized and so no one had to bow to it. On the contrary, the secretary for native affairs, Edward Dower, replied tersely to a similar request that the government had "no power to compel Natives to come out to work in any particular branch of industry." And Stanford explained his wards' logic to other farmers: they were immobilized "by their unwillingness to leave their families unprovided with food."[35]

Despite such references to African "children" learning from their "fathers," the exchanges between ruler and ruled offered precious little evidence that African initiative would be rewarded. Whenever a member of the political elite of Pondoland—its paramount chief, councillors, and headmen—suggested using its own power and tax monies to address the famine, the idea was vetoed by the administration. The justification for the rejection was sometimes legal, at other times practical, but the message was clear. The responsibility of the Amampondo was "to send their young men out to work."[36] Beyond this initiative, the "children" were to remain children.

While members of the chief's court must have found this implicit attitude frustrating, they carefully framed their responses in tones of gratitude and deference, only occasionally revealing their dissatisfaction. Because Marelane, the paramount chief, was often indisposed by either drink or illness, his well-educated and capable secretary, E. Tshongwana, a former teacher at Lovedale, had to handle these encounters in his stead, and did so with remarkable persistence and grace. "The Pondo could now only seek the shelter of their father the Government," he would say before proposing a detailed scheme of action, generously seasoned with praise for the chief magistrate's help. In November 1912, Tshongwana proposed that the Amampondo be allowed to send their wagons across the Umtamvuna River to Paddock and Kokstad where grain cost less.[37] Such autonomy had no precedent, and his proposal was refused. The reasons for refusal had nothing to do with the proposal itself; they amounted to an explanation of what the NAD had already done—communicating with East London merchants so a sufficient supply of grain would be brought in, facilitating mule transport, getting mine advances increased, as well as the assurance that competition, especially from overseas grain, would cause prices to fall eventually. The formal explanation for rejection is less significant than the pattern: no African initiative succeeded.

The following year, in April 1913, when yet another calamity visited—in this case, grub worms infesting the mealies—Pondo opinion was said to run strong on the subject of famine relief. People could not see why the Pondoland General Council should be denied the right to use its own funds to "turn itself into a temporary merchant" by purchasing relief grain.[38] The official reply was that they would be obliged to charge even higher prices than the traders charged because they would have to pay for transport, build grain stores, and hire officers, and so the offer was refused. Fearing that Pondo disappointment in their failed scheme would be bitter, the chief magistrate ordered "a sympathetic reply . . . be sent to soften the edge of the refusal."[39]

Undeterred by this rebuff from the secretary for native affairs, Tshongwana led another deputation to the chief magistrate's office on a related issue in June, only three months later. He congratulated Stanford for enabling eastern Pondoland to survive the "time of famine" by filling the hands that "his children" had extended for relief even while the traders had tried "like bulldogs" to restrain him from giving them anything. Then he began to argue, unsuccessfully because the tax had been passed by parliament, against the administration's efforts to impose a new dipping tax hard on the heels of the recent famine. The Amampondo were too deeply in debt to traders already and their stock continued to be plagued by disease. Why did they need more dipping tanks, some wondered, when their cattle kraals were empty except for the pumpkins growing in them? Tshongwana strategically and eloquently expressed his loyalty and his dilemma in the following words: "In their opinion there was no other Native tribe like the Pondos which evinced the same pride in and loyalty to their Government. No matter how heavy the stone round their neck they had been taught by Faku [their founding chief] to endure it."[40] Tshongwana was too diplomatic to say so directly, but it is not far-fetched to imagine that he thought the "stone" around the neck of the Amampondo was the heavy hand of the father—the chief magistrate or the government—guiding them benevolently and stifling their initiative.

Tshongwana refused to see the law as immutable. Given his deferential circumlocutions it would be possible to see him as a simpleton, failing to understand that parliament was accountable to its electorate, one that, of course, excluded him. In 1919, for example, he told the chief magistrate that in Cape Town he had asked to be shown the law "but people could point only to the leaves of trees." He was actually arguing that since proclamations were written they could easily be altered by the chief magistrate and the prime minister; it would be a mistake to regard the laws as "a God." The case in point was the school inspector's intention to shut down a Pondoland school by denying it funds that were properly allocated only to primary schools (ones teaching through standard six). Tshongwana wanted this higher school to receive money from the Tank Fund, but the chief magistrate said funds could not be transferred from one purpose to another in this way. Tshongwana replied that people had lost their cattle, which they had formerly pledged to build schools, and they were facing famine next year. In this case the chief's secretary seemed to be using famine as a metaphor for poverty; he was implying that people needed higher education to gain skills that would earn money in order to survive lean times ahead.[41]

If judged by their own ideals of service and trusteeship, a flattering portrait of NAD officials emerges from this tale. Individual magistrates carefully monitored the food shortages experienced by their wards and lobbied energetically and creatively for them to be filled. Their respect and sympathy for African society may have been based partly on their own role as paternal figures, but it was real and it did produce concrete results in famine relief. These early magistrates were willing to modify their free-market principles in emergencies. They demonstrated no racial chauvinism by siding with labor-hungry white farmers whom they saw as unethical or white traders whom they believed were price-gouging. In fact, there appears to have been a good deal of collusion between magistrates and older African men; both were intent on keeping the patriarchal social order intact.

The portrait of the NAD itself is not without forbidding blemishes. The higher levels of the department were vulnerable to direction by certain powerful national constituencies, notably the gold mines, though not yet by white farmers. Their faith in the colonial hierarchy allowed them to veto reasonable African initiatives and to misunderstand the reciprocities, such as beer brewing, that made African agriculture work. When some magistrates, at this time a minority, criticized Africans for their "improvidence," they were ignoring abundant evidence of Africans' determination to provide for themselves during periods of dearth. The Amampondo stored a good deal of their 1913 harvest, and they needed it the following year when borer worms as well as drought afflicted their crops; they gathered along the roadsides to buy small quantities of grain from transport wagons to tide themselves over until their crops were ready; they traveled to neighboring but less badly affected districts to buy cheaper grain; they lied about how much grain they had in their storage pits in order to keep pressure on the NAD. While some magistrates criticized young men for failing to remit money to their relatives, the Pondo chief actually did something about these failures of support; he sent two headmen to Johannesburg to urge Pondo laborers there to send money home.

As in a similar Zululand case—a threatened famine from 1911 to 1913—the only official word of judgment leveled against local society was phrased according to the Victorian distinction between the undeserving and the deserving: improvident men are undeserving of relief; they should rather work in the mines.[42] Ironically, the low wages paid on the mines were fostering that very improvidence, if we accept its contemporary definition as beer brewing. No one, though, was calling the hungry people ignorant.

Defending the Hungry: The Lebombo Flats, 1927

In the 1927 famine on the Lebombo Flats of the eastern Transvaal the NAD came up against a slightly different and potentially more formidable lobby than the trader-labor recruiters they had blamed for profiteering in 1912. Officials now saw as local enemies the farmers who strenuously resisted relief efforts because they wanted to sell grain to hungry Africans and to hire them to work on their farms. But, while strident and possessing some political clout, the farmers were not particularly well organized and thus were unable to block the paternalism-in-action of the NAD, which remained as energetic and solicitous at the local level and as sensitive to cost at the higher bureaucratic levels as in 1912. No NAD denigration of African culture occurred, and no African initiative was vetoed; on the contrary, the chiefs in question knew how to manipulate their native commissioner, to make him represent them forcefully within the state bureaucracy. Although none of the actors in this particular drama drew attention to white farmers' need to organize nationally, that is the direction in which the farmers would have to move in order to make a successful end-run around the paternalism of the NAD.

The landscape here was radically different from Pondoland, on the undulating Lebombo flats in the eastern Transvaal, a hot and drought-prone part of the lowveld near the Komati River on the Mozambique border. The winters are warm and dry, the summers hot and rainy. The area is plagued by East Coast fever, controlled only by dipping stock. Its ability to support stock rearing is inhibited also by the presence of nagana, animal sleeping sickness, which can be controlled only by clearing the bush and destroying game infected by the tsetse fly host. People depended for their subsistence principally on maize. Because little rain falls on the flats (fifteen to twenty-five inches a year), local Africans, a mixture of Sotho, Shangaan, and Swazi-speaking people, tended to farm in clusters along rivers where the soil was rich.[43]

Between 1922 and 1935 the people living there drew dangerously close to famine on three occasions, as drought compounded damages wrought by locusts or the pest known as "army worm," by high-priced mealies, by low wages, and by cattle too sick or weak to walk through dipping tanks unassisted or too thin to be sold to the Johannesburg quarantine market. During each of the crises individual native commissioners sympathetically represented their people's plight to administrative superiors in Pretoria, urging the department to take forthright and dynamic steps to relieve the suffering by buying African cattle, fixing grain prices, opening a depot to sell grain at fair prices, and distributing mealies to the hungry on credit.[44] In 1927 this active paternalism nearly provoked bloodshed.

The antagonists were a benevolent local magistrate, G. F. Bennett, and his African wards, on the one hand, and local white farmers, on the other. In the eyes of Africans living on the flats the whites, with few exceptions, were exploitative. Often doubling as local traders, they charged high prices, in cash or bartered cattle, for their grain when African harvests were poor. They paid low wages to their farm laborers, sometimes holding back their pay at the end of the month. And so, young African men from the region preferred to migrate to the cities to find work. Perhaps for these reasons a radical workers' organization with rural appeal, the Industrial and Commercial Workers' Union (ICU), had had some success in recruiting new members in the nearby small gold-mining town of Barberton. The white farmers would have denied the charges made against them, arguing instead that they suffered from a chronic labor shortage the government should remedy by allowing them to recruit migrants from nearby Portuguese East Africa, or alternatively that the government should simply let local Africans be driven by hunger to work on their farms, not try to help them get enough to eat.

Although Bennett had known since 1926 that drought and the pest known as army worm would shrink the maize harvest to a fraction of its normal size, he was alerted to the full gravity of the situation when eight local chiefs visited him in March and April 1927, to ask for mealies to distribute to their people for repayment when times were better. By the middle of April some families had plowed and sowed five times for nothing.[45] They feared that the few local traders willing to buy their cattle would offer them unfair prices. Saying they had used up all their money buying expensive grain, the chiefs suggested that Bennett emulate the republican government of Paul Kruger that had provided them with grain after the 1896 locust invasion.[46] They went on to air the common patriarchal complaint that the majority of their young men laboring away from home squandered their earnings by spending them on themselves rather than sending them to their families. While the praise of President Kruger, not often remembered for his generosity towards Africans, may have startled Bennett, he supported the request for relief grain, sending it upward for approval in the NAD hierarchy.[47]

However, Bennett's superior in Pretoria, E. R. Garthorne, the undersecretary for native affairs, demanded proof more tangible than the testimony of eight chiefs that starvation loomed and that all able-bodied men had gone to work in the cities and mines. "They should be advised," he wrote to Bennett, "that on no account will the Government come to their assistance until they have exhausted every means of helping themselves and particularly till every able bodied man who can be spared has gone out to work to supply funds and is not sitting at home consuming food that should be given to the women and children."[48] Undaunted by this austere lecture and clearly fired by an ideal of service, Bennett managed to win Garthorne's approval for spending the profits of the local dipping fund on grain for families he personally knew to be hungry.[49] A couple of months later Bennett requested "a very liberal supply" (nine thousand bags) of white mealies to distribute for repayment in a year.[50]

Bennett's act of charity falls within the long-standing NAD tradition of resisting involvement in farm labor recruitment. Magistrates tended to blame white farmers for causing their own labor shortages by offering their workers poor conditions. Even the secretary for native affairs J. F. Herbst, a Natalian who has been called a stern bureaucrat without the liberal sympathies of his predecessor, E. Barrett, accepted the NAD's role as a protector rather than a procurer of labor. A recent political change had modified but not transformed his stance: when Hertzog was elected prime minister in 1924 and assumed the office of minister of native affairs he did not want the department to be seen as hostile to the farmers, a significant part of his constituency. And so, Garthorne acquiesced to farmers' pressures, saying the NAD would be willing to cooperate with a farm labor recruiting bureau under the auspices of the department of agriculture "in every way possible short of identifying itself with the actual recruiting of natives."[51]

Despite this recent breakthrough, Bennett's charity smacked of the old paternalism and ignited the tempers of local white farmers, already living under stress as they struggled to grow maize on dry land. They had only recently won the battle against the tsetse fly that had infected their herds of cattle with trypanosomiasis, and malaria on the lowveld had continued to thwart their attempts to grow cotton.[52] Three farmers' associations—Lowveld, Komati Agricultural, and Middelburg Farmers—now marshaled their talents for agitation and for exerting political pressure and fought back. They complained directly to Secretary Herbst that the distribution of relief mealies prevented local folk from having to work in the farmers' labor-starved fields and from having to buy their grain. (The local farmers tended to be traders as well; the Africans living in the vicinity were "a natural market for their products."[53]) They also wrote to the Nelspruit member of parliament, W. H. Rood, asking that the gifts of grain be stopped because "we have orders on hand for 150 men and boys and are unable to fill them, in consequence local farmers are having to curtail their output." Bennett disagreed, and the following day he shot off a telegram to the NAD office in Cape Town calling the farmers' depiction of the problem "quite incorrect." There was no justification for denying assistance to Africans. Herbst himself was more impressed by the farmers' pressure and asked Bennett to modify his proposals; when Bennett refused, he cut his allocation from the nine thousand bags requested to two thousand.[54]

While these bags were being transported by rail to the eastern Transvaal, the Komati Agricultural and Industrial Society (KAIS) formed a vigilance committee to take them by force. Its secretary, H. S. Webb, who prided himself on his forceful oratory, maintained that the farmers felt betrayed "in favour of pusillanimous petting of the natives, and of encouraging the natives in indolence and evasion of man's duty to labour." He "proceeded to gather a number of farmers of standing and long residence in the district, to proceed, unarmed, to prevent any distribution" until Major Herbst had investigated the issue. "There is emphatically no need for immediate distribution," the society wired to Pretoria, "no distress and no famine." Webb swore that "if mealies are issued to the old and impotent they will be eaten by the hale and lusty." The farmers argued that distributing the grain would constitute unfair trading competition and interfere with their labor supply. (They usually drew their labor from Portuguese East Africa or from local folk who were forced to work by "the pressure of a bad season.")[55]

A crowd of local Africans had gathered at the siding and threatened to take the grain to the native commissioner's camp and guard it there "to prevent any white man from interfering." Webb warned that any bloodshed would be on Bennett's head. The following day the secretary for native affairs wired a conciliatory and vaguely cautionary reply: "Confident your association will not allow possible misunderstanding form basis of precipitate action," at the same time wiring Bennett, "Please get in touch with association and endeavour arrive at understanding."[56] Bennett's reply was swift and dismissive: "Owing [to the] determined and defiant attitude" of the society, there was no hope of arriving at any understanding.[57] Perhaps because the authority of the NAD was being challenged, Garthorne told Bennett to proceed with the distribution and suggested calling in the police. Webb's tendency to hyperbole cannot have inspired much confidence in the NAD, and when he alleged in his letter of 17 July that the drought was "caused" by overstocking, one official circled the word in apparent amusement or consternation. Africans' love of cattle and small stock was said to be guilty of almost all ecological damage, but rarely the cause of lack of rain!

The principal impulse within the higher levels of the NAD was to react defensively rather than assertively against the attacks. Herbst not only cut Bennett's grain request by more than a quarter and urged him to account for the money he had spent from the dipping fund in case there was an inquiry, but he also acceded to the farmers' wishes that the district not be opened to mine recruitment as a form of famine relief. Prime Minister Hertzog, replying to Rood, the local member of parliament, displayed the tension between the triple imperatives of bureaucratic consistency, paternalism, and service of an enfranchised constituency that had characterized the whole affair. Apologizing for the "unpleasantness," he said that it was too late for the NAD to investigate the trouble since nearly all the mealies had been distributed by local officials "really convinced" of the threat of hunger. In the future, he concluded, no further mealies would be purchased for distribution, and "where there is a healthy Kaffir that can work he will have to do so."[58]

Hertzog's pro forma display of sympathy did not mean that every farmer's future wishes would be granted. Nearly a decade later, in 1935, when the people of Komati suffered from an invasion of locusts hard on the heels of two drought years, they would again need a relief supply of maize. Their cattle were in danger of growing too thin to be salable, and the price of mealies had risen from sixteen to nineteen shillings a bag. Despite Webb's earlier attack on its "pusillanimous petting of the natives," the NAD did distribute relief grain. It, too, distributed maize in the aftermath of a foot-and-mouth epidemic in 1938, again in the face of KAIS protest, because "it is far more equitable to assist the Natives by the introduction of a relief scheme than to allow them to incur debts which they may possibly never be in a position to liquidate."[59] Local paternalism retained its vitality and even continued to resonate upward in the state bureaucracy.

Not until the 1940s would these frightened and angry white farmers find their situation easing. Only then would large-scale bush-clearing and irrigation schemes develop the local cultivation of subtropical fruit, tobacco, citrus, winter vegetables, and sugarcane to the extent that substantial numbers of new settlers would move to the region. The hard land of South Africa needed to be tamed by money, and, in 1927, farmers were still struggling to tap the capital the mines had produced.

No blood was shed in 1927. Neither is there any evidence that the drought developed into a killing famine; in this sense, the white farmers may have been correct in denying that a genuine famine was occurring. Despite their access to the highest political circles, they had proved unable to stop the distribution of relief grain. At best, they succeeded in keeping the level of relief low. The fact that their organization was local rather than national considerably weakened their impact. That they organized at all was their most significant achievement, one whose meaning would soon become clear.

Politicized Hunger and Bureaucratized Paternalism: The Eastern Cape, 1946

During the famine of 1945–1946 in the eastern Cape, NAD paternalism turned sour. Officials' tones were changing, and they now spoke harshly of African culture, while, paradoxically, launching larger and more creative schemes than ever before to relieve hunger. The reasons for this newly impatient and denigratory attitude were various. The crisis of rural poverty had grown in magnitude while the fiscal structures for redressing it had not, and thus NAD officials seemed genuinely fearful of the cost of fulfilling the widespread postwar hopes for a better-fed world. Further, their department had lost its monopoly on expertly addressing the problem of famine and communicating it to the wider public.

In the eastern Cape in 1946, the harvest failed, as in much of South Africa, for the second year in a row. Its precise effect on people's health was, as usual, hard to gauge. Some said a famine was occurring, others called it "distress." Visitors to the eastern Cape, one of the worst hit areas, tended to describe the consequences in pitiable anecdotes. A man walking east from Alice was picked up so exhausted from starvation that he did not know his own name. Perhaps he had been searching for the dirty water that people could now find only after hiking five miles or more. Mothers on similar treks ran the risk of exposing their infants to infections like measles, as well as to intestinal parasites; both readily killed the weak. Children were coming down with scurvy; as if advertising their need, some were seen eating orange peels discarded by people studying their plight. "Small numbers" were dying.[60]

Cattle were dying in droves (over 50 percent of the entire Ciskeian herd according to one official assessment), while most of the survivors were too weak to pull plows. Milk supplies had dried up, and even ewes had trouble producing enough milk to keep their lambs alive. When rain finally fell in February 1946, it came so late that no wild food, such as spinach, prickly pear, and pumpkins, had grown to tide people over until their mealies became green. Further, the impact of the rain was so weak that it barely penetrated the ground. For all these reasons the drought was said to be the worst the eastern Cape had experienced since 1927.[61]

Drought was only one catalyst of hardship. An invasion of army worms and an attack of East Coast fever in 1945 also helped to blight subsistence. In the immediate aftermath of World War II, as in 1912, there were too few motor vehicles to carry grain from railway terminals into remote areas. Dearth had marked the entire span of the war, especially in rural areas. The reasons for the shortages extended beyond inflation and ordinary deprivations of wartime. By 1946 international food distribution networks had still not adjusted to peacetime: the U.S. was sending grain to Europe; Canada's granaries were said to be empty; it was hard to get supplies from Argentina; Kenya had already sent its surplus to South Africa; and Rhodesia had none. Internationally there was unprecedented alarm about food shortages, as if Malthus were finally going to be proved right. These global disruptions were compounded in South Africa by the national control white farmers had managed to win in the late 1930s over the prices and distribution of their crops. Marketing boards made food expensive in South Africa. In this particular case, the Mealie Industry Control Board was partly responsible for the shortage because it skewed mealie distribution in favor of cooperative societies—six of the twelve white farmers' representatives on the board came from farmers' cooperatives—which created distributive bottlenecks and in this way encouraged a black market to flourish.

Lying underneath all these conjunctural causes of food shortage was the fact that land allotments in the Ciskei were too small to provide subsistence for the number living on them. As Margaret Ballinger, a natives' representative in the lower house of the South African parliament, observed in 1943, the Glen Grey Act of 1897 had laid out small parcels "and they have simply been getting smaller under the new pressure" of a growing population.[62] In 1945, D. L. Smit, secretary for native affairs, had told the Ciskeian General Council that, even if the government actually bought all the promised additional land in the area, "there would never be enough land to enable every Native in the reserves to become a full-time peasant farmer."[63]

Though the wartime economy had opened up employment to a large number of workers, either as laborers or soldiers, this newly expanded labor force had not necessarily eaten well. The cost of living soared beyond the reach of many of these beneficiaries of the wartime boom. The price of food had been rising steadily from 1936 to 1939 and steeply from 1940 to 1945. Many employed Africans could no longer afford to buy meat. The gap between earnings and basic costs was widening, as report after report during the early 1940s testified.[64] Most African men over eighteen years of age resented having to pay annually a one pound poll tax, not in itself excessive but a significant proportion of their already stretched salaries. Prewar attempts to lower the tax foundered in parliament when nationalist M.P.s such as J. G. Strijdom and J. J. Serfontein lobbied vigorously against it on the ground that the money spent on Africans should come from African taxes.[65] In addition, high duties levied on foreign agricultural produce to protect South African farmers from competition led the price of food to increase while wages did not.

In the face of such threats to the livelihood of its "wards," the NAD continued to provide relief along the lines that had guided its rural policies earlier in the century. Its initial response was extreme caution. When food shortages first appeared during a drought in 1941 the chief native commissioner of the Ciskei, stationed in King William's Town, refused to provide relief work—paying people to carry kraal manure to their fields—when requested to do so by one of his subordinates: "Only when famine conditions are imminent will the Department be prepared to consider provision of relief."[66] The upper echelons of the native affairs bureaucracy feared attracting public criticism if they provided relief when labor was in short supply. At that particular moment during World War II, service in the Native Military Corps had not proved popular. Perhaps hunger would encourage more African men to sign up.

Lower level magistrates, as before, tended to be more sympathetic to local needs.[67] They continued to condemn as "unscrupulous" trader-farmers who sought to exploit hunger by buying African cattle at low prices or selling grain at grotesquely inflated prices. Some quarreled with farmers who withheld rations from their employees, and refused to prosecute Africans who deserted those farms. Other magistrates blamed the agricultural marketing boards for driving up food prices and failing to serve African consumers' needs. One nutrition officer visiting the eastern Cape during the 1945 "distress conditions" was moved to pay a backhanded, though accurate, compliment, that no matter how "trivial" its efforts may seem, the department was unfailingly "sympathetic."[68]

Scrupulous monitoring of local conditions continued to be the strong point of NAD administration.[69] Two programs, pauper rations and drought relief schemes, had long reflected the paternalistic ethic of the department, and each month the native commissioner would distribute rations (one pound of mealie meal daily in 1946) to individuals living on the edge of survival, usually the very old and sick, often widows. The state had defined poor relief in minimal terms, as "foodstuffs . . . calculated to maintain the recipients at slightly above starvation level."[70] Most of the poor were expected to work for their own rescue and, during crises, a magistrate would formulate local development schemes and employ the needy, paying them in cash or food. He designed public works projects such as road repair to provide local relief without inculcating habits of dependence. These plans also involved building dams and contour walls against erosion or carrying kraal manure to the fields on sledges. Men received higher rates of pay than women (one shilling for men as opposed to nine pence a day for women, plus pauper rations that amounted to three-quarter pounds of maize weekly until December 1945), presumably so that they would be encouraged to retain patriarchal responsibility for their families' welfare. The same logic informed the decision to deny to Africans old-age pensions: "the guiding consideration has been that benefits should not be provided in such a form or in such amount as to conflict with or break down their tribal food-sharing habit."[71] This aspect of African culture was one that most white observers praised in tones of wonderment.

Pauper rations and drought relief schemes continued to be accompanied by paternal criticism and advice. Vernacular messages to the mines and barracks exhorted absent wage earners to send money home. In tones of exasperation magistrates tended to urge their "wards" to stop thinking of their cattle as wealth and start thinking of them as meat. For the time being these exhortations remained only words—there were no organized stock markets in most rural areas—but their tone was ominous, carrying the threat of "rigorous and regular de-stocking."[72]

Destocking was one component of the development schemes variously called "reclamation," "rehabilitation," and "betterment" that the NAD had begun to launch in the 1930s. Proclaiming a location as a betterment area entailed dividing it into several residential and arable zones as well as different grazing camps. People would be relocated into villages, which were, like the pastures, fenced, and within them, they were expected to plow on the contour and rotate their grazing paddocks in order to prevent the soil washing away and to ensure that it would rest. While such planning aimed at making the reserves self-sufficient, its initial stages entailed spending more, not less, money. And so, unprecedentedly large sums of money now had to back NAD projects; in 1945 the department spent ten thousand pounds in the Ciskei alone on imported seed potatoes and wheat seeds, as well as on tractors and plows that could help, as some critics observed, at most a few families.[73] The money for these purchases came originally from the South African Native Trust (SANT), an organization set up in 1936 to enlarge the reserves and develop African communal agriculture on expropriated, formerly white, commercial farmland. Betterment to stoke reserve economies and make them self-sustaining in the long run was one thing; the immediate cost of feeding hungry people was another. Who was to foot the bill?

The department of social welfare and the Cape provincial government both denied responsibility for "mass starvation of children." The process of state denial was protracted but inexorable. In May 1945, the Lovedale hospital board had complained to the native commissioner in nearby Alice that it needed another "medical man" and government funds if it was going to care for and house in military huts or tents the twenty to thirty thousand undernourished children needing help. The NAD referred the request to the Public Health Department, which in turn forwarded it to the Cape provincial administration. The province replied that mass starvation of children was a matter for Social Welfare or the NAD. Social Welfare denied that it was involved. The NAD again asked Public Health for advice and for another medical officer. Public Health "replied that the Province could hardly be expected to provide accommodation for children suffering from nutritional deficiency" and that it had no jurisdiction in such provincial matters. And so, an NAD bureaucrat advised his own department in August 1945, "In the circumstances it seems that nothing further can be done in the matter."[74] The secretary for native affairs tried once more to exert pressure on the Cape provincial secretary, stating that the responsibility belonged there; there was no money left in the SANT fund in any case. The problem of hunger was left in the hands of the NAD, where it had always been. But need was mounting faster than resources in the immediate postwar world and there had to be some way to define state responsibility toward poor Africans so narrowly that the electorate would not find the fiscal burden intolerable.

In the 1946 famine, children alone were made the beneficiaries of extraordinary famine relief. Paternalistic rhetoric that had until recently framed Africans as children was changing to focus only on Africans who were, in fact, children. In response to needs defined by the board of the Victoria Hospital (Lovedale), the NAD set up a scheme to feed 25,000 preschool children in the southern Ciskei. After receiving a report from a nutrition officer, the head office of the NAD established more than two hundred cooking centers there at the cost of £23,000 a year.[75] Only children under seven years of age were to be fed by these field kitchens "erected on a military pattern." In an attempt to prevent dependence on their philanthropy, workers at the feeding centers warned African mothers that they should not "refuse to feed the children at home upon the grounds that they had already received food."[76] (Semifit men and women would continue to be paid a small wage and receive rations for repairing roads, constructing dams, and eradicating noxious weeds, as well as planting spineless cacti.) The porridge offered at the field kitchens was intended to be supplementary, not a completely balanced meal, and it contained what proved to be a surprisingly palatable mixture of ingredients—fish oil, sugar, peanut butter, milk powder, yeast, and three different kinds of meal (soy, whole, and mealie)—that would have been expensive to buy. This unique and innovative program arose out of the collaboration of one nutrition officer, J. M. Latsky, with the NAD. In a 1946 issue of the medical student journal *The Leech,* Dr. T. W. B. Osborn, referring to the Ciskei famine, praised the government's communal feeding scheme as the only way to avoid famines like those that had just occurred in the European theater of the war.[77] Osborn was equating the social suffering in a war-torn continent with a country that had known no internal combat.

Part of the effort to fight starvation entailed introducing the commercially processed food people had earlier spurned. Sometimes the foods donated as famine relief were memorably bizarre, and surprisingly popular, such as shark biltong (dried shark meat).[78] Officials urged oatmeal upon local consumers as an adequate substitute for mealie meal or sorghum porridge. Occasionally, advocates of new types of processed foods pressed their ideas on government; one enthusiast wanted officials to subsidize for African consumption the manufacture of "predigested" (hydrolyzed) protein from cattle too inferior to be butchered or from whale meat, and he angrily blamed his lack of success in launching his scheme on vested interests in South African agriculture.[79] Less eccentric plans entailed fortifying existing foods by, for example, treating mealie meal with soya meal, fish liver oil, dehydrated vegetables, government sugar, and powdered milk.[80]

The problem with all these new foods was that, unless they were to be distributed free during a famine, they all cost money. This issue alone should have highlighted the problem of wage rates. In the Ciskei famine, the only people to call attention to how little money people were earning in the mines and industries were liberal and African critics. As Margaret Ballinger, natives' representative since 1937, lamented, "[S]o long as the mass of the people are unenfranchised and the enfranchised are a privileged minority who suffer little from any dislocation in our food market, I am not hopeful of the results."[81]

If the people of the Ciskei were at all fortunate in 1945 and 1946, it was because they had a couple of exceptionally engaged observers trying to figure out and then broadcast the significance of their hunger. One was Dr. Roseberry Bokwe, educated at the University of Edinburgh, a district surgeon in the small town of Middledrift. During the worst of the famine he corresponded with Margaret Ballinger, joking that as one of the natives' representatives she was branded as a communist, agitator, and troublemaker "just because you choose to state the bare facts as they are!"[82] Together they sought to link this particular misfortune to increasingly urgent issues for the future of the nation, such as wages and land rights. One sign of their success is the vigor with which the Keiskammahoek Rural Survey sought three years later to discover and document the extent of malnutrition in the area.[83]

Both Bokwe and Ballinger were determined to define what was happening as "gross starvation" rather than as a particularly bad bout of malnutrition. They tried to use the drought to publicize what Bokwe called "the steadily deteriorating health of the people, owing mainly to increasing poverty." To win this definitional struggle, they had to bring into their camp experts sent by Pretoria to determine what was going on. Ballinger frankly stated that her own goal was to get South African land policy redefined as providing "an economic unit on which a family can make a living in order to stop the migrant labour system."[84] She and Bokwe selected as one nemesis Dr. Latsky, the Department of Public Health officer in charge of its nutrition section since 1943, who visited the eastern Cape three times in 1945.

A definitional struggle was launched. After his first stay, Latsky reported back to the secretary for public health, "I saw no children dying of actual hunger or starvation. It is more a question of chronic *mal*nutrition or lack of proper and enough food than one of actual famine and starvation." Latsky lacked neither sympathy for the victims nor awareness that the problem was grave, but he did feel hampered by the absence of reliable statistics revealing whether the situation was deteriorating. He also believed that "the problem of the Native *remains* an economic and educational one." The longer term dilemma, as he saw it, was to make nutritionally sophisticated cooks out of African women and progressive farmers out of African men. Latsky believed that the "ignorance of Native mothers especially is appalling" and that "the root problem [was] overstocking with scrub cattle." He summed up his view of the origins of the crisis: "Only 5 per cent of the Ciskeian Native communities are at present settled on betterment areas. Too late they have realised the value of proper veld management, rotation grazing and of avoiding overstocking. Unfortunately the Ciskei is now reaping the fruits of ignorance and deeply ingrained tribal tradition and the Government is handicapped by [sic] coming to its immediate rescue by several factors chief of which is the world shortage of food." A dietician named Miss Taute, sent out in June, also by the Department of Public Health, to devise recipes for the feeding centers, concluded her evaluation report by wondering what would happen when the next drought occurred. "To this I can see only one answer," she wrote, "and that is that the Natives in the Ciskei will never be able to face a bad drought under existing conditions. They are not producing enough food to feed themselves at present; and it is doubtful whether they ever will unless their whole point of view and system of farming is radically changed very soon."[85]

Ballinger met Latsky upon his return to the Transvaal and urged him to extend the preschool feeding scheme with maize that the manager of the maize marketing board had agreed to donate, thanks to her intercession. "All he did (not being a conspicuously strong man)," she wrote to Dr. Bokwe, "was to send my letter to the N.A.D. and so far I have heard nothing more." (Latsky did indeed express more idealistic and activist goals at a medical student conference that same year than he did in his correspondence with the secretary for public health.[86]) Ballinger sought from Bokwe a fuller sense of what was happening on the ground. A good publicist, she also wanted to "make all the noise we can about the present position so as to get all we can while emotions are fluid."[87] Bokwe did provide a far more comprehensive portrait of life in a famine-stricken area, his analysis extending beyond the bodies of the hungry to the range of their fears and suspicions, and to the state of the nation.

According to Bokwe, the source of the problem was "NOT 'Overstocking' but 'Overpopulation' or congestion and what is therefor needed is just more land for THEM and their already LIMITED amount of stock." Like Latsky he lacked figures, but he felt certain that each family had, at the best of times, too few stock and too little land to provide itself with "the bare minimum necessary to enable it to have milk and to plough its land." The drought had simply worsened or highlighted this underlying poverty. Instead of responding to this structural crisis, the government had failed to deliver on its 1936 promise to provide more land for African occupation. "The people," Bokwe reported, "ask, naturally where the land is that Hertzog promised."[88]

This failure made Africans suspicious of the "Govt.'s present war cry" of "rehabilitation," that is, erosion control, stock limitation, and settlement in villages. "Why," Bokwe asked, "this sudden unholy rush to ask the people to accept a scheme which is to revolutionise their past and present mode of living? Are the millions to be voted for this to go the same way as those voted for the Native Trust, mainly into European pockets by way of enhanced prices for their farms and salaries for numerous agricultural officers of the Trust? Very little of this money has come our way and that mainly by insignificant grants to Hospitals etc and the employment of a few hundred poorly qualified and under-paid agricultural demonstrators." Meanwhile, Bokwe wrote after yet another unproductive encounter with Latsky, he was having to parry official dismissals of the situation's gravity. "These people did not look starved, at least not the Belsen type," Latsky and another visitor told him in November; rather, they looked simply hungry. When asked where the line should be drawn between starvation and hunger, Latsky replied that only those with "swollen ankles" and "puffy faces" were actually starving. But, Bokwe said, "It [is] my duty to intervene long before those conditions become apparent." Bokwe blamed the local and chief native commissioners for having, in conversations with Latsky, minimized the importance of the shortages in order to deflect "criticism of their administration."[89]

The fiscal ethos of the time had probably primed the visitors to oppose the expansion of state welfare. No one wanted to hang a dead weight of dependents on the national exchequer, especially before the economy recovered from the war effort. This conservatism was sometimes explicitly stated but more often glossed with a peculiar interpretation of African culture: it had to be protected from certain kinds of social change. And so, welfare or charity could be seen as evils if they broke down the "Native Custom" of sharing. During Bokwe's encounter with his visitors, this perspective emerged in an argument against feeding a widow whose sole support, a brother, had gone to Port Elizabeth to find work. "Oh yes," one of the visitors imagined, "the Brother has now said, I am not going to do anything more as Bokwe can feed you!" Bokwe found the NAD official's analysis that he was breaking down African custom to be "amusing under sad circumstances." He was left to wonder, "Now, what is their long term policy to be?"[90]

If NAD paternalism was cheap, there were other organizations trying to bridge the gap between hunger and plenty in the aftermath of the war. Missionaries and a few new philanthropies acted as catalysts. In 1945 the NAD had been spurred to act because medical doctors at Lovedale, founded by the Free Church of Scotland, had warned that they were about to be overwhelmed by local need; they had 250 beds for a population of perhaps 200,000, the hospital was running a deficit, and parents were increasingly dumping their malnourished children there.[91] The following year the Presbyterian church urged that food stocks unused by the Union Defense Force be sent to the area. It also argued that the price of mealies be lowered by subsidies and by importation from the United States. In addition to pressures exerted by such accustomed groups, dynamic new philanthropies had emerged in the postwar world. One, the African Children's Feeding Scheme, founded in Johannesburg, operated soup kitchens mainly in cities. In rural areas emergency aid was often supplied by the Red Cross, though its offer to help in the Ciskei was spurned by the NAD in 1945 with the defensive explanation that the "situation was well in hand."[92]

Two newcomers to the field of philanthropy had unusual backgrounds. One was the African Drought Relief Fund Committee, chaired by Dr. A. B. Xuma, president of the African National Congress; its personnel was entirely African and its scope was national. It collected funds to buy mealies, mealie meal, and sorghum to distribute in the Ciskei, the northern Transvaal, northern Natal, Zululand, and the eastern Orange Free State. The second was the African Food Fund, initiated in 1945 by the *Guardian* newspaper (a communist weekly printed in Cape Town) specifically to meet the famine conditions in the Ciskei; it supplied free food to district surgeons and organized soup kitchens. Like Ballinger and Bokwe, the fund linked Ciskeian hunger to persistent social conditions like migrant labor and overcrowding. In the process of setting up the soup kitchens, its employees carefully observed the conditions around them. One, C. Papu in Middledrift, counted the number of people who owned no stock and held no land. His figures, he said, "give the lie to two misrepresentations about conditions in the reserves," proving that a large proportion of the people were landless and that "the Reserves are not as overstocked as is often asserted."[93] Wide-ranging social criticism was part and parcel of postwar philanthropy.

The father-child metaphors that had once signified local deference toward NAD officials by their wards were less in evidence in 1946 than during the previous famines. The black middle class was growing more radical and assertive, and, alarmed by the process of impoverishment that threatened to level African wealth, it made little use of paternalistic concepts either up or down the social hierarchy. Just before the drought began, a councillor on the Transkeian Bunga eloquently expressed the growing political economic perspective. Asking for a commission of inquiry into the "root cause of poverty, indebtedness and starvation" of Africans in the neighboring Transkeian territories, Councillor T. Ntintili noted that, "To-day people who used to be rich men before and who rose in the morning to hear the lowing of their cattle now get up at the sound of their poultry." Despite the government's appointment of agricultural demonstrators, establishment of a department of agriculture, and subsidy of seeds, starvation still existed. Worse, it was "becoming rife." "If a man starves," he argued, "it is because he is poor and there are circumstances which have placed him in that position—conditions that tie men down so that they are not able to move freely, conditions which call for investigation."[94]

The debates in the Bunga reveal the widening chasm between black and white assessments of what was to be done. They also reveal the coming together of middle-class and poor Africans in their analysis of what was wrong. Some white liberals and radicals were indeed forging links with African leaders; Margaret Ballinger, for example, urged such luminaries as Z. K. Matthews and D. D. T. Jabavu, highly educated members of the black middle class, and Roseberry Bokwe to complain directly to the minister of agriculture, J. G. N. Strauss, about the inadequacy of the recent food subsidy, restricted to maize and wheat. Meanwhile, the NAD rejected item by item the range of welfare benefits proposed by delegates to the Bunga: pensions and schemes for invalids, workmen's compensation, the supply of stud bulls to indigent Africans, the establishment of markets for African produce, the purchase of additional land for the reserves, the payment of doctors' salaries, hospitals for the aged and mentally ill, and school feeding schemes. These proposals ranged from the imaginative to a simple plea for extension of welfare benefits already enjoyed by Europeans. Instead, the Bunga delegates complained, their animals received better health care than the people of the Transkei did. Money was being thrown away on education because people were too poor to put into effect what they had learned. As Councillor Ntintili observed, starvation existed because people who wanted to rise were unable to do so.

Bunga delegates argued that their poverty was becoming inescapable. The government would deny a pension to a man who owned five head of cattle. If he complied with the government's wishes and sold his cows, which he kept for their milk, he was likely to become malnourished. Another dilemma arose around the issue of beer brewing. When an NAD official, J. J. Yates, tried to enforce greater thrift by legally restricting brewing "in excessive quantities," he ran the risk of damaging the local economy. Councillor B. Siroqo argued, in 1947, that he brewed beer precisely because he did not have "enough money which I am getting as my wages from the Government to be able to afford to pay people to plough my lands. If I want to fetch my wood supply from the plantation I have to brew beer to pay for the supply, because I cannot afford to employ servants and pay them money."[95] In these cases and many others, the Bunga delegates implied, the government seemed to want the people to be poor.

The NAD's behavior towards its wards exhibited many outward signs of continuity in the postwar years. Some lower level magistrates did take unilateral initiatives to feed the hungry, scrupulously monitoring local conditions so pauper rations and famine relief could be doled out fairly. At the same time, they continued to veto African initiatives in the 1940s just as they had in the

1910s. But there were significant changes. Instead of referring to all Africans as their children as noted above, magistrates made African children the chief objects of their benevolence. Although larger sums of money—£26,000—had been made available for famine relief in 1946 than ever before, the need, too, appeared to be greater. State bureaucracies, frightened by the likely expense posed by the growth of indigents, sought ways of keeping costs down, leading not only to the stress upon children but also to the advocacy of nutrition education and fortified food, not of higher wages. It also encouraged a static vision of African culture—as a food-sharing entity—that must be protected from disruptive change. One of its highest officials, the undersecretary, attributed the crisis not to drought worsened by marketing problems but to "overstocking combined with ignorance in regard to how to live." He urged upon a delegation of missionaries that they "should do [their] best to persuade the Natives to kill and eat their surplus stock." Betterment schemes to improve rural productivity were a logical response to this definition of the problem; "the position clamours for further desperate efforts by the [NAD] to effect rigorous and regular destocking."[96] Such solutions, especially when backed by force, proved to be so unpopular that they helped to kill the father-child metaphors that formerly gave a natural gloss to rural power relations.

Conclusion

The three famines of 1912, 1927, and 1946 do not fit conventional notions of famine. There were no "walking skeletons." It is safe to say that few people starved to death. Nevertheless, the word *famine* was used freely by the press, the hungry, liberals, and the NAD, reflecting what could be called a famine syndrome, a tendency to think of African social suffering as famine, but with no consensus about what the word meant. People engaged in an intense struggle to define what was happening (distress or poverty) and its causes (ignorance or land shortage).

As John Iliffe has observed, "improved measures for combatting famine coincided with increased susceptibility to it"; this process occurred a generation earlier in South Africa than in the rest of the continent.[97] While famine was waning in the twentieth century because of trade and technological innovation, growing numbers in the reserves were hungry largely because they had either too little land or none at all. The many preindustrial strategies for surviving in a difficult landscape were dwindling to one: access to cash. Families depended on migrants' cash wages.

The cause of famine's decline was intimately related to the rise of hunger in one other way, as well. Access to state monies had allowed commercial farms to produce more food, but organizations representing white farmers' interests kept the cost of that food high, enhancing the risk of hunger among South Africa's poor. Famine excites pity, while hunger invites expense.

As the nature of famine changed, the South African government confronted two stark choices. It could either follow the paternalistic imperatives of its inherited "native policy," or it could repudiate them. Erecting an umbrella of welfare to protect all South Africans would have been expensive for white taxpayers, and the fiscal structures to oblige them to pay up simply did not exist. Denying responsibility, on the other hand, entailed remolding images of African famine that had existed for decades. The image of improvidence endured, but it was being superseded by a new scientific rationale for denying welfare: Africans were unscientific farmers whose actions starved their own children.

CHAPTER FOUR

Scientific Paternalism

Hunger and the Measurement of Urban Poverty, 1910–1948

> With the control of Nature with which modern science has endowed us, any economic system must be accounted a failure, root and branch, if with proper planning it cannot [give the workers a "human" or "civilised" standard of life].
>
> *Alfred Hoernle, 1942*

A YOUNG WHITE WOMAN entered the squalid Johannesburg township of Alexandra in 1944, armed with a notebook and pen. The Alexandra Health Centre and University Clinic had sent Gertrude Kark to survey that black residential area, set in the white sea of northern Johannesburg, so that it could establish a welfare center for African families living there. For two years she described, measured, and tabulated their way of life. She found the record-keeping hard. When she visited one overcrowded "hovel," for example, she needed a flashlight "to identify the mass of huddled limbs" of people so wary of intruders that they kept the window—she measured it to be two feet square—closed during the daytime. She struggled to keep accurate figures of people's income and employment, even though she was reduced to writing in the column beside "Beer Brewer" the words "fearful of revealing details," because that profession, common among African women, was illegal. She discovered that measuring the "food intake" of the very poor was "impossible" because they depended on gifts, rations, and free milk.

Gertrude Kark was one of a small number of social scientists who had been trying since the late 1920s to measure black poverty in South Africa's cities. Supported initially by liberal organizations and later by universities, these researchers set out to record the kinds of statistics—what people ate, how much they spent, what maladies they suffered—that the government showed no interest in collecting. They wanted to document the social changes occurring in South Africa's rapidly industrializing cities. They were also struggling

4. World War II accelerated Africans' "drift" to town, their reliance on purchased food, like the golden syrup being sold in this Langa shop in September 1941, and therefore their vulnerability to falling below the "bread line." (*Cape Times* Collection, National Library, Cape Town)

to understand what *subeconomic* and *sub-subsistence* really meant. In a sense they were attempting oxymoronic research: to quantify the "subeconomic" as if precise numbers had the power to reflect the reality of surviving on unquantifiable gifts and illegal earnings, to discover how people subsisted at "sub-subsistence" levels. Faced with such daunting complexities, they chose to emphasize an index of poverty called the "bread line," that is, the minimum level of food consumption necessary to ensure that a man or woman could work. This measure conveniently suggested to social reformers that poorly paid and, therefore, weak workers could inhibit the productivity of the nation. And it conveyed in unsentimental and scientific terms the concept of decency, so that social reformers could use it to lobby on behalf of African welfare.[1]

These social scientists were not only struggling to define and measure African poverty in towns, they were also in effect searching for an idea on which to base an urban moral economy. Paternalism enjoyed a degree of popular acceptance in the countryside: its father-son metaphors facilitated

communication between social seniors, whether they were chiefs or magistrates, and the juniors who were begging for largesse. In the cities relationships between governor and governed lacked any mutually acceptable
metaphor or ideal. This lack was reflected in the ethos of urban native administration. As one NAD official observed, that administrative spirit had evolved
through four phases: between 1910 and 1923 it was preoccupied with super-
vising urban Africans so that they "did not become a menace to the health of
the European population"; from 1923 it had emphasized control; and during
the 1930s it had been animated by the "importance of ensuring that the conditions under which [the urban African] lives are such as to enable him to be
physically and mentally fit to do the work required of him."[2] None of these
fashions enjoyed the consent of the governed. None made even an allusion to
morality. And yet, implicit in the efforts of the social scientists who were investigating subsistence was a search for decency and justice in South Africa's
towns.

The Idea of the Bread Line

The idea of the "bread line" originated far from southern Africa. In the north
of England at the turn of the twentieth century, B. S. Rowntree struggled to
define the poverty he saw around him in the city of York, and every South
African surveyor of urban poverty subsequently quoted his work. Rowntree
latched on to food, or, more precisely, its lack, as a convenient and revealing
means of measuring socially unacceptable levels of deprivation.[3] He drew an
absolute poverty line; below it, people did not earn enough to buy the "minimum necessities for the maintenance of merely physical efficiency." If working
men did not consume 3,500 calories of food energy daily, and women four-
fifths that amount, their intelligence became dulled and their stature stunted.
This quite pragmatic definition of hunger, the "underfeeding" that would
destroy a person's stamina, served for Rowntree as the index for judging
Britain's "social progress."[4] Unlike medieval ideas connecting poverty to spiritual salvation, this idea of progress reflects the industrial era by being explicitly tied to labor.[5] Food allowed the human machine to work efficiently. From
the point of view of international commercial competition, an underfed working class could retard Britain's development, but the issue was not simply utilitarian. It also had a moral dimension.

Rowntree suggested that his findings were related to British national ethics.
He concluded his study by first noting that the "dark shadow of the Malthusian philosophy" had "passed away"; people no longer had to worry that their
numbers would outstrip the world's food supply. Then he alluded to the ethical challenge of living in a post-Malthusian age. "[N]o view of the ultimate

scheme of things," he wrote, "would now be accepted under which multitudes of men and women are doomed by inevitable law to a struggle for existence so severe as necessarily to cripple or destroy the higher parts of their nature."[6] While leaving undefined exactly what he believed the state ought to do, he was effectively challenging well-fed British people to take care of the bodies and therefore the spirits of poorer Britons. His challenge raises the question of how concerned citizens living in a situation of racial domination would deal with poverty.

Rowntree's "poverty line" is today more interesting for what it reveals about his hopes for society than for its ability to define decency. He set his line extraordinarily high; today between 2,000 and 3,000 calories are accepted as an adult's minimum daily requirement, and even these figures exceed what the average person needs.[7] He probably estimated 3,500 calories as the daily minimum because he was writing at a time when western European caloric consumption had reached its peak; in the twentieth century better-off Europeans showed their affluence by changing the composition of their diets rather than increasing the amount of calories they consumed.[8] Furthermore, caloric levels do not reveal how food is distributed within a family, whether the father is given more meat than his children, for example, or from what food types the calories derive; it is likely that diets eaten at the time Rowntree was writing—high in sugar and expensive cuts of meat—were, in the words of the anthropologist Sidney Mintz, "unhealthy and uneconomical."[9] For all these reasons, applicable with equal force to the surveys in this book, poverty lines represent the perception of a social problem more accurately than its actual dimensions.

For reasons other than their crudity, Rowntree's measurements and his heart-searching references to the poor did not appeal to all his contemporaries, many of whom continued to blame the inadequate diet and therefore weak physiques of the British urban poor on their improvidence, laziness, and ignorance. A commission set up in 1904, for example, to investigate the "deteriorating" physiques of British men, recently recruited to fight in the South African War, denied that a crisis was at hand, but it did chastise the perverse preferences of the poor for eating pickles and vinegar, as well as their generally wasteful expenditure on pleasure rather than on good food. It concluded that remedies like cooking classes would "reduce evils which are not only a standing reproach to certain classes of the nation, but constitute a serious menace to its general well-being."[10] Despite this widespread impatience with the working classes and their profligate habits, Rowntree's implication—that it was morally unacceptable for a nation to allow its people to engage in a severe struggle to survive—would dominate British policy nearly fifty years later.

Rowntree was part of a trajectory in early twentieth-century Britain that would lead to the creation after World War II of a welfare state. The ideas of its chief architect, William Beveridge, that all individuals should be guaranteed social security from the cradle to the grave, flowed logically from Rowntree's pairing of national health and ethics. Rowntree had used the concept of nutrition, the minimum calories needed to preserve physical efficiency, to draw tight the link between the two. When Beveridge first publicized his scheme for social insurance in 1942, he defined his goal as redistributing the national income so that all citizens benefited "up to subsistence level, as of right and without means test." No one would be excluded. By this time, the "bread line" was commonly referred to as the poverty datum line. The change in language reflected a shift from focusing mainly on food as fuel to a more full-bodied conception of physical want and minimal living conditions, one that included abolishing the giants blocking the road to postwar reconstruction, that is, "disease, ignorance, squalor and idleness."[11] While hunger was subsumed in this litany of pressing social ills, it had been explicitly at the heart of early attempts to deal constructively and humanely with modern urban poverty.

In mid-Victorian Britain social science associations had been popular among socially active members of the middle class. They had inquired into the conditions of the poor—their housing, crime, health, prostitution—analyzing society in a highly positivist manner and setting its improvement as their goal. They believed that middle-class progress could be made universal. This ethos affected people who still thought in terms of evolutionary models of social development; they argued that societies had "spiritual personalities" with a "moral will." Rousseau's ideas about human perfectibility influenced this movement more than Hegel's brand of potentially nationalistic idealism, argues the intellectual historian Jose Harris; most influential was Plato's idea that society was "an organic spiritual community" over which the state should exercise justice rather than force. Although British idealists differed on the precise relationship between the individual and the state, they all seem to have agreed that the highest purpose of social welfare was "inculcating citizenship." In Britain, especially around the time the Union of South Africa was created, many social idealists argued that the state's proper role was to remove the causes of ill health and malnutrition, as well as low wages and unemployment, in order to allow the full flowering of popular "ethical self-fulfillment and participation in public life." This ethos became professionalized in Britain prior to World War II, but popular idealism remained strong. William Beveridge, Harris notes, was part of this idealist tradition.[12] There was no such wider culture or heritage of social reform within South Africa.

What happened to these measurements and the social welfare trajectory from Rowntree to Beveridge when they were transferred from the metropole to the periphery in South Africa? A 1909 article by a Grahamstown physician, J. Bruce-Bays, suggests how metropolitan ideas were being modified by colonial experience. Bruce-Bays warned that Africans were adapting so badly to urban living, specifically to their new housing, diet, and clothing, that their race ran the risk of being "doomed to speedy extinction." While the 1904 British dietary commission had specifically rejected Darwinian analogies, they were alive and well in provincial South Africa, and early in the century they were clearly more popular than the scientific moralism of Rowntree.[13] Bruce-Bays avoided calling urban Africans poor. They were, rather, adjusting badly to conditions brought about by "contact" with whites.

Bruce-Bays's thoughts reveal that it was possible then to define poverty along racial lines, and so to exclude Africans. This racial division was based on the sentiment that Africans were not so much poor as members of cultures occupying lower rungs on the ladder of civilization, ones that they might or might not ascend to greater heights. The study of hunger in South Africa would, therefore, beg basic questions: Who is poor? What are the nation's responsibilities to those living within its borders? Who must be fed, and who could be left alone? The movement of Africans to cities made answering these questions increasingly important.

From the time of Bruce-Bays's article throughout the Union's first three decades, food, or more precisely pauper rations, defined national welfare policy toward Africans.[14] They were meager. An official committee of inquiry reported in 1937 that material relief was measured by "foodstuffs calculated to maintain the recipients at slightly above starvation level."[15] NAD officials feared that any benefits given out in the cities would encourage an urban influx it would have to stem. And so, during the drought and depression of the early 1930s, relief food that had begun to be distributed to Africans in town was stopped. The NAD had strict standards for choosing worthy recipients of its rations or its small monthly payments: the blind had to prove they lacked an income; invalids and the destitute had to prove they had no supporting relatives; and the elderly who had lived in the city for less than five years did not qualify for pensions.

Certain welfare benefits were extended to every South African under the Children's Act of 1937 when J. B. M. Hertzog was prime minister, though the levels of state support for "orphans, widows with young children, deserted families and families whose breadwinners are incapable of earning" differed according to race. Two years later the Justice and Native Affairs Departments withdrew these grants from African rural children, saying that they would "probably lead to an evasion of the responsibility resting upon the Natives under their own customs." No cash allowances were to be paid to women in town, either, because they would provide "an incentive to Native women to flock to the urban areas." For this reason, indigent children would be repatriated to the care of rural relatives; where there was no rural family, the child would be sent to a crèche subsidized by the Department of Social Welfare or be given food paid for by the South African Native Trust.[16] Jan Hofmeyr, then the great hope of South African liberalism, appreciated both sides of the welfare debate. Especially when he was minister of finance from 1939 to 1941, he feared mainly that social security's cost, if extended to everyone at equal levels, would be more than the government and the economy could afford, but he also believed that too few benefits were being extended to urban Africans because of the tax structure. (Since 1923, when native revenue accounts were set up for each township under the Natives [Urban Areas] Act, money spent on Africans' social welfare derived almost exclusively from the fines and rents they paid and in many places from the sale of African beer.) Hofmeyr rhetorically asked his National party opponent J. G. Strijdom in 1944, "Which country in the world would tolerate a position under which the money for social services for the poorest section of the population had to come from that section of the population only?"[17] The experts who sought to apply the lessons of Rowntree or Beveridge to South Africa's urban poverty inevitably ran into Hofmeyr's question.

The Social Scientists

In the late 1920s, efforts to collect and analyze "native budgets" in Johannesburg and Durban marked the beginning of the movement to assert that African urban poverty, as opposed to maladjustment, existed, and that it was a South African problem.[18] To these ends, a number of intrepid researchers, most of them female, went into the townships from about 1928 armed with questionnaires and the determination to measure how representative households spent their money. The budgets they collected were part of a real struggle to define—and, perhaps, to act upon—a social problem that others wished to ignore or dismiss.

The four researchers whose stories are told below exemplify different contributions—Fabian socialist, Christian humanist, anthropological, statistical—to the growing idea of an inclusive welfare state in South Africa. Together these perspectives would help to forge a new kind of paternalism, one appropriate to an urban setting. The social scientists all were, or would become, social meliorists involved in efforts to improve the quality of African life. Their budgets reveal more than dietary data. They also looked at education, crime, leisure time, housing, sanitation, and interracial relationships. But food was central. Just as Rowntree recognized, food was the sine qua non for analyzing and comparing physical want. They all used evolutionary theory as a more or less unconscious starting point for their recommendation: welfare policy should aim to educate people to adapt to social changes already undergone in

European history. Their efforts reflected far more than self-interest, as they sought to improve South Africa's race relations and ensure a future without conflict.

Fabian Gradualism

The Durban survey, launched in 1928 by the Joint Council of Europeans and Natives, a liberal forum for interracial discussion and some socializing, marks one of the first surveys of urban African household budgets in South Africa. It was part of an attempt made by the Joint Councils of Johannesburg, Bloemfontein, Cape Town, Potchefstroom, and Cradock "to ascertain the cost of living for natives and the native family budgets." The Wage Board in turn used these budgets as part of its 1928 inquiry into the adequacy of African wages.[19] The Durban sample was so small that its findings have mainly curiosity value today. Its organizer, Mabel Atkinson Palmer, was fully aware that the data she collected on the scant eight households, divided into three classes (intelligentsia, artisan, unskilled), were no better than "estimates," and "defective" ones at that, though "not without sociological interest," that is, insights into the psyches and health of urban Africans.[20]

Born in the north of England in 1876, Mabel Atkinson became an active member of the Fabian Society in her youth. Its most eminent leaders, the Bernard Shaws and the Sidney Webbs, had personally encouraged her. Fabian ideas about gradual, government-regulated social change would influence her work as a member of the Joint Council and its offspring, the South African Institute of Race Relations, a liberal research organization and pressure group founded in 1929. She is best known for her commitment to education, having taught economics and economic history at the Workers' Educational Association, Durban Technical College, and Natal University College. Her bluntness won her admiration but probably few close friends, especially among the Indian and African women she most wanted to help.

Sixteen years before arriving in South Africa in 1920, Palmer had produced an M.A. thesis on local government in Scotland that clearly bore the stamp of Fabian socialism. She had written in 1904 that the task of modern social reformers, working "in the plain daylight of our modern world," was no longer the romantic one of destroying hierarchies of privilege that had been handed down from the Middle Ages. The twentieth century was a time for building institutions so that people could work in railways, factories, and mines "without self-destruction and self-demoralisation." An efficient administration and "well-made laws" would "gradually raise the nation from step to step."[21] What happened to these ideas when they were transplanted from an industrialized society with a dynamic and mature labor movement to the divided and rapidly industrializing society of South Africa?

Palmer's thoughts on South African poverty continued to reflect her Fabian background, especially in stressing the necessarily evolutionary nature of both social change and social reform. She gave a speech to the South African Society for the Advancement of Science in 1930 that clearly derived from her earlier gradualist perspective. In her view South Africa was passing through stages that Europe had undergone in previous centuries, subsistence economies naturally giving way to money economies. Arguing that South Africa was inextricably bound together by one evolving productive system, she declared, "We cannot indefinitely preserve in the same country the machine-, money-, and capital-using civilization of Europe and the primitive subsistence economy of tribal communities." It was, in fact, "impossible" to preserve the primitive. The road to be traveled in the twentieth century led in one direction—toward private landownership and market economies and, she was aware, to evictions and indebtedness as well. "The complaints one hears of the vagrant native flocking into the towns carry a distinct echo of the early sixteenth-century laments in England over the perverseness of the evicted labourer in persisting in taking himself into the centres of population where work might be found, or charity, or at the worst, where thieving was likely to be most profitable." The distant echoes from the British past could be instructive, she implied, if properly used. Experts could "help the [African] community as a whole to adapt itself" by sharing modern economic wisdom through, for example, setting up native treasuries and credit societies.[22]

Displaying the Fabian aversion to revolutionary change, Palmer noted that while "difficulties of this transition" were presently acute, they were "often mistakenly attributed to wrong governmental or educational policies."[23] She emphatically did not advocate attacking South Africa's hierarchical structures in the romantic manner that, she said, had been appropriate in medieval Britain. Perhaps her reticence was due to the gradualism of her Fabian political faith, or perhaps she found it difficult to romanticize peasants when seeing them at close quarters. As Shula Marks has pointed out in her edited collection of Palmer's letters, Palmer displayed surprising ignorance about the ethnic geography of her region, thinking, for example, that the Transkei, a Xhosa area, was a "Zulu reserve."[24] What is most important here is that she presumed African development would follow the European model and that political tampering could not help this difficult but inevitable process. Given the paucity of her data, she seems to have been engaging in social science by analogy.

Though Palmer failed to criticize openly the government's policies in 1930, she did raise troubling questions about the way the transition was proceeding: Was male labor migration ruining families? Were African schoolmasters going to teach efficiently on such low salaries? Why did Africans alone have to pay school fees? Did it make sense to subsidize African housing and thereby justify their low wages? "Is the diet of natives in town adequate, and does it contain all the food values necessary? In particular, do native children in towns get sufficient milk?"

Palmer's economistic spirit animated her efforts in 1928, eight years after arriving in South Africa, to collect African budgets in Durban with the aid of "an intelligent native woman, Mrs. Charles Dube." Palmer thought, as Fabians were wont, that people were not spending their money wisely. In this observation she was in accord with Beatrice Webb, though Webb went on to observe that because consumers were poisoning themselves by responding to their appetites, they should ideally be restrained by sumptuary laws. Without going this far, Palmer was unable to restrain a chiding tone; she noted that one man spent an "unnecessary" ten shillings a month on medicines, another family an "excessive" amount on tea or coffee, and a rickshaw puller a lot on drink and tobacco. She "very much doubt[ed] whether this budget," compounded by such unwise purchases, "provides the necessary food values." She also observed how high a proportion of the income of even the best-paid man was spent on food, a "point always characteristic of low incomes"; in every case the largest proportion of the budgets (between one-third and two-thirds) was devoted to food. Consequently, she noted, people could make no provisions for their old age, insurance, holidays, or edifying leisure via books or games.[25] We have no record of what Mrs. Dube thought.

Although Mabel Palmer was helping to introduce African poverty to public debate, her evolutionary perspective on historical change allowed little room for political economic analysis. She made no explicit mention of exploitation, referring rather to the precedent of low wages laid down by the first white settlers "to which industries and the commercial agriculture of the white men naturally adjust themselves." She was also evenhanded rather than accusatory in her recognition that the changeover to wages capable of supporting a family "must, for a time, cause acute difficulties, indeed suffering, both to the African worker and to the European employer." Employing male labor alone, separating him from his family in the reserve, was "most unsatisfactory," but, she added, "it is defensible as a temporary expedient, designed to introduce the native a step at a time, to money economy." This help was imperative because "their wages are not full subsistence wages [for an entire family]. And to this extent South African industries are parasitic on the labour expended on land cultivation in the reserves." She described the moral consequences of these policies harshly: "It is unnatural to divorce working men from family life, and the country which practises it will pay for it in inefficiency, discomfort and almost certainly, in the long run, immorality and degeneration."[26]

European social commentators in the nineteenth and early twentieth centuries, as noted, frequently used "degeneration" to connote moral decay that could also be apparent in the human form. In this sense, although Palmer did not draw the connection so explicitly, a malnourished person embodied the consequences of the gradual but inevitable process of transition to a money economy, as if the human body were exhibiting the weakness and decay of an outmoded social order. Conversely, healthy, well-fed bodies could be read as signs of efficiently run modern societies.

In the person of Palmer, among others, Fabian ideas traveled easily to South Africa and contributed to the process of documenting the impact of industry and city living on the lives of the poor. Reflecting on what her household survey meant, she maintained that the road to future progress followed the European historical path. Her faith lay in the remedial power of education more than in social services or the church.

Christian Social Reform

When Ray Phillips first went to South Africa in 1918, one year after graduating from Yale University as a bachelor of divinity with a specialty in "social service," he brought with him a background of experiences and associations quite different from those of Mabel Palmer's Fabian past. He took care to remark in the preface to his book *The Bantu in the City,* published in 1938, that he was an American who had spent his youth in the racially mixed city of Duluth, Minnesota. The fact that he highlighted this aspect of his background suggests that he believed race was a more important attribute than culture and that the American experience of race relations was directly translatable to South Africa.[27] During the sixteen years he lived in South Africa (1918–1926, 1927–1935) before publishing his book in 1938, he sought to "assist in the development of a social welfare program" on the Witwatersrand, initiated by Frederick Bridgman, an American minister of the Congregational church. He was an urban missionary. For this reason alone, his book is connected to the moral earnestness of a world of Christian social reform that Palmer simply did not share. As Bridgman noted, their goal was to save the body as well as the soul of the African.[28] To this end, Phillips went on to head the Bantu Men's Social Center in Johannesburg, to found the first school to train African social workers (the Jan Hofmeyr School for Social Work in Johannesburg), and the first meeting of the South African Institute for Race Relations took place in his Johannesburg living room in 1929.

And yet, Phillips's efforts to document African urban life reflect many of the core values animating Palmer's work. He believed that factual knowledge, of which there was a "paucity," could help Africans to make the "transition from the tribal state to the civilised life." Because so little data existed, few Europeans realized how much Africans had to economize in order to make

ends meet. Armed with a questionnaire, he set out to measure the extent of
African urban poverty among the 200,000 Africans living permanently on the
Rand in the mid-1930s. He collected data on African wages, savings, expenses,
and debts, as well as their religious affiliations and views on marriage, their
thoughts on local organizations ranging from the police to debating societies.
His final question summed up the spirit behind all his queries: "What changes
must be brought about to make life—fine, clean manhood and womanhood—
zestful and worth while to the coming generation of Africans in the cities?"[29]
In this way, he threw the weight of his experience and conviction behind a
vision of South Africa as one country, not two or many, where Africans had a
right to live permanently in the cities. Four years after Phillips arrived in South
Africa, Frederick Stallard, chairman of the Transvaal Local Government Commission, had laid down the famous dictum that became the basis for South
Africa's urban racial policy: "The native should only be allowed to enter urban
areas, which are essentially the White man's creation, when he is willing to
enter and to minister to the needs of the white man, and should depart there-
from when he ceases so to minister."[30] The American urban missionary implicitly rejected this proposition.

The size of Phillips's sample was, like Palmer's, too small (forty-eight families "of educated men") to reveal the full dimensions of African urban poverty.
Even more important, most Africans had too much at stake to admit the
extent of their informal earnings and debts, despite his gentle admonition to
those filling out their household budgets, "This is not easy to do, but we
would greatly value an honest estimate."[31] Phillips seems to have been aware
of the factors inhibiting honesty.

The question of what it would cost an African family to buy a "well-
balanced food supply" had "never been seriously discussed," he noted. "And
yet it lies at the heart of this whole problem of the ability of the African people
to adjust themselves to the new social order in which they find themselves."
Hungry men, frequently sick, worked inefficiently.[32] Phillips named their
sheer lack of means, rather than ignorance, as the cause of their reliance on
mealie meal, bread, and sugar. Quite simply, people with higher wages could
afford to eat more meat, fruit and vegetables, and fresh milk, and they did.
Even though individualistic competition was growing, urban Africans continued to share their food and, for this reason, starvation was rare in South
Africa's cities.

His language, like that of most of his meliorist contemporaries, was carefully apolitical, as in his references to the "problems of transition" or "cultural
adjustment" or "contact" that bedeviled South African race relations. These
words reflected his determination to control his emotions, especially when he
felt "human rights" had been trampled on.[33] His word choice reflects not only
his efforts to encourage whites and blacks to "see" one another; it also displays

his view of world history, that civilized life and individualism were destined to evolve out of tribal life and communalism. He shared Mabel Palmer's evolutionary vision. Individualistic competition was "transforming the more primitive life of so-called backward peoples" in South Africa, as it already had in Europe and America. "Is the transition from tribalism to a civilised type of life being easily accomplished or are there maladjustments?" he asked disingenuously in his preface.[34]

It is easy to lose sight of the vigor of Phillips's critique of South African society by overstressing his devotion to uplifting leisure activities. Paul Rich has accused the American board generally of using such palliatives as film shows to divert urban Africans from politics, and founding social clubs to instill docility.[35] Phillips did argue that Africans could gradually accommodate to urban living through such private ventures as those he himself had launched— the Gamma Sigma debating society, for example. But he also argued that Africans were in the cities to stay and should be paid a civilized wage. Concluding *The Bantu in the City,* he implicitly rejected the Stallard doctrine by naming African poverty as the core dilemma that the Stallardist restriction on permanent urban migration would be unable to solve: "The poverty of the people is the problem."[36]

Neither Phillips nor Palmer was posing as a social scientific expert. Rather than flaunting their expertise, they were trying as laymen to understand current reality by using contemporary social survey techniques as best they could, without making excessive claims for their findings. Their efforts were pioneering and even valiant in the face of evasion, on the part of many Africans, and indifference, on the part of many whites. Though their belief in the stages of civilized development was arguably conservative in the sense that it crowded out talk of a political solution, they were also opening the way logically for the eventual importation of European ideas of the welfare state and for the inclusion of Africans within it.

Their work documenting and measuring African poverty also represents the gradual process by which evolutionary theory was being refashioned by social reformers. The explanation of poor urban diet was shifting from ignorance to poverty, and education rather than the struggle to survive was identified as the way the species should rightly adapt. With these two exceptions, however, evolutionary theory remained the unquestioned starting point for these efforts to shape an urban moral economy.

Anthropological Study of Culture Contact

When Ellen Hellmann, a candidate for a master's degree in anthropology at the University of the Witwatersrand, began to visit the Johannesburg slum called Rooiyard each morning in 1933, she mingled chiefly with the women living there, asking them questions about how they managed their homes. The object of her study was "culture contact and change."[37] The women generally regarded her, she noticed, with "amused indifference," finding the chocolates she was carrying far more interesting than her notebook. At times, though, people greeted her queries with outright hostility. They called her "that rich young woman who comes here in her grand motor car and looks at you as if she didn't see you properly. They say she is a spy working for the police. . . . She asks questions all the time; silly questions about what we eat, how many children we have, what money we earn, and so on."[38] Sometimes she would discover that an informant who had been carefully trained to "keep a daily budget of expenditure—a valuable index of confidence" had been warned by her neighbors that any recording of vital statistics was "reckless" and would bring "dire consequences." They had legitimate cause for their fears. Because they brewed beer, the denizens of Rooiyard were technically "a criminal class," as Hellmann knew, and they were so suspicious of her purposes that some blamed her for the increasingly frequent police beer raids. Because of this hostility and the constantly shifting population among the nearly four hundred people housed in the triangular yard with a row of back-to-back rooms running down its center, she was able to collect only fourteen household budgets from the 107 rooms. Soon thereafter the slum was bulldozed, a casualty in the war the Johannesburg City Council was waging against such unsanitary and criminal pockets in the midst of the white city center.

Hellmann's twelve months of research nevertheless allowed her to produce a detailed portrait of African urban life, cited by subsequent researchers as a classic. Her analysis resoundingly advertised the poverty of her subjects. The urban African, she wrote with reference to diet, was caught between two contradictory pressures: "the expansive influence of assimilation," on the one hand, and "a restrictive influence in the shape of poverty," on the other. As if to demystify some of the choices made by African consumers, she wrote, "It is only his utter poverty that restricts and hinders him and gives rise to the malapropisms of culture contact as exemplified by the picture of half-naked children huddling together for warmth under a piano." Her choice of this image bears some relation to a common middle-class vision of cultural "maladjustment": in the words of J. D. Rheinallt Jones, then secretary of the South African Institute of Race Relations (SAIRR), new arrivals in town preferred to "put money on their backs instead of into their stomachs."[39]

When in 1948 her thesis was published in the Rhodes-Livingstone series of anthropological monographs, she expressly regretted the "political immaturity" that had guided her research. In 1933, she wrote, she had not been aware of the "implications of national policy in this country." Her subsequent career more than atoned for this period, as in 1949 when she edited the massive annual survey for the SAIRR and went on to become a stalwart in the organization; she would later call it "passing strange" that the SAIRR did not regard its recommendations as "political" until after 1948.[40] It is true that she drew no connection in her text between what she was observing and the laws of South Africa. She ignored the color bar that limited black earning power. She did not mention the Natives' Land Act of 1913 and the Urban Areas Act of 1923 that prohibited Africans from owning land in cities. Nor did she allude to Prime Minister Hertzog's long and strenuous campaign to exclude all Africans from the vote.

And yet, despite her relatively apolitical analysis, Hellmann effectively advanced the argument that Africans were in South African cities to stay. "A new composite culture" was being born there, one that would not allow "detribalization" to be equated with "Europeanization." "The Bantu of South Africa," she wrote in the conclusion to *Rooiyard,* "are not a supine people. They are not succumbing either physically or morally to European domination and colonisation." These words were at odds with her warning that a paralysis was "creeping over many Native customs as a result of contact with a newer and superior culture."[41] Her use of the word *superior* was probably suffused with pride in modern technology, a pride she shared with many contemporaries whose political views she would come to oppose.

Whatever ambivalence characterized the work of its individual practitioners, it is clear that the discipline of social anthropology was attacking scientific racism or the idea of essential racial difference. As Saul Dubow has recently remarked, it did so by celebrating "cultural interaction," albeit between "superior" and "inferior" cultures, and cultural "complexity."[42] People like Hellmann were bringing the study of African societies within the ambit of history. They knew that anything they witnessed was a function of historical circumstances rather than an immutable characteristic of African culture. The ferment of life in cities rendered absurd any argument that African races or cultures had certain essential traits. Too much change was visible in town, and Hellmann's discipline was documenting it richly, even if she and others would later rue the apolitical nature of the observations they made in the 1930s.

The Quest for Social Security

Edward Batson, professor of social science at the University of Cape Town and a follower of Beveridge, was one important link between the movement to establish social security in Britain and in South Africa. In the mid-1930s the Cape Town City Council had supported the establishment of his chair for purposes of researching poverty in Cape Town. W. H. Hutt, professor of economics, had instigated hiring Batson away from his job at the London School of Economics because of his expertise in statistics, gained there as a student of the renowned statistician Arthur Bowley. Other members of the UCT faculty doubted the validity and feasibility of scientific research into contemporary society, but Batson's own regard for his methodology was little short of enthusiastic. Understanding social science to be "the application of scientific methods to the investigation of social phenomena," he described its innovative powers with pride: "We are now far from the days when pundits could . . . assert that there were no scientific laws of the social world, or that, if there were, it would be impious to inquire into them. We recognize now that just as the nineteenth century saw the extension of scientific method from the inanimate world to the world of living things, so we in our turn are witnessing its further extension into the still more complex world of social relations." And so he went on to replace the "bread line" with the more scientific poverty datum line, "raising the general level of welfare so as to assure to every human being that standard of living which our consciences at present prescribe for paupers."[43]

After arriving in Cape Town in 1935 at the age of twenty-nine, Batson immediately began conducting the first systematic survey of black urban poverty in sub-Saharan Africa. Local charity needed his expertise. The previous year H. F. Verwoerd, chair of sociology and social work at the University of Stellenbosch, had criticized the Cape Town Board of Aid for unscientifically distributing its money so that it failed to encourage "the ultimate aims of real charity—rehabilitation and prevention."[44] By 1938, Batson had surveyed 808 Cape Town households to discover how much they spent on six essential food groups, and compared their diet with the still rather inflated minimum daily standard recommended in 1933 by the British Medical Association. His figures revealed that half of Cape Town's Coloured people lived below the poverty datum line. The massive social survey continued so that by the early 1950s he and his research team, funded initially by the Department of Public Health and subsequently by the Center for Scientific and Industrial Research, had documented Cape Town's habits of consumption spanning about fifteen years.

Besides proving that a large proportion of Cape Town's population was living below healthy and "decent" standards, Batson refuted some common social scientific assumptions such as that ignorance determined the poor diets of poor Capetonians, a perspective that, he said, had recently become "fashionable." He had in mind the words of F. G. Joslin, the secretary of the Cape Town General Board of Aid, the agency distributing civic and provincial poor relief, who wrote that, "Present-day poverty is caused to a large extent by thriftlessness and the desire to possess furniture, radios, etc., comparable with a neighbour's, and regardless of the future." On the contrary, Batson wrote, most people simply could not afford to eat better.[45]

His research enthused his students, who knew him to be a "captivating" lecturer and famously engaged scholar.[46] He encouraged their participation in voluntary aid agencies running clinics, night schools, and a welfare community center that Mayor Hyman Lieberman had set up in the central city slum, District Six. And yet he was aware that such efforts were palliatives. In 1943, participating in a symposium on poor relief organized by the Cape Coordinating Council of Social Welfare Organizations, he called attention to a peculiarly South African dilemma: how low could the dole be set in a society with such a low standard of living? He drew the conclusion that there could be no Beveridge-like comprehensive system of social security in a socioeconomic system where poverty was widespread. Only a long-term policy of minimizing the need for the dole would do. Like Beveridge, he wanted the existing social services to be integrated boldly and scientifically with a national system of poor relief that excluded no one. And yet he knew that there were limits to which poorer countries like South Africa could emulate Britain's efforts to guarantee social security. After all, the cause of South African poverty was not unemployment but "maldistribution of our potential labour capacity." The Social and Economic Planning Council, appointed by Prime Minister Jan Smuts in 1942 to draw up plans for postwar "planning and reconstruction," had recently proposed an examination of the country's social services and the conduct of nationwide social surveys. In Britain such research techniques had led to the Beveridge Report. In South Africa the causes of poverty were "already becoming known; we are even approaching the stage of measuring them by scientific methods." While South African social science was lagging behind Britain's and the poverty of the country kept its social insurance in the "experimental stage," there was no evading the imperative of ensuring some form of welfare to everyone: "To provide for one section of her people and neglect the other will not give South Africa social security," that is, a future without conflict.[47]

All the above social scientists were making three potentially radical statements: nonwhite people were in the cities to stay; they had no essential social or biological traits that were racial in origin; and their social suffering derived from poverty as well as ignorance.[48] The "bread line" was important largely as a transitional measure of urban poverty. It lay between traditions of famine relief and the wartime ideas of a poverty datum line to which some all-inclusive form of state welfare was proposed as a solution. It derived from traditions of paternalism that played little part in South African urban life, and it led to calls for government action in a system where the vast majority of the needy possessed no political leverage. The surveyors apparently believed that the social order would respond in an appropriately minimal but positive manner to the demonstrated need of Africans, and, given the rarity with which they referred to legislation, they seemed unaware of the role national policies played in creating the conditions they were witnessing. Especially prior to 1948, they seemed blinkered by their faith in white benevolence. They could not see, as Ellen Hellmann later recognized, that their calls to conscience were feeble in a society where no laws or structures had given rise to collective responsibility for the poor.

Out of a mixture of evolutionary theory, self-interest, and ethical vigor, the surveyors were busy fashioning a new, scientific paternalism. Their faith that it would meet the needs of their times foundered also on the realities of township life.

The Failure of Urban Paternalism

The idea of the bread line was fine moralizing rhetoric, but it did not reflect urban reality in a particularly accurate or vivid fashion. Its numbers suggested precision that even their collectors could not endorse. Neither did urban Africans name hunger or malnutrition as a major grievance. In addition, the issue invited solutions—education and pauper rations—that were simply inadequate to address the gravity of the challenges South Africa's cities increasingly faced.

The Shortcomings of the Bread Line

If the researchers' findings are studied apart from their judgments, a picture emerges of urban diet that was not as dire as some researchers alleged in the 1930s, though it did worsen dramatically in the 1940s. People tended not to starve in town. In fact, one reason for moving there was to escape the fragility of subsistence in peasant economies, subject to lean seasons and famines. Urban hunger had an entirely different meaning from rural hunger; in the countryside a person might be forced to eat grass in order to survive a drought, but in town she might be fed by neighbors who, in turn, expected her to share food with them when their times were lean. People could earn wages or steal in order to survive, and transportation networks brought in foreign foods during a regional subsistence crisis.

Many of the social surveyors mistakenly believed that urbanization was the problem, whereas sometimes it was the solution to rural malnutrition. Over the course of the twentieth century the trend was toward less poverty in South Africa's cities than in rural areas. It is difficult to date precisely when moving to town improved one's life chances. Risk depended on the rural area and season, as well as one's new circumstances in town. For example, malnutrition was likely to be least present in the families of an urban wage earner and more prevalent in what some researchers called "fractured families," that is, urban households headed by widows, abandoned wives, or young unmarried mothers. These were the sorts of urban families likely to suffer from pellagra because they had forsaken the stone-ground mealie meal and home-brewed beer of their rural homes. The urban-rural dichotomy posed by many surveyors was thus diversionary from more formative issues such as wages, prices, and familial coherence.[49]

People did feel hunger in the cities, partly because they expected food to make them feel full. They spoke of not wanting to eat vegetables and fruit when they were hungry because spinaches and apples did not fill their stomachs.[50] As one "progressive Shangaan" eating-house proprietor said in the early 1930s, "If a man is hungry, he wants to fill himself for 6d. and this he does by eating mealie meal or rice and stew. If he is not so hungry, then he can afford to take vegetables."[51] Eating mealie meal without relish (a stew of meat, potatoes, onions, and occasionally tomatoes) could give rise to the sense of being hungry, of living below an acceptable level of consumption. A child from a poor family could feel hunger while watching a better-off child devour a slice of bread covered with butter and jam. People were growing to need sweets, whether in beverages such as heavily sugared tea or in cakes and jam. Foods made with sugar were losing their luxury status, just as they had during the European industrial revolution. A modern sense of hunger, one that sociologists would call "relative deprivation," was being born.

In the countryside people commented on the wide range of subtle distinctions that could be drawn between grains of different types depending on whether they were roasted or boiled or baked, but people with money found that purchased sugar, salt, and curry powder overwhelmed these subtleties with their sharp, emphatic overtures to the tongue. Like meat, sugar had a compelling taste that town life afforded in abundance. Many household budgets reveal that people consumed a pound of it weekly. This sweet seduction was undoubtedly what rural children had in mind when they threatened their parents, "I can go to town and get better food there than you give me."[52] Shopkeepers sometimes gave sweets free to children who made purchases in their shops, just as Ellen Hellmann carried chocolates into Rooiyard to ease her way.

And yet, rather than complaining about their city diet, people often preferred it to what they had eaten in the countryside. Tastes such as meat, that people already found compelling and delightful, were more readily available in town. Even poor urban households were able to consume meat several times a week, although that often meant watering down a stew made with what Europeans considered inferior cuts of beef, the forequarters and offal.[53] In the reserves, on the other hand, people consumed meat mainly when game had been killed or when a festive occasion demanded the slaughter of one of the household's goats. People seemed to regard drinking less milk, especially fresh from the cow, and eating fewer greens and no fruit as a tolerable compromise for gaining meat. Europeans rather than Africans were the ones to comment on the "monotony" of their diets.

African urban cuisine was, indeed, made from a small range of food types and spices. The household budgets reveal that they amounted mainly to meat, sugar, mealie meal, or bread or rice. In this sense, Africans displayed as cooks little of the flamboyant initiative and ingenuity that they showed in other aspects of their new urban lives, such as their beer brewing, their "cafe de move on" carts (vendors selling tea, coffee, and cakes), and their evasion of regulation.[54]

The reasons for the simplicity of African meals were simple: one of them was that women, especially, suffered from shortages of time, energy, fuel, and most other resources; most women worked as domestic servants, laundresses, and beer brewers in addition to caring for their families. As a result, they preferred quick cooking methods, such as frying or boiling porridge for a short period of time over a Primus stove. That no high cuisine developed among these early urban Africans made African cooking the butt of white jokes.

The social scientists' budgets do suggest the precarious hold on subsistence of even the most prosperous and acculturated African families, such as those headed by teachers. They were all in the habit of sacrificing food to pay rent. They all depended on "undependable" sources of food: gifts from neighbors, relatives, parishioners, and strangers; the sale of eggs; beer brewing.[55] Even the poorest families gave food away. The cost-of-living index adopted during World War II was said to have no relevance to African households because they all earned less than the minimum that Europeans considered necessary to guarantee decency and health. The net effect was that they spent a consistently high proportion of their incomes on food (well over half in two of Batson's Cape Town surveys dated 1938 and 1951), and if their incomes went down so did the amount of food they bought.[56] The prices they had to pay in township stores were high both because they tended to buy in small lots—paying three pence for an ounce of tea, for example—and because the stores charged higher prices than in white areas. This meant that they consumed fewer calories than Europeans did.

Fear of hunger was only one stimulus of the generic sense of anxiety that was part of urban living. The stresses of adapting to urban life must have made attractive such promises as pills that purified organs (Partons' Purifying Pill, De Witts Kidney and Bladder Pill, Feluna for women, Chamberlain's Colic and Diarrhoea Remedy) and tonics (Ashton and Parsons' Infants' Powders, Virata and Phospherine—the last "used by white people all over the world for

5. This Xhosa and English advertisement for Nutrine baby food was aimed at mothers reading *Imvo Zabantsundu,* a Xhosa newspaper, in 1938.

many, many years"). Medicines took up at least half of the advertising in South African newspapers oriented to a black readership. Throughout the 1930s commercial images also lured people to buy processed foods like Ovaltine, sweetened condensed milk, brown sugar, coffee, tea, and *incumbe* (fortified milk powder) produced by a firm in Durban.[57] Along with the adoption of European fashions of dress, food was one major way that Africans became absorbed into the consumer culture of town soon after their arrival.

The specific sense of anxiety over hunger may have been growing more acute after 1940. The events and conditions of that decade showed that the solution to basic problems of African urban welfare was bigger than private philanthropies themselves could achieve. The urban influx of the 1940s threatened to overwhelm South Africa's urban infrastructure as well as the ideological structures of the 1930s and earlier that had conceptualized welfare in terms of education and poor relief.

How these structures were breaking down can be seen in Alexandra, the township Gertrude Kark began to survey in 1944. It was studied not only by Kark, but by many other researchers of the bread or poverty datum line. It is worth examining, too, because its existence in white South Africa was insecure, and its present and future generated a good deal of vociferous debate as elements in white Johannesburg tried to get its residents removed to a township controlled by the NAD. Because the township was one of only four in Johannesburg where Africans could own land, they found it an attractive, because relatively secure, place to live. Alexandra illustrates the limited ability of aggregate statistics to reflect community conditions; a look at the township makes the poverty datum line seem mainly an index of consumerism, and so an inexpressive and, in the end, inadequate indicator of social well-being.

Standards of decency more than survival were at stake in South Africa's cities. For the people who live there, slums are probably best defined by what they lack, and Alexandra is no exception. For all intents and purposes, Alexandra township had no "civic amenities" at all, because its residents were poor and its local government, the Alexandra Health Committee, received almost no monies from sources other than the sanitation fees its property holders paid. A visitor in the 1930s would have seen no ambulance; because the roads were poor the ambulance would come only as far as the clinic located on the western boundary. There was no police station; one staffed by fifteen white and three black policemen was located in the neighboring suburb of Wynberg. There was no cinema until an African entrepreneur built one in 1942. There was no hospital. There was no post office, so the non-European lines at nearby Bergvlei were so long that people complained about them. There was no library, and black people were prohibited from visiting city or local libraries. There were no law courts and, with the exception of three public squares and the cemetery, no land was set aside even for municipal or public purposes. The dirt or mud roads were not graded. There was no waterborne sewage system or piped water, so people drew their water from wells. There were no streetlights, garbage cans, or garbage removal, though a partial removal system was introduced in 1937.[58]

Perhaps the most graphic, and certainly the most pungent, illustration of Alexandra's squalor comes from the world of sanitation. By the mid-1940s three buckets might serve as latrines for one stand in which a hundred people could live, a decline in standards since 1932 when four to six families per bucket had been more common. Initially once a week, biweekly by 1933, night-soil collectors sloshed the fetid contents of these brimful, if not overflowing or leaking, buckets into the back of ox-drawn scotch carts. Frequently spilling the night soil because the flap doors leading to the buckets tended to break and the roads were always badly rutted, they then drove the oxen on a low bridge or causeway across the Jukskei River to the depositing site, located next to the cemetery, on its eastern bank. In August when the grain supply for the oxen fell short, in January if the river flooded, or at any time of the year when the wagon sank in the muck, they struggled to dump their load in trenches, often succumbing to the temptation to fill them completely instead of stopping at two feet below the surface. (This latter technique was a surer method of preventing flies from breeding in the rainy season and carrying bacteria away to the food on the other side of the river.) The collectors were instructed to throw earth and a liquid disinfectant over their deposit to prevent maggots from growing on the surface, and they performed their work before sunrise, when the flies became active, for the same reason.

In other places in the township insects could also breed. People scooped out their yards, for example, in order to make raw building bricks from the soil, and they threw their garbage into the resulting pits, which filled with water when it rained. Thus each household made its own cesspool. In addition, because the whole of Alexandra lay on the west slope of the river, it was scarred with *dongas* or gullies caused by erosion; at the bottom of them lay such detritus of the township as tin cans and dead dogs. Because Alexandra's water supply came from wells, there was always the danger that it would be polluted by such refuse.[59]

Throughout its history, this square mile patch of land, located nine and a half miles north of Johannesburg's center, offered its inhabitants so few amenities that its squalor should surprise no one. If its population had remained small—only nine hundred people lived there shortly after it was founded as an African and Coloured township in 1912—it could perhaps have maintained some standard of civic decency. Instead, its population was periodically swamped by newcomers. These influxes occurred most notably in the mid-1930s, when five thousand people arrived from bulldozed spots elsewhere in Johannesburg such as Ellen Hellmann's Rooiyard, and in the late-1940s, when six or seven thousand squatters tried to settle in its open squares. The story of Alexandra is the story of a physical space and its services being repeatedly overwhelmed by economic refugees from the countryside and from other urban areas.

The township was poor because, throughout its history, little money had come into it from anywhere, neither through its denizens' wages, state aid, nor charities. Because it existed outside the Johannesburg city limits, it was not served by the Native Revenue Account set up for such townships by the Urban Areas Act in 1923. In other townships this account received money from rents and profits from services and municipal beer halls to fund slum clearance and the building of subeconomic housing. Without its own revenue account, local government in Alexandra amounted to enforcing health regulations by spending the residents' sanitary and license fees.[60]

Although a few well-to-do Africans did live in Alexandra, earning their money as owners of real estate, buses, or a cinema, the vast majority of its people earned very little. In fact, variations in acculturation were said to be wider than variations in income. If they were lucky enough to have a job in Johannesburg, most men worked as messengers, gardeners, or builders or in factories. Even when wages rose and were supplemented by a cost-of-living allowance during the war, especially for those employed in the formal (municipal, building, commercial) sector, they continued to fall under the poverty datum line. Because women tended to earn money as washerwomen and domestic servants, unprotected by wage regulation, their wages rose not at all in the early 1940s, even while the price of fuel, soap, and starch did. The township itself afforded only limited and occasional employment, much of it clandestine, such as beer brewing and gambling (particularly a Chinese game of chance called *fah fee*), and no researcher managed to quote the level of those earnings accurately.

During the war the cost of living in Johannesburg escalated faster and higher than wages. The cost of living index rose from 100 (1938) to 104 (1941) to 161.1 (1949). Prices for staple foods increased 91 percent between 1939 and 1944, partly due to profiteering. And when the local bus companies tried to raise their fares a penny, they put such pressure on already strained budgets that they precipitated bus boycotts in 1940 and 1943. Rent was high partly because land was expensive: the stands sold for artificially elevated prices because there was a limited amount of land available for purchase by Africans in Johannesburg. The average price of one of Alexandra's attractively spacious stands (80 by 140 feet on average) in 1940 was higher (at two hundred pounds) than the asking price of a similar piece of land in a neighboring white suburb and among the highest priced in the Union. Since large banks refused to lend to such risky ventures as purchasing a house in Alexandra, individual whites offered loans to blacks at what one official commission of inquiry called "extortionate rates of interest," that is, 12 percent rather than the 6½ percent banks offered to white home buyers; and they offered no grace if payments were late. Rent increased in the early 1940s because urban living space was growing more scarce as thousands moved to find work in the city during World War II. Summing up the cumulative effect of the rising costs of maintaining a household, the 1944 commission inquiring into the bus boycotts concluded, "since 1940 the gap between family income and the cost of meeting the essential needs of the family has widened considerably, owing to higher prices."[61]

Consequently, the township's fee collection generated very little money to spend on local services. The chairman of the Alexandra Health Committee, the township's local government, summed up in about 1940 the fiscal implications of its residents' poverty in the following understated way: "In the case of Alexandra almost the whole population is living below the breadline and cannot contribute to rates except to a very modest extent." Far more evocative of the extremity of Alexandra's finances than the word *modest* were the debates the health committee conducted over how to spend its paltry revenue. Its calculations were minute. Wouldn't it be cheaper to repair leaking two-year-old sanitary buckets than to buy new ones? Shouldn't old sanitary-cart oxen be sold so that their thirty shilling monthly upkeep could be saved? Weren't garbage cans too expensive to provide? Stand holders, that is, people in the process of buying land as opposed to their voteless tenants, paid for these amenities in the form of an annual sanitation fee, as well as various local taxes (water, land), and everyone was liable to pay some other fees (cemetery, planning) and licenses (bicycles, dogs, and trading). They paid more in taxes than they received in services.[62]

The health committee did manage to improve some of the township's conditions in the 1930s and 1940s, but beside the enormous scale of Alexandra's poverty and the continual influx of more poor people, these improvements could only seem paltry.[63] By the mid-1930s, the committee had graded some of the roads, sunk a couple of wells, and provided a two-pail sanitary service. Its other services included raids on unlicensed dogs, inspections of building plans, milk and dairy inspection, and the burning of disreputable shanties. By the early 1940s, it was replacing the old water supply system of wells and water carts with a few metered standpipes. Meanwhile Alexandra's population grew by about 10,000 to 15,000 thousand people between 1939 and 1944, and this pattern continued after the war as nearly 59,000 more African men found work in Johannesburg between May 1945 and September 1946; some of them had to cram into Alexandra township. The result was greater squalor.

Resources flowing into the township from charities augmented the paltry services it was able to buy with its own revenues. Throughout the 1930s the money tended to originate overseas. These gifts sometimes galvanized local donations, but their foreign origin meant that they were readily interrupted by the depression or war. The Alexandra Health Centre is a case in point. In the late 1920s the only medical help available in the township had been provided by a Swiss woman, Dr. Marguerite Crinsoz de Cottens, who made rounds part-time from her base in the inner-city neighborhood of Doornfontein; the city of Johannesburg offered no medical services to the township. Then, in 1927 the Boston-based, Congregationalist American Board of Missions sent Ruth Cowles to open a clinic in Alexandra. In 1936 the Johannesburg municipality reversed its long tradition of refusal and made a grant—of one hundred pounds—toward health care in Alexandra, a gift that led Cowles to observe that it was "the first time that the Municipality has ever taken responsibility for the thousands of workers who daily labour in her midst."[64]

Local charitable organizations became more active around the time the war began. The University of the Witwatersrand Medical School gave the greatest boost to local services in 1939 when it first affiliated with the health center and a full-time medical officer was first appointed. In 1942 the university's newly established social welfare department began to investigate needy cases, a research effort that expanded two years later into Gertrude Kark's systematic study of the township's needs. In 1944 a family welfare department occupied one wing of the new, expanded clinic building, and its work was funded both by student charities (the "Rag Fund Committee") and by the Johannesburg branch of the Union of Jewish Women. In 1945, Cowles organized Alexandra's residents to solicit funds from their employers in white Johannesburg and netted over £816 from these efforts. The burst of local philanthropy could not meet the township's burgeoning needs, with its population growing and the cost of living soaring.

Dr. A. B. Xuma, medical officer of health in Alexandra for roughly a decade between the early 1930s and the early 1940s, reflected on these conditions and found the social surveyors' categories of analysis wanting. He thought malnutrition to be a denigratory term, as used in South Africa. He angrily attacked the national minister of public health, Richard Stuttaford, for saying that Africans would squander higher wages on "cinemas, drink and finery" rather than on "protective foods." Of course people spend a lower percentage of their incomes on food when they earn more money, Xuma wrote. "Man, especially twentieth century man, has many other wants and inclinations than food," but most black South Africans were paid so little they were having to "stint themselves on food." Due to their low wages, they were failing to meet the "minimum nutritional requirements."[65]

Xuma also thought the concept of hunger was vague. In 1934 he could only suggest that the diet of urban Africans was "possibly deficient" in qualities necessary for the increased activity of modern life, as he wondered how the new "soft carbohydrate or starch" diets, made from refined rather than bulky meal, would affect people's health in the long run. In explaining why tuberculosis was on the rise in the late 1930s he did find malnutrition a useful concept. Oceans of medicine would prove useless, he wrote, if people could not afford to provide themselves with good food and housing. In a lengthy and meticulous annual report written in 1939, he blamed tuberculosis on "bad socioeconomic conditions," that is, a much more general state of deprivation than the bad sanitary conditions that produced enteric fever. Tuberculosis was a disease emblematic of the general phenomenon of poverty, rather than one like enteric or even the causes of infant mortality that could, misleadingly, be attributed simply to unclean habits. "[I]f only certain depressed classes are the victims [of tuberculosis]," then this disease must result from the "bad distribution of economic benefits."[66]

To prove the danger posed by hunger, or any malady, required precise medical and demographic figures, and they did not exist. In 1940, Xuma dismissed South African vital statistics as being "misleading and valueless to one who wishes to know the whole truth" about the country. He had been making the same point to the Alexandra Health Committee since at least 1933. In that year, he expressed his frustration with the police at the nearby Wynberg police station who frequently registered deaths as "Cause of Death Unknown or Not Mentioned," thus preventing any "reasonable figures for calculating even the 'Infant Mortality Rate.'" Because most people never bothered to register the birth of their babies and did not have to do so, he was unable to quantify the net effect of the unclean food and water in the form of an infant mortality rate. He noticed that half the reported cases of enteric fever did not hold up under clinical examination; he was irritated by a local medical doctor who persistently diagnosed malaria in cases that likely had other causes. The following year in a speech entitled "Changes Taking Place in Health and Diet of Natives in Urban Areas and Their Effects," he condemned the "[l]ack of reliable official vital statistics." Ticking off four points under this heading, he complained that "African native health, socalled [, was] treated as something distinct and apart from European health," that only the gold and coal mines kept African mortality rates, that the last census of the African population was in 1921, and that the registration of African births and deaths was not compulsory.[67]

Due to the dearth of statistics, he could say with certainty only which infectious diseases were most lethal: that gastroenteritis killed mainly in the summer and bronchopneumonia in the winter. To combat intestinal infections killing the vast majority of infants, he inspected and reprimanded local dairies for pouring milk into dirty cans or diluting it with unclean water. He condemned leaking or blown cans of condensed milk sold by local shops as well as the offal that local butchers hawked even when it was unfit for human consumption. He lobbied for a clean biweekly pail service and ordered wells filled if they seemed likely sources of infection. By 1938 the health committee was negotiating to get its water supply from the mains at the nearby white suburb of Orange Grove. "If this plan is accomplish[ed]," he told his welcome-home party in Alexandra, when returning from a trip to the United States and

London, where he had received his doctorate in public health, "we shall have gone a long way in preventing certain infectious diseases that are now still too prevalent in Alexandra Township."[68]

Although Xuma's job was defined as controlling disease, he wanted principally to prevent it. Perhaps his years as a medical student in the United States, Hungary, and Britain had put him in touch with modern ideas of preventive medicine. Certainly his years as president of the African National Congress (ANC; 1940–1949) provided him with ample opportunity to publicize his belief that the root causes of South Africa's health problems were economic, and that higher wages by implication would be the best preventive of all.

In 1940, the year he was elected president of the ANC, Xuma gave a speech elaborating this economic and political perspective to a joint meeting of two sympathetic groups, medical students at the University of the Witwatersrand and the Joint Council of Europeans and Natives in Pretoria. The speech carried an implicit reproach to those arguing that African physiques and physical needs were different from those of Europeans, a view held by many Africans as well as Europeans. (Kark would discover that many of her African informants in Alexandra believed their bodies and needs were indeed different from whites.) While medical officers of health recognized that "disease is democratic and colour-blind," those who "held the purse-strings in the country" did not, and so "we must educate white South Africans for a proper and intelligent attitude toward the Native Health Problem." Disease patterns, Xuma stressed, could be tied to specific pieces of legislation, that is, the Natives' Land Act (1913) and the Urban Areas Act (1923), which caused African poverty in rural and urban areas, respectively, and the color bar in industry. Quite simply, the low income level of Africans was responsible for their illness.[69]

While Xuma is today remembered primarily as an elitist former president of the ANC, he was a democrat on health issues and a fairly radical analyst of political economic conditions. "First and foremost," he said, "the economic status of the African must be raised. The African must be paid an economic wage. . . . If, the legislative, the land, and the industrial restrictions against the African were removed, he would thereby be enabled to be better housed, better fed, better clothed and therefore healthier."[70] Senator Hyman Basner remembered Xuma for his timidity, accusing him of displaying militancy only when he ran no risk of clashing with the authorities, who would not, for example, have been present at this Joint Council meeting in 1940. Xuma, Basner believed, had no faith in or stomach for mass action, instead hoping that such speeches would bring about change if only they were heard in the right quarters, that is, by Smuts and his cabinet ministers.[71] Despite Basner's impatience with Xuma for staying clear of Alexandra during the bus boycotts, the doctor's analysis was more radical than that of any meliorist social scientist.

And yet, he was ministering to the health of a township that was about to leave him and the paternalist world behind.

The Politicization of Township Poverty

Certain conservative elements in white Johannesburg displayed no interest at all in the township's hunger, because they saw themselves faced with a human flood that threatened to deluge them. They measured African poverty in terms of the crime and disease with which it could afflict whites. The very imprecision of their allusions to African poverty was a source of their strength. Appealing to vague fears of pollution and invasion, they demanded the township's abolition. Their response to Alexandra's squalor demonstrated the real shortcomings of hunger as an issue capable of provoking reform.

The conservative goal was to destroy Alexandra. The spearhead of the movement to remove Alexandra—an organization called the North Eastern Districts Protection League, founded in 1938—became exceedingly active in 1942. Reacting particularly to the alarming influx of new residents during wartime, the league organized meetings calling for the "early abolition of Alexandra Township with its attendant danger and evils, and the reestablishment of the inhabitants in healthy and congenial surroundings" to the southwest of Johannesburg.[72] The chairman of the league, G. Hibbert, a poultry farmer whose land lay just outside Alexandra, spoke to such local groups as the Rotary Club, exhorting them not to take their health for granted. "The health of our native servants, delivery boys, who handle most important foodstuffs, workers in shops, abattoirs, dairies, factories, chauffeurs, nursegirls, washerwomen," he said, "is a matter of vital importance in maintaining the health of the white population, as is the[ir] efficiency." His language was infested with medical metaphors. Calling the township "the greatest potential plague spot in the Union" and a "cancerous growth," he warned that "a major operation" was necessary to remove the danger, quoting the minister for native affairs for whom Alex had become a "running sore of evil." And yet, the only disease he specified during this speech was venereal disease.[73]

While such exhortations did make extravagant, though largely metaphorical, use of health issues, the fliers and speeches also called attention to the threat that the township posed to material security. Hibbert, for example, would quote the police as having stated that "there was more crime in Alexandra Township than in any other Native Township in the Transvaal, and with the advent of Native taxis and buses it has become the greatest centre of crime on the Witwatersrand, the police being powerless to prevent it." Hibbert cited no statistics. In his Rotary Club speech he hinted at "the repercussions upon the white population of an uncontrolled native township in its midst," one where, in the words of Deneys Reitz, the minister for native affairs, "the King's Writ runs with difficulty" and "toughs and roughs and criminals congregate." The league also republished an August 1942 article from *Libertas* magazine, modeled on the American magazine *Life*. Though the article tried to galvanize remedial action against Alexandra's squalor, presenting it as "an immediate challenge to democratic action" and part of "the general problem of the exploitation of the African and Eurafrican," the league's new covers told a different story.[74] Full of exclamation points, they warned that only abolition could bring "security" to the entire community. Similarly, the *Rand Daily Mail* paraphrased the native commissioner of Johannesburg, reporting that "the township is a refuge and harbourage of native criminals of every type and degree." He blamed the newly rampant vice on "growing lawlessness, the lack of parental control, the prostitution, the defiance of authority and the signs of moral degradation," especially of the young.[75]

Like the white Johannesburgers who wanted to get rid of Alexandra, urban Africans rarely mentioned hunger in talking about their poverty. They expressed their grievances increasingly loudly in the 1940s and with reference to other issues, indicating once again both the weakness of hunger as an index of urban poverty and the lack of a moral economy binding the two races together. Whenever African groups broached the subject of urban squalor during this period, they focused on money rather than health: How much money was actually in the health committee's coffers? Why were plot prices escalating? Would the government subsidize the township's services? The Standholders Committee of Alexandra Township was made up of property owners or people in the process of buying their stands, and their gravest fear was that they would lose their investment either through inability to pay their bonds and taxes or through the abolition of the township. These issues crowded out health concerns, except insofar as people argued that the township was not as peculiarly unhealthy as its white neighbors made it out to be. After all, they argued, the health committee was ensuring that all new buildings conformed to a healthy building code, and it was also overseeing the demolition of old, unhealthy dwellings. In the African townships of western Johannesburg (Sophiatown, Newclare, Martindale), "more overcrowding exists and even worse conditions prevail," but no one was agitating for their removal because speculators were not eyeing that land as they were coveting Alexandra's square mile.[76]

Even while suggesting that the health committee be made more accountable to the people it governed, the Standholders Committee glossed its requests with the residual language of patriarchy. Its members had written to the minister of native affairs in 1935 "as our protector" because, they explained, they had no other form of redress.[77] Seven years later, another "vigilance and protection" committee earnestly stated its desire to "become a model native township."[78] And when the principals of Alexandra's schools asked the chairman of the health committee to release them from having to pay water and sanitation fees, they addressed him as a "sympathetic Father." They even used the rural idiom for requesting patronage by referring to the schools as "starving."[79]

The conventions of verbal and behavioral deference tell only part of the story. Far more significant, because it advertised the advances of African nationalism in the early 1940s, was the increasingly restive, even resentful, tone of Africans, ranging from Dr. Xuma to women protesting the poor quality of the new water supply, toward the paternalistic white leadership of the health committee. In 1942, for example, Alexandra's stand holders expressed to the minister of native affairs their frustration with "the delay in returning to us our democratic right to elect our own rulers in the township," especially in light of the current war "we are fighting [against] dictators in defence of democracy throughout the world."[80] They frankly disliked the presumption that they could not represent their own needs to government.

In 1943 a group of Alexandra residents, calling themselves the Alexandra Anti-Expropriation Fund Committee, decided unilaterally to visit the minister of native affairs, Piet van der Bijl, in Cape Town and present their case against removal. (According to Senator Basner, van der Bijl was a singularly inappropriate minister of native affairs, a wealthy Cape Afrikaner who probably only encountered Africans when shopping in Cape Town and meeting delegations like this one.[81]) Their memorandum gave a highly critical view of South African history: "Since the day the Whiteman landed in South Africa the Non-Europeans of this country have never had any security of tenure, they have been driven from pillar to post in order to make way for European interest, and they now feel that the time has come when they should no longer tolerate such a state of affairs particularly in the land of their forefathers. Alexandra Township," they went on, "is one of the many Townships which came into being as result of the policy of the Whiteman of depriving Non-Europeans of their land for the purpose of control and exploitation." They drew attention to their belief that, by "investing their meagre and hard earned wages in this Township," they had "at last . . . secured a home from which no Whiteman should drive them away." Any attempt to abolish Alexandra now would be "a retrogressive step, dictated by the desire to suppress their progress, to deprive them of the right to develop their life to the full and the right to manage their own affairs."[82]

They concluded with a hard rhetorical blow to the integrity of the Johannesburg City Council's proposals to take over the township as a prelude to abolishing it in a time of world war: these proposals conflicted "with the principles of democracy in defence of which Non-Europeans are shedding their precious blood in the fields of battle and . . . they are inconformity [sic] with the methods practised by the enemies of democracy in their dealings with the defenceless and helpless."[83] At least two hundred men from Alexandra were serving in the non-European units of the army, and the committee was hinting at the consequences of their disloyalty in wartime.

Significantly, several of the signatories of the memorandum to van der Bijl were conservatives within the context of African nationalist politics: Selope Thema, for example, was hostile to boycott tactics and the radical left of the ANC, and Richard Granville Baloyi, as the owner of a real estate agency and bus company, was one of the richest men in Alexandra and an unpredictable political figure. The reference to "exploitation" may well have come from J. B. Marks, an ANC and Communist party member, who was also a member of the deputation. Clearly, the removal threat was forging a coalition of African nationalists holding diverse political points of view. None of them referred to the township's squalor or to the menace it possibly posed to their own health, except perhaps indirectly when they referred to the need to prevent the growth of "evils which may challenge its continued existence."[84] Some actually denied it, as when Dan Gumede wrote to the *Star,* "The residents wish to point out that Alexandra Township is one of the healthy native townships on the Witwatersrand and that is why some of the Europeans are agitating for its removal."[85]

Paternalist leadership was under assault. Upon their return from Cape Town, the Alexandra Anti-Expropriation Fund Committee angrily upbraided Alfred Hoernlé, the chairman of the health committee since 1941 as well as president of the SAIRR, for having prevented their success by corresponding secretly with the NAD.[86] They were accusing him of something he had not exactly done, though he had written confidentially to Donald Molteno, a natives representative in the House of Assembly, and to Harry Lawrence, minister of the interior, saying the committee represented "only a minority section of the standholders." Hoernlé advised both men to avoid encouraging public action on the abolition issue since it would only play into the hands of the *"swart gevaar"* (black peril) element in Johannesburg politics.[87] Dr. Xuma, he said, agreed with him, though this support would not have reassured the stand holders who were known to distrust the doctor. They also feared Hoernlé was willing to tolerate Alexandra's removal if it would lead to improved conditions.

Hoernlé, on the other hand, suspected Africans of being unable to represent their needs effectively to white authorities.[88] "It would be foolish to argue," he wrote in 1943, "that a Health Committee of purely African membership, employing purely African officials, can, here and now, undertake the running of the Township without European advice and assistance"; but the franchise should be extended to include longer-term tenants, and more money should be devoted to advancing the material improvements that the health committee had already begun. This money must come from the Union government; it had to tackle such social problems as juvenile delinquency and crime "on a national scale."[89] The urban crisis was leading inexorably to meliorist calls for state intervention, even though still short of Beveridge-like welfare measures.

All the above actors—the philanthropists and the people they were trying to help—were about to be deluged by a human wave that none of them could control. In January 1947, the stand holders of Alexandra were threatened not by abolition but by an invasion. Six or seven thousand squatters poured into two of the three open squares in the township and built several hundred shacks of sacking. Their numbers included people from Alexandra who could no longer afford to pay the rent for their rooms in the backyards of stands, as well as men and their families who had moved to the city in the war years to take advantage of the explosion in jobs. They were organized by one Schreiner Baduza, chairman of the Bantu Tenants Association of Alexandra, a man who earned his living by installing burglar bars on local homes, and a twelve-person committee that, official investigators recognized, had "assumed many of the functions of government." The squatters had, in other words, slipped into the yawning hiatus of local government, overwhelming by their sheer numbers the Standholders Committee and the Alexandra Health Committee itself. In the process, they evoked "extreme bitterness" from Alexandra's stand holders who threatened to occupy one of the squares in central Johannesburg if they were not removed. Because these six thousand or so people shared only three standpipes and some pit latrines covered with sacking, they presented another and familiar menace. The Union Department of Public Health rushed into the breach confronting the underresourced Alexandra Health Committee, inoculating the squatters against typhoid and smallpox. Then the city council intervened and from the end of June until mid-July moved the squatters to Klipspruit, a new location to the southwest of the city. In this way, they averted an epidemic that could have threatened not only the squatter population and the inhabitants of Alexandra, but "the people of Johannesburg for whom many of the squatters and other inhabitants of Alexandra work."[90] The political strategies of less well-off Africans had dragged the reluctant government in.

Conclusion

Using imported techniques to define and measure decent subsistence, social scientists had raised public awareness of African urban poverty. They asserted that Africans were in the cities to stay and that their poverty was a South African problem. They came out of a meliorist political tradition that defined good social policy toward the poor in terms of pauper relief, nutritional education, and soup kitchens. Following this imported trajectory, they found themselves after World War II conveying rising expectations for a welfare state. They helped push the issue of wages into the public eye before popular urban movements of the 1940s made it and the cost of living impossible to ignore. Even within the government, they won converts to the idea that the state should play a larger role in ensuring public health and welfare.

These experts' efforts were riven with unresolved struggles. They debated but never quite decided whether urban malnutrition resulted from ignorance or poverty. While asserting that a new urban culture was arising, they never abandoned a European model of the right and proper direction for South Africa's future development. They imported a welfare trajectory to a country whose political and fiscal realities opposed its adoption. Their remedies—education, hygiene, a healthy diet—never dealt with the magnitude of the social problem, as defined by Africans. Without supporting evidence, they believed that people in power would respond to their findings.

The communist senator Hyman Basner excoriated the experts for having sold out to the gold mining industry; most of the money in the SAIRR, he believed, came from the Chamber of Mines. The NAD did maintain almost daily contact with the SAIRR, which, in Ellen Hellmann's words, "enjoyed easy access to Cabinet Ministers." The meliorists' blinders, however, came not from money, I believe, but from their pride in their own paternalism and the scientific achievements of European society. The European model of historical development was great and dominant, they believed, because it contained moral and scientific progress. This core belief is reflected in the following words written by Alfred Hoernlé in 1942: "With the control of Nature with which modern science has endowed us, any economic system must be accounted a failure, root and branch, if with proper planning it cannot [give the workers a 'human' or 'civilised' standard of life]."[91]

By the late 1940s, the rising numbers of the African urban poor were rendering paternalism ineffectual in terms of both ideology and organization.[92] Attempts to modernize and make a science out of it were demonstrably failing prior to the 1948 elections. The meliorists and their search for a new, scientific paternalism were about to be swamped by the rising tide of urban poverty, as exemplified by the 1947 Orlando squatters; these homeless people were controlled by none of the three parties—the social surveyors, bourgeois Africans, and white conservatives—who were publicly discussing African poverty during the interwar and war years. An African language of rights was similarly swamping meliorist discussions about welfare.

Part Three

People without Science
A Modern Rationale for White Supremacy

CHAPTER FIVE

The Threat of "Race Deterioration"

Nutritional Research in Industrial Context

> It is by no means an exaggeration to affirm that comparatively the average Zulu can boast of a larger share of pure scientific knowledge than the average European.
>
> *A. T. Bryant, 1909*

> Mostly and fundamentally, the causes [of African hunger] are overstocking combined with ignorance in regard to how to live.
>
> *F. Rodseth, 1946*

IN THE EARLY TWENTIETH CENTURY, many leaders of South African white opinion, reflecting popular insecurity about the destiny of the new nation, worried openly that both whites and blacks were degenerating physically. Answers to the questions—who was deteriorating, in what ways, why, and what should be done about it—changed over the course of the century, but the concern endured deep into the era of apartheid.

The objects of nutritional research shifted in tandem with political and economic needs, specifically to sustain a strong labor force and to maintain a sense that South Africa was a civilized nation. In the course of responding to these two pressures, medical researchers produced ideas with far wider impact than the state could control.

Early South African medical journals reflected a general malaise about the medical destiny of the new country. Faced with epidemics of smallpox (1882–1883), plague (1900–1904), and influenza (1918), doctors worried about how to contain infectious disease and also how to improve the sanitation of the poorest so that all would be free from dysentery. Could habits of eating and dressing be altered to withstand the rigors of industrial life in a subtropical setting? Some concluded that the low wages and high rents in South Africa's cities might make adaptation not only difficult but perhaps impossible.

6. These miners at Welkom gold mine in the Orange Free State were dining in 1955 on porridge and the acidulated beverage meant to protect them from scurvy. (*Cape Times* Collection, National Library, Cape Town)

One doctor reminded his *South African Medical Journal* readers in 1893 that "the large earning power of a nation is indissolubly bound up with its vitality." Such nationalistic imagery had long been current in Britain, where virtually all of South Africa's first doctors had been educated. As early as the sixteenth century, according to Paul Slack, European humanists had used the "analogy of the body politic to underline the dangers of civic and national disease and decay," perhaps reflecting anxiety about the consequences of belonging to an increasingly wide community.[1] In this new colony a sense of national community was tenuous at best; perhaps inevitably in these colonial circumstances, fear of deterioration, of loss of vitality and, therefore, of prosperity was expressed in terms of race.

Around the time of Union (1910), many medical observers warned European immigrants of the dangers of failing to adapt to their new environment. Reflecting the vogue for the evolutionary schemas of Charles Darwin and Herbert Spencer, they defined what standards for fitness would guarantee survival. "[W]ant of adaptation to environment . . . in a living species, is believed to presage its extermination," Dr. Wilfred Watkins-Pitchford told the South African Medical Congress in his 1908 inaugural address as its president. He suggested the colonists eat the fresh produce of the region rather than canned food. "We must admit that the physique of our savage races is at all events as good as our own, and the deduction seems allowable that their diet is as serviceable—it is certainly much cheaper." Nor should the colonists try to duplicate in the heat and humidity of Durban the physical exertion and dark clothing appropriate to life in Glasgow. Also, they could prevent their own "moral and intellectual degeneration" by organizing cultural events that would invigorate "the mind of the community." Watkins-Pitchford's definition of "community" excluded black people, whose "moral ideals and social habits [were] widely different from those of educated Europeans," and who, therefore, should live apart from whites in their own "specially allotted district of the town," thus helping to contain communicable diseases and uphold social standards and feelings of community.[2]

In 1909 an article in the *South African Journal of Science* by J. Bruce-Bays, the Grahamstown physician, bore the unmistakable stamp of social Darwinism. The "unfittest" were perpetuated in Britain, Bruce-Bays wrote, with charities keeping "puny" Londoners alive. The same fate—"constant deterioration"—awaited Africans in South Africa, if tuberculosis and other respiratory and digestive diseases of civilization took their toll. In rural areas, no one could have found "as regards their physique finer specimens of humanity" than Africans, or so Bruce-Bays assumed, but those who moved to town dressed so poorly that their skin lost its "self-regulating" mechanism. Further, mothers began to feed their children tea and white bread, and even adults became enfeebled by this diet. Africans' ability to resist disease was eroded, and their mortality rate soared. Bruce-Bays gloomily predicted, "unless the natives are able to acquire some immunity and power of resistance as the result of the survival of the fittest, the present native races of this colony may . . . in course of time become as extinct as the dodo." He reverted to the common theme of the body politic or national destiny. "[T]he provision of a supply of strong and healthy labour is one of pressing importance in South Africa, where from racial and social causes the supply is unable to keep pace with the demand, and where in consequence undertakings of great importance to the commercial prosperity of the country languish or collapse." Bruce-Bays, like many other Darwinians, was proposing that the process of adaptation was essentially biological and hence no one could interfere with it. Some of his contemporaries were so convinced that the Bushmen, for example, were a "dying race" that they searched villages to find human specimens to photograph before they were extinct and make plaster casts of their bodies for display in Cape Town's South African Museum.[3] Neither Bruce-Bays nor Watkins-Pitchford had much data to support their theories. On the eve of its birth as a nation, South Africa lacked not only medical schools and sufficient laboratories, but also the information that might have laid to rest, or at least focused, these diffuse anxieties about the future.

In the following decades with the rising standard of living, fears of white degeneration waned in some quarters, but the fate of blacks continued to draw wide medical attention. Even after the social Darwinist vocabulary of "degeneration" became unfashionable, the underlying ethos remained: Could primarily rural people adapt to modern conditions of work and urban living so that South Africa could thrive? On the eve of World War II, the concept retained some vitality. In parliament Dr. K. Bremer, a medical doctor and also a nationalist M.P. for Graaff Reinet, defined the duty of the Department of Public Health as protecting "the individual health of every member of the population so that the people will not be threatened by inferiority or retrogression"; he added thoughts appropriate to the brink of war, that all South Africans had, in fact, "retrogressed physically until in times of crises we have reached an alarming state of affairs."[4]

During South Africa's first fifty years, people commonly expressed fears of degeneration in terms of malnutrition. The belief that South Africans were deteriorating because they ate badly was so widely held that it was used to explain a wide variety of maladies, so pervasive that it might be called an intellectual syndrome. From about 1900 to 1930 scurvy gained the lion's share of attention from nutritional researchers; thereafter and through World War II investigation into general debility dominated research; and from the late 1940s into the 1960s protein deficiencies led nutritional research agendas. The double-edged heritage of scientific authority gave rise to an analysis that could support the status quo, on the one hand, and, on the other hand, created provocative, new knowledge about the consequences of political and economic inequality.

Scurvy

Scurvy provoked the first nutritional research in South African history. The stigmata of the disease are difficult to ignore: gums bleed and teeth may fall out, legs swell, skin and tissues hemorrhage so that people suffer easily from nosebleeds, and their skin may be blotched with broken blood vessels. An injury may give rise to a wound that will not heal. Death may ensue from the sheer inability of the body to maintain the walls of blood vessels and tissues. In less extreme cases a person may simply be too weak to work hard; "muscular weakness," one health official wrote, was "probably as important a symptom as any in Scurvy," and, for all these reasons, the mining industry found scurvy a scourge.[5]

The precise catalyst of South Africa's first phase of nutritional research occurred in the summer of 1902. Between November 1902 and April 1903, 12 percent of the miners, or 186 men, who died on the Witwatersrand gold mines succumbed to scurvy.[6] These deaths provoked the mines to investigate causes and possible cures. A second upsurge in fatalities occurred between 1918 and 1920, and scurvy incapacitated many miners through the 1920s.[7] With their labor supply under threat, the mining companies funded and controlled research into its causes; one pressingly important quandary was to determine whether scurvy originated in the home reserves or on the mines.

The incidence of scurvy on the mines in the late nineteenth century is not known. In this period the mines suffered from an erratic food supply, as southern Africa was unable to produce enough to feed its miners. In 1889 drought and the heightened demand for food caused by the sheer proliferation of mining companies led to shortages in the mining camps and in the city of Johannesburg. The new companies—none older than three years—begged the South African Republic to lift import duties on mealie meal, flour, butter, and canned goods, so their employees could be fed more cheaply. Paul Kruger's government responded by donating five thousand pounds to the newly established Chamber of Mines, which used the money as a bonus for owners of wagons carting supplies from the nearest railheads on the line being laid from Cape Town to the Rand. The health consequences of relying on grain imported from Argentina and America and hauled long distances by train or cart soon came under critical scrutiny. In 1899 the medical plague officer told the secretary of mines that miners should be fed fresh South African, rather than dried imported, mealies as well as vegetables and fresh meat, and lime juice, not alcohol, in order to avoid scurvy.[8] When the Anglo-Boer War broke out that year, scurvy was reported in besieged towns, internment camps, and jails.

After the war, when the supply problems began to be solved, the goal of eradicating scurvy among South African miners confronted a more intractable, economic obstacle. Considering the great expense of mining low-grade ore at deep levels and the fixed price of gold, the dietary remedies had to be cheap. One way of trying to control the cost was to lobby the government for lower railway tariffs and maize prices; another was to feed the miners no more than necessary to safeguard their health and strength.[9] A commission of mine medical officers in 1903 decided that "kaffir beer," known to possess "an antiscorbutic value," was a "useful" but "not necessary" part of miners' diets, and a "rather costly" one.[10] Similarly, because meat was "a most expensive article of diet," another doctor wrote, its issue on the mines was necessarily restricted "to the smallest amount compatible with health," and African desire for more meat was "not . . . likely to be met with"; mealie meal was the black miners' staple "because of economic factors," as well as "the native's habits."[11]

The second obstacle to ending the threat of scurvy was sheer ignorance. Researchers had to learn more about the cause than that scurvy was a "dietetic disease."[12] The long history of naval encounters with scurvy, and the earlier effective prophylactic of lemon or lime juice, suggested that the miners' diet needed to be improved, but not exactly how. Most persons with some medical knowledge were convinced, like the plague officer of 1899, that fresh meat and vegetables would help, but early twentieth-century doctors were uncertain whether scurvy was contagious, a nitrogen deficiency, or the consequence of ingesting tainted or rotting grain. Autopsies on corpses of men with swollen legs, loose teeth, bleeding gums, and bleeding gastrointestinal tracts revealed cases of scurvy. A few suspected that such conditions were symptoms of rheumatism provoked by the wet conditions on the mines, or from a contagious form of beriberi brought in by Chinese miners in 1904. In 1912 one Johannesburg physician wrote that "the origin [of both beriberi and scurvy] seems to be unsuitable food." Others arrived at such vague or confusing explanations as "impoverished blood brought on by low diet and scurvy."[13]

Not all conditions diagnosed as scurvy were scurvy. During the first several decades of the twentieth century in South Africa it was a fashionable disease to identify. In mines and jails autopsies of men dead of many other diseases might read that death occurred as "the result of scurvy, occurring in a weakened constitution, caused by old tubercular disease of both lungs."[14] It could have been said instead that the man died from tuberculosis, a disease becoming rife in rural areas of South Africa, where it was spread by returning miners. In one 1903 case, also drawn from a prison, the men listed as dying from scurvy may have died from unclean water or from an infection. The Kenhardt jail in the northern Cape served its prisoners one and three-quarter pounds of mealie meal daily and nothing else. Many were compelled to undertake extraordinarily hard physical labor and to live in crowded, unclean conditions (the Kenhardt jail drew its water from a shallow open well and allowed no light into its cells). Six other people were diagnosed as having died of "scurvy" there that year and twenty other men as afflicted with it, but it seems unlikely that scurvy alone killed or disabled them.[15]

Were diets predisposing workers' blood vessels to break down? This question cannot be answered definitively; rations varied widely from mine to mine within the gold mining industry, and on diamond and coal mines, all of which produced cases of scurvy. There were discrepancies between what miners ate and what was said to be served. "It is common knowledge among us," one mine medical officer said, "that there are considerable variations on the mines in the quantity and quality of food issued."[16] The one constant was heavy reliance on mealie meal porridge. Before the Anglo-Boer War, in the words of the commissioner for native affairs, Sir Godfrey Lagden, "it was the custom to feed the native absolutely and entirely on one article of food, namely, mealie meal; it was thrown to him, he cooked it, ate it, and suffered."[17] Even after the war, when some efforts were made to vary the rations, cornmeal porridge remained the principal item of the miners' diet, accompanied by one to three pounds of inferior meat a week. Similarly, the coal mines of Natal in 1905 fed their black miners mealie meal all week long, with meat at one meal only.[18] The word most frequently used, even by the mine managers themselves, to describe this diet was *monotonous*. One doctor accused colleagues, who had blamed the 1902–1903 outbreak on American mealies that were "tainted and musty," of seeking a foreign culprit: "In my opinion the monotony of the food is by far more responsible for scurvy than even this scape-goat for all diseases among Natives—the American mealies."[19]

If official provision lists are to be believed, throughout the first decade of the twentieth century the gold mines fed their black miners daily only mealie meal, beans, and coffee.[20] Some supplemented this limited fare with weekly rations of meat (a few mines offered three pounds of raw meat to each miner for grilling in his free time), "kaffir beer," and a soup made from meat and vegetables, while lime juice was issued "when required."[21] More men might have come down with scurvy had they not sought out eating houses, located outside the mine compound, to buy bread and soup or bread and meat for a few pence. Two pounds of mealie meal daily served by the mines may sound gargantuan, but this was normal African fare in early twentieth-century institutions. Around 1902–1904 hospitals fed their patients a half pound of mealie meal three times daily, with a supplement of lime juice (four ounces) and sugar (two ounces) for scurvy patients; and a jail in the northern Cape served one and a half pounds of mealie meal daily with no supplements at all.[22]

On the gold mines, black miners worked extraordinarily hard—hand-drilling, shoveling, trammeling—on only one meal a day. White miners ate breakfast and were brought to the surface for a midday meal, but black miners arrived at the shaft heads at about 4 a.m. without having eaten anything, and labored underground for up to ten hours, still without food. One mine medical officer, Abraham Orenstein, who did not approve of this regimen, later explained that the lack of a morning meal was the result of "a prevalent belief that natives do not care for food early in the morning, partly because of the disinclination of natives to rise earlier than absolutely necessary, but perhaps principally because of the difficulty of distributing food so early in the day on mines where the average barracks house about 4,000 natives, most of whom go to work at almost the same time." Africans were thought to "dis-like taking food down the mine to eat" and to consider it "not healthy to eat down in the darkness underground." And so, Orenstein argued in a pamphlet designed to serve as an operating manual for compound officials that they must be "educat[ed]" to eat a substantial meal before going underground and also to eat something—a loaf of bread, for example—in the middle of the shift.[23] Such opinions suggest that mine doctors tended to regard the mines as essentially benign organizations, and African habits, not their own parsi-mony, as the cause of hunger.

Yet mine managers, in providing meager rations, were disregarding the protests of African miners themselves, who had a history of striking and com-plaining when labor recruiters fed them poorly—with less mealie meal than promised, for example, or with meat from a lungsick ox.[24] In 1903 miners were said to "grumble at being kept constantly on mealie meal porridge and nothing else; all the natives grumble at that," according to the report of a Durban-based missionary, F. Suter, who visited the Rand mines.[25] Complaints about diet came in tandem with other grievances such as broken promises, rough treatment, and, mainly, low pay. The investigator of the 1913 miners' strike, H. O. Buckle, chief magistrate of Johannesburg, acknowledged "some complaints of insufficiency of food"; in particular, "natives who had been detained underground exceptionally late came up to find the food all finished" and, of course, "a large number of natives will always want more meat."[26] In 1923, three thousand miners picketed a compound kitchen saying the mealie meal was of such poor quality that they couldn't stomach it. Many miners absconded, leaving few records of their disgruntlement or maladies and no redress.[27]

The Chamber of Mines largely disregarded the dietary advice of the one government agency charged with protecting African interests. The NAD, and after 1911 its native labor section, seldom intervened on dietary issues, and, in addition, had no clout. In the early twentieth century most NAD officials were unprepared or unwilling to tell industries what to feed their workers. The only legal backing for requiring dietary improvements was a masters and servants act, the legacy of the first British administration in the Transvaal (1877–1881), an act stipulating that employers were to provide their workers with "good and wholesome food." In 1903 the commissioner for native affairs, concerned with "the great mortality," that is, the 186 miners who died during the summer of 1902–1903, organized a committee of six mine medical officers. Like subse-quent NAD efforts to regulate diet in 1911 and 1922, the improved ration scales drawn up by such experts were simply suggestions. The 1911 minimum ration scale suggested a hot morning ration, recommended providing miners with a loaf of bread to take down into the shafts with them each day, and urged compound kitchens not to undercook beans. There was no bite to its provisions since any employer could make changes, "provided that in the opinion of the medical officer such changes do not reduce the physiological or calorific value of the diet as a whole."[28]

Each mine prepared its food differently, and the factor determining quality or quantity was often the whim or parsimony of the compound manager more than the ration scale. As one mine medical officer said in 1941, "I regret that there are still compound managers who are inclined to consider that keeping feeding costs low is one of the most important things they have to do—more important than the health of their boys!" Another mine doctor noted that "practically all mines issue foods in considerable excess of the quantities laid down," but about half of his sample of ten mines failed to feed their men groundnuts, a food mandated in the 1922 ration scale. Rations were so irregularly apportioned that men coming up to the surface at the end of their long shift could be fed a thin, meatless gruel, after having had no breakfast. And sometimes the fermented grain beverage *lambalaza* was served in the morning too hot to be drunk by miners rushing to catch the elevator going underground. The large amount of discarded food, especially samp, indicated that monotony was not a characteristic of African tastes but of the mines' own dietary regime. Most significantly for scurvy, the food tended to be overcooked because it began to be cooked in the morning, with the result that much of the antiscorbutic value of the fresh vegetables was lost by dinnertime; in any case, neither oranges nor fresh vegetables were available throughout the year.[29]

When the 1922 diet revision was first mooted, the cost of adopting it shocked mine management, so the Chamber of Mines' actuary and labor adviser wrote to DNL Pritchard, calling it "a most alarming increase in cost." The extra expense to the mines would be "not far short of a quarter of a million sterling per annum!" In addition, "many mines contend that an excessive quantity of food is required under the new scale and that a great deal of waste occurs."[30] Mine managers protested that calling for an increase in quantities of specific food types, such as whole wheat flour, cocoa, peanuts, and germinated beans, would necessarily lead to a decrease in others, such as the old staples of mealie meal, meat, malt, mealies, and beans. In fact, the impact of this new regime depended utterly on the responsiveness of mine management to the reports made by NAD mine inspectors and the inability of those inspectors to prosecute offending mines. According to Matthew Smith's history of health on the mines, "inspectors' reports were seldom acted upon."[31]

Nor did international scientific authority prove to be more effectual in changing mine diet than African and NAD complaints. The attack on a nearly exclusively mealie meal diet had been given a substantial boost by the visit of an eminent foreign visitor, Colonel W. C. Gorgas, in 1913, the year before he became U.S. surgeon-general. Because he was famed for eradicating diseases like malaria and yellow fever during the construction of the Panama Canal, the Chamber of Mines had invited him to the Rand to recommend means of ending a pneumonia epidemic then claiming so many African lives that the British government was threatening to curtail recruitment in its neighboring territories.[32] While Colonel Gorgas focused on the need to improve sanitation and the desirability of housing workers in small villages rather than in barracks, he also investigated mine rations and appears to have been appalled. "I have never seen," he wrote, "so large a proportion of the ration supplied by one article as is here [on the mines] supplied by mealie meal. . . . [It] is too large a portion of carbohydrates for men doing the hard manual labor that the natives do." His report, in the words of H. O. Buckle, the man investigating the 1913 strike, "has thrown doubts upon [the ration's] adequacy, and I presume that the question will now be reconsidered by the medical authorities."[33] But the Chamber of Mines was committed to a migratory labor force and thus ignored Gorgas's recommendation that it pay miners enough to buy and prepare their own food.[34]

Although Gorgas had cited the diamond mines at Kimberley as having solved the problem of industrial feeding by employing a settled labor force, evidence of worker health there belies his praise. It also shows how intimately nutrition was influenced, not by African family life itself, but by wages and the individual worker's strategies for saving money. Especially during a time of recession when wages were dropping, the rates of scurvy could soar as alarmingly as those on the gold mines. In 1920 on the alluvial diamond diggings at Taung, north of Kimberley, the tin, wood, and sack shanties of the African locations on the diggings within the Taung reserve were perched above the Harts River on a hillside so strewn with boulders that the land was difficult to cultivate. Workers' subsistence was, therefore, unusually dependent on their earnings. As more workers arrived at the diggings and as the price of diamonds dropped by an astounding 40 percent in early 1920, white diggers paid black laborers lower and lower wages.[35]

The local registrar of deaths recorded five fatalities from scurvy in late 1920, four cases were apparent to the NAD inspector at the time of his visit, and there was no telling how many people were sick at the diggings themselves. With their waning incomes, Africans had to buy water as well as food; they bought cheap cuts of meat—sheep's heads, legs, and offal—that had been grilled over a fire outside the butcher's shop.[36] One disapproving NAD inspector, visiting the Taung diggings from Johannesburg, reported, "[while] the Native is the back-bone of the Alluvial Diamond Digging Industry, the [licensed, white] Digger is generally a person of straw and impecunious, [taking] little or no interest in his employees welfare, he expects his men to work long and arduous hours and does not scruple to omit payment of wages should his week have been one of many blank washes." Workers scrimped on vegetables and supplemented their mealie meal with meat only when they could get it "without purchase," a sign that stock theft may have been rising in the area.[37] Gorgas's idea of settling the workforce foundered on the fact that poorly paid workers had to cut back on their purchases of supplementary food.

Employers, and even some civil servants, were evolving a story to justify their disinclination to spend more money on rations. Whether they fed their employees or not, they blamed them for their own ill health. Laborers on the Natal sugar fields were said to arrive from the Transkei "prone to scurvy." A little work in the field, not poor rations, was said to precipitate them into the sickness itself. Also, because African men from some regions of the country were not used to eating spinaches, considering them women's food, they picked the leaves out of their porridge, and thus the secretary for public health testily suggested to the director for native labor that men who contracted scurvy by discarding spinaches be punished by deducting their sick time from their pay.[38] It was rare for a government official to suggest such stringent punishment, but individual employers often did; some in 1927, for example, repatriated scurvy-ridden Fingo canning workers from Lüderitz (South-West Africa) for malingering, and others explained after a scurvy outbreak at a Saldanha Bay whaling station that those sick employees had been "overindulging in whale meat." A canning worker in Lüderitz complained to the NAD, "our employer took no notice of complaints of sickness and the result was that I and three others of the same company contracted scurvy." One of the workers, Ndandani, complained that he spent one week, and others six weeks, confined to bed before a doctor came to examine them. When they were discovered to be suffering from scurvy, the employer shipped them back to Cape Town, saying that he had never promised to provide food and quarters. Ndandani said the food on sale in the local shops was too expensive to buy and so he had lived on stamped mealies, bread, and meat.[39] The resulting investigation lost its momentum in the workings of the NAD bureaucracy, which was ill equipped to impose standards on industry, and the sick man received no redress. The same story was played out that year in Durban when some employees of South African Railways and Harbours were hospitalized with scurvy; their diet consisted only of mealie meal. When a physician told them that the mealie diet was the source of their sickness, other employees demanded a pay raise from the compound manager so they could buy their own food. The Durban police, investigating the incident because an African union, the Industrial and Commercial Workers Union, was involved, found the diet grievance to be legitimate, but the secretary for native affairs decided "the Railway authorities must be left to determine what diet scale they will adopt."[40]

Substantial changes in workplace diets were initiated neither by African protesters nor by compound managers nor, for that matter, by the NAD, but rather by mine medical doctors and, more specifically, the world of scientific research. Before the 1920s, medical doctors were as prone as others to blame Africans for coming down with scurvy. After working among the Tswana since 1903, D. M. MacRae, principal medical officer of the Bechuanaland Protectorate, analyzed "tropical residence and food in relation to health and disease." "The Native," he wrote, "shows the languor and inertia due to climatic effects, and does not work from inclination, but under compulsion, and if not well-nourished under European conditions of labour, will . . . develop scurvy or some other disability." His ideas were not unusual for his time, though by 1920, when he submitted his thesis to the University of Glasgow, they were on the brink of becoming outdated by the new understanding of vitamins. Because the Tswana loved eating meat, going so far as to cut up dead horses and mules and cattle and even devour locusts avidly, he concluded that they were suffering from "nitrogenous starvation," that is, lacking an element to replace worn tissues. They lived "in a constitutional condition little removed from scurvy," a state glaringly evident whenever their supply of milk or grain ran short. Prisoners in Gaborone jail (usually incarcerated for stock theft, another sign of their craving for meat) became so sick from scurvy that their teeth fell out during their sleep. MacRae recommended returning to the wisdom articulated by David Livingstone fifty years earlier, that people protect their health by consuming plenty of meat and milk.[41] Because MacRae had lived seventeen years in Bechuanaland, he was proud of basing his thesis on experience rather than on research in books. Nevertheless, the theme he touched upon—that rural folk were weak and languid because they lived, at best, in a subscorbutic state—was widely shared. It was also applied to pellagra, a niacin deficiency found frequently among people whose diet is super-refined maize. One doctor, investigating pellagrins in a Natal jail, claimed that "a large portion of the native population are in a subpellagric state," a condition worsened by the admittedly deficient prison diet coupled with hard labor in the hot sun.[42] A pattern was emerging in scientific writing that rations played a role in sickness but that blame had to be shared with peasant diet at home.

An early allusion to the "subscorbutic state" of rural people appears in the writings of G. A. Turner, a medical officer employed in 1909 by the mine labor recruiting agency, the Witwatersrand Native Labour Association. Turner had already studied an outbreak of scurvy in and around Kimberley in 1898, and the hardships he had witnessed there led to his observation that "certain races on account of their anatomical development are preeminently suited to withstand prolonged periods of famine." This idea of profound racial—anatomical and evolutionary—difference, like MacRae's focus on nitrogen, was becoming distinctly old-fashioned. How was it, then, that people who appeared to be resilient in the countryside came down with scurvy on the mines? Turner answered the question in this way: "if after such privations [of a limited food supply] they are given severe muscular labour, even when supplied with a good nutritious diet, they are very liable within the first few months of commencing work to develop scurvy."[43] Thus, the fault lay not in diet on the mines but in rural life. He was not alone in this judgment: a Johannesburg doctor, H. A. Loeser, observed that Africans developed scurvy despite a good nutritious diet on the mines because they had previously endured privations and then on the mines had undergone severe muscular labor; and a public health officer, E. H. Cluver, wrote, "in the lazy life [Africans] live in the kraals, scurvy may not develop," whereas "they develop scurvy during work."[44]

To what extent were miners arriving through the 1920s at the mines in a subscorbutic condition? Could their propensity to develop scurvy be fairly blamed on poor eating habits in the countryside? The idea was not absurd because the rates at which people from different areas came down with scurvy did differ.[45] There may have been some truth to the suggestion that recruits, weakened from drought or winter shortages, readily came down with scurvy after only a little work in the sugarcane fields of Natal or on the mines. In preindustrial times scurvy would have occurred during the winter months; the months following a poor harvest or the last weeks of winter in a normal year were times of great susceptibility. Fortunately these times also required the least labor. Mine schedules, on the other hand, paid no attention to these seasonal distinctions, and neither, initially, did miners' diets; men fell ill at a markedly higher rate during their first three months of mine service, perhaps because the stress of labor and of fighting off infections raised their need for vitamin C, which their diets were not meeting.

These experts who blamed rural areas for producing scurvy-prone men were about to propose a rural remedy: African beer. Ironically, beer brewing was attacked by NAD officials as a sign of improvidence at precisely the same time that the government was investigating its health-promoting qualities. Turner was thus caught in a contradiction. While positing an image of people barely able to provide for themselves, he argued at the same time that Africans were brewing both a cure and a prophylactic for scurvy. He urged the mines to adopt "kaffir beer"—as well as meat and fresh vegetables—because of its strong antiscorbutic properties. His views gained wide currency because they were published in the *Transvaal Medical Journal* and issued as a pamphlet by the government printer in Pretoria. By the time Turner published his report, both the mines and the government had already been testing the powers of African beer for at least six years.[46] Around 1910 the mines began to brew and issue beer in order to control scurvy. In 1916 the director of native labor was so impressed when commissioners investigating tuberculosis advocated "kaffir beer" that he recommended employers brew it and issue it to their employees for free.

Dr. Marion Delf, a biochemist with a D.Sc. degree from the University of London, was hired in late 1919 by the South African Institute for Medical Research (SAIMR), whose founding in 1912 was initiated and largely funded by the Chamber of Mines. Her presence in South Africa resulted indirectly from Gorgas's visit six years earlier. The Rand Mines had invited back an American member of the colonel's party, Dr. Abraham Orenstein, to serve as a medical adviser, and Delf arrived to work at the SAIMR on Orenstein's recommendation; he wished her to carry out "certain researches into the vitamin content of the diet of black mine labourers."[47] Only three vitamins had been identified as of 1919—A, B, and C—and none had been isolated, that is, made available in any form other than nature provided. In September 1921, fewer than two years after her arrival in Johannesburg, Delf published "Studies in Experimental Scurvy," arguing for the addition of fruit and vegetables to miners' diets and warning against the damage done by overcooking. She had reached these conclusions by inducing scurvy in guinea pigs, a technique pioneered at the Lister Institute in London, and then trying to cure it by feeding common South African foodstuffs to the animals.[48] Oranges, lemons, and pineapples proved to be of higher antiscorbutic value than pumpkins and squash. Green mealies, cabbages, and sweet potatoes were also valuable; and so, the miners would be happy to learn, was sorghum beer, though its precise antiscorbutic power depended on how it was brewed. Her report laid out the implications for changes in mine diet and stressed that prevention was cheaper than cure.[49] Pumpkin, sugarcane, and beer may have managed to stave off scurvy in rural African households, she wrote, but they had failed to do so in the hard labor conditions of the gold mining industry. Even though the mines' ration scale was immediately amended to reflect Delf's findings, the problem of scurvy persisted.[50]

The director of the SAIMR, Wilfred Watkins-Pitchford, prefaced Delf's report by raising the old alarm of race deterioration. He stated that the health of everyone in South Africa was at risk of being undermined by infections against which they had no protection with a diet periodically lacking fresh vegetables and fruit. However, "town-bred people" were most in danger; their growth was stunted and their teeth were decaying because they, like people "throughout all the civilised nations," had diets deficient in vitamin C. The official historian of the SAIMR referred to Watkins-Pitchford's judgment with some embarrassment as a sign that "the best of scientists can have lapses," but these ideas were continuous with others Watkins-Pitchford had expressed soon after his arrival in South Africa, and they were commonly held. This fundamental unease, not backed up by any scientific evidence, preceded and informed the later focus on the black "race" as in danger of "deterioration." As the food historian Harvey Levenstein has observed, people in early twentieth-century Europe and America commonly feared the impact of modernity or industry on popular health through artificial or patented foods.[51] In South Africa this fear was transmuted by the developing patterns of wealth and poverty into a concern that a particular race was facing degeneration to the point of extinction.

Despite Delf's research revealing that more vegetables and germinated pulses needed to be added to mine diets, and not overcooked, the problem remained how to improve mine diets cheaply. F. W. Fox, a British biochemist trained like Delf at the University of London, began to tackle this problem at the SAIMR when he arrived in 1925. Recruited by Watkins-Pitchford to start the biochemistry department, he was introduced to the field of nutrition by the scurvy problem, and went on to found the study of nutrition in South Africa. For the following five decades, Fox wrote more than seventy articles principally on the properties of South African foodstuffs, discovered by running biochemical tests, not the more complicated and time-consuming animal tests Delf had used. In 1934, the year after vitamin C was isolated and synthesized, Fox and his SAIMR colleagues began to measure the amount of the vitamin in common South African foodstuffs and especially in sorghum beer.[52] Fox's colleague L. F. Levy confirmed Delf's finding that cooking foods like cabbage in a lot of water and for a long time reduced their vitamin C content.

Even though by 1929 improved diet, following Delf's recommendations, had lowered the incidence of scurvy among mine laborers, the symptoms of this deficiency persisted, and this fact puzzled researchers. Was it caused by mine recruits arriving from rural areas in a "depleted state," especially during the early summer months when they had been eating food from last season's harvest?

In 1939, Fox set out to find the cause. In a study of the livers of victims of fatal accidents he found that black miners showed a lower level of ascorbic acid than that occurring in either urban Africans or Europeans. Maybe rural areas and not the mines were to blame. Or were the mines, even in 1939 after all their dietary improvements, still responsible for the debilitated and hemorrhaging state of some African workers? Fox determined that the persistence of scurvy among African miners was a result not of their home diets, but of the "precarious" nature of their "border line" or "minimal" mine rations, which left them "little or no margin of safety." With less than 10 percent of scurvy cases contracted within the first month of service, he concluded that "scurvy is not so much brought to the mines, but develops there as a result of the Native's reactions to mine conditions." (This article is not cited in the official SAIMR history of important breakthroughs in scurvy research.) Systematic attention had to be paid, he wrote, either to the "choice, storage and handling" of the vegetable ration or to the administration of an additional daily dose of a measured quantity of ascorbic acid (via orange juice or concentrate or synthetic ascorbic acid). Eventually, according to the official history of the Mine Medical Officers Association, ascorbic acid was added to an acidulated cold beverage (fermented maize flour called *marewu*) offered daily to the African miners.[53]

This story is one that would make Adam Smith happy. The invisible hand of the profit motive had reduced, perhaps not speedily, morbidity rates in the case of scurvy, and medical researchers had served as major catalysts for this improvement. Delf's and Fox's research reveals that mine revenues, indirectly through their expenditure on the salaries of mine medical researchers, did help to improve miners' health through better rations. Scurvy never occurred again at the high levels of 1902–1903 and 1918–1920, though it did not disappear, and this nutritional deficiency, as well as the term *subscorbutic* itself, virtually disappeared from the pages of South African medical journals, at least when doctors discussed the health of miners. From the 1940s on, statistical data demonstrated that miners gained weight, and fell ill from scurvy less frequently, hardly ever dying from it.[54] Scurvy was the first focus of South African nutritional research because it was a serious medical problem, a visible sign of gross malnutrition during an era when the discovery of vitamins shaped scholarly agendas and understandings internationally. Two ironies emerge from this tale. First, rural African diet, in the form of beer so frequently linked to proverbial improvidence, provided the favored, because cheap, cure and prophylactic. Second, despite Fox's research the idea of rural debility resulting from African laziness and dietetic ignorance persisted.

Research into scurvy may have facilitated a shift from one way of marking differences between the races to another. In the early twentieth century, the idea lingered that the bodies of Africans and Europeans might be essentially different. G. A. Turner, for example, had suggested, in 1909, that African bodies might withstand famine better than white bodies. H. A. Loeser, on the other hand, wrote three years later, "If [the African] were entirely capable of living on vegetable food we should, from analogy with lower animals, expect to find that the alimentary canal of the negro differed materially from that of the European, which is not the case." Rather, "when through abnormal conditions, such as famine, war, or unsuitable dieting by his employer," the

African, like all other men, "is deprived of one of these [dietary] essentials, the result is marked by physical breakdown, indicated by an outbreak of scurvy or by an increased tendency to contract infectious disease." "The feeding of the coloured labourer," Loeser wrote, had become "deservedly . . . a matter of public interest as well as of industrial economy."[55] Nutritional research was helping to propagate the idea of physiological equality. African debility needed other explanations.

Debility

One potential, and two actual, catastrophes helped to launch the second phase of South African nutritional research. In the late 1920s and early 1930s a severe drought dried up many of the springs and rivers that fed the fields and stock in that already arid land. The international depression coincided with the drought. Only when South Africa left the gold standard in 1932 did the economy begin to grow again, but the recovery threatened South Africa's resources in one new way. Secondary industries were being developed, creating a demand for unprecedented numbers of laborers. What if the health of rural Africans had been so undermined that they were simply too few or too weak to serve the country's burgeoning need for more labor? The question reflected the tenuous confidence in the South African economy's ability to grow.[56] Medical men and employers voiced this malaise when they took note of the spread of tuberculosis among black miners and when they learned from rural doctors that half the African children born in the reserves died before the age of five. (They, of course, had to rely on their own observations because the state did not register African births and deaths.) These specific indices of African debility, together with more general fears of a stunted and inefficient labor force, fueled a nearly two-decade-long spate of investigations into the nutritional well-being of all South Africans.

About twenty surveys of South African nutrition produced between 1929 and 1945 reflect the redefinition of "race deterioration." The social Darwinist phrase was going out of fashion, as was the concept of extinction, but the insecurity remained. The researchers chose indices of the condition often as diffuse as the fear itself. Some researchers did focus on, and try to enumerate, such observable symptoms as dental decay, rickets, pellagra, and infant deaths. The earliest South African research on malnutrition, published in medical journals before about 1937, tended to examine these precise defects.[57] After 1937 there was an increasing tendency for researchers to measure height, weight, and the circumference of forearms in an elusive search for numerical indices of normality and nutritional health. But it was often impossible to learn whether and how such measurements were connected to ill health or weakness. The word *debility* captures the generic sense of alarm extending throughout both these phases.

What is remarkable about the researchers' efforts is that as they broadened the scope of their search for a medical definition of *deterioration,* they were giving the imprimatur of scientific authority to discussions of social conditions. By the early 1940s nutritional research was not only proving correlations between poverty and malnutrition, it was helping to bring the concept of African poverty into public discourse. Science was validating inquiries that had a political trajectory.

Before examining the studies to discover what they reveal about South Africa's interwar malaise and the sense that nutritional experts were making of it, it must be stressed that South Africa was not alone in these concerns. In fact, the desire to define and bring about nutritional health was imported to South Africa from Europe, especially from Britain. The 1904 study of British physiques had been followed by others reflecting the belief that working-class diets—heavily biased toward tea, bread, and jam—needed to be made more robust and that such time-honored British staples like oatmeal and milk should be added. However, during the 1920s, when people in Britain and America talked about nutrition, they mainly focused on the health of infants and invalids. (Adults ideally ate well simply by responding to their appetites.) Curative medicine was, in any case, the order of the day; eating well to prevent disease was not a common medical concept.[58]

In the late 1920s concern about nutrition was burgeoning, and it spread to the empire. John Boyd Orr, head of an animal research institute in Scotland, joined John Gilks, head of medical services in Kenya, to compare the value and impact of Masai and Kikuyu diets. Their conclusions owed more to their preconceptions that it was unhealthy to eat blood or simply vegetables than to the rigor of their logic. Measuring muscular strength with a dynamometer or recording the incidence of tropical skin ulcers, after all, revealed very little about the labor value of either group. Nevertheless, Orr and Gilks thought that a "general improvement of agriculture and animal husbandry amongst the Akikuyu will almost certainly be accompanied by an improvement in the health and working capacity of the natives themselves. . . . [T]he loss of health and efficiency attributable to deficient diet," they concluded, "is, therefore of considerable economic importance."[59]

The League of Nations took up the subject of the quality of colonial diets in 1933, encouraging further research in both the French and Belgian empires. Anthropologists adopted the inquiry with enthusiasm, and, in 1936, an entire issue of the journal *Africa* was devoted to studies of food consumed throughout the continent. The nutritional interest of Audrey Richards, author of one of the articles, stemmed from her work with a family welfare settlement in Frankfurt in 1924, yet another indication that nutritional concerns originated in European cities in the 1920s among middle-class persons worried about the fate of the working class. Richards, a student of the anthropologist Bronislaw Malinowski, was eager to apply what she learned from the social sciences to improve colonial societies.[60]

The effusion of international interest in nutrition during the interwar years resulted from the discovery and isolation of vitamins around the time of World War I. Biochemists were the heroes of these scientific breakthroughs, well into the 1940s. Scientists who applied their vitaminic insights to the colonies tended to focus on soil quality, maintaining that if people were malnourished, it was because they had overused the land where they grew their crops and herded their cattle, and so depleted it of essential minerals.[61]

In brief, this story about the degradation of African land came to prominence in the 1930s from diverse roots. One was nineteenth-century missionaries seeking, according to William Beinart, "to legitimise their activities by projecting their task as one of restoring ecological balance and plenty to a devastated land of unbelievers." Another was drought commissions criticizing white and black farmers for overfarming the land. Yet another was propaganda from the United States, where Department of Agriculture officials were coping with their own dustbowl. Finally, there were "the political imperatives of segregation." This last point is well illustrated by the words of I. B. Pole-Evans, a senior official in South Africa's Department of Agriculture, who wrote in 1938 that the greatest social problem in South Africa was urban migration caused by "poverty and hunger." "Land that formerly produced virile whites and healthy and contented natives," he went on, "no longer continues to do so. The original valuable vegetal cover has been removed, the soil has lost its fertility, and much of the precious land has been washed away. Man has misused the land that formerly gave him health and wealth." The consequent drift to town, lamented by segregationists, had resulted in a "competitive association of the races in the struggle for existence." As Beinart has argued, the narrative bears greater truth with reference to some overpopulated areas, like the Herschel district of the Transkeian Territories, than others. It also slights "the rich experience of practical experimentation [with soil types and planting times, for example] in the African rural areas."[62]

The story that South Africa's land was deteriorating framed virtually every discussion of African diet during the Union's first fifty years. The medical officer E. H. Cluver wrote thankfully in 1939, "The marriage of health and agriculture, as it was felicitously phrased at a historical meeting of the League of Nations, has certainly proved advantageous to health." Three years later, Dr. Sidney Kark warned, "all our efforts to combat malnutrition were doomed to failure if soil erosion continued to devastate the land." Most analyses of African debility could be traced back to the assumption that the land in the reserves was dying.[63]

Nutritional knowledge from Europe transplanted to the colonies contributed to another major interpretive stress. The study of diet had led European researchers away from biological determinism, that is, from any conclusion that the working classes had inherited certain physiques and capacities. If Europeans were scrawny, it was probably because they ate too many pickles and too much vinegar, as the 1904 parliamentary inquiry suggested, rather than that they had inherited meager physiques. In South Africa the biochemists, whose work presupposed that human bodies were essentially the same, succeeded in demolishing the logic of racial determinism so that it played virtually no role in clarifying the causes of the perceived physical degeneration of Africans. The weight of explaining malnutrition thereby fell either on wage rates or on African culture. In the former case, there were unavoidable political implications. In the latter case, eating poorly could be read as a sign that time-honored African habits were not up to the challenges of modernity. If this interpretation were true, then science in general, and nutrition in particular, were among the greatest gifts that the imperial powers had to give to the colonized.

Between 1929 and 1946 researchers produced at least seven significant studies of the nutritional health of white South Africans. The fear that whites could not live in South Africa had clearly died. In place of this definition of race deterioration—to which the only logical solution would have been to return to Europe—a new idea appeared: how to save the poorest whites and assess the damage poverty had inflicted on their bodies and minds. The first study was launched in 1929 under the auspices of the Carnegie Commission's investigation of the "poor white problem" in South Africa. The six-member commission devoted one volume of its report to "health factors." The author of that volume, Dr. W. A. Murray, sent by the department of public health, used data—chest, weight, and trunk measurements—similar to those Orr and Gilks had collected among the Masai and Kikuyu.

Murray, nevertheless, complained that his data were too subjective, and much of his chapter on malnutrition laments the impossibility of making comparisons across time and space. The few extant figures did allow him to inquire, inconclusively as it turned out, whether malnutrition retarded the onset of puberty among "necessitous" youth. He also noted that children who lived on the high Transvaal plains seemed to be bigger than those in Natal, probably because the atmospheric pressure on the coast inhibited "the increased assimilation of nitrogen." He did not check out the labor potential of poor white adults and how it was affected by their nutritional status. In fact, Murray expressed frustration with his data far more frequently than he conveyed a sense of urgency about white strength. He even suspected the situation was improving: the continuous decline in the proportion of the malnourished segment of the white population in the Cape from 1918 to 1929, he observed, was probably a result of "the excellent work done by local committees, with State support, in providing necessitous school children with a daily nourishing meal at or near the school."[64]

White-focused studies such as Murray's appeared often after his volume was published in 1932. The authors shared Murray's desire for anthropometric data and, like him, drew conclusions that the measurements themselves did not quite support. The paucity of their data highlights their preconceptions. When parliament mandated a survey of European schoolchildren in 1937, using three different kinds of examinations (clinical, somatometric, dietary) as recommended by the League of Nations, it discovered "malnutrition . . . in minor forms," but no gross deficiency or starvation.[65] Without a historical baseline of data, researchers were left to draw comparisons between the provinces: Natal schoolchildren had apparently grown heavier over the 1930s, for example, though the significance of this observation is hard to define. Not only did careful measurements fail to reveal what change over time meant, they also had no clear nutritional significance. Their interest lies partly in documenting that whites in South Africa decreasingly feared they were facing extinction or even a physiological crisis.

A 1941 report by F. W. Fox, the SAIMR biochemist, and Douglas Back, an agricultural researcher, explicitly confirmed this sense that the white nutritional crisis was passing. "We see no reason for supposing," they concluded, "that malnutrition is on the increase, or that, speaking generally, conditions in the rural areas are deteriorating; in fact many of those best in a position to judge assured us that conditions in their own areas were at least better than some time ago, or were even steadily improving."[66]

Reports on whites, in contrast to studies of black health, tended to stress less explicitly their labor potential. Dr. C. Louis Leipoldt, for example, urged that poor rural whites be "husbanded for the State" by being cured of malaria, and "fed, trained and disciplined properly." The results would repay whatever "treasure" had been spent to uplift them. With this exception, poor whites and poor blacks tended to be discussed in similar terms. Fox and Back wrote about the "poverty of knowledge, ambition and industry as well as poverty of purchasing power" among rural Europeans. Once again targeting soil erosion as "the first and greatest nutritional problem," they implied that poor white management of the soil was no better than black efforts.[67] No nutritional study after Murray's drew attention to the specific ethnicity of the European poor, that is, that they were disproportionately Afrikaners.

The eleven or so studies of nonwhite people during this period demonstrate the belief that the physique of Indians, Coloureds, and Africans was worsening, unlike that of poor whites in the above studies. The first such survey was also conducted by Fox and Back on a five-thousand-mile journey in April 1937 in the Transkeian Territories. They collected data on infant mortality and the heights and weights of African children in areas where milk was abundant and where it was not. Their three-and-a-half-month trip was clearly inspired by concern that rural children would not develop strong bodies. It was likely that the labor force would shrink just as labor needs were increasing; the infant mortality rate was widely believed to be high. On the first page of their survey, Fox and Back quoted the Witwatersrand Native Labour Association's 1936 report: "it is being increasingly realized that some of these [factors guaranteeing the continued availability of African labor] are altering appreciably and not always for the better." The Chamber of Mines had sent them to the Transkei and Ciskei for the explicit purpose of ascertaining such facts. With the local Native Recruiting Corporation offices as their bases, they established contact with the local magistrate, medical men, and hospitals, as well as "Native chiefs, village groups or kraals, getting in this way into fairly close and frequent touch with Native life and the Native point of view."[68]

Many Africans, so Fox believed, considered their traditional diet cheap, satisfying, and nourishing. However, its very simplicity was making it vulnerable to "contact with Western civilization," especially with local traders from whom Africans, imitating European consumer habits, were buying machine-ground mealie meal, white bread, tea, canned fish, and condensed milk, as well as a considerable amount of sugar. They were growing to despise traditional dishes such as wild spinach. The major problem looming in the future, he considered, was rapid deterioration of the land from overgrazing, especially by the sheep of the small wealthy minority and by cultivation of steep hillsides. He did not mention the Natives' Land Act that had established the small size of African reserves, but noted that shifting cultivation and communal grazing were viable agricultural techniques only as long as the land was unlimited. Fox credited Orenstein with "the happy thought of combining the agricultural with the nutritional approach"; linkages between health and agriculture were already common in dominions like Australia. The Native Economic Commission report of 1932 had influenced his analysis by noting that "[b]efore the time of the present disastrous overstocking, milk was plentiful."[69] The narrative of degeneration was spreading from concern with deterioration of the people to the deterioration of the land.

When Mrs. K. Malherbe, a member of parliament, asked the South African House of Assembly in 1937 to sponsor nutritional research, she was giving voice to all the above influences: the contemporary international trend to investigate vitamin deficiencies; the fashion of linking malnutrition to impoverished soil; anthropologists' efforts to facilitate the modernization of colonial societies; and South African white fears about the shrinking of the local labor supply caused by the high infant mortality rate and by the incidence of tuberculosis. The same vectors primed government officials to respond positively, and parliament in 1937 directed the Department of Public Health to set aside six thousand pounds to fund nutritional surveys. The amount of money was not large; it was simply unprecedented. Over the next four years researchers spent that money documenting the food status of segments of the body politic. Each of the four racial groups was studied independently. In 1938, one-fifth of the white schoolboys throughout the four provinces were measured and placed in one of the four categories on the Dunfermline scale: nutritional status that was excellent, adequate, needing attention, or requiring immediate hospitalization. Given the vagueness of the measures, it is perhaps not surprising that malnutrition of one degree or another was said to exist in fully 40 percent of this white schoolboy population. Also in 1938 the Bantu Nutrition Survey, conducted by Sidney Kark, a medical officer, and Harding LeRiche, an anthropometrist, focused, with the same techniques of measurement, on the incidence of malnutrition among schoolchildren: 71 percent of African boys and 66 percent of girls were found to be suffering from malnutrition. Meanwhile, Dr. B. A. Dormer studied one thousand Indian schoolchildren in Durban for evidence of disease caused by food deficiency. The remaining thousand pounds went to Dr. John Fleming Brock, professor of medicine at the University of Cape Town, for his Cape Nutrition Survey, similarly devoted to measuring schoolchildren, though Brock included blacks, whites, and Coloureds and ran biochemical (vitamin C saturation, hemoglobin and blood, x-ray of bones, and calcium and phosphorus metabolism), not only somatometric (body measurement), tests.[70] His study found that, in selected districts, approximately half of the children in each group were malnourished. Nevertheless, he expressed doubt about the reliability of conventional indicators of nutrition.

Nutritional concern pervaded discussions of South Africa's future. The South African Institute of Race Relations held a conference in Cape Town in 1939 whose proceedings were published in a special issue of its journal, *Race Relations*. The institute credited that gathering, which called for a national survey of food resources, for the creation the following year of the National Nutrition Council, which had been advocated five years earlier by the League of Nations.

After 1940, in a significant new direction, many researchers, frustrated by the unreliability of such categories and measures as the Dunfermline scale, began to seek causes and consider remedies. What caused the patterns of malnutrition? What correlations could be drawn between those patterns and other social variables? And what could be done to improve them? A biochemist, Leon Golberg, wrote in a 1942 issue of the *South African Medical Journal* that since the existence of malnutrition had been proven, the postwar task must be "remedial . . . reconstruction."[71]

Scientific research was becoming linked with social science. When Miriam Janisch, a social research officer in the Non-European and Native Affairs Department of Johannesburg, surveyed African income and spending in Johannesburg in 1941, Fox contributed an appendix on diet. J. L. Gray, head of the Department of Social Studies at the University of the Witwatersrand, discovered a "regular and formidable increase in malnutrition" accompanying a decline in family income among Europeans on the Rand. Edward Batson, with Carnegie Foundation funding for a socioeconomic study of the Cape peninsula, found a positive correlation between poverty and malnutrition.[72] Soon their findings would be cited by government commissions of inquiry— into the conditions of urban Africans (1942), miners' wages (1943), and the creation of a national health service (1944), for example—and by parliamentarians debating such issues as school feeding.

In 1939, Henry Sigerist had carried the message of social, or community, medicine to South Africa. Invited to receive an honorary degree at the University of the Witwatersrand, Sigerist delivered about fifty lectures during his four months in the country, and the SABC radio broadcast his farewell address, urging South Africa to develop the public services that would protect the health of *all* South Africans. "You are a nation, not of two, but of ten million inhabitants." Regretting that no vital statistics were available for Africans, he referred to the commonly stated figure that half of all children born never reached maturity. He appealed to white self-interest: "Disease knows no colour bar, and a sick native population is not only an economic handicap, but a direct menace to the health of Europeans." The mines seemed to have grasped that fact, he said, because, by feeding their workers scientifically and providing medical services, they were earning large dividends. This apostle of socialized medicine—two years earlier he had written a study of it in the USSR—named low wages as the "basic evil." His broad and inclusive vision apparently inspired a generation of South African doctors; when, nearly sixty years later, I asked Dr. Sidney Kark to name the origin of his own holistic view of medicine, he mentioned Sigerist.[73]

The rising tide of tuberculosis proved to be another potent catalyst. In 1937 physicians were calling attention to the "astonishing" increase, and the

7. Shops near miners' hostels carried processed foods to supplement mine diet, such as the imported malt extract praised in this *Imvo Zabantsundu* advertisement (1938) for its energizing powers and quick preparation.

following year an NAD commission on indigent tuberculates reported that the mines played "a less important role than formerly" in the spread of the disease; rather, the low milk supply in the reserves brought about by soil erosion and inferior stock was stated as the cause. By 1945 a state of "white public hysteria" had arisen about the tubercular threat to the labor supply and public health. Randall Packard has argued that, by the late 1930s, doctors commonly linked this incidence to overcrowded housing and poor diet, whereas, he wrote, earlier in the century, medical opinion had tended to conclude that black people were peculiarly susceptible to the disease. After his Transkeian tour, Fox was convinced that a definite deterioration in people's resistance to tuberculosis had occurred since 1935 "due to the prolonged drought" with shortage of milk seriously damaging health. Nearly 2 percent of Natal's urban Africans were suffering from TB, Dr. Dormer found in his 1938 study of twenty thousand Africans, because of overcrowding, hard work, and a diet inadequate in vitamins and calories.[74]

Perhaps because of the tuberculosis scare and certainly because of fears of future labor shortages, some mines were caring for their workers' health more assiduously. Wartime enhanced this concern. In July 1941, L. S. Williams reported on his "investigations into the food and feeding of the Native labourers on a certain group of our mines [five mines within the New Consolidated Gold Fields Group]" to the annual meeting of the Transvaal Mine Medical Officers Association, of which he was then president, noting "the almost frenzied efforts and research" of wartime. Based on the "immense advance in the science of dietetics" by Fox and others, Williams had devised an improved diet for miners at New Consolidated Gold Fields, one he hoped would become standardized throughout the industry so that feeding could be "more scientifically controlled." He ordered an increase in the daily ration of meat, fat, and vegetables by adding "whole orange juice," soya bean flour, and "a definite sugar ration." The miners were facing greater stress by requirements to work deeper underground, but their health improved on this new diet: the morbidity rate per thousand laborers fell from 257 in 1938 to 211 in 1940.[75]

The doctors listening to Williams's talk, the first on the subject in the twenty-year history of the mine medical officers' association, must have greeted his paper with enthusiasm because two months later, in September 1941, they devoted their general meeting to a laudatory discussion of the paper. Fox proposed establishing a "centralized food laboratory." One doctor suggested sending the paper to the Chamber of Mines in the hope that the chamber would ask the government to revise its minimum ration scale. Would the added expense of an improved diet be justified? "I think it may be generally accepted as a scientific fact that physical efficiency depends largely on wise and adequate feeding" and the miners were, after all, "such an important cog in the mining industry's machine." Also, a "shortage of labour" would soon result from the development of secondary industries, and "it behoves us to conserve the health of the labour we get."[76] By 1943 the contribution of manufacturing to South Africa's GNP surpassed that made by mining.

Referring to the significant increase in miners' weight upon their discharge, Williams noted, "One may merely infer that the Natives respond very quickly to any form of diet which is better than the one they receive at their homes." Dr. Goldsmith also put forward an opinion widely shared at the time but never demonstrated, not even in Williams's study: "I am of the opinion that the majority of Natives are all in a state of slight malnutrition, due to a general lack of protective food elements, in which they are not actually ill but in which at least they cannot give maximum efficiency, and are predisposed to a larger degree of illness."[77]

Despite putting this spin on their discoveries, nutritional researchers were contributing to potentially explosive knowledge by documenting the physical consequences of privilege and poverty. Even the smaller studies of the late 1930s revealed with startling clarity the discrepancy between the quality of black and white urban life; in Benoni in 1938, for example, C. C. P. Anning, a medical officer, revealed that Europeans consumed one thousand more calories daily than Africans did, by eating twice as much meat and drinking more than twenty times as much milk. As long as South African industries needed many strong African laborers, this discrepancy would have pressing practical importance; one authoritative medical voice after another called attention to the danger in speeches and in the pages of medical journals. The Pietermaritzburg medical officer, M. Maister, warned in 1940, "Apart from humanitarian reasons, we cannot afford to stand calmly by, for the cost of repairing the damage consequent upon this malnutrition is already enormous. South African economics depend upon cheap Native labour, yet that labour must be drawn from neighbouring countries because enough of its own Native labour force is not fit." Cluver extended this economic observation into the realm of politics when he wrote, "malnutrition, the cause of most of our ill-health, [is] one of the main causes of inadequate citizenship." And the National Health Services Commission noted that malnutrition demanded a broad-based, society-wide attack; "Nutrition, we found, was a field so broad and so interwoven with every phase of modern life that no single approach can, by itself, prove effective."[78] The mid-1940s marked the end of the research inquiring whether Africans were debilitated, because by the end of the war, the problem had been revealed. Now was the time to do something about it.

Kwashiorkor

In the 1950s kwashiorkor dominated medical research agendas in South Africa and also in the international arena. The word came from the Ga language of West Africa, describing the sickness an elder child may get when a younger one is born. The child, typically between the ages of one and four, becomes slightly swollen with fluid, at first at hands and feet, then patches of skin darken and thicken, then fall off, exposing raw pink skin. The child may develop diarrhea and grow irritable or extremely listless. Death commonly follows.

Since 1933, when the condition was first publicized under that name, researchers have debated its causes. Earlier, it had been called atrophy or "malignant malnutrition" or "infantile pellagra," revealing that its origins were commonly believed to lie in vitamin deficiencies. The symptoms did bear a good deal of resemblance to the "butterfly cast" on the skin of adults who suffered from pellagra. In 1944, H. C. Trowell, a British doctor who had worked in Kenya, suggested that the cause was protein deficiency, but two years later, working in Uganda, Trowell said he was still unable to answer the question whether "this syndrome [is] confined, almost exclusively, to Africans and their descendants, occasioned largely by race and heredity?" Some subsequent researchers, such as Rhodesia's Michael Gelfand, thought its origin lay in an unknown toxic factor in certain batches of corn and cassava; how else to explain the fatty liver, the sole abnormality found in postmortems? Research in 1950 swung the balance of opinion toward a lack of protein. But was that the sole deficiency? Five years later, the diverse histories of young patients suggested that the absence of certain key minerals might also be at fault and, even more important, that their diets may have been lacking in calories, that is, children fell ill because they ate too little. Reflecting the staying power of that observation, medical opinion still holds that the condition is caused by "protein-calorie malnutrition." Early warning of its onset is provided by tracing a child's rate of growth against North American standards of weight, height, or arm circumference, correlated with age. It is treated by boosting the number of meals the sick child eats daily. Having been variously regarded for most of the twentieth century as a condition arising from a toxin, the lack of a B vitamin, deficiencies of either protein or calories or both, it is now commonly seen as "a problem whose complexities have not yet been fully unraveled."[79]

The ultimate causes have been as contentious as the proximate ones. The fact that most cases occurred in the Third World led researchers to pose the question: Was kwashiorkor caused principally by maternal ignorance or by poverty? Cecily Williams, the British physician in the Gold Coast who had first publicized the Ga name, attributed kwashiorkor to mothers' feeding their weaned children only maize gruel and seldom high-protein foods like milk, eggs, fish or meat, or a protein-rich mixture of vegetables such as beans and rice. Like scurvy and debility, protein-calorie malnutrition led directly to questions about the nature of South African society and even the global distribution of wealth.

The prominence of kwashiorkor internationally from the late forties stemmed directly from the lessons on nutrition World War II had taught. Once again, war had revolutionized how people thought about food.[80] Men with experience in relief operations in postwar Europe now assumed important positions in the World Health Organization (WHO). The American physician Nevin Scrimshaw, for example, had seen emaciated children in Europe and, subsequently, in Guatemala, and helped to push protein issues high on the agendas of the new United Nations organizations concerned with world poverty. At nine meetings of the United Nations Food and Agriculture Organization/ WHO Joint Committee on Nutrition, held between 1949 and 1975, kwashiorkor was featured. UNICEF was founded in 1949 primarily to distribute surplus American dried skimmed milk to the hungry of the developing world, a strategy based in part on the efficacy of such a distribution program in postwar European schools. In the late 1950s, UNICEF added $100,000 to the $250,000 given by the Rockefeller Foundation to WHO's Protein Advisory Group, its purpose "to advise on the safety and suitability of proposed new protein-rich food preparations." It is no wonder that Brock, South Africa's key player in international kwashiorkor research, called the 1950s the "protein decade."[81]

Kwashiorkor struck a responsive nerve within South Africa. It aroused the diffuse fear of race deterioration that experts had been articulating at least since the turn of the century. It reinforced anxieties over the adequacy of the country's future labor supply that had sent Fox and Back on their journey around the Transkei in 1937. The Ga name made more specific the threat of the high infant mortality rate. Also, white taxpayers were apprehensive lest the cost of treatment fall heavily on them. As Dr. Halley Stott, founder of the Valley Trust in rural Natal, noted in 1960, the "tremendous" amount of more than a million pounds a year was spent on urban hospitalization at King Edward VIII, one of Durban's two non-European hospitals, and the vast majority of its kwashiorkor cases came from the reserves. This meant that Africans themselves were making only a token payment of a few shillings "towards a cure which has probably cost the taxpayer a considerable sum of money."[82] Stott's own records at the Botha's Hill Health Centre showed kwashiorkor mounting in 1965 to a peak of 180 cases per 10,000 children under the age of seven attending the center for treatment.

The prominence of kwashiorkor research in South Africa owes a great deal to the energies and international eminence of Dr. Brock. He was also in the forefront of medical efforts to give greater emphasis to the prevention of disease and not to concentrate wholly on cure. Leaving the University of Cape Town in 1926 to study animal physiology at Oxford University as a Rhodes Scholar, he encountered a discipline that was contriving to raise productivity of food—more eggs and milk, and faster-growing piglets—by improving animal diet. The study of human nutrition, on the other hand, was then devoted mainly to concocting diets for invalids. During his entire medical training at Oxford and then at the London Hospital (1926–1932), he said, "I never heard any talk about applying nutritional science to the prevention of disease or to the achievement of good and lasting health except in the sphere of infant feeding." His appreciation of the importance of diet was undoubtedly stoked by his year at Harvard Medical School in the early 1930s; he found American recommended daily allowances for food, and especially dairy, consumption to be phenomenally high, a product of the local food industry's promotional talents. In 1936 he took these American lessons on the importance of diet, however overblown, to Cambridge University where, assisting Professor J. A. Ryle, he developed his lifelong commitment to "social," later known as "community," medicine. Ryle taught that medical science properly looked after a person within the context of his entire environment, that is, "the whole of the economic, nutritional, occupational, educational, and psychological opportunity or experience of the individual or the community."[83] Nothing contextual was irrelevant to health. In 1938, Brock returned to South Africa to apply those lessons there.

Brock's successes owed much to foreign donors. In 1939, the year after he became professor of the practice of medicine at UCT, he received one of the thousand pound grants that parliament had been dispensing for the study of South African nutrition since Mrs. Malherbe's motion in parliament. Research money was generally hard to obtain, however, and much of his subsequent success depended on overseas, especially U.S., support. In 1949 he was appointed to the nutrition panel of the WHO, which sent him and M. Autret the following year around the continent of Africa to collect information on the epidemiology of kwashiorkor. His classic report "Kwashiorkor in Africa" was based on this trip. Also in 1949, the South African Council of Scientific and Industrial Research established a clinical nutrition research unit under his direction at the University of Cape Town, and from that base, Brock led a productive research team that would put South Africa on the international map of leading nutritional research for the next two decades. Funds from the Merck pharmaceutical company and the Williams-Waterman Fund of New York enabled this team to conduct the first South African intercity clinical trial in pediatric nutrition, with special attention to the treatment of kwashiorkor. In 1957 the National Institutes of Health, U.S. Public Health Service, began its decade-long support of the metabolic ward and laboratory at the Red Cross Memorial Children's Hospital in Cape Town.

In between his first trip to Central Africa in 1944 and his return in 1950 under the aegis of WHO, Brock collaborated with F. W. Fox in analyzing how nutritional factors affect human health and welfare in Africa. Their 1949 article in the *South African Medical Journal* suggests how difficult it would be to apply Ryle's lessons to African societies Brock himself knew only as a visitor. Brock noted that "Africa has been backward in applying existing knowledge of nutritional science to the welfare of mankind," its agriculture "wasteful and inefficient"; "apathy, ignorance and superstition" had led to "starvation in the midst of plenty." Undoubtedly influenced by Fox, he noted the need to conserve soil resources in the South African reserves rather than allow them to be depleted by "primitive agriculture and the effects of the *lobola* system on pastoral methods," an allusion to overstocking. While he did say the reserves had "inadequate area in relation to population," he skirted policy issues on the distribution of land. He was more forthright on wage issues. As early as 1943 he had written that the "only final solution is to raise wages" paid to every employed person among South Africa's ten million population.[84]

After his research trip around Africa with Autret, Brock would once again address the question of "backwardness," but now saw it as an effect rather than a cause of malnutrition. "It would not be too far-fetched," they wrote, "to attribute to protein deficiency, at least in part, the backwardness of the African people." He recommended milk as the best prophylactic and cure. Six years later, Brock and John D. L. Hansen demonstrated that skimmed milk was the best treatment; it approximated the combination of amino acids, glucose, and a salt mixture that they had successfully devised.[85] Brock's clinical research pointed out the general need for more and better food for all sectors of the population and gave no support to those who urged that African health should be improved simply by fortifying their staple foods with vitamin additives.

Brock, perhaps sensitive to his dependence on government funding, engaged in no political activity until after his retirement in 1970, when he joined the Progressive party. In his articles and surveys he depicted South Africa as one all-inclusive country, every race within it running the risk of malnutrition. As a doctor he knew he could insist only that politicians reorganize the country's agriculture and economy, rather than decide on the remedies himself. And so, his critiques of policies and the attitudes supporting them tended to be oblique. He told medical students in 1945, for example, "Capacity for hard physical work over a limited number of years is not the sole objective of human evolution," as if to caution them not to think of Africans simply as units of labor.[86] The doctors he helped recruit and train would develop even more explicitly the political implications of their research.

Hansen helped to heighten the sociological tenor of kwashiorkor studies. Returning to South Africa in 1953 after working with a neonatologist in Boston, Hansen was adopted onto Brock's research team and, for the next three years, studied why skimmed milk cured kwashiorkor. While engaged in this project, he observed the high incidence of kwashiorkor patients at the Red Cross Hospital—20 percent of the children there were afflicted—and this insight stimulated his further research. In a paper on the symbiotic interaction between gastrointestinal infection and malnutrition, he drew attention to the differential rates between Europeans and non-Europeans. Virtually no European infants had died in either Cape Town or England in 1957 from gastroenteritis, he wrote, but close to forty of every thousand deceased non-European infants in Cape Town had succumbed to such infections. Taking a leaf from social medicine, he itemized in the *South African Medical Journal* environmental factors like the poor quality of most nonwhite housing, a demoralized and insecure population, and the fact that most people had too little money to meet such basic needs as proper feeding. He backed up this last point by citing research on Cape Town incomes recently collected by Edward Batson. He now suspects that this kind of wide-ranging exploration of the nonmedical roots of childhood disease is what led to him being called a communist in the Afrikaans press in the early 1960s.[87]

In 1962, Hansen noted no material difference in the birth weights of the four South African "races," adding that the retarded growth and weight of poor nonwhite children began after the age of six months. The poverty of their families, not their genes, was taking its toll. Two years later he integrated this perspective into the research design of his study of Bonteheuwel, a Coloured housing estate in Cape Town where, by dividing the household sample by income, he found economic status and protein-calorie malnutrition (PCM) "very closely linked," and concluded that "adequacy of income and the capacity to earn such an income" were basic to improved child health. He explicitly rejected maternal ignorance as the cause of illness: "even if a mother is adequately educated in nutritional and other principles, she has to have sufficient income to buy protective foods to maintain the normal growth and health of her children."[88]

Hansen, like Brock, publicized kwashiorkor so assiduously that the state declared it a notifiable disease in 1962. Neither he nor Brock brought politics into their analyses. Rather than target issues of wage rates and land distribution, Hansen wrote that South Africa's industrial revolution was responsible for its health problems: "rapid industrial development, causing among other things a shift in population from country to town, is producing a demoralized and insecure society that has not yet succeeded in adapting itself to the pace of current change." He did not fault the Medical Research Council, as some of his colleagues did, for shifting research funds after 1970 away from kwashiorkor and toward lipids and fats and the associated diseases of affluence. Instead, he found their awards fair. He accepted that research priorities depended on and hence were highly responsive to government policies because "academics in South Africa are virtually public servants."[89]

Despite such research as Hansen's, the ignorance paradigm remained a formidable opponent of socioeconomic arguments. Its resilience may be observed in the work of A. R. P. Walker, a British biochemist who replaced F. W. Fox at the SAIMR upon his retirement in 1954. After receiving his M.Sc. degree from the University of Bristol in 1939, Walker had traveled to southern Africa in search of better employment opportunities than Britain afforded; he conducted biochemical tests on food purity for the Department of Public Health in Johannesburg before beginning to work with Fox at the SAIMR in 1946. Walker wrote a series of articles taking what a historian would call a *longue durée* (long-term) perspective on the health and physique of South Africa's black people. Walker maintained that change would come slowly and naturally, as it had in Europe, with rising privilege one day improving the admittedly poor "Bantu" vital statistics: life expectancy, tuberculosis mortality, and infant mortality rates. The process would not be fast because it depended on education in "understanding, self-reliance, and responsibility," that is, how to spend their money wisely and live hygienically. Only an idealist would assert, he wrote, that there was a "readily available 'blueprint' whose adoption could guarantee instant or even quick success when applied under South African conditions."[90]

And yet, his historical attempt was married to an ahistorical one. As late as 1960 he was arguing that food resources in the reserves depended on the quality of the land, the presence of parasites, and also "the providence and intelligence of the peoples themselves," as if subsistence farming were still possible in those cash-dependent areas.[91] But the vast majority of his sources were other articles in medical journals; he cited his sources without referring to the time they were written, and he quoted no Africans. While in principle acknowledging regional differences, he tended to speak of "the Bantu" as an undifferentiated category. This tendency was strengthened by his habit of drawing analogies to the health and physique of black Americans, as if race were a superhistorical determining factor.

Walker sought to defend his adopted country from the slings and arrows of international outrage and exclusion. After the WHO excluded South Africa in

1963, international medical journals began to show "hesitancy" about publishing articles by South African authors. Walker perceived this onslaught as unfair and "over-simplified" because foreign critics falsely supposed that the infant mortality rate, for example, could be lowered "by a greater degree of intervention, direct and indirect, by health and other authorities." He marshaled arguments from medical journal articles to demonstrate the real limits to what any program could achieve: a well-nourished mother does not produce better-quality milk, poor women need less calcium than more privileged women do, "country Bantu run well, often despite poor nutritional status and infections," and degenerative diseases like hypertension and coronary heart disease afflict privileged populations. "The benefit of school meals to health status remains unproven," he said, and provisions of pure water do not immediately lower rates of morbidity and mortality from gastroenteritis "until the hygienic practices of the population involved are greatly improved."[92] Walker's profession had trained him to focus on the microscopic and, possibly as a result, Walker missed the wider social context of national health.

This third fashion of nutritional research waned in the late 1960s for a variety of reasons. The archival data to explain why is not yet available. The government withdrew funding from the UCT nutritional unit on Brock's retirement in 1970. Hansen notes in explanation that technical advances in pediatrics had lowered interest in child nutrition and also that good nutritionists, such as his colleague Stuart Truswell, chose to leave South Africa as apartheid came increasingly under international fire. With the government setting up the homelands beginning with the grant of self-government in 1959, African rural areas, where the majority of kwashiorkor cases were now occurring, were becoming the responsibility of Bantustan departments of health. The long-standing problem of an African labor shortage was being transformed by mechanization into a labor surplus. Within this context, a new fashion of nutritional research began when, in the 1970s, cholesterol became the focus of researchers' money and time. Walker had noted that coronary heart disease afflicted the privileged primarily, and it was in this direction that the bias of South African nutritional research now turned. The idea of race deterioration was not dead. Within the context of nutritional research, it had simply swung, over the course of the twentieth century, from a focus on specific vitamin deficiencies to subnutrition to starvation to diseases of plenty.[93]

Conclusion

Kenneth Carpenter writes at the end of *Protein and Energy* that a general principle "can lie so strongly at the back of scientists' minds that it, rather than the observations, is the unconscious starting point of discussion, so that interpretation is not truly open to discussion." One unconscious starting point for discussion of African hunger was the idea of race deterioration. It had multiple origins: diffuse European fears generated by rapid industrialization and urbanization; the unease of those who transplanted themselves to colonies; the lingering popularity of the social Darwinian idea that only the fittest would, or even should, survive; and perhaps what Oliver Sacks has called "the Eden of lost childhood, childhood imagined, . . . an Eden of the remote past, a magical 'once', rendered wholly benign by the omission, the editing out, of all change, all movement."[94] In South Africa, the concept of physical decay seems to have been increasingly defined racially in this period, along lines similar to those by which the upper classes judged the lower classes in Britain. People even applied the concept to the land.

South African research on these matters shifted as international scientific research paradigms changed. This is not surprising: the historian of science Thomas Kuhn taught us to expect such shifts.[95] South Africa's political tensions and the whole question of the national destiny also affected the questions researchers raised about people's health. Researchers talked candidly about the economy's need for a strong and healthy labor force, and the economy had indeed shaped and funded their research agendas. As targets of research, scurvy, debility, and kwashiorkor reflected the toll that industrial development was taking, especially on poor people. Some nutritional researchers deployed evolutionary theory to argue that nothing need be done because race deterioration was a consequence of biological processes. This rationale, in turn, freed them from discussing issues of social and political power. Time alone, they said, would take care of the social aspect of bodily decay; in the meantime, the state should intervene in issues of malnutrition mainly by educating rural folk. Not all researchers subscribed to this evolutionary perspective, but many joined the social Darwinists in bypassing discussion of the role low wages or land loss played in African malnutrition.

And yet from this unpromising nexus of "unconscious starting points" and political and economic needs, understanding of the origins and dimensions of African poverty grew. That knowledge would later prove useful to critics of segregation and apartheid. It ran counter to any state-sanctioned ideology or industrial labor needs. Scientific authority gave weight to statements that Africans were suffering physically because of their poverty, and it documented the consequences of material and political inequality. When international research on nutrition shifted from an investigation of animals to chemicals and from vitamins to proteins, it inadvertently but inexorably led to scientists' testimony on African poverty. Nutritional research was helping to quash the idea that European and African bodies were fundamentally different in their nature. Following this research, racialist analyses of why Africans lived differently from Europeans came to focus less on the inherent limitations of their bodies and more on their unscientific culture. Concern about race deterioration spilled over to the land, and in the process provided a basis for the growing ideology of African ignorance.

CHAPTER SIX

Missionaries of Science

The Growth of the Malnutrition
Syndrome, 1920–1960

> There have been limits to the extent to which non-scientific people can
> take part [in a scientific experiment].
>
> *Halley Stott, 1975*

RURAL MEDICAL DOCTORS treated Africans debilitated by scurvy and tuberculosis, the dementia and sores of venereal disease, and leprosy. They tried to
keep wasting infants alive. As they reflected on the causes of these afflictions,
many tended to see African disease as fundamentally rooted in poor native
diets. The idea that "[m]ost . . . disease has its roots in inadequate nutrition"
was linked to the belief that malnutrition was the "most important [medical]
problem" in rural South Africa.[1]

The malnutrition syndrome was a successor to the earlier paternalistic habit
of thinking of rural Africans' bodily suffering as principally the consequence
of famine. It also followed what Maynard Swanson called the "sanitation syndrome" that characterized South African public discussion of urban health
early in the century. Swanson wrote, "the imagery of infectious disease" was
a "societal metaphor" that "powerfully interacted with British and South
African racial attitudes to influence the policies and shape the institutions of
segregation."[2] In the same fashion, malnutrition gained emblematic power
that influenced state officials' thinking about the problems of rural South
Africa and, therefore, eventually the policies of apartheid.

It is hard to say how much malnutrition really existed in rural and periurban areas during the four decades 1920 to 1960. Symptoms of malnutrition
may be produced by a conjuncture of maladies, from psychological illness to
parasites. Neglect and unhappiness may suppress appetite, and infections,
rather than poor feeding, may prevent a child from obtaining nourishment.

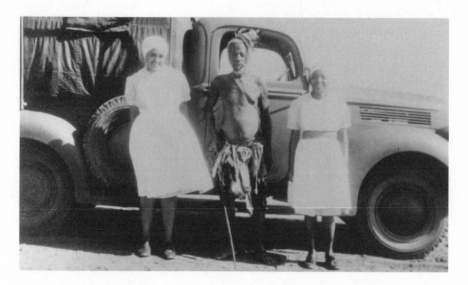

8. Two Holy Cross Hospital nurses pose for the medical missionary Frank Drewe alongside a Pondo diviner (1930s). (The Bodleian Library, Oxford: USPG M. 783)

Accurate statistics on food intake are notoriously hard to collect, and few exist historically for the height, weight, and age, including age at death, of black South Africans. Further, the quality and quantity of milk yield per cow may have deteriorated over time, but this is not a certainty.[3] Malnutrition did afflict the newly poor, whose numbers were probably increasing in rural areas since the 1920s. The problem with the malnutrition syndrome is not that it is inaccurate, but that it can reduce the complex causes and attributes of poverty to a single dimension whose cure can be framed in narrowly technical terms.

The stories of the founding of two rural hospitals or health centers tell a good deal about the distinctly South African face of the malnutrition syndrome. Though one was a standard rural mission hospital and the other was a "socio-medical experiment," both happen to illustrate interpretations of the malnutrition syndrome that were less critical of the South African social order and more impatient with African food culture. The archival record confirms the ordinariness of the opinions expressed within them. Outsiders, like district surgeons or professors, discussed the two institutions fairly uncritically, as if they represented the mainstream of rural medical practice. Individuals and other institutions made charitable donations to their budgets. Critical scrutiny during these four decades focused occasionally on their finances, but rarely, if ever, their philosophies.

The first is Holy Cross Hospital (HCH), located in the part of the Transkei known as eastern Pondoland, and established in 1920 by the Rev. Dr. Frank Swinburne Drewe, who was to serve that area for the next thirty-five years. The second is the Valley Trust and Health Centre in Botha's Hill, Natal, where, in 1951, Dr. Halley Harwin Stott founded a center based on his comprehensive vision of the causes and cures of disease among the Zulu. Both founders had an intense and coherent mission—the former religious, the latter holistic in a secular fashion—to improve the fate of Africans, and their experience gave them extraordinary power to disseminate scientific knowledge about rural Africa.

Precursor to the Malnutrition Syndrome: Christian Healing at Holy Cross Hospital, 1920–1940

Drewe's wider purpose as a Christian missionary helped shape his understanding of the connection of local culture to local disease. He had become a doctor in order to become a missionary. The son of an Anglican priest serving Port Isaac, a fishing village in north Cornwall, Drewe had first studied military history, strategy, and tactics at Lincoln College, Oxford, receiving his B.A. in 1910. Then, following his father's example and probably also the inspiration of a Plymouth Brethren aunt who had raised him, he began to prepare for the priesthood, reading theology at Cuddeston College, Oxford. Learning that medical missionaries were in greater demand than preachers, and hearing one missionary doctor speak about life in China, he asked the Anglican missionary society, the Society for the Propagation of the Gospel (SPG), to pay his fees at St. Thomas' Hospital in London. His training there enabled him in 1918 to pass the exams giving him membership in the royal colleges of physicians and surgeons (MRCP and MRCS). With the exception of refresher courses, also paid for by the SPG, that he thereafter took every five years while on nine months' leave in Britain, Drewe's formal medical education had ended.

Drewe came to Pondoland equipped with a canon, that pagans could be converted by caring for their bodies. He hoped to win over the medicine men, the "brains" of the tribe; he envied them the natural drug they had found for treating epilepsy and enteritis and wished they would share it with him. He photographed "the honourable opposition" smiling for his camera and labeled one print of two nurses standing beside a skin-clad herbalist "nurses old and new," noting, "I feel if only we could get him to use his good qualities and see the error of his ways, we might be shown a fresh approach for Christianity to the native mind." He sought to replace their god, who was believed to "live behind the thunder, knowing of individuals but not caring for or loving them." Converted to both Christianity and, by implication, science, those practitioners would come to see that germs and not the spirits called *tikolosh* caused sickness. Then "the race will rise," Drewe believed, explicitly contradicting an eminent, unnamed doctor who had recently said Africans would never attain the heights of the white man. He foresaw, in 1934, that the hospital would one day be run entirely by Africans.[4]

Drewe had been taught to think of medical remedies for ill health in terms of hygiene and moral behavior. He thought the Amampondo lacked both: he found them "fascinating in their humility and childlikeness . . . exasperating in their unmorality, and lack of ambition, and enthusiasm."[5] His sketches, watercolors, and photographs, as well as the warm memories of local people, attest to his rapport with and affection for Africans generally, but he also grew frustrated caring for people whose language he never learned to speak fluently, relying on interpreters both to preach and to take case histories.

A major preoccupation of the Pondo paramount chief (the head of the royal lineage) was to develop his "nation" so that it would maintain maximum possible independence, despite its colonial status. In 1894, Chief Sigcau reluctantly, under threat of "consequences disastrous to himself and his tribe," submitted to being ruled by the Cape Colony. The Pondo chiefs had tried to select innovations that would make their rule as strong as possible in these dependent circumstances, and a hospital was one powerful emblem of modernity. Chief Sigcau had made it known that he wanted modern medical care in his territory only five years after incorporation when he decided that land should be set aside for lepers. In 1911 his son, Marelane, granted to an Anglican priest, Robert Callaway, the right to establish a mission on a ridge between two rivers where Callaway had already planted a cross. The young chief added, "we want also a school and a hospital." The hospital and its parent mission might become a bulwark against any challenge to the Pondo chieftainship by either educated Africans ("school kaffirs") or Europeans. He wished the hospital to be established for the "entire and exclusive use of the Natives." No doubt wanting to test the power of European medicine more than he craved the Word, a chief cut off Callaway one day in 1912 when he tried to proselytize. The chief instead discussed East Coast fever, a cattle disease then ravaging local herds so severely that the stench of rotting cattle reached to the new hilltop mission. In 1916 Marelane and his councillors urged the visiting bishop of Glasgow to set up a hospital, and suggested to the chief magistrate, J. B. Moffat, that the Amampondo be taxed so that a hospital could be built at Holy Cross Mission. Callaway's death in French trenches during World War I left Marelane and his men on their own to try to acquire a hospital "to uplift and develop the nation."[6]

As the modernizing words *uplift* and *develop* imply, the Pondo chiefs saw medicine as part of nation-building, that is, of keeping the Pondo chiefdom as independent as possible, and Drewe fell in with this agenda. Marelane underscored who were the intended beneficiaries of the hospital when he welcomed Drewe in 1920. He slaughtered a heifer in honor of Archdeacon Walter Leary, who had brought the young Cornish doctor a "gift from the English people to the Pondo race." Drewe, adopting the chief's nationalistic language, fashioned a suitable motto for the hospital—"For Jesus Christ and the Pondos"—a motto every nursing sister at HCH would wear on her badge.[7]

Having accommodated the chief's political goals, Drewe had to come to terms with local medical beliefs. Drewe's first patients wondered why he needed to ask questions about their health. Why couldn't he tell without asking, as an African doctor could, how many children a woman had borne and what they had died of? When Marelane took Drewe to see his ill daughter, he expected him to explain what was wrong without asking any questions. "I told them that I was not a native doctor but an English doctor," Drewe said, "and that the English custom was to ask questions." The Pondo also loathed the idea of being hospitalized. Staying at HCH not only separated them from their families, but also made them vulnerable to malign forces possibly lying around the mission. Some patients moved around the hospital grounds to avoid the invisible snakes *(ntlwanti* or *canti)* that might harm them. Drewe, in turn, was ignorant of the forces conjured up by the medicine men: the short, stout, hairy man with superhuman strength *(tikolosh),* the bird that caused thunder and lightning *(mpundulu),* the flying baboon *(mfene)* that carried people vast distances at night on its back. Disease was believed to derive from a relationship gone sour. A man with venereal disease, for example, may have thought that a jealous man had baited a girl to make her carry the infection to him. "No doubt it is the question of bewitching that is going to be our great difficulty," Drewe wrote in 1922.[8]

Many Amampondo, maintaining their beliefs in the spiritual causes of sickness, sought to mix indigenous and imported techniques for protecting their health. Pondo medicine was by nature an eclectic combination of strategies. There was no canon of "witchcraft," as Drewe and other Christians called local "methods of causing sickness to other people" by targeting enemies.[9] People did not believe that all diseases were caused by ill will; they would have found laughable, for example, the idea that the common cold was sent by an enemy. At first, Drewe was used as the doctor of last resort. Witchdoctors sought out Drewe for their own illnesses and brought patients to him, expecting to get paid for their efforts at referral. But patients came only after a local diviner, the man charged with finding the sender of malign forces, had failed five or six times, or when a homemade mixture of patent medicines, sometimes combined with Drewe's or a witch doctor's drugs, had failed. Drewe's early cases tended to be so advanced as to be hopeless.[10]

When Drewe gave priority to faith over science in his proselytizing efforts, he earned a gentle rebuke from the African overseer of the hospital farm, H. S. Matee, in a fascinating critique of missionary methods. In a 1935 report entitled "Witchcraft from the Native Point of View," Matee eloquently urged missionaries to teach science rather than dwell on evil spirits: "The best advice is that the native should be led to see that there are disease-carrying germs and that they are those things that he has been calling by such horrible names [e.g. *tikolosh*], but now he is a bit civilised he must call them by scientific names." Instead of genuinely teaching science, missionaries tended to "aggravate the position" by incorrectly calling the *tikolosh* "evil spirits," thus helping to spread rather than dampen a "spirit of fear"; the *tikolosh* were not evil spirits but messengers sent to do harm by people with evil intent. "The Church with all its Medical Missions should not find it difficult to arrange for lectures on Health by Medical Experts," Matee concluded, "so that the intelligent natives should be led to know the real causes of sickness."[11] Matee was taking care to distinguish himself from the uneducated, but he was also asserting that everyone was capable of learning science if approached in a less adversarial way than the missionaries when they derided local spirits.

Drewe's efforts were lonely. The nearest hospital lay more than one hundred miles away in Umtata. As the district surgeon in Lusikisiki, W. P. Nicol, had complained in 1915, "In these wild native districts there is practically no such thing as Public Health." The Cape Colony had once "quite seriously considered" establishing small "native" hospitals throughout the reserves, but nothing had been done. "It is strange," Nicol added, "that whereas special provision is made for the care of cattle, sheep and goats, man himself should be neglected."[12] The district surgeon (DS) in each of the four magisterial towns of eastern Pondoland—Tabankulu, Lusikisiki, Flagstaff, Bizana—provided skeletal public health services, designed mainly to prevent epidemics: as an employee of the Union Department of Public Health, the DS periodically inoculated people against smallpox, certified lepers, performed postmortems, and tended to the health of people on white farms and in the towns. They serviced very few rural people. The state continued mainly to ignore rural hospitals throughout Drewe's career at HCH and, as a result, the hospital came close to closing on several occasions.

The hospital had been founded when church wardens collected one hundred pounds from members of a Wimbledon congregation one Sunday in 1919 as they filed from the Anglican church where Drewe was priest; subsequently, the managing director of a Durban drug company agreed to help him found the hospital after learning how little capital he had. These spontaneous gifts apparently set the pattern for funding in the decades to come. For most of Drewe's stay, private donations pulsed into Holy Cross in fits and starts. When the hospital appeared about to close for lack of six hundred pounds, white farmers in Kokstad, Natal, were persuaded to make the necessary donation. The SPG made small annual grants, but the level of gifts from Britain fluctuated with the fortunes of the British economy. The patients themselves had to contribute two shillings for medical care, which in lean times they paid with their scrawniest sheep or goats, or in mealies. Local people contributed their labor to erecting the hospital buildings and, in a way, so did Drewe. Devoid of personal venality though he invested wisely in the stock market to ensure his wife would be provided for after his death, Drewe himself donated directly to the hospital his pay from the health department for working with lepers and for helping a district surgeon. He canvased for funds so relentlessly that a Pondo praise song depicted him as "shooting with his lips at a conference [so] a ten shilling note will pop out."[13]

For three and a half decades Drewe's efforts to provide a wide range of Western medical services to cure and prevent disease were weakened both by his isolation and the lack of official support. Initially, Holy Cross received small amounts from the NAD for building and to defray deficits. The Bunga contributed funds each year from the mid-1920s on, collected from Transkeian taxpayers. The Union Department of Public Health paid, in 1938, three shillings daily for the hospitalization of patients with infectious diseases. The Cape Provincial Council gave a small amount (£150–£300) each year, but in 1938 its executive told Drewe that it would not consider paying for African hospitalization until it could tax Africans for this purpose.[14]

Mining companies and their labor recruiters gave small targeted gifts irregularly, as well as more regular support to TB victims. Holy Cross Mission, as distinct from the hospital, had started because Callaway had lobbied the heads of the mining companies in 1911 and obtained a five hundred pound check that paid for its first buildings.[15] Medical emergencies evoked further gifts. In response to Drewe's request for help the Native Recruiting Corporation (NRC) donated one hundred pounds in 1922, a "starvation" year. From 1923, the year the hospital officially opened, the NRC did donate one hundred pounds annually for the upkeep of chronically sick, usually tubercular, miners it had transferred to Holy Cross. A typhoid epidemic provoked donations from the NRC as well as the Union government; an isolation wing was added to the hospital around 1931. The Deferred Pay Board, spending the interest earned by miners' wages before disbursement in rural areas, funded the construction of the maternity wing, also in 1931. The mines were more generous than the sugar estates of Natal. The secretary of the Sugar Association in 1937 dismissed Drewe's personal appeal, made on the advice of the Paramount Chief, after failing to reply for three months: his business, the sugar official said, was sugar, not philanthropy.[16]

The low level of funding available for his hospital periodically depressed Drewe's sunny and creative temperament. At first, he could remark with pride that he had successfully operated on a gangrenous appendix by scraping it with a spoon, or that packing cases had served as his operating table, or that the former home of a "witch doctor" served as his surgery. The thrill eventually palled. By 1932 lack of financial support caused him to take leave on the verge of a breakdown.[17] Over the years he never stopped struggling hard for money to keep the hospital open. He must have been distracted by the dilemma of always being short of cash and by the indignity of going hat in hand to ask for donations from South African businesses that, failing to see African health as their responsibility, rebuffed his pleas.

Drewe was a creative man, and he devoted a good deal of energy to tuberculosis, a tough enemy to defeat. He established a tuberculosis ward in 1925–1926, purchased an X-ray machine in 1935, and set up a laboratory for testing sputum for the tuberculosis bacillus. Most notably he established a training program for African nurses, some of whom went on to pass the nonracial state exam and become registered nurses. One of the major innovations, in harmony with the large role that the chief's permission and initiative had played in the founding of HCH, was the hospital committee, jointly run by the hospital and the paramount. It dealt with all African affairs such as debts and complaints. Mothers who were furious that their children had been left unattended inside the hospital complained to the committee, which responded by setting up the children's ward in 1938. In addition, there was a board on which sat members of the mission, the four local magistrates, the paramount chief, and four district councillors. In 1939 the NAD requested the board's appointment, noting that it should bear responsibility for finance.[18] While this tactic safeguarded the government from claims on its resources, it appears to have been an unusual example of African participation in hospital management and did signify Drewe's dream that the hospital would one day be run by Africans. Drewe started clinics in remote places, as well, such as in Lukanyisweni, Ntafufu, and Palmerton, and organized weekly visits to them. Over the years the numbers of people willing to try his innovations grew; 5,783 patients visited HCH in 1942, up from 3,200 in 1926.

People felt increasingly attracted to Drewe's hospital perhaps because of the respect he showed them. Three weeks before Drewe was due to return from leave in 1932 the nurses went on strike. In his absence they were taken to the paramount chief who learned that their grievances were essentially two: hospital censorship of their letters to certain young men, and food. The chief cautioned Drewe upon his return to "understand that these girls were drawn from the chief's kraals," that is, their status merited greater respect. Drewe acknowledged that "our personal contact with these girls was poor" and that they needed better housing and food.[19] There is no record of his precise reforms except that he did institute study groups and devise the Holy Cross badge, a blue cross on a white ground, symbol of Drewe's personal responsiveness to the nurses and their acute need for respect commensurate with their status. One Holy Cross nurse, later the wife of ANC activist Robert Resha, praised Drewe and the British nurses as "sympathetic to all the nurses and devoted to their work of teaching us and seeing to our welfare and that of the patients."[20] Not only did I hear these sentiments echoed by older nurses remaining at Holy Cross in 1989, I have never heard or read any complaint against Drewe. His devotion and his achievements, especially in the face of his chronic lack of resources, were remarkable.

While Drewe's devotion was unimpeachable and he appears to have had an good deal of respect for local people and in return to have been highly respected, there remains the question of how efficacious this early and weak, because underresourced, effort to introduce Western medical care really was. The answer to that question lies in the maladies he treated and the way he conceptualized African health problems in the years leading up to the malnutrition syndrome.

Medical ideas like the diagnoses of scurvy that were precursors to the malnutrition syndrome were absent from discussions of HCH's founding. For one thing Pondoland rarely suffered from dearth and hardly ever from famine. Having expected "dry, red, dusty sandunes [sic]," Drewe was pleasantly surprised by the green rolling landscape before him. Soft, soaking rains falling mainly between October and March appeared to keep the area well supplied with grain (maize and sorghum) and free from erosion.[21] Over the next quarter century Drewe saw it visited only two or three times by "acute distress" and only once by "real starvation," in 1922 when people ate one meal every day or two. Far more problematic and frequent than drought were rains so plentiful that a profusion of weeds choked the maize and sorghum. Heavy rainfall swelled the rivers and made the paths so slippery that horses and oxen fell in the mud. At such times Holy Cross became more remote and inaccessible than usual, and the journey of sick patients, whether an adult on an ox-drawn sledge or a child on its mother's back, was prolonged. The six days it ordinarily took for Drewe to travel to Durban, the nearest city, where he bought his drugs (antiseptics and anesthetics such as ethyl chloride and ether) could then multiply. The remoteness from town led many outsiders, African and European, to call the area and the people around Holy Cross primitive and wild.

Drewe had been forewarned that the three most prevalent diseases he would encounter would be leprosy, syphilis, and tuberculosis. Each could be attributed to a hygienic or sexual lapse. The palliative for each one—there were no cures in the days before sulpha drugs and penicillin—was confined to modifying the patient's behavior.

To treat the lepers and prevent the spread of their disease, Drewe isolated them in his government-funded Mkambati Leper Institution on the coast. There he made them take daily baths in a stream of clean water and rub their bodies with chaulmoogra oil, an Indian medicine that at best eased sores and prevented infections. He hoped that antimony would help prevent further ulceration of fingers and toes, paralysis, and violent outbursts. Drewe's responsibility at Mkambati, he was told by a government official in 1920, was to make the patients comfortable, but he knew "they would all die inch by inch." He could not cure them; not until the time of his retirement was the cheap and highly effective antibiotic known as dapsone introduced to Africa, and it became widely available only in the 1950s. The importance given to leprosy seems to have derived partly from European images of the dark continent; the number of times British donors mention leprosy in their gifts to the SPG mission is out of all proportion to the number of patients actually residing at Mkambati; in 1941 only forty-two certified lepers lived among the seventy thousand people of Lusikisiki District.[22] One is tempted to think that paramount chief Sigcau was shrewdly assessing the disease's appeal to British donors when he named leprosy in 1899 as the primary scourge of his land.

The second part of the deadly trinity was syphilis. Initially, Drewe had been shocked by the "terrible immorality" of even those Pondo who had converted to Christianity; he sent away communicants who had been found guilty of it. He delicately avoided specifying the precise behavior that had given rise to the disease, but, as the years passed, he attributed the disease not to all Pondo, but mainly to the *dikazi* or sexually promiscuous single women who frequented beer parties and, more generally, "to the low status of women in many African minds." But, in 1930, when he gave Wasserman tests to his patients, he determined that the prevalence of syphilis had been exaggerated. Only 7 to 10 percent of the Pondo suffered from it, he estimated. "We do something to combat [the conditions giving rise to the disease]," he wrote, "by continually teaching the nurses of their duty and the part they can play in the lifting of the African view on the women."[23] In the absence of a nontoxic cure for syphilis until penicillin became commonly available, Drewe's and the Western medical profession's best remedy was, perforce, moral exhortation; meanwhile, local medicine men achieved some success by treating less advanced cases with poultices and boiled extracts from local leaves and roots.

Drewe considered tuberculosis "the scourge of the country," and he made it the object of his "chief energies." Its prognosis was as grim as leprosy; only severe TB cases would consent to admission, and the ward where they stayed was known as the "house of death." Drewe found the Pondo susceptible to a particularly virulent form of the disease. "The disease gets hold of them quickly and completely, there seems hardly any holding of it," he wrote in 1922. Many died within months of showing symptoms. He tried to prevent the spread of the bacillus by urging people to ventilate their homes and schools, rather than keep them closed, dark, and filled with smoke. He was concerned that people slept with their heads wrapped in blankets. While never directly blaming the mining industry for the spread of the disease, he was fully aware that men who had returned to Pondoland from their fourth or greater mine contract "are liable to silicosis of a very, very acute type . . . [that] will progress so far as to kill them in ten or fifteen years." He wondered whether Africans should be allowed to go to the mines more than four times, even though he thought they liked working there and their first four visits actually developed their physique. He regretted that "our results have not been startling. . . . In any case we are able to show the family that little can be done when the disease is advanced."[24] Once again, there was no cure.

Malnutrition fell far below the aforementioned trinity in Drewe's roster of common Pondo maladies. He did not ignore it, but he failed to treat it as centrally important. He more frequently attributed the high infant mortality rate—half the children born in Pondoland died before the age of three, he estimated—to common infections such as gastritis, enteritis, pneumonia, measles, and whooping cough, as well as a narrow birth canal, the result of women carrying heavy weights on their heads.[25] Drewe was not alone in thinking about infections to the virtual exclusion of nutrition.[26] So, too, district surgeons writing reports in the 1920s focused on diseases like typhus and smallpox without mentioning the nutritional status of those who fell ill. Nor had his medical training stressed it. As the drugs he brought in from Durban testify, his principal medical strength was his ability to operate hygienically and to relieve pain.

Although Drewe did not blame most infant deaths on poor feeding, he did judge some Pondo mothers harshly, like many European doctors of his time. He thought mothers were wrong to feed their infants on demand; the child might be crying simply because he had a stomach ache.[27] Soon after Drewe's arrival at Holy Cross, a mother carried her dying nine-month-old child seventy-five miles on her back to seek Drewe's cure. She believed all her earlier children had died from "rainbow"—bewitched by crossing a stream that a rainbow had touched; she had been feeding the infant sorghum beer and pork. This sort of incident would lead Drewe to testify to the Native Economic Commission in 1930 that "the feeding of the children is wrongly done." Mothers left infants in the care of younger children in order to cultivate their land. They were "ordered off to the lands," presumably by the older women in the household.[28] While the new mother was hoeing or harvesting, a sibling would hold the infant on his or her lap and scoop handfuls of *amasi* (thick sour milk) into its mouth. Given the impurity of the milk, this method undoubtedly did cause enteritis.

Belief in witchcraft could indeed kill infants. The deadly chain of events might be forged when a woman believed her milk to be "bad" and withheld it. "The heathen woman and her child," Drewe wrote, "are prey for witchcraft should the baby sicken, as the trouble is more often than not put down to the mother's milk. The child has the only food that might save its life taken from it, and the mother may be told by the Witch-doctor that she is responsible for the child's illness, in fact that she has bewitched the child. This is the most terrible state of affairs. . . . The mother is left with her child, she watches it die firmly believing that she herself is killing it and can do nothing to arrest the tragedy."[29] To avoid this tragic scenario, Drewe, by 1930, had set up four or five huts at Holy Cross where women were "taught to look after their children." Still, people continued to believe that a thin and sick child or one with a bloated belly had black matter in its stomach *(iplate)* and should be washed and given an enema to purge its stomach of its poisonous contents; the evil entering the child at night had been sent by a jealous person.[30] Malnutrition, Drewe believed, existed largely because such superstitions still ruled women's lives; these beliefs would continue to kill young Amampondo as long as their mothers resisted the lessons of modern science and of Jesus Christ.

Local medical logic was at loggerheads with Drewe on the issue of milk. Whether from women or cows, milk signified social boundaries in Nguni societies both in abstract and quite concrete and powerful ways. Sour milk was often associated with semen and so was said to produce virility. Perhaps for this reason, a man would eat sour milk only in neutral places such as the homes of his closest relatives; he could not marry a girl where he had eaten sour milk. No one who was ritually impure could, in principle, drink cow's milk: a new mother had to avoid it for ten days; a bride could drink it in her husband's home only after completing her ritual incorporation into that home and severing her ties to her father's *umzi* (household); and after a death, milk was spilled from all calabashes except, interestingly, those of the children. Before putting her child to breast, a new mother, after walking in areas where malign forces might lurk, would chew on a charm made from a root, spit on her child's body, and squirt her own milk on the child and on the ground. In this way, and also by wearing a special charm for the first three or four months after giving birth, she would try to ensure that her milk had not been bewitched.[31] It is not surprising that such a potent signifier of social boundaries could also be seen as carrying malign power.

Educated Africans like Mr. Matee, the overseer of the hospital farm, joined the chorus blaming mothers for neglect, "superstition," and "ignorance." An African medical doctor, Dr. M. R. Mahlangeni, explicitly tied the 60 percent infant mortality rate he had estimated in his Mount Frere practice to maternal neglect, implying that this negligence occurred most grievously in matters of hygiene. Based on a careful twelve-month survey, Dr. Mahlangeni reported in 1930 that the most prevalent cause of infant death was enteritis because mothers were "very backward in the way they handle the children, the feeding and the care are bad." Another African witness to the Native Economic Commission, B. S. Ncabene, spoke as harshly: pregnant rural women did not know how to treat themselves and their infants, and because there were no midwives no one looked after them, "just like a wild beast in a field"; they became pregnant again too soon after giving birth, and consequently mother and child never became strong; their huts were unhygienic; newborns were not properly fed because "children, even of seven months of age, are allowed to eat cooked mealies and to eat nearly everything."[32] In 1944, the paramount and two of his chiefs asked Drewe to give advice on infant feeding and welfare to women in their locations each month. These local judgments indicate that the malnutrition syndrome had local roots lying partly in men's judgment of women's work; African men, used to looking for the causes of disease in social relations, were now phrasing their blame in social scientific terms by suggesting that uneducated women were poor mothers. The idea of culpable mothers was not simply transplanted from metropolitan medical circles.

The Fiscal and Medical Crises of the 1940s

During the 1940s the malnutrition syndrome grew from a conjuncture of forces, some medical, others financial. The net effect was that by the time the National party won the 1948 election many were primed to see rural African life in a state of disarray deriving from basic cultural deficiencies. In this decade can be seen the seeds of change that led from the qualified respect for African culture characterizing Drewe's first twenty years to the common tendency in the 1950s to denigrate it and to blame sick Africans for their own suffering.

The first crisis hit South African medicine when donations from Britain were cut off by World War II. HCH fell into an eight hundred pound debt in 1940, and Drewe was forced to travel to Johannesburg to appeal for more money to the NRC and the Chamber of Mines. In newly straitened circumstances, he met a familiar response. The general superintendent of the NRC, H. C. Wellbeloved, told Drewe he was frankly fearful that if he gave money to Holy Cross, he would be inundated with appeals from other missions.[33]

Perhaps because private industry remained cautious, the government was slowly repudiating its heritage of neglecting African health. Its assumption of greater responsibility was partly financial but mainly rhetorical because the question of who was fiscally responsible had still not been sorted out. In response to Drewe's 1940 plea, the NAD did pledge seven thousand pounds for new wards, a water supply, and maintenance. The big push to modernize and extend South African medicine came in August 1942, when Henry Gluckman was charged with drawing up plans for a national health service. The following year Gluckman visited Holy Cross bearing the promise of more government aid. He praised the inclusion of Africans on the hospital committee and board, adding that if Drewe wanted regular and guaranteed official support the government would require fuller representation on the board. More government aid would come with more government control. The prospect frankly worried Drewe, not because he foresaw apartheid, but because government, with its emphasis on efficiency, could not offer the mission's moral commitment to "service, sympathy and religion."[34]

The 1940s saw the crisis and impending defeat of the old mission order as it faced new bureaucratic as well as medical challenges. Government officials were clearly growing impatient with those missionary attitudes that could hardly be described as modern. In 1942, Holy Cross was inspected by the Department of Public Health employee Dr. Rijno Smit, who criticized it for hospitalizing patients on average for thirty-seven days, in contrast with fifteen at Umtata hospital. Drewe explained that he wanted to win the confidence of patients and to treat them humanely.[35] These goals cost money, and some state officials felt the overcrowded hospital could not afford this luxury. In the late 1940s, Drewe went one step further: he refused to allow the Cape provincial administration to take over the hospital entirely because he believed "we must keep our missionary character. We must be allowed to preach the Gospel."[36]

The second crisis was also economic. Government officials feared that South Africa was losing strong African laborers and that weakened men would put a burden on the state in the form of disability payments. Better nutrition was a cheap way to ensure the survival of a strong labor force. The magistrate of Bizana complained about one malnourished sugar estate employee—the man was "otherwise perfectly healthy [but] could barely walk"—in the following terms: "the native . . . was given exemption from taxes and might apply for a pension, and would live the rest of his life in idleness—a complete loss to industry—in this case, the sugar farming, one which is crying out for labour."[37] It would be much cheaper, he argued, for the government to supply vitamins such as nicotinic acid (niacin) to the district surgeons than to pay for hospitalization of such sick men. Given the imperviousness of the sugar industry, it is not surprising that the magistrate failed to suggest that the sugar estates improve their workers' diets. These concerns for worker health, framed in peculiarly South African terms, built on the increased attention being paid internationally to malnutrition from the 1930s. The magistrate's solution—that the government provide vitamins—may reflect either his aversion to criticizing employers or his disbelief that the mines and sugar companies would assume responsibility for their workers' health. Whatever the origins, some government officials were clearly worried that the country would not only run short of laborers, but would also have to shoulder a prohibitively expensive bill of caring for broken men.

The tuberculosis epidemic of the 1940s sparked the greatest official alarm. District surgeons' annual reports from Pondoland at the time frequently linked tuberculosis and malnutrition; one district surgeon noted, for example, that the "chief factors in the hitherto uncontrollable spread of [TB]" were malnutrition "caused chiefly by the lack of a well balanced diet, and overcrowding in the huts."[38] In 1947 the Department of Public Health even set up a course in Johannesburg where district surgeons could be lectured on, inter alia, infant feeding. Many of these rural doctors blamed the upsurge of tuberculosis on mothers and the African love of cattle or "cattle complex," rather than on the mines.[39] A Bizana magistrate worried, "until we can get them to regard cattle as *cattle* and not as wealth," children would be fed milk only after the calves had drunk their fill, and they would be susceptible to tuberculosis.[40]

South African businesses were generating new kinds and levels of disease, but African agriculture was branded the culprit. The transfer of responsibility occurred in the following way. The malnutrition syndrome was growing along with the scare that African agriculture was turning the reserves into deserts. A 1941 circular entitled "Save the Veld," drafted for Transkeian schools, drew this anxiety to its logical conclusion: "if we do not preserve the veld the Bantu may yet disappear from the list of the peoples of Africa." State officials explicitly blamed overstocking—Transkeian stock had nearly tripled between 1918 and 1939—for precipitating this decline by ruining pasture so that the ill-fed cows had nearly dried up: that was "why so many children die before they are two years old and why many of those who do survive grow up to be thin and ill-nourished boys and girls." With more imagination than accuracy, Dr. Mary McGregor testified to the 1941 Overstocking Commission that infants suffered from diarrhea "of the fermentative type" because they ate too many carbohydrates. Adding that children readily got infections because they lacked "fat soluble vitamins," she concluded that "the biggest enemy" of medical work in the Transkei was "malnutrition: and the greatest lack is fresh milk."[41]

The malnutrition syndrome provided useful ammunition in the armory of native administrators trying to cull Transkeian cattle, a policy to which local

Africans were "distinctly hostile." The officials drew tight the causal link between malnutrition and overstocking. Mr. Hyde, the agricultural supervisor at Umzimkulu, argued that "overstocking and resultant erosion" had led to "the undernourishment so evident among the people"; their harvests had recently declined, and "because Native stock are to-day subsisting on a starvation diet, milk at the Native kraal is a thing of the past." The chief magistrate justified his support for culling by calling the provision of milk "the most urgent need for action," stressing "it is no kindness to the Native himself to allow him in his thoughtless ignorance to destroy for ever the heritage of his children."[42] Without scientific farming and feeding, there would be no African future.

This scare penetrated the confines of Holy Cross, and in 1942 when the chief magistrate of the Transkei, W. Mears, visited Holy Cross to open the Drewe wing, he urged people to take greater care of their stock and lands so that there should be no malnutrition, as if wages were not an issue. In 1945 the manager of the Holy Cross farm, P. Peppin, wrote that it was imperative to teach the Amampondo good farming so that their children would grow into strong adults. Africans had to be taught that farming was a year-round job that involved rising early and working late, "something to teach a cheerful, happy-go-lucky race like the Pondos."[43]

Africans, too, seized upon the malnutrition syndrome and used it to express their opposition to culling. One Bunga councillor linked the infant mortality rate to "babes sucking milk from underfed mothers." Since mother's milk actually remains healthful long after the health of the mother has begun to suffer, this analysis reflects popular alarm more accurately than it conveys fact. Some councillors blamed the practice of dipping for keeping alive beasts better left to die than to breed and produce inferior offspring. Others named the state-mandated castration of inferior bulls: the shortage of bulls was encouraging bull owners to charge "service fees" from those wishing to get their cows impregnated; many poor were having to go without milk, even if they owned cows, because they could not afford the fees. In 1940 several African witnesses to the overstocking commission presented an alternative vision of the causes of their "abject poverty": they needed more land rather than fewer cattle; if they were paid a "living wage" many would abandon agriculture and stock raising; the rules of the veterinary department governing the dipping and inspection of cattle had increased erosion by causing them to drive the cattle along the same routes.[44] Malnutrition was proving useful to both sides in the political fight about culling.

Drewe appears to have been reluctant to join this nutritional clamor. He had rarely drawn a connection between agriculture and health; to the Gluckman Commission he simply stated that people's health would improve once they recognized the value of proper cultivation, especially of vegetables, but he continued to stress the importance of teaching Africans more about disease and the value of fresh air.[45] This perspective would soon be overwhelmed by the malnutrition syndrome and its agrarian corollary even at Holy Cross.

Drewe's career at Holy Cross marked the last phase of the syndrome's precursor when the emphasis was more on Christian mission and less on science. Perhaps Holy Cross was too remote from urban centers to be easily reached by such fashionable currents. In addition, Drewe's medical training had occurred during World War I, before the isolation of most vitamins, hence his stress on hygiene. Certainly he was preoccupied with raising money for his mission hospital, an enterprise that even at the time of his retirement in 1949 was being replaced by more modern—that is, technological and state-funded—hospitals. Though he was aware that mine service was connected to tuberculosis, his professional bias was toward belief systems; his focus on African beliefs led him to slight factors other than culture that affected such practices as infant feeding. Because his career took place almost entirely before antibiotics became commonly available, Drewe reflects an era when medical attitudes were not as marked by the hubris that would come to characterize them in the 1950s when his legacy at Holy Cross Hospital of relative respect for Africans and African culture would be overwhelmed.

The Rise of the Malnutrition Syndrome and the Biomedical Clinic: Holy Cross Hospital in the 1950s

When Drewe formally retired as superintendent of the hospital he had founded nearly thirty years earlier, his farewell ceremony lauded his achievements and ominously foretold many of the developments in the decade to come. In December 1949, he rode on horseback, accompanied by the men of the hospital, to the Great Place of the paramount chief, Botha Sigcau, to be honored by dancing women led by the chief's wife, and by the slaughter of a black and white ox. In words undoubtedly aimed to flatter the sixty-two-year-old missionary's life of Christian service, Sigcau explained the symbolism of its coloring: the white represented Drewe's clerical collar and the good things Drewe had taught the Amampondo, while the black stood for the black fever of ignorance and superstition pressing down on the people when Drewe first arrived in Pondoland. Despite these symbols of continuity with the old paternalism, the moment contained seeds of a new order. Drewe ceremonially handed his stethoscope to his replacement, James E. Cawthorne. A young doctor from suburban London, Cawthorne had three months earlier visited the provincial administrators in Cape Town in order to discuss the hospital's perpetually parlous finances. (The hospital was in danger of closing.) One of the officials had surprised him by asking a question in Afrikaans. Not only had an Afrikaner nationalist regime come to power, but the internal ethos of the hospital was changing. Cawthorne and the doctors who followed him in rapid succession would refer less and less frequently to their Christian mission in their letters to the SPG. And so, in many respects, internal and external, a new order was coming to Holy Cross, its land then turned by drought, Cawthorne noticed, into a "sunbaked expanse of dust and rock," just as Drewe had expected it to look thirty years earlier.[46]

During the 1950s malnutrition gained unprecedented prominence as a major malady afflicting Pondo life. Every report sent back to the London office of the SPG mentioned it. Many diverse maladies were attributed to it. By the end of the decade some Holy Cross doctors were even citing a new deadly trinity in their reports, replacing Drewe's with, first, tuberculosis, second, wounds incurred by young men in "faction fights" (a term used to describe, though not to explain, armed clashes between groups of young men, often beginning at beer drinks), and, third, malnutrition caused by "poverty and ignorance." When Cawthorne blamed what he called an African tendency to do only as much work as could not be avoided, he attributed this laziness to the climate and also to malnutrition that had lasted "for decades, if not for generations."[47] This innovative perspective—that malnutrition lay at the root of much rural behavior—was thus linked to the age-old colonial judgment that Africans were lazy.

British nurses, like African men in the recent past, blamed Pondo mothers. Eileen Hope wrote in 1950, for example, "One of our great difficulties is trying to teach the mothers how to feed their babies properly; they have an awful habit of giving porridge, sour milk and sour porridge to babies of a few weeks old. Mother's milk (or any other) is not considered food. That is just an extra!" Doctors believed Pondo women fed their children either too little milk or milk that was unclean, making them fall prey to infections like tuberculosis and dysentery. Dr. Dennis Patient expressed amazement in 1961 at the prevalence of tuberculosis of the chest, which, he said, "springs mainly from malnutrition." His wife buttressed his statement that children fell prey to tuberculosis and dysentery because they were given a bare minimum of nourishment, adding "children do not often have [milk] though the dogs may like it." By suggesting that people preferred feeding milk to their dogs, Mrs. Patient was revealing her ignorance of the historic centrality of sour milk in the Pondo diet, as well as a warped version of the cattle complex. She was also choosing to blame Pondo maladies on an inadequate diet rather than on parasites from unclean drinking water. Failing to exempt the educated, who so keenly wished not to be grouped with uneducated heathens, the medical missionaries saw all African mothers as equally afflicted by this peculiar ignorance.[48]

And so Holy Cross started a baby clinic in July 1954, open to all babies, with the special object of preventing malnutrition. One doctor remarked that the "phenomenal" amount of dried milk consumed on the hospital grounds was "only a palliative of course for the immense amount of malnutrition around here." In 1958, Dr. Spalding told the story of a mother who brought in a baby with swollen legs and abdomen, peeling and ulcerated skin, diarrhea, vomiting, and pains; she had fed it only mealies and water plus herbs from the "witch doctor" and balked at admitting the baby to the hospital without asking her husband's permission. The staff interpreted the incident as a sign of regrettable Pondo patriarchy. But, despite having to fight premodern attitudes of this kind, the medical staff saw signs of progress. They noted that mothers appreciated their formula-fed babies gaining weight, an impression confirmed by my own interviews in 1989 with mothers in the Holy Cross area. "Generally they come," Spalding concluded optimistically. "We have not had many children with this trouble lately and they improve dramatically with a few weeks of good feeding."[49]

The tone of medical reports from Holy Cross had become newly triumphant in the immediate postwar years, in marked contrast to the more tentative and spiritual victories recorded by Frank Drewe. The era of wonder drugs had reached Pondoland. Medical science at Holy Cross had won indisputable victories in the baby clinic through use of new antibiotics that cured such diseases as whooping cough and syphilis. In addition, dried milk, with which Britons themselves had been unfamiliar as recently as the 1940s, had become available.

There was, however, a dark side to the hospital's record in the 1950s. A new tone of impatience began to permeate its reports as medical personnel, drawn principally from Great Britain, vented frustration, that Drewe had rarely expressed publicly, with the beliefs and habits of the Pondo. This attitude could lead doctors and nurses to blame patients for their own misdiagnoses. A case in point occurred in 1950 when a two-year-old child weighing only eleven pounds was brought to the hospital by his pagan grandmother. "The size of a miserable six month old baby," the child had been fed on skimmed milk. Diagnosed as malnourished, the child was dosed with water, glucose, salt, and vitamin B every two hours when he was admitted. After two weeks, Nursing Sister Hope fed him spinach, carrots, minced meat, and gravy, but he showed little sign of improvement. The nurse asked the grandmother about the child's mother and was told she was being injected for syphilis. Exclaiming, "They had not thought it worth telling us!" the nurse began to administer penicillin and the syphilis-infected child did begin to improve.[50] Diet was emphatically not the cause of the child's sickness, and the "malnutrition syndrome" clearly impeded the cure. In this case the syndrome had crowded out the taking of a useful medical history, the result of a failure to locate the malady in its broader context.

Holy Cross's European nurses treated infant feeding as an orthodoxy that knew no fashions. In fact, they were as enmeshed in culturally determined habits as the people they were advising and were even somewhat behind the times. Since the beginning of the century medical people had debated whether infants should be nursed on schedule or on demand. African mothers were seen as too ready to respond to their infants' tears with more food rather than realize, in the words of one South African doctor, "a good cry is the baby's mode of taking exercise." This perspective was popularized by a New Zealand pediatrician named Truby King, whose criticism of indulgent Western mothers during the 1910s and 1920s had influenced the nurses who came to Holy Cross and persisted there even after the perspective was beginning to lose favor in Britain. Until 1920, European doctors had taught mothers to offer no solid foods to infants under the age of twelve months. From the mid-1930s this advice was beginning to change and, by the late 1950s, doctors were finding no reason to avoid supplementing milk with solid food when feeding infants over three months old. Ignoring this shift in medical fashion, Holy Cross nurses continued to oppose feeding infants anything but mother's milk before at least eight months.[51]

What was actually happening? The chart on the next page suggests that, in the late 1950s, malnutrition afflicted infants seasonally. The peak months for admission to Holy Cross Hospital for malnutrition were between September and November, the time for planting and weeding, and March to June, when green and then dried grains were harvested. The first period conforms to historical expectations of hunger; people were most likely to be malnourished when the remnants of the previous year's harvest were being scooped out of the mealie pit and the new year's crops were not ready to be picked. The second period is more puzzling because the period from March to June represents the months of plenty.

Many hypotheses could explain these patterns, but the HCH staff raised none of them, too wedded to the cattle complex to look further than Pondo values. In their eyes Amampondo health was undermined by preference for feeding milk to calves rather than children and, in addition, they blamed the Pondo practice of feeding sour milk to infants. Because these explanations ignore time they fail to explain the seasonal flux. My own conversations with Holy Cross staff suggest that nurses accepted cultural explanations to the exclusion of observing or formulating time-sensitive ones. Occasionally their explanations did take time into account, but these usually entailed condemning Pondo values. Some medical missionaries accused mothers of neglecting

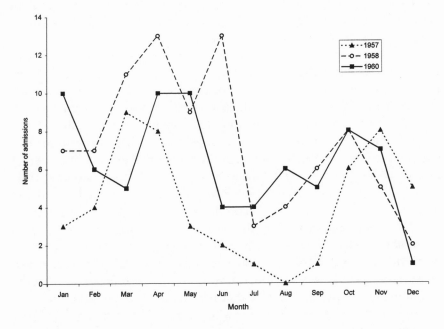

9. Holy Cross Hospital inpatient admissions for malnutrition for 1957, 1958, and 1960. Total inpatient admissions: 1957 = 1,884; 1958 = 2,069; 1960 = 2,681. (Holy Cross Hospital, Inpatient Register)

their children to attend beer parties, generally held after harvest ended in June; in any case, the chart fails to confirm this interpretation as the number of cases drops then.

One plausible hypothesis concerns the steadily mounting demands on women's labor. Increasing numbers of Amampondo men were leaving to find work in town in the 1950s, and so, the number of people living in each Pondo household was declining. Harvest was, of course, a labor-intensive time; Dr. Spalding noted in 1958 that during harvest there were empty beds in all the wards, an indication that every hand was needed in the fields. Why would the peak period for malnutrition occur then? Was it perhaps because a mother was absent from her *umzi*, working in the fields from sunrise to midafternoon? In that case her infant, instead of nursing, was probably being fed on *inembe*, the water in which maize had been boiled. Another noncultural and time-specific hypothesis may explain the first peak of malnutrition cases between September and November. These months occurred roughly nine months after migrants had come home for the Christmas holidays. Perhaps the impending birth of another child had caused the preceding one to be weaned.[52] The waning of polygamy decreased the time between births.

Other women may have been under such stress—worrying about their failure to receive remittances, for example—that they produced little milk themselves. Still other mothers might have left their children with their own mothers when they departed to find paid work. Mothers who went to work in Durban or Johannesburg usually had to rely on the energy, wealth, and wisdom of other family members for the proper care of their children. In cases where these qualities were in short supply or embattled the returning mother might well find her infant sick. One former cook in the nurses' home at Holy Cross got a better-paid kitchen job in Benoni after her husband, a cattleless man working initially at a hotel in Port Saint Johns, had deserted her. She left a seven-year-old son with her brother and a one-and-a-half-year-old son with her mother. Both children died. She did not know the cause of the elder boy's death, but she believed that the younger one died because he did not live with his parents. She had weaned him on tinned milk. Despite the fact that the grandmother was married to the local chief, she was "very poor" because she was the fourth of five wives. The first wife controlled her and the other junior wives so tightly that they had to beg her for milk, which, in any case, hardly existed in winter.[53]

Such tragic stories are not uncommon among families left behind by wage-earning women. They are even present among the families of better-paid women, such as teachers. In these cases, malnutrition was likely to be caused by the age and energy of the grandmother and her understanding of the ways in which processed milk can and cannot substitute for mother's milk. In this way, the separation of the generations may well have inhibited the exchange of systematic understanding, whether inherited or modern, about the link between diet and health. In the poorest and most severely disarranged families in which children or enervated and weak old women were effectively raising babies, the sharing of such wisdom may not have taken place at all. The "cattle complex" crowded out all such questions about women's time, and they were never asked.

Associated in many medical missionaries' minds with unscientific attitudes toward infant feeding were unprogressive spending habits. As P. Peppin, the manager of the Holy Cross farm, had observed, "[p]rimitive natives are quite capable of selling their milk to buy beads for their personal adornment at the store."[54] In this way, images of Africans as poor mothers and poor farmers spilled over into harsh judgements of them as poor consumers, reminiscent of the way the working classes in London were judged by the well fed at the beginning of the century.

While these ideas were not new, there were signs that medical personnel and Amampondo were becoming newly estranged: after Dr. Drewe's retirement doctors increasingly cut their contracts short. Dr. Cawthorne stayed for only four years, leaving after such acrimonious disputes with local people, including the paramount chief and chairman of the hospital board, that the board called "his biggest achievement" the installation of a new lighting plant with all new wiring. Subsequent superintendents stayed roughly as long. After only two years, Dr. Patient, unable to live up to his name, explained his decision to leave in the following terms: "Endless patience in the face of persistent provocation" was needed in the job, because the Pondo were "still largely ignorant, lazy and sometimes stupid; but you love them because of their complete honesty and absolute integrity."[55]

Dr. Patient's reference to "provocation" came during a decade when the mobilization efforts of African nationalists were being felt throughout Pondoland. It presents an illuminating contrast with the way Drewe handled the strike nearly twenty years earlier. In 1953, twenty-six trainee nurses left the hospital shouting "Afrika!" because their grievances had not been redressed. These complaints, mainly against the educational and disciplinary system at the hospital, included criticism of the "appalling" diet fed to both patients and staff— "baptised girls being made to eat beef which at their homes would be cast to the dogs"—and of the generally "tyranous [sic]" attitude of Cawthorne.[56] The protest reflected the estrangement and mutual mistrust of the doctors and the African people: the Europeans were expressing their low opinion of the material standards of all Africans by failing to recognize status distinctions among them. Each party was expressing its distrust of the other in terms of food. The African nurses were not defending African diet but protesting against reducing all Africans, including those who adopted bourgeois norms, to one low status. Food was a potent vehicle for conveying this lack of respect, as we have seen as far back as the 1932 nurses' strike.

The problem was bigger than Cawthorne and poor meat. Coming only a few months after the African National Congress had launched the Defiance Campaign against discriminatory laws in 1952, the young women of Holy Cross were fired by a sense that they, too, were victims of discrimination. The Lusikisiki magistrate backed Cawthorne, noting that the fracas was "probably engineered by the patient Jackson Hanxa." Hanxa, a pulmonary tuberculosis patient, had written several letters criticizing the food: "I am starving here," he wrote the native commissioner in Pretoria. "I only get crushed mealies and porridge. . . . Truly speaking this place is really primitive because we are taken as red Pondos."[57] Hanxa was angry that he was being treated as an uneducated and pagan native, the kind who would smear his blanket and body with red ocher, rather than as the literate wage-earner he was proud to be. While

neither Hanxa nor the nurses mentioned the ANC or larger political or economic issues, they were seen to reflect ANC mobilization. They managed to
communicate with a ferocity unprecedented at Holy Cross that European disrespect was a matter of pressing concern. This incident differs from the 1932
strike, to which it was otherwise so similar, because it took place within a
highly politicized context.

We have been looking at what the anthropologists John and Jean Comaroff
have called the shift from the moral economy of the Christian mission to biomedicine. In his urge to offer salvation through Christianity, Drewe was in
greater harmony than his successors with local medical beliefs, especially the
power of the spirit to affect health. He was also personally more responsive
to the need for respect than the people who followed him, bringing wonder
drugs, irritation, and denigration in their wake. Drewe notably lacked a modern approach to medicine: he kept patients in the hospital for an unusually
long time in the hope that he would convert them. He resisted accepting state
money if that would entail losing the ability to proselytize, even though traditional mission donors simply could not provide the funds necessary to update
his facilities. After he retired, his successors displayed such weak commitment
to his ideals that their tone is memorable mainly for its impatience. They designated malnutrition the source of most maladies partly because it fit logically
with their view of rural culture as suffering from a "cattle complex," the obdu-
rate overvaluing of cattle.

The story of HCH is the story of the mission declining as a galvanizer of
rural change. In the postwar world the times were ready for a new approach
to rural medicine.

The Malnutrition Syndrome and a Holistic Reaction to Biomedicine at the Valley Trust and Health Center, 1951–1960

Halley Harwin Stott, founder of the Valley Trust and Health Centre in Botha's
Hill, Natal, exemplified the postwar zeal to tackle health problems compre-
hensively. Stott wanted to use his organizational skills and modern nutritional
wisdom to combat malnutrition effectively for all time. He exuded visionary
energy similar to that displayed around the same time by Henry Gluckman,
architect of South Africa's plans for a national health service, as well as by the
doctors Sidney and Emily Kark, in 1940 the founders of a comprehensive
health project at Bulwer in rural Natal, and even by the white South African
war veterans who wished their memorial to be not a statue but funds to build
hospitals for Africans.[58] Compared to these people, Dr. Drewe belonged to a
different generation, one whose faith in the powers of science to cure social
ills was less zealous. Stott's commitment and tone bore traces of the mission-

ary spirit as he sent out disciples to convert rural Zulus to holistic agriculture, but he never referred to God or Christ. Independently funded and allied to no religious organization, he disseminated a message that was resolutely secular and scientific.

Named after the comet, Halley Stott was born into an old Natal family in 1910 and so, unlike Drewe, he was truly South African. Stott founded the Botha's Hill Health Centre in 1951 and the adjacent Valley Trust in 1953 to fulfill his holistic vision of what causes sickness. His environmental perspective ran counter to the popular medical approaches of the immediate postwar years, an era when wonder drugs were curing many infections. To Stott good health originated in a good diet. The regrettable commercialization of medicine had resulted, he thought, in doctors treating sickness with drugs, rather than teaching people to take responsibility for their own well-being through improved farming and feeding. His inspiration came partly from his experience in the mid-1940s at King Edward VIII Hospital in Durban where he observed doctors ignoring the social and economic conditions of their patients, particularly the many African children suffering from kwashiorkor. Modern concepts of preventive and promotive, not simply curative, medicine were at the heart of his work.

"Most of the disease" Stott saw in his practice, he wrote, "has its roots in inadequate nutrition, largely due to the misuse of available facilities, poor agricultural methods, defective soil husbandry, bad cooking practices, and increased reliance on processed foods." He had not forgotten that there were other problems complicating African well-being: he listed such diverse factors as "customary practices and beliefs, social disruption, lack of economic opportunity, poor education and amenities. . . . [T]he immediate need," though, was "improved nutrition."[59] Valley Trust personnel paid far less systematic attention to complicating social factors, but Stott was fully aware that people lacked capital and secure land tenure and transport and that overworked Zulu women now had less time to hunt for wild food and cultivate their crops. He was also alive to questions of injustice. He addressed these social issues mainly by commissioning social scientific research and by personal acts of kindness.

Stott nailed responsibility for the deterioration of African health to several causes: nutritional ignorance and superstition, consumerism and commercial interests driven by the profit motive, and soil erosion. "Ignorant as he was of the importance of food for health, the Zulu had no option but to accept the refined and processed productions easily obtainable at the trading store," Stott wrote, "notably the nutrition-deficient, refined maize products (sifted mealie meal, samp and mealie rice), white flour products, commercial sugar, tea, curry and condiments."[60] People were buying white flour dumplings, fat cakes, sweetened condensed milk, synthetic cool drinks, biscuits, cake, and buns, and they were frying onions, spinaches, cabbages, and beans. They were no longer eating fresh vegetables, sour milk, and peanuts. Infants were fed watery sifted maize meal gruel. Stott blamed industrial food manufacturers, in particular, the fertilizer and sugar interests, for robbing food of its value by overprocessing it. Because sugar took minerals and nutrients from the undernourished, it was effectively a poison. In addition, people had not adapted their agricultural and cattle-keeping practices to accommodate their own population explosion; they continued to cut down trees, overgraze pastures and fail to replant them, burn grass, sell manure to white gardeners on the ridge above the hospital, and generally misuse the soil.[61]

Stott's Zulu patients had lost the robust health their ancestors had once enjoyed. He tried, in treating malnourished patients, to praise the traditional Zulu diet and to explain good health in terms of the Zulu idiom of strong blood. Much of the good in Zulu culture—social security, cohesion, solidarity—was being lost, Stott believed, because missionary education discredited and ridiculed ancestor worship and parental authority. Lost collective and cooperative patterns had been replaced by the "more selfish and exploitive outlook of urban natives." But there was still time to stop the decay in the "relatively intact" valley. The story of the Zulu fall from nutritional grace is part of the broader narrative of "race deterioration" that preoccupied so many European thinkers from the nineteenth century. Stott and others saw their task as educators to halt degeneration so that the "natural process" of slow evolution toward modernity—"[it] cannot be hurried"—could take over. The vast majority of the people living in the valley, he wrote, were culturally "marginal, drifting away from tribal beliefs and customs but not yet ready for Christianity and full westernization."[62] He was asserting his belief in the inevitability of their passage along this one-track road to the future, and the ability of Europeans to judge African preparedness.

The widespread evolutionary perspective of Europeans had tended to present African ill health as an inevitable consequence of urbanization. The secretary of health, G. W. Gale, wrote in 1952 about the anthropologist Eileen Krige's report on malnutrition among Africans in Durban: "Gross ill health of the kind described by Dr. Krige is almost inevitable in any area which is undergoing rapid changes of both a demographic and cultural nature." Stott himself presented the causes of the "almost inevitable" suffering as cultural rather than political. "Today," Stott told a British audience in 1958, "these once-proud people are one of South Africa's social problems." Instead of adjusting to "modern western civilization," he said, "their way of life seems to combine some of the worst features of the old and new orders."[63]

Stott's holistic perspective on health derived more from his experience than from his medical education in the early to mid-1930s at the University of Edinburgh, where he remembers reading only one study of nutrition as part of his medical course.[64] And yet the power of his conviction that, medically speaking, "you are what you eat" was so strong that, in the 1950s, he did not have his own five children inoculated with the polio vaccine. He was supported in this decision, as in his work generally at Valley Trust, by the devotion of his wife, Joyce. None of his children fell ill, thus vindicating his belief in holism, that good health was a function of a healthy environment rather than drugs. Halley Stott practiced what he preached. He placed his faith generally in the capacity of scientific thinking, not wonder drugs, to cure maladies.[65]

The Valley Trust, which he called "a Socio-Medical experiment" in an effort to draw attention to its vanguard role, embodied his holistic ideals. If successful, this registered welfare organization could serve, he believed, as a model for the development of medicine throughout postwar South Africa. In the late 1960s he would draw up maps covered with arrows shooting out from the Valley Trust to show how far its trainees and influence had reached. The trust's first objective reveals the wide scope of its aspirations: "to promote the health and well-being of the local Bantu population with due regard to the significance both of their social, economic, educational and nutritional customs and of their total social environment as factors in the aetiology of ill-health." Its other goals stressed the importance of gaining local cooperation and not simply imposing innovations from above, using what was valuable in local culture, securing the active participation of local people, cooperating with like-minded official and private bodies, such as medical schools, promoting relevant social and agricultural research, establishing producers' cooperatives, and setting up "social amenities" so people could play, worship, and study in a healthy atmosphere.[66] Though Valley Trust represented an intensive effort to realize these holistic ideals, its definition of "social environment" fell short of "total" since its publications seldom discussed political and economic influences.

An early promotional pamphlet summed up two key traits that the trust was designed to inculcate: "self-reliance and self-sufficiency in food, energy and technology."[67] To this end, a home produce market was set up in 1956, a maize-grinding mill in 1957. Freshwater fish were introduced to small ponds to augment the protein in local diets. Five subcenters were set up, and nursing teams, armed with three-legged cooking pots, visited them and remote homes of "heathen and illiterate" families, bringing lessons on the nutritional treatment of disease and how to cook cabbage properly. A food-preparation teaching unit was built in the trust itself. In 1959 a rotating pool was initiated to offer interest-free loans to those wanting to build houses and erect fences, an activity that local people initially considered antisocial. The agricultural demonstrator R. T. Mazibuko introduced a demonstration garden based on the trench principle: "costly and dangerous" chemical fertilizers could be avoided if local compost—grass, weeds, and topsoil—instead filled the two-and-a-half-foot trenches where vegetables could be grown. The trust urged people to buy only foods they could afford and to eat food within their resources to grow.

The goal of using only local resources reflects the sort of postwar utopian spirit that could at the same time be found, for example, in the kibbutzim of Israel. The trust itself justified its effort to build self-sufficient communities by quoting an ancient scholar: "The noblest charity is to prevent a man from accepting charity, and the best alms are to show and enable a man to dispense with alms." And yet, ironically, within the South African context, these goals fit neatly into the vision articulated in 1955 by the report of the Tomlinson Commission, urging that African areas of South Africa be more independent from white South Africa. Stott himself did not intend to support apartheid ideology, and subsequent editions of the promotional pamphlet dropped the exhortations to "self-reliance" and "self-sufficiency," but he did endorse the expectations of his friend, J. D. Scott, professor of pasture management and soil conservation at the University of Natal, that agricultural "betterment" schemes like those the NAD was then promoting would make it "possible to accommodate in the reserves all those who are domiciled there today, if not more, without having to acquire more land." He hoped race relations would be improved by the lack of European self-interest in the experiment. In 1966 the member of parliament for Pietermaritzburg district, W. T. Webber, drew the attention of the House of Assembly to the benefits of the trust's scheme: "[T]he rural Bantu people are taught to be independent of outside sources of supply for their food requirements."[68] Proponents of the homeland scheme of grand apartheid can only have been pleased.

Stott's vision was backed by a talent for fund-raising, though the trust was always strapped for money because of the small amounts given by local people. In the eyes of donors his plan must have had an appealing clarity and his organization a reassuring transparency. Entirely a voluntary organization, the trust received generally small donations of a few rand from individuals among Natal's white population and larger sums from organizations like the Rotary Club, the South African Police Golf Committee, and the Staff Charitable Fund of Stanley Motors (Natal). Four trustees were assisted by a management committee that included representatives of important local bodies (the University of Natal, the adjacent tuberculosis settlement, the district white women's institute, and the NAD). The trust publicized its work and successes in glossy annual reports that, along with illustrated articles in magazines, won it an international reputation. Not until the 1960s, however, did larger sums begin to flow into the trust, first from foreign donors like Oxfam (1962) and after 1966 from South African corporations like Anglo American. The South African

Sugar Association in 1970, in a remarkable retreat from its earlier refusal to contribute to African health care at Holy Cross, gave funds that allowed the nutrition education unit to expand.

Stott received no pay from the trust, and he himself purchased the fifty-five acres on which it sat from his father's development company, Botha's Hill Estates, transferring ownership immediately to the trust. He was proud to receive no aid from the state or province, but when J. M. Latsky, the chief adviser to the national Department of Nutrition, visited in late 1955, he was so impressed by Stott's efforts to "integrate these people into a community able to withstand the impact of Western ways instead of leaving them in their migration to the cities to drift to that which is false," that he urged the nutrition department to send a dietitian to help.[69] The donor lists at the end of each annual report produced by the trust attest to Stott's inspirational power and to the general popularity of his vision, one that Latsky's quote captures well.

Of vital importance to Stott's experiment was social science. The anthropologists Jack and Eileen Krige, who had attended planning meetings in the Stotts' living room as early as 1946, remained an influential force at the trust. Jack Krige was alive to the dangers of engaging in social engineering without expert knowledge and training. By the late 1950s, he said, Africa was littered with failed social experiments that "left an aftermath of disorder, suspicion and often fierce hostility to the white man." These failures and the models provided recently by British and American research councils suggested that researchers should be encouraged to delve into the social heritage of the valley because "[t]here are many Bantu beliefs and practices that, in the light of modern knowledge, must be changed. They range from bad land management and culinary practices that destroy vitamins, to taboos restricting the use of resources and mystical conceptions of the causes of disease, from defective child rearing techniques, to inadequate notions of the destiny of man and the nature of the universe." Thus, psychologists' and anthropologists' reports on the valley reflected this supremely confident era in social scientific research. The head of the Department of Psychology at the University of Natal, R. C. Albino, studied "thinking in Africans" by asking them to classify toy animals, for example, and presenting "a highly standardized series of questions which only permitted of a few unequivocal responses." He also designed a very simple task that demanded "a high level of attention and persistence," watching a revolving pointer for 108 minutes. Albino explained African resistance to these tasks not in terms of boredom or irritation, but as a possible consequence of life in a rural environment that did not require persistence and attentiveness. Another psychological study, based on mere observation rather than testing, concluded that children who have suffered from kwashiorkor "appear intellectually backward," a conclusion contradicted by subsequent medical findings that "there is no evidence that [kwashiorkor] *alone* stops children from learning."[70] Like inconclusive soil analyses performed for the trust by J. Lintner, this research demonstrated faith in the scientific method more than it produced useful knowledge.

The anthropological studies overseen by the Kriges were more revealing, partly because they were undertaken by Zulu speakers. In the 1950s the Kriges obtained fellowships from the Nuffield Foundation to support fieldwork by two African students of anthropology, Absolom Vilakazi and Mrs. M. Malie, who was later replaced by Harriet Sibisi Ngubane. Vilakazi and Ngubane published their research in, respectively, *Zulu Transformations* and *Body and Mind in Zulu Medicine*. All three researchers drew attention to the social changes already apparent in the valley: tension between Christians and "heathens," the increased incidence of witchcraft accusations, the victory of the cash over the subsistence economy, the changing regard of labor migrants for their reserve homes and wives. In reporting these findings, Jack Krige noted that, "as scientists," he and his fellows were interested not simply in practical results but in "arriving at principles that will have universal validity and be applicable in situations anywhere in South Africa or even further afield."[71] Krige's words captured postwar social scientists' confidence that they had the tools to understand and change reality around the world, a professional pride analogous to that of postwar physicians. Both had to confront the question: Was the valley already so enmeshed in South Africa's industrial economy that the goals of self-sufficiency and nutritional well-being would be impossible to attain?

Care of the Land as Cause and Cure

The trust buildings sit on a hilltop in the Valley of a Thousand Hills, a location as spectacular as the name implies. From a high ridge in white Natal now occupied by the Rob Roy Hotel, the land drops away into seemingly endless folds of steep granite hills and deep ravines. Its natural beauty does not reflect natural wealth. Absolom Vilakazi wrote dismissively of the agricultural potential of the valley: the land was too rugged, the soil too granitic, the slopes too steep; "highly leached and erodible soils seriously limit the amount of land suitable for agriculture."[72] In a footnote he explained why this land was designated a native reserve by quoting the *Natal Regional Survey:* Europeans had settled the undulating land suitable for agriculture that lay just to the south. Stott, less pessimistic about the potential of the land, believed the area could become self-sufficient in food if terraces stopped the erosion, and if manure and compost enriched the soil. He deliberately chose the worst agricultural land in the reserve as the site for a demonstration plot in order to prove his point.

The chiefdoms occupying the immediate and more distant hinterland of the trust buildings, Qadi and Nyuswa, both trace their origins to near the

Tugela River in northern Zululand, which some of their ancestors left in the 1830s to escape the wars of Zulu imperialism. Toward the late nineteenth century the relations between people living in the two chiefdoms became strained, erupting occasionally into "faction fighting," as colonial administrators called it. The shortage of good land played some role in the deterioration of their relations. Some of the Qadi had settled on the rich red soils of the Mabedlana Hills to the north and refused to follow the leadership of the Nyuswa chief. Colonial reports of the faction fights show women quarreling over the boundaries of their gardens and men having to drive their cattle across the footpaths of their enemies as early as 1895. The local tension was complicated by the fact that neither people actually had a chief living among them: the secretary of native affairs in Natal, Sir Theophilus Shepstone, had sent the Nyuswa chief and some of his followers to live on the south coast at Harding in the 1850s to serve as a buffer between the Natal settlers and the Amampondo; the Qadi chief lived a few miles from the coast in nearby Inanda. The local political system was, in any case, clearly in disarray. The waning powers of chiefs in a colonial situation made it hard for any one of them to win popular approval. To complicate matters further, with the development of commercial agriculture in Natal, African tenants were constantly moving away from white farms either because they had been expelled or because they wanted more control over their working lives. Many of these former farm laborers sought independence by moving to land in the valley, thereby increasing the pressure on the land; still, the refugees appear to have been readily accepted, in part because they could prove useful in shoring up the numbers and boundaries of the faction they joined.[73] One notorious faction fight between two neighboring clans occurred over a boundary in 1934, when 460 huts were looted and burned and eleven men were killed, an incident reported even by the *Times* of London. Such incidents inspired little sympathy in the NAD. Five years later, the native commissioner of nearby Camperdown told a meeting of fifty or more, "You natives who are living in the Reserves are constantly complaining that you are short of land but unless you are properly handling the land you already possess you cannot expect the Government to give you more."[74] The area where Stott established his trust had, in short, been growing increasingly crowded and violent during the first half of the twentieth century.

When Halley Stott praised the dietary habits of his patients' forebears, the culinary traits he had in mind were the nineteenth-century staples of fermented milk, stone-ground cereals boiled as porridge, and cultivated vegetables. One can easily compare inherited dietary beliefs and practices with those the trust tried to influence because in 1956 the trust, true to its goal of fostering research, had Malie, under the supervision of Eileen Krige, carefully record the names of the local foods and how they were produced. When Malie broached the subject "To what extent the land supports the people," she noted losses of sour milk and maize variety. People planted a narrower range of crops than their ancestors had done, and their yields were also lower since each household had an average of only two acres to farm. "A striking feature of Nyuswa," Mrs. Malie noted, "is the absence of *izilulu*—grass storage baskets or grain tanks. People tell you there is no need for these as they never have much grain to store."[75] They now bought a good deal of their food: cabbages, potatoes, tomatoes, tea, spices like curry and chilies. Purchased food tided people over seasonal food shortages, but Stott had called it "dead food" because manufacturers preserved grain by overrefining it and they had pushed so much lard onto the market that people were no longer eating enough protein, in particular, or protective foods, in general.

The origins of this new diet lay at least as much in land shortage and low wages as in ignorance, but it was a point Stott himself never raised. Buried in her report, Malie indicated the agrarian effects of what her adviser's husband, Jack Krige, would soon label a "pathological economy," one in which the men worked in town, leaving the farming to women able to engage only in "inefficient supplementary cultivation." No longer were fields allowed to lie fallow since land was so scarce, and the yields were bound to decline as the land became exhausted. There were so few cattle that not many people had manure to scatter over their seeds, and milk was no longer a staple. They even offered to weed in exchange for being allowed to plant crops among those of a landed person—running beans up the stalks of mealies, for example. Plowing was rare; only three in a group of twenty families owned plows, and owners kept borrowers waiting until sometimes too late in the season to plant. Hoeing was traditionally women's work, but workers now had to walk farther over the deforested hills in search of firewood, and their husbands, Malie noted, were often of little help. Most men worked in town and came home on weekends to drink "and compare their [wives'] attentions unfavourably with those of their mistresses." Jack Krige, reflecting on Malie's report and the work of Vilakazi, warned that although programs to improve health education, marketing facilities, and farming would have some beneficial results, "we should be prepared for disappointments" because workers now saw their future in wage labor and found that "the pursuit of farming places them at a serious disadvantage." By implication, he saw limits to "our power to influence trends in policy which we ourselves cannot alter."[76]

Krige had in mind the measures that the apartheid government had been passing for the past nine years, especially the more stringent pass laws allowing legitimate urban residence to the employed only. In its impact on the valley, the Group Areas Act of 1950 was one of the more influential pieces of recent legislation. It held up the establishment of a general market Stott had intended "as a means of encouraging the Bantu to self-help, and [which] directly, and indirectly, would have educated the Bantu participating in the scheme in business methods." Success would have conflicted with the interests of local European traders. When the European owner of land adjoining the trust complained, the secretary for native affairs ruled that the market would have to be located in the reserve and "run by the Natives themselves with the help of the Department if necessary."[77] To do otherwise would have contravened the dictum of the Group Areas Act that trading areas be separated by race. By mandating racial segregation of urban neighborhoods it had uprooted African families from mixed neighborhoods in the area of Durban and Pietermaritzburg, sending many to a periurban refuge in the nearby reserves. This influx undoubtedly worsened the population pressure in the valley, which would grow graver still when people began to be resettled from white South Africa to the homelands in 1960. The valley's population nearly doubled between 1958 and 1981.

Pressure on valley land grew not only from white farmers evicting laborers, but also from the magnet of the labor markets of Durban and Pinetown, particularly apparent during the 1940s. Many of the migrants came to the urban labor markets without official permission, but the records of those who did apply to the NAD for the right to move to Camperdown and Pinetown reveal commonly shared aspirations. Workers applied from across South Africa, though mainly from the Transkei, the Transvaal, and the Orange Free State, to take up jobs in the Durban area. Some had already obtained employment at, for example, the South African Railways, the Durban Corporation, or the South African Police; only a quarter of applicants in the early 1940s wanted permission to live as farm laborers, most probably preferring to commute to urban jobs, or even to retire and live on land they held legitimately. Most swore that they would be bringing no livestock with them. The net impact on the valley was that the human population density increased and the size of people's gardens diminished. By 1962 the average population density was between 139 and 181 per square mile, "too dense for a subsistence economy to be any longer possible."[78] As Jack Krige had written, people no longer saw their future in farming.

The employed could move more readily to the valley in the 1950s because local transport was expanding. Before 1951 people had to take the train or railway bus to Botha's Hill, high on the ridge, and walk down into the nearly roadless valley. By 1957 there were five African and Indian taxis, and, by 1965, a bus route ran down the steep dirt roads. The area was becoming periurban. Stott's anti-industrial bias ran increasingly counter to reality.

The historical process affecting the valley is apparent in Stott's medical histories, which, in keeping with his holistic vision, allowed whole family medical histories to be cross-referenced. These family stories document the medical consequences of the historical process in which the valley was enmeshed. To cohesive families with relatively secure access to wages the Valley Trust offered advice and help allowing them to make the transition from subsistence farming without much damage to their health or fortunes. Other families and individuals were so destitute that the Valley Trust could offer no help at all.

Florence Thabete was a Valley Trust health committee worker whose life steadily improved. Born in 1927 to a farm worker, she had slept under sacks with her entire family in a single hut. In 1939, her father, deciding that his schedule of six months' labor on the farm and six months' work for money elsewhere was "a waste of time," moved his family to Taylors' location, outside Pietermaritzburg near a hostel where he worked, and the family's fortunes looked up. Florence began to attend school, though only for two years. The family bought food from the shops and slept under blankets in two rondavels (round, mud houses). Then, in 1957, she and her husband moved to a small plot of land in Nyuswa because her husband had begged a friend to find a place for him there; they paid the chief nothing for the privilege. Her husband could commute to jobs in local cities, first to a Pietermaritzburg kitchen, then to a bakery in Pinetown, and, finally, the thirty kilometers to Durban, where he worked as a driver. Because he had a car, he was able to come home each night. His income now allowed them to educate their six children to become policemen and teachers. Since 1987, Florence Thabete has supplemented his wages by weighing babies for the trust.

Florence Thabete enthusiastically endorsed the lessons of Valley Trust. When I visited her in 1989 she proudly displayed the new fencing she would use to keep cows away from her garden patch of potatoes, sweet potatoes, spinach, carrots, beetroot, and onions. She lamented that one of her infants had died at the age of six months because, instead of breast-feeding, she had fed the infant poorly measured lactogen. The head of Valley Trust, and not her mother, she said, had taught her to eat for health. She did not, however, measure her former poverty in terms of diet. Sleeping under sacks had been a hardship, but she did not complain about the stone-ground mealies, spinaches, and homemade beer that had characterized her family's rural diet. At first, she had not liked sour foods like tomatoes available in the location; she had had to learn to eat cabbages and rice. "Now everything I ate when a child, my children don't like," she observed. Tastes had simply changed, and she had the money now to keep up with them. Because the Thabetes could afford to buy seven cows, they ate *amasi* daily in the summer; because they had steady incomes, they bought milk from the shops in the winter along with the food, including dry mealies, that they could not grow on their small plot.

Most women with whom I spoke in 1989 endorsed the benefits of nutritional education purveyed by institutions like Valley Trust, and even herbalists spoke warmly of the lessons they learned about infant feeding, delighted their babies were growing fatter. They also appreciated the ease with which they could procure food in shops. Similarly, the settlement of people in villages under the name of "betterment" schemes pleased many women because village life allowed them easy access to clinics and other services. Setting up a local mill and market and teaching nutrition, the Valley Trust was serving the interests of those who could afford to make use of its lessons.

These beneficiaries of the Valley Trust tended to be older and relative newcomers to the valley who planted their gardens to supplement the money coming into their families from a migrant wage earner. They fenced their gardens, planted fruit trees, ate fish, and bought brown bread. Their ideas about what causes ill health had already begun to change, perhaps because they tended to be Christians. After 1963 the kwashiorkor rate would begin to fall. Research conducted in the early 1980s by Dr. Stott's successor, Dr. I. B. Friedman, suggests that because the people interviewed professed no knowledge of the need to avoid sugar and overrefined foods, the decline may have been connected to other factors like better transportation and higher wages.[79] African wages rose by 6 percent between 1973 and 1977, which might help to explain why, by 1975, people were eating more fresh fruit and vegetables, legumes, and powdered milk. Valley Trust's success stories, like that of Florence Thabete, seem to derive from the resources the trust provided to well-placed people in a dramatically underresourced community.

Halley Stott's admirable honesty led him to reveal in his annual reports the setbacks in the trust's achievement of its goals. For instance, after fish farming was first broached in 1955, people discovered the ponds were too small to allow the fish to grow large enough to contribute much protein to a family's diet. Similarly, torrential rain could damage the trenches and, in any case, they, like the fish ponds, required intensive management and hard manual labor; a minority of people adopted them. By the early 1980s the trust was redefining its goals toward community development and away from a primary focus on nutrition. As the population continued to swell, clean water emerged as a major issue. And trust personnel no longer saw kwashiorkor, for example, as the result of ignorance but of lack of money and social disorder.

The story of one old man named Samu Ntaka illustrates how malnutrition was and also was not at the heart of local people's problems. Samu Ntaka was born around 1879, the time the British army inflicted its final defeat on the Zulu army. Ntaka had spent his working life on a white farm called Assagay, managing to acquire a few cows and a team of oxen with which he plowed for other Africans. By the 1950s he was alone; his wife and son had died, and he had tried in vain to find a daughter who had disappeared. From 1952 he began to visit the health center for treatment of rheumatism, an enlarged prostate, spinal arthritis, bladder and kidney problems, in addition to malnutrition. On August 12, 1955, he returned to the center with further symptoms of malnutrition. He had a practical problem that was at least as grave: at the age of about seventy-six he had just been turned off the white farm where he lived. A brother refused to help him, and another lived in an inaccessible place, high up in the hills of Ndwedwe to the north, though that brother's son, a driver employed by a friend of Joyce Stott, probably alerted Dr. Stott to the old man's plight. Ntaka managed to find a new home for himself and his cattle about twenty miles away on the Umgeni River but could not obtain the permit to move his stock until he had taken up residence. In the meantime, with nowhere to leave the animals and fearful of prosecution, he slept out in the hills with his cattle. Stott, moved by the plight of his patient, who was clinging desperately to pastoral life in an urbanizing situation, got a statement from the stock inspector that the cattle could be moved because they were not scrub cattle, but Stott failed to get him a disability grant because the old man lacked both a pass and exemption from taxes. Ntaka developed pneumonia in his hilltop refuge and died in September 1955, probably from kidney and heart failure.

Many of the records in the trust archives reveal similar tales of exposure of weakened individuals, children or old people, suffering alone without family ties or state aid at the mercy of the elements. The ability of any health center or trust to intervene in such cases was limited. The old man's plight had originated in all likelihood in an economic strategy by the white farmer to rationalize his workforce and by state policy determining that he was ineligible for support. In these circumstances Stott's sense of justice was aroused, but there were clear limits to his ability to intervene and stop the suffering.

Stott differed from the Holy Cross doctors who used antibiotics and from Afrikaner nationalists who subscribed to ethnos theory, but he came to the same medical conclusions and had similar political goals. Their common focus was on malnutrition as the alpha and omega of African health problems, a perspective that they interpreted in such a way as to crowd out political and economic analysis. They treated the reserves as if, even in the 1960s, they were still capable of autonomy from a money economy. Halley Stott's story reflects postwar pride in the power of scientific thinking to cure social ills, a scientific hubris that was not even dependent on wonder drugs.

Conclusion

The malnutrition syndrome possessed three principal actors: soil, women, and tuberculosis. The ostensibly apolitical or scientific version of this narrative of South African history went as follows: Africans readily fell victim to tuberculosis because they were poorly nourished; they ate badly because their mothers or wives needed nutritional instruction; overstocking had damaged the soil to the extent that crop yields were poor, and the supply of fresh milk from scrawny, underfed cows was waning. Halley Stott and Frank Drewe's successors contributed to this story, and it probably had a wider impact on the fortunes of their patients than the cures they dispensed. By lending their authority, they helped make this rationale the orthodox medical version of South Africa's modern history and, in so doing, they kept in relative obscurity a more overtly political version of that same history: that the mines had spread tuberculosis; that milk and produce yield in the reserves was declining because of an increasing man-to-land ratio related to the static size of the reserves; that some women were caring for the nutritional health of their children less effectively because they themselves were bearing the economic and physical burden of maintaining their households in the absence of their poorly paid husbands.

The problem with the orthodox medical version of South African history is that it was diversionary, the malnutrition syndrome providing a useful defense against spending money on African rural health, except to cure soil erosion through betterment schemes. Doctors joined other experts in attributing to African culture—especially the "cattle complex"—the cause for increased African poverty and for their own failure to cure all the maladies arriving at their clinic doors during this period. This denigration of African culture occurred at the same time as the increased politicization of African poverty by African nationalists and those whites who made an entirely different use of the malnutrition syndrome, interpreting it to show the damaging effects of labor migration.

Three representative quotes highlight changes in the evolving story. The first came from the pen of a missionary, A. T. Bryant, describing Zulu medicine. In 1909, Bryant wrote, referring to Zulu pharmacoepia, "It is by no means an exaggeration to affirm that comparatively the average Zulu can boast of a larger share of pure scientific knowledge than the average European." By the 1940s this respect had all but disappeared. Instead, one could hear the undersecretary for native affairs blaming African hunger on "ignorance in regard to how to live." The third quote comes from the 1975 annual report of Stott, perhaps in reaction to his chief disciple's failure to live up to his own high standards of personal honesty and self-sacrifice, especially where money was concerned: "[T]here have been limits to the extent to which non-scientific people can take part [in a scientific experiment]."[80]

The idea that Africans were people without science would prove useful in excluding Africans from the common institutions of South Africa in the same way that the "sanitation syndrome" had justified segregating cities at the turn of the century. This apolitical version of the malnutrition syndrome was, similarly, a "societal metaphor" that interacted with local racial attitudes to influence the policies and institutions of apartheid. It did so when its focus on soil erosion helped keep the idea of the political causes of African poverty at bay. It expressed medical impatience with African society, especially during the high modernist period of the 1950s. It could be used to justify supplanting an evolutionary model of African history with a static ethnic one: because African culture was rural, the cure for African problems like hunger lay in rural areas. Politicians would use these ideas to great effect.

Part Four

The Triumph of Scientism and
Cultural Essentialism

CHAPTER SEVEN

Denial and Coercion

The State Response to the Malnutrition Syndrome, 1940s to 1960s

If we continue to spoonfeed the Native we shall spoil him utterly.

J. J. Serfontein, 1949

WHEN PEOPLE ARE LESS than full citizens, experts define their problems and propose the solutions for them.[1] What were the consequences for Africans of having had their poverty defined for them in particular ways? Answering this question entails discovering what policies the South African government implemented with reference to hunger, and with what effect.

The apartheid state embodied cultural racism by basing its separate development schemes on the idea that each people has essential cultural traits or "national characteristics." In the postwar world this stand would eventually win it the status of pariah. And yet, its ideology might also be seen normatively as an example of "authoritarian high modernism," James Scott's phrase for the hubris that allows modern states to meddle in the intimate details of the lives of the governed. Bureaucratic states colonize their countries internally. Officials place grids over the land and its people, trying to enforce conformity to the categories they understand and through which they can exercise control. They are able to do so because of the supreme self-confidence with which they regard their society's material achievements, especially ones that are scientific and technological. The utopian urge goes wrong, Scott writes, when the subjected people lack the capacity to mount determined resistance against state control over the smallest details of their lives—such as what food they eat, where they sleep, how they farm—and they cannot assert the value of their own systems of knowledge. The meliorists and hunger experts who are the subjects of this book were among those who gained that right instead. The impact of their ideas was mediated by vested interests, whose power sometimes seemed to strike them unawares and sometimes appalled them.[2]

Bantu Pictorial

SUPPLEMENT TO IMVO ZABANTSUNDU

NO 2

MARCH, 1946

JOHANNESBURG

VEGETABLES ARE GOOD FOR US
(See Story on Page 2)

10. When World War II ended, campaigns to educate Africans to avoid hunger began in earnest, as seen in this 1946 exhortation.

The Entrenched Interests of White Farmers

The depression had given rise to official efforts to regulate agricultural markets in South Africa as in the rest of the Western world where governments were overwhelmed by mounds of surplus agricultural produce their citizens could no longer afford to buy. South Africa's regulatory bodies tended to be framed in explicit emulation of those already adopted by Great Britain, by other British dominions like Canada and Australia, as well as by the United States. These bodies variously set prices, subsidized certain foods, and decided what to do with surpluses. Their tight control over production and distribution coexisted oddly but easily with official rhetoric that praised the free market.

The Marketing Act of 1937 shaped South Africa's agricultural markets by subsidizing cheap exports with high domestic prices. The origins of the low export prices charged for South African agricultural produce lay initially in the protective tariffs erected by western Europe around its own produce in 1925; South Africa had had to set its prices low simply in order to compete on the world market. The act also grew out of the failed cooperative movements of the 1920s and the more successful marketing boards of the early 1930s that had sought to develop reliable export markets for South Africa's surplus produce. It was an attempt to develop a long-term agricultural policy that would smooth out the effects of good and bad years, ensuring farmers a decent income whether they were suffering through a drought or reaping a bumper crop. This stability was achieved, under the 1937 act's authority, by establishment of many marketing boards, one for every major crop, overseen by the National Marketing Council. Each board became the sole legitimate channel for the marketing of that crop and set both domestic and export prices. One of the act's architects, S. J. J. de Swardt, argued that the period between 1929 and 1936, when the precursors of the act were set up, as well as the 1937 act itself, marked "the end of pioneer farming" and the opening of an "umbrella of confidence" that allowed large investments in commercial production. He later credited the Marketing Act with subsequently allowing South African agriculture to meet local food needs during "the enormous mining and industrial expansion from about 1955 onwards."[3]

The marketing boards made food expensive inside South Africa.[4] Rich and poor alike were charged high prices for maize, dairy products, wheat, and meat. At the same time, parliament passed legislation setting tariffs, quotas, and restrictions on imports. The net result of these controls was strangely unpatriotic in the sense that South African consumers paid more for their own maize and butter, for example, than they would have paid in Europe.[5] Because guaranteed high prices were not accompanied by restrictions on output, acreage under cultivation steadily expanded. That growth, in turn, provoked farmers to demand more labor, even though the effect was to create a food surplus priced too high for the majority of South Africans to purchase. This situation caused some economists to pepper their journal articles with exclamation points and emotive words like "absurd" and "ridiculous."[6]

Especially from the late 1930s to the late 1940s, members of parliament used that forum to advertise their concern over the poor "distribution of foodstuffs," rather than specifically against the control boards. In 1938, for example, Dr. Karl Bremer (National party, Graaff Reinet) urged, "we must put foodstuffs under the control of the state, to the extent that the state itself will be concerned with the business of producing foodstuffs and making them available." He was supported by M.P.s decrying the export of butter, cheese, sugar, and dried fruit for purchase in London at prices lower than people paid inside South Africa. His motion for a commission of inquiry was seconded by another M.P. who wanted to know "how we can disperse the surplus products which we are now sending overseas." He was joined by others who urged government to buy fruit and vegetables that remained unsold in local markets and distribute it "among the poorer section of the population."[7]

The few left-wing members of parliament criticized these earnest pleas. Duncan Burnside, for example, scoffed at his fellow parliamentarians for talking about food to the virtual exclusion of wages. Burnside, a self-described supporter of the "workers' movement" (he had founded the South African Socialist party earlier that year), named "the Marketing Act and the various control bills" as the culprits, or more precisely as signs of the "crass stupidity of farmers making money by the growing of foodstuffs, . . . in order to get a higher price from other people and by exporting the surplus and selling it at a loss."[8]

At first the effects of the Marketing Act were not depicted in racial terms. By presenting the problem as a case of national "physical retardation," parliamentary critics included poor whites among those who would cause the country to "retrogress" and be unable to defend itself. Perhaps for this reason, the National party registered no dissent, even when the cost of having the state fulfill, as Bremer urged, the "duty of a father or of a bread-winner" to a nation of ten million people was likely to be astronomical.[9]

Some local extraparliamentary critics protested the inequity and injustice of the marketing boards by saying that they benefited only the wealthy farmer. Producer subsidies gave small farmers too little capital to pay off their debts and invest in expensive projects like irrigation schemes, whereas rich farmers profited without having to increase production.[10] Representing producer rather than consumer interests, the boards were said to push up prices by creating scarcity. It became more expensive to buy food for humans than feed for cattle. Equitable distribution was so ill served by marketing boards that surplus food would be destroyed rather than sold, as happened notoriously in 1943 with a bumper crop of maize and more frequently with fruit. The result was a chronic food shortage, worsened by the increased consumption of the war years. Just after the war ended, South Africa found itself in the peculiar position of producing more food than ever before and of watching its number of hungry people grow larger and larger.

Through the Mealie Industry Control Board (MCB), white farmers most dramatically affected African welfare; twelve of the board's members were farmers, and only two of the other seven represented consumers' interests. Since maize was the staple of African diets, the MCB ran the risk of harming the health of the majority of the population, especially people who relied on maize purchases, such as widows, township dwellers, or anyone during a time of drought. Neil MacVicar, medical superintendent of Lovedale's hospital, specifically blamed the upsurge of starvation in 1937 on the newly high price of maize: "The action of the Maize Control Board in forcing up so enormously the price of this staple and only cheap food of the poorest people during a time of drought has been a scandalous misuse of power."[11] By 1946 the MCB had managed both to raise the price of maize and to diminish the quantity available on the market. These dubious achievements resulted from the monopolistic powers that the Marketing Act of 1937 had vested in the board. The act prohibited local barter of mealies, even between neighbors. In addition, the board was reluctant to allow newcomers to enter the mealie trade and had halved its number of authorized agents in order, some said, to force the mealie trade into the hands of cooperative societies.

Searching for reasons why there was an acute shortage of grain for purchase by Africans in 1945, Margaret Ballinger, a maize board member, made some unpleasant discoveries. She found that a few milling companies were incorporating large quantities of maize into their cattle feed. Other maize found its way onto the black market at higher prices than were paid by the MCB; black market trading sometimes stemmed from the sheer inconvenience farmers experienced when sending mealies to centralized depots instead of selling them by cash or barter to Africans living nearby. Further, the board was unresponsive to local demand, delaying or reducing the issue of permits to sell mealies while traders faced the prospect of empty shelves and hungry customers carrying ready cash. In Nqutu, Natal, for example, each trader sold his full quota of maize in a few days and was told to wait six weeks for the next consignment to arrive.[12]

Similarly, large quantities of butter and margarine were exported to London before the war, by the Dairy Industry Control Board, for less than the sale price within the Union. When local fat shortages occurred during the war, the control board agreed to allow the production of margarine as long as the Ministry of Agriculture set a low limit to the quantity that could be legitimately manufactured. Initially the dairy industry proposed that a means test be instituted to ensure that only lower income groups would be able to buy butter's cheaper competitor. After the war, the minister of agriculture consulted with the dairy control board and then allowed margarine to be available for purchase by anyone, but only if it was colored white and sold from special food vans.[13]

Shortages of other foodstuffs such as sugar were caused less by bureaucratic inefficiency and corruption than by the logic of the market. Sugar, a commodity whose absence was lamented more by tea and coffee drinkers than by doctors, was similarly in short supply for Africans after the war even in the form of cheap sweets. Supplies went, rather, to manufacture more profitable lines like expensive candies that African traders themselves could not even afford to stock.[14] Shops in remote areas tended to be stocked last.

The political power of commercial farmers that resulted in the 1937 Marketing Act went on to control the movement, pricing, quality standards, and marketing supply of most South African farm produce until the 1980s. The Wage Board, on the other hand, was somnolent during the 1950s. Responding to white farmers who wanted to ensure that large urban pay increases did not lure away their laborers, it did nothing to stop real wages from falling.[15] Because they were researchers and not politicians, the hunger experts had seldom chosen to focus attention on the price and wage issues that lay at the heart of malnutrition. As a result, their optimism was able to flourish in the 1940s.

Wartime Idealism and the National Nutrition Council

World War II escalated rather than interrupted the prewar promises that more and better food for everyone was within reach. The imperative to devise improved field rations for soldiers has long led embattled nations to search for and discover new approaches to healthy eating. Canning, for example, was a French innovation discovered during the Napoleonic wars. In the South African case, soldiers' biscuits were much improved by advances in milling and additives such as wheat germ and powdered milk, and their diet benefited from the mass production of dehydrated vegetables. When the Allies gathered at Hot Springs, Arkansas, in 1943 to plan the United Nations Food and Agriculture Organization, they passed a recommendation that all Allied governments establish national nutrition organizations to advise them on sound food and nutritional policies. The rhetorical urge toward a better postwar world was international, and its wellsprings were partly strategic and partly primeval: strong bodies made good defenses.

South African policy-makers were pulled in two quite different directions as they contemplated the shape their country might take after the war. On the one hand, documents like the Beveridge Report fed them images of big government tackling and solving a wide range of social problems, including malnutrition; on the other, they were reminded that such dreams could easily outrun the state's ability to pay. One vision of postwar South Africa focused on the need to make the country more prosperous by serving the interests of new secondary industries; between 1948 and 1958 the number of private manufacturing plants rose and the value of their gross output more than doubled. As canning and automobile assembly plants developed they would need more skilled and efficient workers and not simply men strong enough to wield jackhammers. In the words of people researching physical efficiency, these firms might require help in devising "scientific supervision of feeding" so that they could "transform human raw material into specialised precision workers." And yet, some officials saw such schemes, and the "zeal for Native welfare" generally, as in danger of "outrunning financial discretion."[16]

During the war years themselves, no one had to resolve this tension. They were free to devise creative and innovatory plans for a new South Africa. For example, when Douglas Smit, secretary for native affairs, and a seven-member committee reported in 1942 on the living conditions of urban Africans, they proposed that the government become involved in providing free communal meals "on a selective basis even if only as an interim measure, pending a really adequate rise in wage levels." The Union government would pay half the cost. (They did note that Europeans found this idea more attractive than Africans who argued instead, "Give us higher wages and lower prices for food and let us feed our families ourselves.") Clearly well versed in the malnutrition surveys, the committee went on to recommend that municipalities distribute at cost protective foods like milk, vegetables, and fruit, and encourage the keeping of poultry. They concluded by urging that any surplus foods, such as oranges, be distributed among urban Africans, an idea that would gain greater publicity in the following decade.[17]

A prime national example of these innovative wartime projects was Henry Gluckman's 1944 plan for a national health service that would overturn South Africa's history of providing skeletal public health services. The report deplored the government's precedent of intervening in public health only to redress specific crises. Over the course of its three and a half decades, the Union of South Africa had managed to devise "an uncoordinated [health care] system [dealing] with each problem as it arose, or . . . became . . . acute." The government had, of course, left a great deal of its health initiatives to private enterprise, whether missions or businesses; Transkeian rural clinics, for example, had been established from a base in Umtata only because the Native

Recruiting Corporation had taken the trouble to fund them. Such efforts on behalf of Africans were, nevertheless, rare. The Department of Public Health had noted "widespread apathy or even opposition" to the serious considera-tion of non-European health issues. Gluckman and his commission wanted to reverse that history and they wanted to do so quickly. They no longer had the patience that characterized the 1936 Collie report on national health insurance: "with tactful administration and sympathetic treatment by medical officers genuinely interested in the life and customs of the native people, there is no doubt that the methods of western medical science will in the end prevail to the immense betterment of the native population."[18] Characteristic of the times, Gluckman's tone, employing words like "drastic" and "desperate," was more urgent.

The Gluckman plan proposed that the government levy a health tax on all South Africans according to their means, so that a preventive health service would be available to everyone. No one was to be excluded, a virtually revo-lutionary proposal. Such a preventive scheme was preferable to a curative one because "unless there were to be drastic reforms in the nutrition, housing and health education and recreation of the people, the mere provision of more 'doctoring' would not lead to any real improvement in the public health." Gluckman said the commission learned that nutrition "was a field so broad and so interwoven with every phase of modern life that no single approach can, by itself, prove effective." Malnutrition was, in Gluckman's case, a means of getting at the broader issues of national health. Within a few months of the report's completion, Smuts responded by rejecting the health tax as financially impractical, and dismissed central state control as interfering with the consti-tutional rights of the provinces. The plan, he said, was "idealistic and imprac-ticable." As Shula Marks and Neil Andersson have observed, the plan may genuinely have "exceeded the capacity of the political economy, which was still so heavily dependent on the primary sectors of farming and mining."[19]

The sense of innovation and urgency also characterized wartime efforts to plan for reconstructing state structures after the war. In 1942, Smuts appointed the Social and Economic Planning Council with the mandate to make admin-istration more rational and efficient. As Ivan Evans has observed, its reports were part of a comprehensive modernizing project, one shared by many gov-ernments at the time and one that should not be reduced to "devious strate-gies formulated by state and capital to rationalize the 'superexploitation' of blacks." In 1944 the council's report on social security appeared, inspired by the international movement to achieve "freedom from want." It called the cur-rent level of pauper rations "below minimum subsistence needs." It predicted that school meals and food subsidies, then in their infancy, "must in time become of considerable importance in view of the high food prices in the Union and the seriousness of malnutrition." In a single phrase tucked into a paragraph on the reserves, the council's 1944 report noted that Africans needed more land. Flirting with Soviet-style solutions as Douglas Smit had done, the authors suggested collective farming experiments in the reserves. They also explicitly rejected ignorance as the "dominating" cause of malnutrition "in urban areas, amongst rural employees, small farmers and Reserve Natives," naming instead "inadequate family incomes relative to the price of necessities."[20]

No doubt alarming to a tax-wary electorate was their call for "a redistribution of income, not only from the wealthy but also from the middle and better paid working classes, in favour of those in primary need." The council members themselves thought the social security scheme would reduce future capital supplies to a dangerously low level, so "[t]he only possible solution is that production per head be raised sufficiently by unremitting effort." Hofmeyr, the minister of finance as well as education, agreed, specifying that national income would have to increase 50 percent in order to support such an ambitious plan.[21]

Among the dangers to the idealistic plans of wartime was the potentially explosive power of newly politicized populations, Afrikaner and African, already signifying their disapproval of a vision of South Africa's future defined simply in terms of social security for all. Speaking in parliament in 1944 on behalf of the National party, J. G. Strijdom objected to providing old-age pensions for Africans while there were still poor whites. African nationalists, on the other hand, were expressing a more activist idea of their role in postwar South Africa than the concept of welfare suggests. Responding in the Natives Representative Council to Hofmeyr's 1946 budget, the African nationalist Z. K. Matthews said it ignored "the burning questions of the day" such as pass laws, the color bar, and political rights.[22] None of these issues could be addressed by the National Nutrition Council (NNC), a body that epitomized the highest hopes of the 1940s that hunger might be ended.

When the minister of public health, H. G. Lawrence, introduced a bill into the House of Assembly in June 1940 to set up the NNC, he was warmly welcomed "by all sides." The new council's function was "to investigate and report to the Minister of Public Health, upon all matters relating, directly or indirectly, to the prevention of malnutrition in and improvement of the diet of the inhabitants of the Union." This nonpartisan effort was addressed to the needs of all the young, rather than to any particular group, as the authors of the bill signified by naming the "inhabitants" rather than the citizens of the Union. Lawrence acknowledged that the initial impulse to found the council had come from overseas, that is, from the League of Nations in 1935 when it recommended establishment of such bodies. Its creation was a source of pride to one of its members, J. M. Latsky, the full-time nutrition officer in the Department of Public Health, who wrote in 1944: "I believe that the Council is the largest permanent statutory body which has ever been created in this country for a single purpose. Indeed, I am not aware of a larger permanent body in existence anywhere in the world which has been established for the sole purpose of championing the cause of nutrition. I have reason to believe that, among the United Nations, the National Nutrition Council of South Africa is regarded as a national example and is highly thought of."[23]

Like Henry Gluckman's national health service, the eighty-three-member council was designed to achieve a "coordinated approach" advising the government on how to prevent malnutrition and improve the diet of all South Africans. It comprised a war committee to give advice on feeding the Union Defense Force, as well as committees devoted to research, agriculture and economics, and education and propaganda. Its members were scientific and lay experts from different disciplines intent both on pooling all available knowledge and on launching new investigations. They included many of the men whose work produced the malnutrition syndrome: the biochemist F. W. Fox; J. F. Brock; the head of the SAIMR, E. H. Cluver; the former secretary for native affairs J. F. Herbst; Henry Gluckman; two former members of the Carnegie poor white commission, E. G. Malherbe and J. F. W. Grosskopf; as well as "the highest officials of the social service departments of the state, Health, Agriculture, Native Affairs, Labour, and Social Welfare, and experts from the universities and other scientific institutions."[24] In addition, L. S. Williams, the mine medical officer then working on improving African mine rations, advised the war emergency committee on rations for non-Europeans in the army. If the ideas about African hunger that experts had been publicizing throughout this book were to have any impact on people's lives, it was likely to be through this body.

The council's first reports warned that the country's nutritional situation was one of "extreme gravity," its definition of risk embracing all those who lived within its borders. Most surveys, it swore, had under- rather than over-estimated the problem. Money should be spent on a "unified national health policy" and should include the teaching of preventive medicine, another sign that Gluckman's ideas had gained favor on the council.[25] Other comprehensive recommendations included free meals for certain classes of schoolchildren, availability of foods at sufficiently low prices, and the distribution of surplus food to poor sections of the community. The council recommended that the Department of Social Welfare be named the sole distributing agent for agricultural surpluses and that the Citrus Board, in particular, be asked to donate its surplus oranges to the poor. The council requested its propaganda committee to prepare an informational pamphlet on vegetables, asked the Department of Agriculture to give marketing advice to urban housewives, and instructed its own research committee to assess the adequacy of the country's milk supply and to investigate such ingenious new examples of fortified food as fish flour. Arguing that the position justified expenditure without limit was bound to alarm even those who were not fiscal conservatives.

The council's proposals, which it had no power to enact, merged new scientific insights with old concerns for South Africa's prosperity. Malnutrition was now understood to result from a multitude of factors, including disease, parasites, overcrowding, defective hygiene, insufficient sleep, and emotional and psychological maladjustment. It made sense to stress food, because "diet is the one factor which can be adequately controlled," and, of course, diet is a politically safer issue than housing or disease. The implications of the situation were alarming because, with South Africa sparsely populated, "manpower must be regarded as the greatest [national] asset."[26]

The researchers themselves maintained that their goals were not outlandish because the wartime government was already heavily engaged in economic planning through the various marketing boards it had constituted and through the subsidies it had applied to certain foods. They did not attack the boards but stressed that their own views should be represented. Dr. C. H. Neveling, an NNC member, deputy chairman of the National Marketing Council, and soon to be the secretary for agriculture, said the council had to formulate practicable proposals and stop passing ones that would have no effect. On the face of it, he was correct. The council did have a propensity to pronounce ideals, but there was another rationale. Whenever anyone talked of reforming the marketing boards, farmers' profits were at stake.

One inauspicious note was sounded by the council when it accepted that African health was linked to farming in the reserves. It supported the NAD's policy of vigorously restricting the numbers of African livestock and thereby reclaiming the land. Partly because Africans were "more amenable to restrictive legislation than Europeans," the council decided that "it should be a comparatively simple matter through Government or Native Trust guidance to improve the self-sufficiency of the Native in relation to his nutrition." Plowing African fields communally by tractor, for example, would allow African cows to be reserved for milk production. In addition, agricultural holdings might be set aside for Africans outside cities so that "the wage earner [would be able] to frequently visit his family [living on those farm plots]."[27] The NNC was thus tacitly accepting the doctrine that Africans would live in town only

as long as they were employed there. It was also retaining the focus on the
"cattle complex" as if it were the cause of rural African hunger, and as if the
cure must be rural.

The council was caught in a further bind: it was devising some foods that
its target population disliked and that its own research revealed were unlikely
to cure malnutrition. Only occasionally did council members discuss African
food preferences, and then they expressed frustration with African resistance
to their guidance. In 1944, for example, Africans were refusing to buy a new,
improved type of mealie meal in which white and yellow mealies were mixed,
with yeast and soya bean meal added, and the germ and bran left in. Calling
this mixture "cattle food," African consumers preferred to buy mealies whole
and grind them themselves. One perplexing attribute of this thwarted scheme
is the slight advantage that even the council members believed could be derived
from the yellow maize. Fox said it was only "somewhat" better nutritionally
than white maize, and Dr. D. Haylett of the University of Pretoria's Agricultural Research Institute called its value "small." The point was to increase
Africans' intake of vitamin A as a defense against eye disease. Meanwhile, Dr.
Joseph Gillman of the University of the Witwatersrand Medical School, who
was conducting tests on laboratory rats, discovered that the addition of a single vitamin to a poor diet was likely to undermine other aspects of the animal's
health.[28] For rats as for humans, a balanced diet was the best preventive. His
findings were interpreted to mean Africans needed to be taught to eat in a balanced way.

In 1952 the NNC issued its last report, its disheartened tones offering a stark
contrast to the grand hopes of its founding just over a decade earlier. The
report began by emphasizing the council's advisory role and its lack of responsibility for implementation. Its members must have been acutely aware of its
ineffectiveness. In 1944, for example, they had even had to sit through a meeting presided over by three different chairmen as each one left for more important meetings. The minister of public health explicitly lamented the council's
flawed structure, undoubtedly a result of the wartime rush to set it up. The
council was deeply inhibited by its advisory status, reduced to naming problems more than formulating policy. The few suggestions it recently made had
been spurned. In deciding for the time being not to subsidize foodstuffs the
government had in 1950 explicitly rejected the NNC recommendation that the
state pay for enriching mealie meal. Further, the Department of Agriculture
had not "seen its way clear" to transfer the subsidy on white to brown bread.
Other disappointments stemmed from the apparent intractability of South
African poverty: improved milling was unlikely to ensure a robust diet because
"maize meal was still a poor food" if it constituted nearly the entirety of some-

one's diet; iodized salt was unlikely to reach the poor who chose unrefined salt instead, because it was cheaper.

What then is the significance of the NNC? The council's brief career illustrates the inclusive impulse of wartime idealism. Its minutes also show what the times to come would reveal as flaws in its collective thinking: it linked African health with farming; it treated black and white health separately; it had no power like that of white farmers. It could only tinker with the details of inequality.

Denial of Responsibility for African Hunger

The 1948 elections brought the National party (NP) to power with a small majority of seats in parliament. Its electoral vulnerability—most whites in big cities had voted for the United party (UP)—meant that it would spend its first four years in power trying to broaden its appeal for the next election. Because white farmers formed an important part of the NP's constituency one of the party's main tasks was to help channel more labor onto commercial farms. This meant trying, unsuccessfully as it turned out, to get urban employers to hire first Africans who were already living in town. It also meant ignoring the development of the reserves in any vigorous way, so that, in consequence, peasants would be obliged to become labor migrants, whereupon state labor bureaus would divide them between urban and rural employers. To appeal to urban voters, the party tried to keep spending on urban native administration to a minimum and to devise no development plans that required tapping white taxpayers' moneys. As Deborah Posel has argued, through most of the 1950s this electoral dilemma was coupled with an internal debate among party members about the desirability of complete, in contrast with partial, economic segregation between the races; as a result, there was, initially, no grand plan governing the implementation of apartheid, only a unanimous commitment among NP members to the principle of political segregation. This stand contrasted with the UP's "middle way." Inheritors of anti-Stallard opinion, UP supporters were more tolerant of Africans achieving limited political rights in town, though the party had long avoided addressing the question of who was to pay for the urban infrastructure that would allow them to live there.[29]

Ivan Evans has suggested that Jan Smuts was defeated at the polls in 1948 because he lacked a clear native policy: the urban wing of the NAD was in a state of bureaucratic confusion, and the rural wing was trapped in paternalist inertia. This pattern began to be overturned when Hendrik Verwoerd took over the department in 1950. He set out to provide all Africans with labor bureaus to help them find jobs and only those who had the right to live temporarily in town with affordable housing in planned locations. The NAD precisely calibrated the cost of providing this housing according to what its numerous socioeconomic surveys had divined about African spending capacity. Evans argues that the rapidity of their construction won the admiration of even liberal administrators. In the eyes of white taxpayers their merit must have included the fact that the construction cost them nothing. Social services apart from housing were to be limited by what Verwoerd called in 1955 the imperative to teach Africans "how to take responsibility for themselves. . . . The government has moved away from days of spoonfeeding the Native."[30] With the single exception of its housing policy, the official ethos of the apartheid era was devoted to denying that the state had responsibility for African urban welfare.

The Assault on School Feeding

In 1935 European, Indian, and Coloured schoolchildren had begun receiving government-subsidized milk and cheese, the result of overproduction in the dairy industry, but African schoolchildren had to wait until 1943 to receive milk and butter donated by the South African government. Before then, certain African schools consumed food provided by ad hoc local charities. Schools in the area around Alice in the eastern Cape in 1937, for example, got milk, vegetables, and fruit from nearby South African Native Trust farms (bought by the state to enlarge the African reserves under the 1936 Natives Trust and Land Act). Dr. MacVicar, the head of the local hospital, was convinced that such donations improved the health of local children, because he had observed his mission feeding nearly 100 poor children since 1924. Fear of tuberculosis had provoked many of these early attempts to ensure that African schoolchildren were well fed, and milk was commonly seen as the best defense. In a similar local effort, the citizens of East London in 1940 began to send £675 a year to feed "520 small Native children" in its two locations or townships, selected according to whether they were likely to be tubercular or were demonstrably "semi-starved."[31]

These efforts bore a strong resemblance to feeding programs in American schools from about 1912 until the depression. In the United States, too, the initial impulse had come from local philanthropists who, alarmed by reports of a great malnutrition crisis, footed the bills in selected cities. In 1936, the federal government, through the Works Progress Administration (WPA), began to provide cooks and helpers to school feeding programs, though not food or money. Two of President Franklin D. Roosevelt's chief advisers, Henry Wallace, the secretary of agriculture, and Harry Hopkins, soon to be the secretary of commerce, favored treating hunger with work relief rather than donations and involving state and local as opposed to the federal government. Farmers and food retailers opposed free food handouts to the poor, but after World War II began the Department of Agriculture overruled this long-standing resistance and started providing to schools surplus food purchased from farmers unable to sell their produce on the open market at a good price. The history of school feeding in South Africa, similar in many ways to the American case, particularly in terms of the government's response to farmers' needs, indicates that social policies about poverty and welfare were not influenced by racism alone.

As in the case of the NNC, the school feeding idea had been adopted in South Africa in a rush of optimism but with little apparent forethought about how it would operate. As a result the conditions of the scheme were chaotic because it lacked staff and sufficient preparation. The 1943 feeding scheme for African schoolchildren in South Africa was modest. While the Union Treasury did pay the full cost of African schoolchildren's meals, the state contributed a larger amount of money to each European child (six pence per child daily) than to each African (two pence per child daily). Similarly, Coloured and Asian children received less milk, fruit, and vegetables than European children. But even this differential level of funding provoked parliamentary concern about the rising costs borne by white taxpayers. The NP opposed the scheme from its inception, offering the following arguments: it was unfair to deny food to the majority who did not attend school; children were seen taking food home from schools; and schools were reported to be empty on nonfood days.[32] When the Nationalists won the 1948 elections they were in a position to act on these concerns, and they formed a committee to report the next year on school feeding. In the meantime, no new schools were to be added to the existing scheme, a decision that excluded schools in the new townships now mushrooming around South Africa's cities.

The committee's 1949 report on school feeding managed to straddle two points of view while giving greater weight to the negative. It admitted that the scheme was necessary, due to the "deterioration" of African physiques, but resisted it on the grounds that it reduced parental responsibility and incurred "state pauperism," the common expression for dependence. It asked "how long the little over two million of the European population will be able to carry the responsibility for the development of the approximately nine million of the Bantu population." Echoing NP complaints that had greeted the inception of the program six years earlier, the minister of education observed during the parliamentary debates that the scheme was trying to bring about improvements "at the expense of the European taxpayer [and] must be counteracted because it fails to observe the important educational principle of self-help and creates the danger that the Bantu community may become accustomed to the dole system." Since government currently had no means of controlling spending on the scheme, the report recommended setting a limit of £1.2 million for the coming fiscal year, the expense to be balanced by withdrawing equipment grants from African schools. The minister of education, A. J. Stals, told parliament this sum was "unduly high" and tightened up the provisions even further: native school feeding "would have to be limited and gradually decreased until eventually there would be nothing left."[33]

By cutting the school feeding program begun by the Smuts government in wartime, the new NP government incurred the wrath of liberals who gave impassioned speeches in the 1949 parliament. While Nationalist members of parliament failed to speak with the eloquence of their opponents during this particular debate, their stated opinions did starkly reveal that party thinking on the subject of African welfare was governed by dread of the tax burden. Also worrisome was the impact school feeding would have on the influx to the cities—and the loss of labor to white farmers—should the program be continued in urban areas alone. According to M.P. Labuschagne, "We farmers experience the drift of our Natives from the farms to the towns because there are no school facilities on the farms. They drift to the towns where they are loafing and where the children receive their gratis school-feeding."[34]

The Nationalists parted company with the UP not in its concern for cost and dependency, because Smuts shared these worries, but in their elaborate cultural rationale. Glossing, but hardly obscuring, their preoccupations with money and labor, the NP members stressed the welfare of African culture and the African psyche. Feeding would destroy self-esteem: "[You must not] destroy the native's self-respect," M.P. Maree argued. "If we continue to spoonfeed the Native we shall spoil him utterly," added member J. J. Serfontein. By maintaining that the state would stunt parents' sense of responsibility for their own children they ignored the fact that the two pence daily subsidy to African children was only one-third what the state spent on European schoolchildren's meals. This amount was spent mainly on milk and cheese in European schools, while African schools served starchy foods—bread and mealie products—and sugar and jam, because they were cheaper.[35]

Apartheid ideologues' devotion to ethnos theory emerged in statements warning that the "white man's food" was destroying the formerly balanced customary diet of Africans. To Nationalists, it was another example of Smuts's UP "destroying the Native's self-esteem and his national characteristics"; the "dole system . . . [was] crushing national characteristics under the cloak of philanthropy." And so, according to Dr. Hertzog, the "child of nature who moves away from his people and who thus also moves away from the balanced food of his people becomes sickly and decrepit. . . . [T]he children of the so-called half-baked Christian . . . [are] weak and sickly and shrunken." He queried whether Africans were hungry at all. Wasn't the problem, rather, that they were malnourished because they were squandering their incomes through "incorrect eating . . . [and] incorrect spending?" He went on, "the father and mother spend their money on gramophones and nice clothes rather than on the sound feeding of their children." He quoted a 1947 Johannesburg municipality survey saying that it lost £25,000 a year because the African—with a white loaf in one hand and sugar water in the other—was so ill-nourished he could not do the work of an ordinary man. Further, if Africans flocked to town because children were fed in schools there, the urban murder rate would rise. Whites could protect themselves against these various aspects of race deterioration only by offering medical and social welfare services to Africans in the reserves, and by making them pay for it.[36]

Given the force of these sentiments, it is not surprising that the 1950s saw a rapid scaling back of the state's involvement in feeding schoolchildren. In 1951 the government terminated its preschool feeding schemes in the Transkeian territories and cut back its subsidy for African, though not for European, school meals.[37] In 1953 the amount of money funding the scheme declined still further, but the heaviest blow was dealt in 1955 when schools were offered the choice of receiving state money for a feeding scheme or for extending their facilities so they could take in more pupils. The majority of school boards chose the latter alternative. In 1957 the minister of native affairs reported to parliament that the feeding scheme operated in only 20 percent of the school board areas, adding, "I have no doubt that without any pressure being brought to bear upon them they will also abandon it. Rather than giving this double benefit to a handful of children they would also prefer to see that the amount involved is spread out more fairly; in other words, to make room for new pupils." It would, he said, cost the government £3 million a year to provide for every African school child a meal costing three pence a day.[38] For this reason, in just over one decade the state had moved from accepting to denying responsibility for protecting African preschool and schoolchildren against malnutrition. The meliorists had elicited crude expressions of cultural essentialism from the Nationalists in the course of debating school feeding, and yet, the ideas underlying the references to "national characteristics" were not radically different from those of the UP: the dole bred dependency, and feeding all African schoolchildren would be prohibitively expensive.

Palliatives: Food Fortification, Subsidy, Surplus

The government's principal interventions in food markets into the 1960s were palliatives. They fell under three main categories—fortification, subsidy, the disposal of surplus. The Department of Nutrition, founded in 1951 and terminated in 1959, spent its energies devising fortified foods that consumers themselves often disliked.[39] Mealie meal and bread were the prime targets for fortification. Bremer bread, named after Minister of Health Karl Bremer, and introduced by the Department of Nutrition in 1952, was said to be nutritionally improved by the addition of groundnut flour, skim milk powder, calcium carbonate, and fat, while mealie meal was enriched and whitened with soya bean meal, milk powder, casein, food yeast, and calcium carbonate. Both foods were, in 1954, "improved" by the addition of a tasteless and colorless "fish flour." Though none of these foods appealed to African consumers, the department could not be deflected from its preoccupation with marketing, and in 1955 recommended the selling of milk in Coca-Cola–styled bottles so that Africans would buy it instead of mineral waters. By 1956 the Center for Scientific and Industrial Research reported that these enriching programs cost more than they were worth, and in 1959 a member of parliament noted this fact in parliament as the Department of Nutrition was being abolished.[40]

In 1960, Prime Minister Verwoerd announced that attention was going to be paid to providing more nutritious food for Africans, but subsequent governmental intervention amounted to mere exhortations to employers to provide one meal for their workers daily and to Africans to eat a better balanced diet.[41] At the time the government had failed to convince employers to hire, preferentially, Africans already living in the city, because the managers of the burgeoning manufacturing sector preferred the more docile labor force of persons newly arrived in town. In these circumstances, Verwoerd was in effect telling employers that, since they had persisted in ignoring the government's Urban Labour Preference Policy, the well-being and efficiency of their workers rested on their shoulders, not on the government.

Plans in the early 1960s to distribute surplus food were related to fears of losing agricultural markets more than to consumer need. South Africa's ability to export its surplus food began to founder in the 1960s for two reasons: commodity prices were declining on world markets, and countries were increasingly closing their doors against South African produce. In November 1961, Britain tried to protect its own producers by asking South Africa to cut back its export of subsidized dairy products to Britain. They were sold overseas at a loss because there was no market for them in South Africa. In the words of the SAIRR, "a large proportion of the population cannot afford . . . [butter and cheese], and many have as yet not developed a taste for them."[42] The situation was expected to worsen when Britain joined the Common Market. The Dairy Industry Control Board responded by dropping the consumer price of butter by 14 percent. In the hope that a local market could be developed in the townships the board even hired an African public relations officer to advertise the product.

Rather than redirecting the surplus of fruit and maize internally, as parliamentary critics had been urging the government to do since the late 1930s, farmers were given incentives to produce less. The maize surplus was attributed to its high guaranteed price, that is, farmers received a guaranteed price per bag through a price stabilization fund to which they made contributions. In 1961 this fund spent between 10 and 12 million rand on maize that was exported at a loss. To reduce production, the producer price of maize was lowered in 1961. The consumer price stayed the same. In 1963 the Maize Board sent a mission to the United States to study curbs on production and also to set up a marketing promotion department to boost domestic sales. The size of its surplus was so "huge" that South African Railways lacked the capacity to carry it to local ports for export. A similar story applied to the fruit industry. Because the return on exported fruit was five times higher than on fruit sold locally—one hundred cents as opposed to twenty cents a pocket—it was considered "bad economics" to sell citrus at home rather than plow it under as compost.[43] Thousands of pounds of surplus citrus fruits and bananas were therefore dumped to rot in early 1962.

Local charities were left to devise schemes for the needy. They did so by flying in the face of the NP's attempt in 1954 to ensure that welfare would be given and received within one's own group, while churches confined their ministry to spiritual matters.[44] In 1962 after the SAIRR failed to convince the government to buy and distribute farmers' surpluses of oranges and bananas, a group of concerned "personalities" formed a corporation to do just that on a private and nonprofit basis. They moved on to develop outlets and markets for other surplus food as well, selling food at prices lower than normal while covering their operating costs.

Eager to reassure businesses that it would not clash with their interests, the corporation, calling itself "Kupugani," a permutation of the Zulu word for "uplift yourself," proposed buying surpluses in bulk and distributing them to welfare and voluntary organizations, which would, in turn, sell them to undernourished people. The founders of Kupugani—Oluf Martiny, Carl Keyter, Neil Alcock—suggested that the price of mealie meal be dropped so that Africans could buy more protein-rich food with the savings. Health educators from the rural health center at Pholela were to be used as agents to distribute the foodstuffs and to teach nutritional lessons to the recipients. Kupugani also hoped to popularize foods so that new internal markets would be opened up, and it wanted to "run centralized kitchens in industrial areas where employers can obtain foods for their canteens and workers can buy food to take home to their families." In 1964 Kupugani, aided by Oxfam and the NRC, managed to pay the costs of transporting from the eastern Transvaal surplus fruit then being offered to charity by the Citrus Board. While the government was sufficiently impressed by the organization's successes that year to adopt its relief tactics during a drought in the northern Transvaal, it turned against Kupugani in 1965, attacking it as leftist and foreign-funded. When Kupugani failed, however, the cause was financial; some of its branches had simply gone bankrupt, according to Oluf Martiny, because it was hard to collect money from donors.[45]

Kwashiorkor: Data Collected and Suppressed

Nutritionists in South Africa and elsewhere called the 1950s "the protein decade," and the high profile given to kwashiorkor internationally was, in part, a result of research by eminent South African doctors. In addition, the Food and Agriculture Organization (FAO) of the United Nations called conferences on world hunger to focus attention on the consequences for children of living on a diet low in milk. This postwar fashion in understanding malnutrition had been given a substantial boost by the creation in 1949 of UNICEF for the purpose of distributing surplus American milk in the developing world, a logical sequel to the American policy of donating milk powder to help European schoolchildren emerge healthy from the ravages of World War II.

On September 12, 1962, the South African government, declaring the disease "notifiable," officially recognized the importance kwashiorkor had gained as a valuable indicator of overall nutritional status. All medical doctors now had to report to the state every case of kwashiorkor they found. In 1963, 5 white, 230 Coloured, and 7,170 African cases were identified.

The government responded to this crisis by subsidizing the distribution of fortified food and by supporting kwashiorkor research mainly through the new National Nutritional Research Institute (NNRI). These efforts led to milk distribution as a way of combating the disease. To extremely needy cases the department reluctantly gave the powder for free, noting that 100 percent subsidies would be unappreciated. The cost rose from R20,000 in 1962–1963 to R64,600 in 1967, when a further R250,000 was earmarked for distribution of powdered skimmed milk through Bantu Authorities, African administrators in the homelands. The other component of the government's anti-kwashiorkor campaign was the funding of research by the NNRI, part of the Center for Scientific and Industrial Research (CSIR), into deodorized fish flour and dry skimmed milk. The CSIR proved that one pound of skimmed milk powder a week was enough to prevent malnutrition. Kwashiorkor thus was a disease that could be prevented for fifteen cents a week. The alternative of not doing so was said to be a workforce of mentally retarded, listless, apathetic people with short attention spans. The South African Medical Association had urged urban employers at its annual conference in 1953 to emulate the rations served by the mining industry so their workers would be healthy and efficient.[46]

Shortly after notification of kwashiorkor became mandatory in 1962, the minister of health spoke in parliament in terms that captured the issues at stake. Malnutrition did not result, he said, from economic or socioeconomic factors, but from sociological ones. He explained that there was no famine or undernutrition in South Africa, but some malnutrition caused by Africans buying the wrong kind of food. He spoke in reply to a private member's motion requesting the government to provide nutritional advice to all South Africans, including those "Bantu who cling to old tribal customs, wrong eating habits and, in many cases, moral decline and undesirable living habits." The minister added, in tones whose repercussions would be felt within the decade, that the house should strongly condemn "any misrepresentations made to exploit these conditions."[47]

The minister of health's concern must be understood within the context of the resettlement program the government was then undertaking. From 1960, 3.5 million people began to be moved to live permanently in the homelands. They arrived in rural areas whose resources were already under strain. Doctors practicing there talked of the widespread malnutrition that resulted; the sheer press of the population rendered attempts at preventive medicine a "fairly academic" exercise.[48] It is clear that the government was simultaneously engaged in two mutually reinforcing exercises: it was resettling people in areas too impoverished and too densely populated to support their new populations, and it was collecting statistics on how many children were afflicted with protein malnutrition.

In 1968 the state withdrew its mandate to be notified of all kwashiorkor cases. Government officials offered many reasons for its decision. A spokesman for the minister of health called the requirement "extra work for medical practitioners," and said there was no need to continue counting since a general picture of the incidence had been gained. The head of nutritional services at the Department of Health, Dr. J. P. Kotze, said kwashiorkor would no longer be notifiable because doctors were not diagnosing it correctly and were inflating the numbers in order to boost their salaries. In any case, he added, by applying the same expectations to children of different races, some doctors paid too little attention to the possibly differing genetic potential of the different races; the Boston standard of normal child growth—measured by the ratio between height-weight and age—was based on white children and might not apply to blacks. Others by implication supported the end of notification because, even if the same growth potential applied to whites and blacks, equality in international food consumption was a receding ideal, given the world-wide shortage of protein-rich food and its escalating cost.[49] Statistics on the rate of kwashiorkor, which had been falling throughout the 1960s, were probably not very accurate; after all, the children who were well enough to walk or be carried to the doctor were not those who suffered most from kwashiorkor.

The government's sensitivity to criticism clearly lay at the back of its suppression of kwashiorkor statistics. J. D. L. Hansen reports that when the Afrikaans press labeled him a communist in 1960 for publicizing his findings, he adopted a policy of keeping out of politics and "just reporting facts" so that he could continue to receive financial support and to be listened to in committees; for example, in company with the secretary and minister for health, he was able to draw up a milk scheme for underweight children that parliament passed in 1961. The costs of confrontation were all too visible; when Brock publicly opposed the banning of a senior scientist, R. Hoffenberg, who had been attacking the government in the press and his lectures, Brock was immediately dropped from the Medical Research Council.[50] That the public record contains few explicitly political statements by such doctors cannot be read to mean that they endorsed government policy.

1959 was a watershed year in the South African government's official retreat from responsibility for African hunger because three events concurred: the Department of Nutrition and the health centers providing state-sponsored medical care in the reserves closed down, and the Bantustans became nominally self-governing. Then, in 1968, despite the abundant sense of urgency among medical authorities, the same year that the marketing act was repromulgated, kwashiorkor was declared no longer notifiable. Thus, 1968 looks like the nadir of the state's denial. And yet, despite such public disavowals of responsibility it is clear that costly official efforts to deal with African hunger continued. The Ministry of Finance was still pumping millions of rand into food subsidies; in 1967 it paid out R76 million to keep low the prices of bread, butter, maize, and fertilizer, a sum more than double the R34 million it had paid in 1958. Similarly, while in 1969 the Bantu Affairs Department acquired responsibility for health and hospital services in African rural areas, the bill would continue to be footed by the South African Treasury; in any case, the executive authority for health remained with the Department of Health.

Denial of all welfare responsibility for Africans may have been the stated logic of the apartheid state, but it was a goal impossible to achieve. Holy Cross Hospital, for example, was receiving free gifts of Pronutro (vitamin-enforced bran) from the government in the mid-1960s. The government was even offering to take over the hospital entirely in exchange for title to its land, an offer that led some hospital staff to admit grudgingly that, however much one may dislike apartheid, the government was at least recognizing its financial responsibility toward rural hospitals.[51] In another example of increasing largesse, the government donated massive aid to the drought-stricken northern Transvaal in 1964, breaking all its sworn rules: it distributed free food to schoolchildren, it gave out free milk powder, and it donated surplus citrus, bananas, and potatoes. Though a good deal of this kind of relief aid was distributed through Bantu Authorities, it was still a cost borne by the government in Pretoria. Even though the press had been kept out of the region in 1963 in order to avoid publicizing the crisis, the government's action proved that the total denial of welfare responsibility for poor Africans was simply not possible.

The apartheid state's efforts to divest itself of some responsibility for African welfare coexisted with these vestiges of paternalism. In 1955, for example, the inspector of native pensions began to weed out the undeserving poor from his rolls. His brief was to move around the Transkeian territories, striking off partially disabled workers, such as an epileptic who could still work as a herder despite his handicap, and a crippled man nicknamed "The Butterfly" who could nevertheless work on the surface of gold mines or at less strenuous jobs on the sugar estates. He also struck off the rolls many older men and women who were able to prepare fire belts or dig holes for tree planting, as well as people whom traders reported as owning more stock than they had admitted to him. Though the inspector, V. G. Vermeulen, may have been a particularly uncharitable man, he did reflect the fiscally conservative ethos of apartheid.[52] Three years later, the Lusikisiki paying officer began requiring all pensioners to report to him so that he could register as dead all who failed to show up in his office. Then, in 1959, people applying for pensions had to take a form to the dipping foreman so that the number of their stock could be accurately entered, and married applicants were required to report to the magistrate's office in the company of spouse and headman.

For nearly thirty years the hunger experts had been generating publicity that provoked the apartheid state to deny responsibility for, and sometimes even the existence of, African hunger. They had done so in the faith that South African paternalism was a real force for improving black people's lives. Many were distressed by the state's rejection of its paternalistic heritage, some transferring their efforts to the private sphere and some emigrating. And yet, the idea of Africans as a "non-scientific" people was close enough to the cultural essentialism of apartheid to allow many experts to continue to work within state structures that disappointed them in so many other ways.

Coercion

Without intending to do so, people who disparaged African agriculture were providing the state with a powerful rationale for forcing rural areas to modernize. Most of the hunger experts in this book blamed African malnutrition on African farming, particularly the overstocking that depleted the soil of nitrogen and allowed rainstorms to sweep topsoil into the sea. Only very occasionally did an expert observe that white farms were also overstocked, because this judgment simply did not fit the image of modernity lying at the back of most observers' minds. We have seen, for example, Drs. Fox, Orenstein, Stott, and Kark and all the HCH doctors of the 1950s identify poor soil science as a root of African nutritional suffering. Even a resolutely urban expert like Ray Phillips would join the cry. Several factors make the reduction of rural poverty to a question of soil erosion problematic: it was never clear how improved soil quality would benefit the rising numbers of landless people; it elevated one precondition of a good harvest—fertile soil—above the many other equally important factors such as rain, a plentiful labor force, sufficient acreage, and, increasingly, capital equipment such as irrigation pipes and tractors.

"Betterment" grew out of "reclamation" schemes of the 1930s devoted to arresting soil erosion as well as attacks on overstocking. By the 1940s it was the name given to the cluster of development policies that included contour plowing, culling herds, and the separation of grazing, residential, and arable plots. In time, the reserves were supposed to gain a modern infrastructure—water supplies, roads, bridges, dipping tanks, fodder banks, soil conservation works, and plantations. The precise details would be worked out for each locality by a local committee made up of administrative and agricultural officers, an engineer, a soil chemist, and "a Native member." Their goals were to plan rationally the future of the reserves and to save the land. More precisely, "one of the aims of agricultural development in the Bantu homelands is that every Bantu farmer should be able to produce enough to feed himself and his family throughout the year."[53]

By the early 1950s in the Transkei, the site of the following case study of apartheid-era rural coercion, the plan had mainly amounted to tough discipline, actual or threatened, of the following nature: canceling the land rights of people who did not adopt contour strips and soil reclamation measures, levying annual grazing fees on sheep and goats in order to cut down their numbers, removing stock that had been imported to the reserve without the permission of a man's father (if he was single), his headman, and the local magistrate. Some NAD officials frankly regarded shortages of food as catalysts of "progressive" or commercial change, saying, "The district [Lusikisiki] is inhabited by a very backward people, the majority of whom are quite satisfied to continue in the old way so long as they have sufficient food to eat."[54]

Deborah Posel has suggested that the principal function of state ideology is "to depict the exercise of power in terms which legitimise it as morally right."[55] She was referring to the way the myth of total separation of the races masked the apartheid regime's real purpose, to sustain the benefits of white domination. The same argument could be applied to "betterment." Using force against peasants could be justified as a means of improving African health and efficiency even if fundamentally driven by highly opportunistic imperatives: winning international approval for "decolonization," and allowing surplus African workers to be repatriated to the countryside from the cities where they could fall prey to African nationalism. State ideology, however, was not only a smokescreen camouflaging interests. It was powerful because it built on strongly held popular beliefs validated and partly shaped by scientists.

Betterment schemes drawn up by local planning committees began to be introduced in the Transkei in the late 1940s and, until 1959, they were executed with a curious mixture of tentativeness and force. Not all magistrates approved, some calling them a "farce" when they were introduced in areas that experienced no erosion or food shortages. The acting magistrate in Lusikisiki in 1948 derided the plans because maize was not in short supply during years of decent rainfall, the number of vegetable gardens was increasing, and there were "very few kraals where milk is not available for consumption by the children."[56] Nevertheless, in 1950, a betterment planner visited the area, decreeing that the coastal plain at Lambasi, a verdant grazing area, was in danger of erosion. He drew up rules forbidding any further settlement within eight miles of the coast and restricted access to the forests at Mtambalala and Lower Ntafufu to protect them from people seeking firewood and land to plow.[57]

One major reason for the tentative execution of "betterment" rules was the virulence with which local people reacted to these measures. In the 1950 Ntafufu case they spoke in public meetings of murdering rangers and of going to war against whites, in general, and white officials, in particular. One feisty sixty-year-old subheadman, Mgqinqo Pikani, showed his disrespect by baring his backside to the magistrate in a public meeting. Many of the people under threat of removal from the Lambasi plain announced that they simply would not move. The land was theirs, they said, and they had already plowed. "[S]tarving," they were having to watch other people eat green mealies while theirs rotted in the ground. This grievance became one of many against betterment that an angry crowd of peasants—so large they had to mass outside the crowded meeting room—delivered to the chief magistrate, J. Yates, on his unprecedented journey to Lusikisiki in 1950. Some of their complaints were purely political, as in criticisms of the arrogant behavior of the highly unpopular magistrate in Lusikisiki, A. W. Leppan. A few months later, the chief magistrate received an articulate letter of censure from one Daniel Tabalaza, a Lusikisiki teacher, accusing Leppan of attaching more importance to plant life and land matters than to human life. Back in his office in Umtata, Chief Magistrate Yates scribbled on a scrap of paper that he had nothing further to add to his previous announcements.[58] Such obliviousness could only have stoked the resentment of those peasants who already believed that the forest and coastal preservation efforts were the thin edge of the wedge of hunger and arbitrary rule.

Their protest was not in vain. It provoked the appointment in October 1950 of a new magistrate who found no evidence of erosion at Lambasi at all and who also decided that the boundaries of the forest reserves had been laid too far away from the wooded areas. An official admitted that the "primitive" type of agriculture did prevent soil from washing into streams. "In order to save face and the land," the administration watered down its proposals rather than jettison them entirely. Further settlement at Lambasi was prohibited, though those people already farming more than one mile away from the coastal escarpment could stay; the eight-mile boundary was discreetly dropped. Prosecutions for illegal settlement were to be suspended while an official inquiry into the land question took place.[59] In 1950 local opposition could still persuade the administration to compromise, a situation that would change radically after the Bantu Authorities were put in place in 1959.

The NAD's willingness to make these concessions to local opinion derived in part from its vestigial paternalism. During the 1950s many magistrates continued to seek to protect their wards from unfair practices. T. D. Ramsay, chief magistrate of the Transkei, for example, devoted a good deal of energy in 1956 to trying to exchange defective South African plow parts for better Canadian ones.[60] The NAD's compromising spirit was also a function of the fact that, prior to 1959, the NP government had not worked out its rural policy. In 1950 it appointed the Tomlinson Commission to devise one.

Ivan Evans summarized the commission's recommendations in terms of three major interdependent points: farmers who were capable of producing a subsistence income should be separated from those who were not; the land should be rehabilitated; the reserves should be industrialized so that nonfarmers could be employed. Only if all three conditions were fulfilled would the reserves truly become independent homelands and the stated apartheid ideal of total separation of the races be finally achieved. "In sum," Evans writes, "the program called for state intervention to create, within three decades, an economy and a class structure in the reserves that were typical of industrialized states."[61] The political will to erect this independent structure was missing. None of the prerequisites for development was fulfilled and the homelands continued to be simply labor reserves largely because no one except the idealists—like Eiselen and Tomlinson—among the apartheid theorists wanted them any other way.

The Tomlinson report, and the UP response to it, reflect white pride and fear in the mid-1950s. The overlap between the reactions of both political parties testifies to the report's widespread appeal. While the Nationalists alone raised the threat of miscegenation, leaders of both parties worried that the low level of white demographic growth would lead the race to be swamped. Both parties saw the development of the reserves as an antidote. Bantu "enlightenment," in the report's words, depended on jettisoning the cultural values that allowed men to ruin the land because they left the farming to women and instead focused their attention on cattle, thereby causing overstocking. "The real limiting factor," Tomlinson wrote, referring to the reclamation of the land, "is the Bantu himself." His "essential metamorphosis" was a sociological and psychological task entailing "very far reaching changes in their traditional ways of living and thinking." The UP was unwilling to criticize the modernization program for the reserves, even though betterment would be applied "with the people's consent and cooperation where possible and without this where necessary." On the contrary, the party went on record as willing to "give the fullest and most unstinted support to any reasonable, economically feasible steps that the Government might wish to take" to develop the reserves. J. G. N. Strauss, the UP leader, concurred that the reserves needed to be developed in order to support a larger black population, and he stated in parliament that "the main reason" for their current "agricultural backwardness"—their "undeveloped, overstocked and eroded [state] with millions living in poverty and ignorance"—was the system of communal land tenure.[62] Both parties were blaming African poverty on African culture.

In commenting on the report, Hendrik Verwoerd used patriarchal language to reject paternalistic claims on government. Rejecting land tenure reform, white industrial investment in the homelands, and the £100 million budget Tomlinson had proposed, he said Africans should no longer expect to be "spoon fed." In using those words he not only mocked the African poor as children, he was also keeping the language of rights at bay. It became communist, or deeply foreign to the western European heritage, to suggest that people should vote if they wrongly used the land, farmed inefficiently, and kept themselves at a low standard of health and living.[63] Verwoerd and other defenders of apartheid made scientific claims for the correctness of their program. They invoked sociology and psychology, as well as agronomy, to defend their analyses of what was wrong with the reserves. Citing the authority of these modern scientific disciplines did not set the Nationalists apart from their political opponents. NP programs for developing the reserves differed from their precursors less in their content than in the toughness of their execution.

If NP and UP attitudes to the reserves were so similar, how different was the liberal response? Using the SAIRR as an index, a striking degree of consensus is revealed. Before the report appeared, Hobart Houghton presented a paper at the SAIRR council's January 1955 meeting that could have come from

Tomlinson's own pen. "The whole tribal system of agriculture must go," he said, "and sound farming can only be expected after an enclosure movement analogous to that which transformed the manorial system in Britain into modern scientific land utilization." The institute waited nine months before holding a national conference on the subject, and published only one paper given there. Because the paper was written by two Africans, it may signify the institute taking the political opinions of Africans more seriously than it had a decade earlier when, as we have seen, Hoernle warned officials against taking the Alexandra stand holders seriously. When Leo Marquard gave his presidential address in 1958, he decried the boundary thinking inherent in the plan, but not the nonconsultative social engineering that rehabilitation entailed.[64] While these enfranchised parties to the discussions heralding the birth of the homelands may have prided themselves on finally getting around to thinking creatively about reserve development, they had not reached the point of thinking of African rural areas as other than inert and a problem, or its people as other than infinitely malleable. Within five years their blinders would be ripped off.

The state's resort to force began with a vengeance in 1959 when it first made efforts to establish the homelands. Verwoerd had been prime minister and head of the NP for one year and he brought the Broederbond, the apartheid think tank, into the forefront of political decision-making, including over NAD policy. The NP faction that rejected the strategy of trying to maintain white privilege by co-opting an urban African middle class now held power. All Africans were considered temporary visitors in town; the Stallardists had won. The time was ripe for the South African state to defend itself against the rising international condemnation of apartheid and against the threat of African nationalism. The NAD planned to elevate chiefs to the highest level of local political power, and this strategy meant that chiefs would have to enforce betterment.

The chiefs had to have their power enhanced, it was argued, if they were to play an effective role in "carrying out . . . regulations made for the improvement and betterment of the Native people, their land and their stock." As one of the most important architects of the "Government's policy of building up the power of the Chiefs and resuscitating the tribal system of administration," N. J. van Warmelo explained, the chiefs needed to be rescued from the corruption they had come to display under the colonial system. "In pre-European times," he argued, there had been no money and little opportunity for them to squander tribal property except on a "limited quantity of beer and victuals" for their court. Now, corrupted by money, they were even selling the tributary maize given to them for use by the entire tribe. Van Warmelo stressed that the remedy for the low popular opinion of chiefs was education through gradual extension to them of control over their treasuries and courts. A revitalized tribal system would meld the chieftainship with such modern innovations as a "livestock and maize register" to prevent personal appropriation. Apartheid planners gave their plans the most benevolent veneer by expressing the desire to "generally rais[e] the standard of living all round." The Bunga, one official suggested at a conference of magistrates, had undermined itself by having "done very little to counteract this opposition [to betterment], either by educating the people who elected them or by endeavouring to undertake and pay for the services themselves." Had not the time come, he wondered rhetorically, for a "more progressive system [than the Bunga] . . . which is understood by the Bantu because it would be in keeping with his tradition and eventually lead him to the achievement of his own national aims?"[65] The most basic subsistence issues were made to justify the birth of Bantu Authorities.

The Bunga, in its final days, before being encouraged to vote itself out of existence in 1955, articulated peasant fears that betterment was impoverishing them. Councillors argued that rehabilitation created "difficulties" by "compel[ling] people to reduce the numbers of their cattle whereas they used to be their source of living." The scheme provided no new industries and no more land. Reflecting the gravity of popular fears, councillors frequently raised the issue of food. Councillor Tyali, for example, wanted the rivers dammed so that "our commonages could be irrigated [and then] we could see the result of the production of milk by our cows." People feared that health services, like the provision of clean water from boreholes, would go only to districts accepting betterment. They spoke about this issue, like most associated with betterment, as a life-and-death matter. When Eiselen visited the Bunga in 1950, he heard apartheid rejected in terms reflecting with simple immediacy the perceived threats to livelihood: Councillor T. Ntintili warned that unless more land and industries were given to the Transkeian territories "[their people] will disappear from the face of the earth."[66] The government was taking more care, councillors often said, of the stock than the people, a common refrain for decades.

The final Bunga debates reveal both the administration's and the councillors' apocalyptic visions. They alluded frequently to the death of the land or of its people. While hunger was, of course, a common idiom for poverty, precisely what was at stake depended on the vantage point of the speaker. Officials spoke of betterment and its associated issues, such as the protection of the forests, as a matter for urgent salvation, while Africans spoke equally urgently of the death of their children. The two parties were using the production of food to talk about survival—of the land and of the "Bantu race"—as if Armageddon were approaching. A district officer saw Transkeians facing death by starvation "because they do not help themselves."[67] People were suffering from "starvation," councillors said, because the government was not buying grain at reasonable prices after harvest in July and not erecting grain elevators to store it until people needed to buy it back again in December. After losing his plow oxen either to culling or drought, a man would have to inspan his sons or his wife to the plow, some said. These needs were more pressing than terraced fields. Councillors used the word and concept of malnutrition as a rhetorical weapon in their struggle to divert official attention from the future of the soil and to focus it on their poverty instead.

Confronted with these pleas, officials replied tersely and negatively. The director of food supplies and distribution rejected requests to subsidize more foodstuffs (beans, fruit, coffee, tea) by stating that staples, such as margarine, were "already subsidised"; their cost was "very reasonable," especially in light of the "higher income in wages." Furthermore, new experiments were revealing ways of fortifying staples like mealie meal, and these would be passed on to consumers at no extra cost. Some councillors buttressed their pleas for welfare by agreeing that Africans were to blame for their own malnutrition, but they, too, were rebuffed. When one councillor asked for an inquiry into the increased infant mortality rate among Africans in the reserves "through malnutrition and ignorance," he was told one year later by the Executive Council of the Bunga that his request contained its own answer. The only solutions were increased production and consumption of milk, vegetables, and fruit, and these could be achieved through "soil conservation, reduction of over-stocking, afforestation and improvement of agriculture." The district surgeon of Flagstaff bluntly reflected the idea of rural African culture that lay behind these policies: he attributed the high rate of fatal cases of malnutrition to the "ignorance of the local population," which was "truly fantastic," a judgment that concurred with the now dominant official sentiment that malnutrition was "due to unbalanced diet not shortage of food."[68]

Popular outrage in Pondoland crested early in 1960 in a peasant movement now called the Pondoland Revolt. Its causes lay explicitly in resentment against betterment and the imposition of Bantu Authorities. They probably also lay, as Clifton Crais has argued, in the "moral panic" betterment caused by making it harder to control the movement of strangers who might be witches or stock thieves or both.[69] In diverse parts of the region governed by the paramount chief from his Great Place at Qaukeni men had been meeting on hills for several months in late 1959 and early 1960 to discuss rehabilitation and the paramount's legitimacy. Each group would send a couple of men with remarkably good memories to neighboring hills to report their discussions and listen to others. A lively regional network was set up. The Lambasi people brought news to an area called the Vlei about being cheated of their land to make room for a sisal development project, noting that the district magistrate, J. Fenwick, seemed not only indifferent to their fears, but cruel. They believed that Fenwick wanted to provoke a local fight to assert his dominance, and also to bait people so that the police could justify opening fire on them.

Some men broadened their critique to "the white man must go." Bizana, where the movement began, had helped people articulate their grievances by drawing attention to the way Bantu Authorities "threw" laws at people. Botha Sigcau, never a popular paramount, was seen as a fat and lazy collaborator, arriving in a village in his big car simply to accept a gift of meat and then leave.[70] They targeted men they considered guilty of abetting and profiting financially from the distress of their fellow Amampondo. After attacking two of Sigcau's "spies" the rebels gathered in the protective hollow of Ngouza Hill on the morning of June 6, 1960, to discuss their next move. They were soon surrounded by armed police who had arrived by truck and helicopter; ignoring a white cloth someone had hung from a stick and planted in an anthill, the police fired, and the crowd scattered. More than a dozen men lay dead in the grass. Thirteen wounded men were treated at Holy Cross Hospital.[71]

Pondo resentment had been provoked by the intrusive social engineering that affected them simultaneously at the levels of political life and subsistence. Their stated grievances show that they recognized corruption had spread farther than one chief. The police were taking "our fowls, our eggs and our food." Headmen assigned to try court cases and allocate land were pocketing court fines and fees without accounting for them. They were even selling kraal sites; one man cited four sheep and ten shillings as the going price for land, leading another Mpondo to exclaim in outrage, "We have to buy God's grass and wood."[72] The men of the anti–Bantu Authorities movement calling itself "Intaba" frequently accused the tribal authorities who supported reclamation and rehabilitation of "selling the country." Their metaphors were appropriately basic: "the Bantu Authorities is like a cow with some milk—they say that Gladwin should not be able to milk this cow." Their actions also expressed subsistence issues. When three "kraals" belonging to Gladwin Sigcau were burned, the rebels took care not to fire the hut where the family's food was stored.[73] A similarly focused concept of precisely who needed to be punished, and why, was apparent in the relations between the men of Intaba and traders. Those shopkeepers who contributed money to the resistance kept their customers, but those who refused or traded with soldiers found their shops boycotted. "We even boycotted shops we had grown up with," one man remembered.[74] Intaba asked rich Amampondo farmers to pay money to the movement in order to avoid having their homes burned. Poor people were never singled out.

Many people linked the local issues to national ones by saying, for example, "the government was using the chiefs as a ladder to reach us." Some believed they were donating money to "send people to Ghana and they will employ the services of an attorney, who will come to South Africa and speak to the

Government, so that the native policy should be put right and the people set free. . . . The whole African continent is moving." As one former teacher put it, "All the unrest in Pondoland today has been brought about by the Acts of the Government."[75]

Unlike the Pondoland disturbances of 1950 the state responded in 1960 with a vengeance, seeing Pondo political mobilization as potentially damaging the grand plan of homeland development. The government presented the violence as essentially conservative, blaming the deaths at Ngouza Hill on "tribal" infighting, that is, between followers of two rival claimants of the chieftainship. However complicated the motives of the men involved in the Pondoland revolt really were, the government's response, like its shooting of pass protestors at Sharpeville the same year, was ferocious. It divested the government of any vestigial claims to have benign intentions. It helped to destroy the idea that the causes and cures of African poverty were apolitical.

Conclusion

The apartheid state used science as its handmaiden. It asserted the right to engineer the future of South African society on the basis that its officials knew how farming should be scientifically managed and how social need and services should be scientifically measured and provided. NP planners showed a reverence for numbers and an unquestioned faith in their ability to put people into categories. They represented the pinnacle of pride in modern science that had been building over the course of the twentieth century and that was particularly intense in the aftermath of World War II. It is conventional to blame the coercive policies of apartheid on these ideologues, but closer scrutiny of the ways they justified their acts reveals ideological roots that lay deeper in time than 1948. The malnutrition syndrome, for example, had played its part in preparing the ideological ground for the evolution of segregationist attitudes toward Africans into the institutions of apartheid. It did so by propagating an image of an ignorant, nonscientific Africa that dominated popular attitudes by the 1950s and that helped accommodate even non-NP supporters to the policies of apartheid.

Under apartheid, state paternalism was to be focused exclusively in rural areas, and it was made as scientific as number-wielding bureaucrats could make it. Official claims of benevolence did not disappear entirely, though they were sorely tested by the postwar crescendo of African need and political demands. The problem of African social suffering was too pressing to go away and, as it and African protest grew, so did the level of ferocity with which officials greeted it. Again, this reaction derived no exclusive inspiration from apartheid or the NP. Scientific paternalism of the 1950s and 1960s grew also from the failure of the more personal NAD tradition of paternalism to keep up with the demands placed upon it. This modern, postwar paternalism may have appeared new, but it was based on the same judgments of rural African culture that, in the guise of the malnutrition syndrome, had animated its predecessor: that Africans were essentially rural folk, and did not know how to farm.

Apartheid policies derived from many diverse quarters. Supporters of the NP worried about the cost of implementing the high social ideals that had been born during World War II. They were reluctant to attack one of the party's key constituencies, the white farmers whose marketing boards made food so expensive in South Africa. And, of course, visceral fear and hatred of black people did characterize many adherents of the party. The policies of apartheid derived not only from these readily identifiable and now infamous origins but from professional agendas and popular perceptions of the country's public health problems as well. Even people who did not support the NP could be reconciled to some of its policies because of stories they believed about the African past and culture and about their own identity. Apartheid represents the flowering of scientistic ideology. Support for it did not derive simply from state interests and directives.

The hubris of high modernism suffused politics and administration in the 1950s and 1960s. Pride in Western technological and scientific achievement was undermining even the limited respect for African culture that had existed earlier in the century. The hunger experts thus possessed an ambiguous heritage. They successfully made public and defined African social suffering. Those experts who linked African health to the reserves, denigrated African farming, and failed to publicize points of view from among the suffering were also displaying the pride that helped suffuse the state with such draconian energies.

Epilogue

The Heritage of Disrespect

Kwaf' igul' elinamasi. (The calabash with sour milk is broken.)

Zulu proverb

"THE CALABASH WITH SOUR MILK is broken," goes a Zulu proverb expressing misfortune. This adage could also be understood historically, as an assertion that southern Africans lost their preindustrial way of life. They were no longer eating with the old spoon, to paraphrase another saying that conveys a sense of viscerally significant social change. The late South African artist Thami Mnyele sought to capture this sense of irrevocable transformation in his drawing *Things Fall Apart;* a cooking vessel has slipped from a woman's grasp, and she is looking with shock at the impending and irreversible damage. Perhaps she was sensing that her world would be turned upside down, and that oxymorons—like "starving on a full stomach"—would become the order of the day. What neither Mnyele's drawing nor the proverbs capture is black people's inventive adoption of new ways of working and living, including eating, that were part of the sea change in South African life brought about by its industrial revolution. This book has similarly downplayed the creative and entrepreneurial embrace of modernity that characterized black societies during the twentieth century, though the photographs heading each chapter were included to express that vitality.

We have focused, rather, on how African diet and hunger were interpreted by scientific authorities, that is, by people who made public knowledge and whose words could be used to support or attack policies and acts of state. Their ideas provided a lens for understanding how white supremacy was justified and undermined in modern South Africa.

Cultural racists, Paul Gilroy writes with reference to modern Britain, habitually regard black people as a problem and as unthinking victims. "The oscillation between black as problem and black as victim has become, today, the principal mechanism through which 'race' is pushed outside of history and into the realm of natural, inevitable events. . . . Racism rests on the ability to contain blacks in the present, to repress and to deny the past."[1] Gilroy dates this pattern to the late twentieth century. This South African case study has

11. Thami Mnyele, *Things Fall Apart,* 1977. (National Museum, Monuments and Art Gallery, Gaborone, Botswana)

shown cultural racism evolving over the course of the entire twentieth century, hard on the heels of increasingly discredited biological racism. It has confirmed Gilroy's observations by noting that cultural racism's key components were, first, paternalism or a tendency to see Africans as child-victims who needed to be aided by benign father figures and, secondly, the scientism that allowed African culture to be defined as the problem that led to African hunger. The power of cultural racism is apparent in its ability to inhibit expressions, and perhaps even sentiments, of white guilt that might otherwise have arisen from the contradiction between the inclusionary ethos of such Enlightenment values as liberty, equality, and fraternity, and their transgression in a setting of racial domination. Cultural racism succeeded in making modern black poverty appear to be a cultural trait rather than the result of political and economic policies.

We fail to come to terms with the protean resilience of racism if we associate it only with crude language and ideas originating, for the most part, in the nineteenth century. George Fredrickson has written that, in the case of the United States, the antislavery movement provoked a more elaborate rationale for white domination than had ever before existed: in the mid-nineteenth century scientific authorities were driven to depict Africans as a distinct and unequal species, an inferior race doomed to extinction; while they explained white degeneration as the result of vice and ignorance, they saw black frailties—like "savagery" and "licentiousness"—as inherent defects.[2] Traces of these formerly common European and American ideas could be found in modern South Africa even today, but the respectable or scientific rationale for white domination was being displaced, during the twentieth century, from physiognomy to culture. Biomedical research had indicated that the bodies of Europeans and Africans did not differ in any significant way. Poor whites and blacks could, therefore, be taught to catch up with "the march of civilisation."[3] Their progress would be limited, not by their bodies, but by their resistance to the lessons of modern science.

Prior to and during World War II many government officials argued that hunger would prevent African children from becoming "good citizens," words including black people in South Africa's political future, but the postwar years saw once subtle expressions of cultural racism—as in the chastising of improvident "children"—grow more harsh and exclusionary.[4] Old-fashioned paternalism was damaged by the rising numbers of the urban poor who were shifting to a political language of rights, as well as by rural opposition to betterment schemes. All-inclusive welfare statism could not replace paternalism as a legitimating ideology in a country where there was no heritage of a shared national moral economy and where the expense of guaranteeing social security to everyone would have been greater than the political system, and perhaps even the economy, could tolerate. The escalating cost of redressing black poverty and the increasing scientistic impatience with African culture were fostering crude expressions of cultural racism, even among people who had no affiliation with the NP and did not accept apartheid ideology. Leaders of both political parties, discussing the seminal Tomlinson report in the mid-1950s, agreed that the reserves had been ruined not by national policies but by

African customs like communal land tenure and the cattle complex; both argued that African rural areas must be developed to accommodate black people who would otherwise flood the cities. These development plans were connected to international intellectual currents and, in particular, to the post-war birth of modernization programs and theories. The ideology of African ignorance, growing for all the above reasons during the twentieth century, facilitated popular tolerance of apartheid.

Fear—of unwarranted expense, of miscegenation, of being swamped by people different from oneself, of losing control—obviously lies behind racist sentiment. Whites trying to remove Alexandra township from Johannesburg, for example, deployed all these arguments. Other psychological catalysts of racism are less easy to document, but the yearning to see oneself and one's culture as virtuous is a potent force in social life. As Adam Smith observed, "We desire both to be respectable and to be respected."[5] The power of denial is equally strong. Both tendencies encourage people to ignore the damage caused by their social actions and to develop elaborate stories justifying their privileges. Both give rise to the pride that, like fear, lies behind cultural racism. They help to explain why the adage "men make history but do not know the history they are making" is true.

Many whites felt sincere pride in the plenty and the luxury that Europe's particular historical circumstances had allowed it to achieve. They claimed those material standards as their birthright and as an index of their identity as whites in Africa. Similarly, they pointed to the achievements of modern science as a measure of their worth. They also believed in their own cultural benevolence, sometimes expressing this faith by such elliptical statements as, "Africans will break your heart [by failing to follow your example]." These prideful sentiments lay deep in many white South Africans, preceding their research and shaping their interpretations of what they found. With the best will in the world, authorities were often captive of the dominant mode of contemporary thinking about race and social suffering. Usually without intending to do so, they helped to elaborate an ideology of African ignorance, a more subtle form of discrimination than the crude expressions commonly associated with racism.

White cultural pride blinded many experts to the contradictions between their vision and what was actually happening. The image of white benevolence allowed NAD officials to veto African initiatives at the same time as they called Africans improvident. It also encouraged earnest reformers to advocate social welfare schemes in a system that manifestly would not support those schemes politically or economically. The power of the image of modern science allowed doctors and agronomists to assert its superiority and to enforce its lessons even when they demonstrably failed to cure sickness or develop agriculture. Many scientists mysteriously conflated care of the land with the health of the people.

Expert knowledge was neither uniform nor static, and debates among authorities did occur. We have seen Drs. Hansen and Brock enduring some ridicule and ostracism, respectively, for criticizing the impact of state policies in the 1960s and, thereafter, strategically redirecting or muting the political content of their public statements. Dissent within the loose fraternity of hunger researchers escalated, especially after 1960. For a while it continued to take the form of debating whether the first cause of African hunger lay in ignorance or poverty. For example, by arguing in the 1970s that "the main cause of malnutrition is the broken homes and destitution which often result from migrancy," the pediatrician Trudi Thomas provoked research into whether nutritional education was, in fact, more useful than "economic rehabilitation."[6] Similarly, by the early 1980s, Valley Trust had moved away from its founding nutritional ethos and was focusing more broadly on community development. Some politicized health professionals criticized researchers for lowering the official rate of malnutrition by redefining its clinical indices. Sometimes they believed the *South African Medical Journal* had rejected their articles for political reasons.[7] These rising tensions within the medical profession resulted in the formation in 1982 of NAMDA (National Medical and Dental Association), an organization counter to the more conservative South African Medical Association. By then, the battle to define the causes of African poverty had been joined by foreign funding agencies like the Carnegie Corporation of New York. The knowledge produced by the expert researchers had helped to strip the South African state of its tenuous claims to legitimacy both internationally and among broadening sectors of its own population.

Research about African hunger contributed to disturbing and, in some quarters, even destroying the possibility of faith in white benevolence. Pride in white technological and scientific achievement retained some reassuring explanatory force, as if it allowed people to say, "We rule because we know how to control nature." This pride was useful, because cultural essentialism, with its strong appeals to the corporate identity of the *volk,* failed to win over the section of the South African electorate made up of individualistic children of the Enlightenment. It is common today, for example, to hear English-speaking veterans explain that in the South African Defense Force only Afrikaner soldiers believed in what they were doing.

During the apartheid era, one problem troubling white supremacy was that, justified by cultural essentialism and scientific pride, it failed to address the need of whites to feel virtuous. South Africa's history since 1960 shows whites displaying decreasing faith in the virtue of their own dominance up to the point that they might well have joined the ancient Athenians in saying, "We rule because we can." This loss of confidence in the moral worth of white overrule is one reason why the transition to democracy was accomplished with so little bloodshed between 1990 and 1994. The sense that white supremacy was morally bankrupt was thereafter heightened by the revelations of the Truth and Reconciliation Commission, though the shock with which so many South Africans greeted its testimonies of official brutality against apartheid's opponents suggests that the myth of white benevolence had not completely died.

Cultural racism remains alive in the new South Africa, and it is likely to retain its ability to justify privilege, though on the basis of class rather than color. African culture was denigrated so forcefully that one can find vestiges of it in popular sentiments today. While a couple of city-center restaurants in Cape Town and Johannesburg began to feature African cuisine after the 1994 elections, people commonly refer dismissively to African food. I heard, for example, a young white art historian, certainly not a supporter of apartheid, deride the food rural Africans eat and the basic nutritional ignorance their diet reveals. I met in the South African Library an African university student from the Transkei who swore that he would eat only "quality" food like cultivated spinach, as opposed to the wild greens his parents had enjoyed. An agitated white medical doctor told me in a seminar, where I was presenting a draft of chapter one, that African and European food cultures had never shared a single trait in the past. These anecdotes do not expose any systematic doctrine. The force and longevity of their views probably derive from the fact that, diffuse and deeply felt, they are safe from the intrusions of critical thinking. The apartheid state may have lost legitimacy, partly as a result of the knowledge produced by experts in this book, but some of its rationales will take longer to die.

Since the ideology of African cultural ignorance does not seem to be entirely dead, it will continue to afflict poor rural folk: expertise will go on acting as a muffler and a blinder, preventing the privileged from hearing what the subordinate have to say. As this disrespect accompanies South Africa into the twenty-first century, it may trouble the new government's efforts to forge one nation from the divided past. While the question of cultural respect may matter more pressingly to the middle class than to peasants, antiwhite racists could gain political adherents by focusing on this denigration, especially if the professedly nonracial African National Congress government can show little evidence of raising poor South Africans' standards of living.

Dumo Baqwa, professor of community medicine at the University of Cape Town, has publicly lamented the heritage of disrespect. Introducing his talk on the state of health in the new South Africa, he leaned toward his American audience and summed up his view of South African history in the following words: "[After Africans were defeated militarily in the nineteenth century,] the history of the people was put outside the body of knowledge used for development." For a people to be "outside," he implied, was one of the real tragedies of the segregationist and apartheid eras. Whites considered the culture of Africans irrelevant to the problems of modern life. They dismissed African knowledge as outmoded and worthless, perhaps even dangerous. Denigrating African culture, they idealized their own.[8] They did so despite abundant evidence that in the realms of medicine and agriculture modern practices were not always superior to what they were replacing. Scientists' confidence and their actual successes gave them the power to convert people to faith in Western medicine and technology. (Dr. Xuma, for example, never defended traditional medicine and diet; and Steve Biko said, "because of the ability of the white culture to solve so many problems in the sphere of medicine . . . you tend to look at it as a superior culture."[9]) Western medicine and technology had the effect of squelching public support for prior or alternative points of view.

Baqwa is a member of the new wave of postapartheid medical experts who, like their predecessors, are driven to interpret disease and hunger as a commentary on the health and history of the body politic. A former member of the Black Consciousness movement, Baqwa reflects an Africanist perspective on that history. Like the artist Mnyele, who had embarked on a quest for a non-imitative African aesthetic, he is searching for an authentic African response to the problems of modernity. The work of both men reflects their anxiety to overturn the disrespect for African culture that has been one glaring heritage of South Africa's history in the twentieth century. Both would endorse the poet Mongane Serote's condemnation of apartheid-era mentality and laws intended

> to herd and pen people and mock them
> to mock them and to use them
> to use them
> like a pick[10]

Baqwa backed up his call to redress the mockery and the exclusion of Africans by proposing a new form of medical education, one that includes folk knowledge. Noting that nearly two-thirds of his patients consulted traditional healers, he stressed the importance of working creatively with the areas where the two healing systems—clinical and indigenous—overlapped, so that no one would be excluded. He urged that more medical anthropology be infused into the training of South African doctors. Such proposals, of course, demand vigorous efforts to discover what the best diviners and herbalists actually prescribed. As the anthropologist Harriet Ngubane has warned, "the neglect and scorn of traditional medicine" cannot be remedied by uncritical and romantic adoptions of the ways of the "self-appointed healers, including not a few charlatans" who have flourished, especially in towns. It goes without saying that traditional medicine often proves weaker than biomedicine, and no one is arguing for its atavistic adoption.[11] However, as Gilroy suggested, to suppress knowledge of its strengths is to deny the past, and cultural racism thrives on that suppression.

Baqwa was effectively proposing a return to the greater respect shown for African belief systems earlier in the twentieth century, during the times of A. T. Bryant and even Frank Drewe, than was apparent during the zenith of modernist hubris in the 1950s and 1960s. He was implying that the privileged citizens of the new South Africa, of whatever color, have to be more open to symbiosis and syncretism than they have been, especially since the middle of the twentieth century. If they remain closed to African culture, they help to sustain the long heritage of denigration. They run the risk of maintaining South Africa as a divided nation where the poorest remain vulnerable to the coercion that comes from disrespect.

Notes

Abbreviations

AHC	Alexandra Health Committee
Ann. Natal Mus.	*Annals of the Natal Museum*
BMJ	*British Medical Journal*
BNA	Botswana National Archives, Gaborone
CMT	chief magistrate of the Transkei
CNC	chief native commissioner
CT	Cape Town
DNL	director of native labor
DS	district surgeon
FAO/WHO	United Nations Food and Agriculture Organization/ World Health Organization
HCH	Holy Cross Hospital
IJAHS	*International Journal of African Historical Studies*
JAH	*Journal of African History*
JCAS	*Journal of Contemporary African Studies*
JSAS	*Journal of Southern African Studies*
KAB	Cape Provincial Archives Depot, Cape Town
KAIS	Komati Agricultural and Industrial Society
NAB	Natal Provincial Archives Depot, Pietermaritzburg
NAD	Native Affairs Department
NC	native commissioner
NEC	Native Economic Commission
NNC	National Nutrition Council
OFS	Orange Free State
P&P	*Past and Present*
PDL	poverty datum line
PMMOA	*Proceedings of the Mine Medical Officers Association*
RH	Rhodes House
RM	resident magistrate
SAB	South African National Archives Depot, Pretoria
SAHJ	*South African Historical Journal*
SAIMR	South African Institute of Medical Research
SAIRR	South African Institute of Race Relations
SAJE	*South African Journal of Economics*

SAJMS   *South African Journal of Medical Sciences*
 SAJS   *South African Journal of Science*
 SAL   National Library of South Africa, Cape Town
SAMJ   *South African Medical Journal*
 SAR   South African Railways
 SML   Sterling Memorial Library, Yale University
 SNA   secretary for native affairs
 SPG   Society for the Propagation of the Gospel
 TLC   Transvaal Labour Commission
 TMJ   *Transvaal Medical Journal*
 UCT   University of Cape Town
 VT   The Valley Trust, Botha's Hill, Natal
 Wits.   University of the Witwatersrand

Introduction

1. A. H. Keane, *The Boer States* (London, 1900), 73, quoted in Dubow, *Scientific Racism*, 71.

2. Dubow, *Scientific Racism*, 1. Barkan, *Retreat of Scientific Racism*. Barkan argues that scientific racism began to be repudiated in Britain and the United States before the rise of Nazism, due to changes in the sciences and also in the scientists; their ranks were being joined by outsiders like women and Jews who had egalitarian political convictions.

3. W. M. M. Eiselen quoted in Evans, *Bureaucracy and Race*, 229.

4. Scott, *Seeing like a State*, 89, 93.

5. The man was interviewed in the Transkei and was quoted in the report of J. Herbst, M. G. Apthorp, and F. C. Wilmot on "Starving or Under-nourished Native Children," to SNA, 30 May 1938, 22, Herbst Papers, UCT. The committee had been appointed by the SNA to report on "conditions existing in the various Native areas which have given rise to allegations of starvation and grave distress amongst the children attending schools."

6. Iliffe, *African Poor*, chap. 14.

7. Uday Mehta, "Liberal Strategies of Exclusion," in Cooper and Stoler, *Tensions of Empire*, 60.

8. Slack, *Poverty and Policy*, 17.

9. Headrick, *Tools of Empire*, 209.

10. Dubow, *Racial Segregation*, 180.

11. Evans, *Bureaucracy and Race*, ix.

12. Dubow, *Scientific Racism*, 291.

13. Carnegie Commission, *Poor White Problem*; Wilson and Ramphele, *Uprooting Poverty*.

14. Gelfand, *Livingstone*; Gann and Duignan, *Burden of Empire*, chap. 22.

15. Farley, *Bilharzia*; Turshen, *Disease in Tanzania*, 14; Mushingeh, "Disease and Medicine in Botswana"; Fetter, "Mines."

16. In 1933 the first person was successfully treated with ascorbic acid (synthesized vitamin C); in 1915 niacin was discovered to be the vitamin whose absence causes pellagra. Carpenter, *Protein and Energy*, 187; Carpenter, *Scurvy and Vitamin C;* McNeill and Wheeler, *Basic Nutrition and Malnutrition.*

17. Pacey and Payne, *Agricultural Development and Nutrition*, 25, 69. Sometimes the low intake of food is labeled *undernutrition* to distinguish it from a poorly balanced diet or malnutrition, but since the distinction tends to distract attention from the functional effects of a poor diet, it will not be used here. Roderick Floud, "Medicine and the Decline of Mortality: Indicators of Nutritonal Status," in Schofield, Reher, and Bideau, *Decline of Mortality*, 155.

18. Freund, *Insiders and Outsiders*, 40.

19. Packard, *White Plague, Black Labor*, 215.

20. Porter, *Greatest Benefit to Mankind*, 643.

21. McKeown, *Modern Rise of Population.*

22. Livi-Bacci, *Population and Nutrition*, chap. 2.

23. Post, *Food Shortage*, 28; Livi-Bacci, *Population and Nutrition*, 46–47.

24. The aphorism "Tell me what you eat, and I shall tell you what you are" was composed by J. A. Brillat-Savarin and adapted by Ludwig Feuerbach as "Der Mensch ist was er isst." Fisher's trans. of Brillat-Savarin's *Physiology of Taste*, 3, 5.

25. Roland Barthes, "Towards a Psychosociology of Contemporary Food Consumption," in Forster and Ranum, *Food and Drink in History*, 169.

26. Moore and Vaughan's *Cutting Down Trees* restudies data published mainly in Audrey Richards's *Land, Labour and Diet in Northern Rhodesia* (London, 1939).

27. Moore and Vaughan, *Cutting Down Trees*, xxiv; Arnold, *Colonizing the Body;* Comaroff and Comaroff, *Of Revelation and Revolution.*

28. Cooper and Stoler, *Tensions of Empire*, 10–11.

29. "The strong do what they have the power to do and the weak accept what they have the power to accept." Thucydides, *History of the Peloponnesian War*, book 5.

30. Gilroy, *"No Black in the Union Jack,"* 12.

1. European Cultural Pride

1. The quotes are James Stuart's words, spoken as he conversed with three African Christians in a Ladysmith hotel room in 1900 about the relative merits of European and African civilizations. Webb and Wright, *James Stuart Archive*, 1:258, 256.

2. Transvaal Indigency Commission, *Report*, 23.

3. A. L. Vanderplanck, Acting Principal of Fort Cox Agricultural School, Speech of Welcome to Visitors at Fort Cox on Women's Day, 25 Oct. 1941, SAIRR reel 4, 10.6, film 1044, SML.

4. Undersecretary for Native Affairs Fred Rodseth to SNA, CT, 12 Mar. 1946, SAIRR (AD 843) B3.10.1, Cullen Africana Library, Wits.

5. Harries, *Work, Culture and Identity*, 40, 125; Bheki Sikhakhane, personal communication.

6. Quoted in Montanari, *Culture of Food*, 36.

7. Geremek, *Poverty*, chap. 3; Camporesi, *Bread of Dreams*; Montanari, *Culture of Food*, 108–9.

8. Giulio Cesare Croce's *La sollecita et studiosa Academia de Golosi. Nella quale s'intendono tutte le loro leccardissime scienze* (Bologna, 1602), and Guiseppe Rosaccio's *Il Microcosmo* (1688), quoted in Camporesi, *Bread of Dreams*, 170.

9. Rousseau, *Discourse on the Origin of Inequality*, in *Basic Political Writings*, 42.

10. Brillat-Savarin, *Physiology of Taste*, 3.

11. He even attributed national characteristics to climate rather than to race; the Turks and the Italians, for example, were more choleric and vindictive than the English because they sweat a lot. Willich, *Lectures on Diet and Regimen*, 295.

12. Himmelfarb, *Idea of Poverty*, 366; Himmelfarb, *Poverty and Compassion*, introduction; Levenstein, *Revolution at the Table*.

13. Alberti, *Life and Customs of the Xhosa*, 22–26; Bleek, *Natal Diaries*, 61; John Ayliff, appendix to MacLean, *Kafir Laws and Customs*, 148–52; Mackenzie, *Austral Africa*, 1:29.

14. The revolutionaries' judgment was ironic in light of the fact that Mexican Indians had long before figured out how to soak their maize in lime juice to release its niacin and avoid coming down with pellagra. Becker, *Setting the Virgin on Fire*, 67; Sheldon, "Pounders of Beans."

15. Former Rhodesian prime minister Ian Smith memorably mentioned opera as one index of the superiority of European culture that Africans could never emulate or equal.

16. Goody, *Cooking, Cuisine, and Class*, 210–12; Levine, *Wax and Gold*, 157, 225.

17. These foods were consumed at wedding banquets of the prosperous in the northern Italian city of Piacenza in the late fourteenth century and were described in these words by one Giovanni de Mussis, quoted in Montanari, *Culture of Food*, 71–72.

18. Bourquin and Filter, *Paulina Dlamini*, 26, 28, 45.

19. Grigg, "Nutritional Transition," 252; Livi-Bacci, *Population and Nutrition*, 99; Mintz, *Sweetness and Power*, 198, 14.

20. "Wa z'enza ukuba abantu ba dhle, ba bone nje." H. Callaway, *Religious System of the Amazulu*, 17. Levine has noted that much Amharic verse imagery relates to eating and drinking (*Wax and Gold*, 225), whereas one Pedi proverb says more basically, "I love you as I love salt in my food" (quoted in Fox and Norwood Young, *Food from the Veld*, 44).

21. Montanari, *Culture of Food*, 94–95; Camporesi, *Bread of Dreams*, 80–81.

22. These words concern a Neapolitan famine in 1764. Camporesi, *Bread of Dreams*, 33.

23. Braudel, *Civilization and Capitalism*, 1:33; Grigg, *Dynamics of Agricultural Change*, 32–33. Wrigley notes that the seventeenth and eighteenth centuries in Britain were a period of "advanced organic economy" when population, nevertheless, continued to rise and fall in response to rising and falling food prices (*Continuity, Chance and Change*, 67). This fluctuation was not necessarily due to mortality but to changes in nuptiality and fertility as people adjusted their strictures on marriage to the availability of land and other resources; Laslett argues that age at marriage is a sensitive indicator of social conditions (*World We Have Lost*, 129).

24. Beinart, *Political Economy of Pondoland*, 11; Webb and Wright, *James Stuart Archive*, 2:277.

25. Laslett, 119.

26. Braudel, 78; Bonnassie, "Consommation d'aliments immondes," 1046–50.

27. Quoted in McKeown, *Modern Rise of Population*, 67.

28. Dyer, *Standards of Living*, chap. 6; R.-J. Bernard, "Peasant Diet in Eighteenth Century Gevaudan," in Forster and Forster, *European Diet*, 20.

29. European population had grown most dramatically during the following periods: 1100–1320, 1480–1640, 1750–1820. Grigg, *Transformation of Agriculture*, 64. See Livi-Bacci, *Population and Nutrition*, chap. 1.

30. Eldredge has argued in *A South African Kingdom* that the rather anomalous case of BaSotho export agriculture predated the appearance of the mines and even of missionaries, but was driven by long-standing needs for guns and horses as protection during the early nineteenth-century period of regional warfare, as well as for bridewealth cattle (147).

31. English charity law dates to Elizabethan poor-law statutes based on a royal commission finding that social unrest was caused by vagrancy and food scarcity. Geremek, *Poverty*, 165–67.

32. Slack, "Dearth and Social Policy."

33. Slack, *Poverty and Policy*, 8–14.

34. Olwen Hufton, "Social Conflict and the Grain Supply in Eighteenth-Century France," in Rotberg and Rabb, *Hunger and History*, 105–33.

35. One scholar has even suggested that, in at least one southern African society, rules governing the behavior of younger people changed when the society's resources were overtaxed by population growth and the fertility rate needed to be lowered: by postponing the marriage age of men and women, Zulu age regiments had the same depressing effect on fertility as British customs controlling age at marriage and procreation outside marriage. (Jeff Guy, "Ecological Factors in the Rise of Shaka and the Zulu Kingdom," in Marks and Atmore, *Economy and Society*, 116–17.) According to this interpretation, in those areas of southern Africa suffering from shortage of resources, rules governing the formation of households could be used to keep the population in line with the food supply.

36. Dyer, *Standards of Living*, 59; Livi-Bacci, *Population and Nutrition*, 92.

37. Walter and Schofield, *Famine, Disease and the Social Order*, 32.

38. Wrigley, *Continuity, Chance and Change*, 94; Braudel argues that meat consumption generally fell in Europe after 1550 until the mid-1800s because wages were dropping, and rising cereal prices encouraged farmers to convert their pastures into fields. *Civilization and Capitalism*, 1:194–99.

39. Grigg, *Transformation of Agriculture*, 38–39.

40. Wrigley, *Continuity, Chance and Change*, 32.

41. Livi-Bacci, *Population and Nutrition*, 97; Boserup, *Conditions of Agricultural Growth*.

42. Wrigley, *Continuity, Chance and Change*, chap. 3; Livi-Bacci, *Population and Nutrition*, 21–22.

43. Himmelfarb, *Idea of Poverty,* 18. She dates the industrial revolution circa 1760, adding, "For it was then that poverty was removed from nature and brought into the forefront of history."

44. Laslett notes there is no evidence that the infant mortality rate was higher in nineteenth-century England than under the Stuarts (*World We Have Lost,* 133).

45. The figures refer to 1848–1878, varying with reference to income, size of family, and aspirations. H. J. Teuteberg, "The General Relationship between Diet and Industrialization," in Forster and Forster, *European Diet,* 98. In 1960 the percentage had fallen to 35 percent. Braudel devised a chart illustrating that 72.7 percent of a Berlin mason's family budget was spent on food in 1800 (*Civilization and Capitalism,* 132). Shammas has compiled figures giving the percentage of English household expenditure devoted to diet from 1688 to 1978. For all households between 1688 and 1890 the figures move up and down between 50 percent and 75 percent; they reached a low of 35 percent in 1978 for the poorest category of household and 28 percent for all households. Thereafter a small rise began. (*Pre-Industrial Consumer,* 124–25.)

46. McManners, *Death and the Enlightenment,* 17.

47. Shammas, *Pre-Industrial Consumer,* 127. In late eighteenth-century Britain, a man's earnings were estimated to contribute about two-thirds of his household's total spending, while the difference was made up by other members' self-employment, secondary jobs, or parish poor rates.

48. Teuteberg, "Diet and Industrialization," 82; van Onselen, "Randlords and Rotgut, 1886–1903," in *History of the Witwatersrand,* 1:44–102; Mintz, *Sweetness and Power,* 196. Sugar began to become a commonplace rather than a luxury starting in 1650, especially in England. Mintz, *Sweetness and Power,* xxix.

49. Shammas, *Pre-Industrial Consumer,* 146.

50. McManners, *Death and the Enlightenment,* 20, 37–39; Bonnassie, "Consommation d'aliments immondes et cannibalisme," 1037. According to Dyer, English people in the later Middle Ages saw meat as contributing to their health and strength (*Standards of Living,* 64). In eighteenth-century France, for example, doctors commonly prescribed meat soup for convalescents and warned against immoderate eating. At the time, people generally gave great importance to proper digestion, some even tracing all human psychology to roots in the way bodily organs functioned.

51. McManners, *Death and the Enlightenment,* 19.

52. Carpenter, *Scurvy and Vitamin C,* 46.

53. Sen, *Poverty and Famines,* chap. 1.

54. The Natives' Land Act of 1913, as amended in 1936, set aside only 13 percent of South African land for the legitimate occupation of Africans.

55. Eberstadt, "Poverty in South Africa," 30. Grigg notes that the composition of diets changes with a rise in income: first more of a staple is consumed, then people shift to eat more of a preferred staple, and finally they choose more palatable and expensive food that is higher in protein. "Nutritional Transition," 247–61.

56. James, *Varieties of Religious Experience,* 491, 498.

2. Before the Land Was Lost

1. Turner was a medical officer employed by the Witwatersrand Native Labour Association. Turner, "Diet of South African Natives," 183.

2. Nelson Mandela speaking in his defense at the Rivonia Trial, in Benson, *The Sun Will Arise*, 20; Evidence of Mkando ka Dhlova, 14 Aug. 1902, in Webb and Wright, *James Stuart Archive*, 3:174.

3. J. P. Jessop, "The Ecological Setting," in Hammond-Tooke, *Bantu-Speaking Peoples*, 54.

4. Cranefield, *Science and Empire*.

5. The storage life of grain was highly variable and dependent on damp. When rain fell after a drought had cracked open the earth, water was likely to seep through the cracks and ruin the grain stored in underground pits in a matter of months. B. Mgudlwa, in United Transkeian Territories General Council, Proceedings, 18 Apr. 1945, 33.

6. Richard Harwin, MS, [1864?], private collection, Dr. Halley Stott. I am grateful to Dr. Stott for showing me this letter.

7. Vilakazi, *Zulu Transformations*, 6; Webb and Wright, *James Stuart Archive*, 1:119, 186; 4:49–58, 66. In addition, Zulu brothers who quarreled and sought to live with their followers apart from one another remained fairly free to settle where they wished for most of the nineteenth century; some moved to the valley where they acquired land by swearing allegiance to a chief there.

8. Bryant estimated that people ate about twenty-four meals with meat each year after they had domesticated pigs and fowls. Goat was ranked at the low end of the spectrum, slaughtered for visitors and for minor ancestral sacrifices. Bryant, *Zulu People*, 342, 346–47, 338–39.

9. Webb and Wright, *James Stuart Archive*, 1:99.

10. Fynn, *Diary*, 302; Krige, *Social System*, 68, 53, 56; H. Callaway, *Religious System of the Amazulu*, 181. The ability of anyone who was not the head of a village to cause a feast by simply dreaming about bullocks was limited by the custom of sending him to a diviner first to ensure that that was what the ancestors really wanted. Ibid., 174.

11. Bryant, *Zulu People*, 265–71; Malie, "Nyuswa Crops and Diet," VT, 25. Greens and vegetables were believed to upset the baby's stomach and cause diarrhea. Bryant, *Zulu People*, 286–89. Webb and Wright, *James Stuart Archive*, 4:336, 269.

12. Fynn, *Diary*, 289. According to an 1852 report, the number of huts per household in Pafana location ranged from two to thirty with an average of six; those with six huts had about twelve cattle and those with two or three huts rarely had any cattle at all. Commission Appointed to Inquire into the Past and Present State of the Kafirs in the District of Natal, *Proceedings*, 9. Krige, *Social System*, 47.

13. Webb and Wright, *James Stuart Archive*, 3:302. H. Callaway, *Religious System of the Amazulu*, 444. Elite households would have three threshing areas due to the size of their grain harvest. Krige, *Social System*, 44; Grout, *Zulu-land*, 104. A fire was burned underground to bake the walls hard, the grain was mixed with burnt aloe, and the pit

was lined with bitter-flavored grass to discourage pests. Fox and Norwood Young, *Food from the Veld,* 54.

14. Bleek, "Translation of Callaway," SAL, 51, 53.

15. Bryant, *Description of Native Foodstuffs.* According to Bryant, *Zulu People,* salt was obtained naturally (290). Bleek, *Natal Diaries,* 61 (27 June 1856); and Bleek, "Translation of Callaway," 9.

16. Fynn, *Diary,* 21, 92. Webb and Wright, *James Stuart Archive,* 1:129, 342. One recipe for famine food required the cook to pound and cook grass, the *ingcengce* plant (with berries), and the *uboqo* (like a sweet potato, with black roots; to be cut into pieces with a sharp-edged stone, dried in the sun, then mixed with curds). *Ingoni* grass was beaten, ground, and kneaded into a dough after its seeds had been beaten out and ground.

17. Samuelson, *Zululand,* 180–81. Even a king's messenger might then be only grudgingly entertained by a subordinate chief with a little milk, some corn, and no meat. Isaacs, *Travels and Adventures,* 1:55. In better times, travelers left little cairns of wishing rocks by the side of the path; each stone carried the hope, "When I arrive at the next kraal, I hope they give me plenty of food." Webb and Wright, *James Stuart Archive,* 1:341; 2:8; 4:267.

18. Webb and Wright, *James Stuart Archive,* 4:38; 1:158, 320, 325; 2:120–22. Isaacs, *Travels and Adventures,* 61, 46. Klopper, "Art of Zulu-Speakers," 158.

19. Webb and Wright, *James Stuart Archive,* 3:128–30; H. Callaway, *Religious System of the Amazulu,* 389.

20. Fynn, *Diary,* 31, 284, 125. Webb and Wright, *James Stuart Archive,* 3:81, 83–84, 271; 4:81, 89; 2:14–15, 272.

21. A file (CSO 1477) in the NAB reveals numerous strategies adopted in Natal during a plague of locusts in 1896: sweet potatoes were planted because locusts avoided them, cattle were sold, migrants left to find work, green corn was saved by early harvesting, and "greedy kraals" bought wagonloads of grain. The only communal activities referred to in these letters are beating the locusts off the crops and setting fires to drive them away; this latter activity appears to have been organized by the European locust officer and not by local African political authorities. Frank Goxon (?), Stanger, Report re Lower Tugela Division, 15 and 17 Feb. 1896; Rev. A. Prozesky, Koenigsberg Mission Station, to Sir John Robinson, Prime Minister of Natal, 15 Jan. 1896, CSO 1477 1896/5109, NAB.

22. Bourquin and Filter, *Paulina Dlamini,* 46, 50.

23. Berglund found during his fieldwork in the 1960s few references to the hunger of the ancestors; rather than a sacrifice, confession and the desire for harmony were said to cause ancestral hunger to abate. *Zulu Thought-Patterns and Symbolism,* 314. H. Callaway, *Religious Systems of the Amazulu,* 154–55, 158–59, 190, 197, 183, 218, 175, 173.

24. Bryant, *Zulu People,* 712–13. H. Callaway, *Religious Systems of the Amazulu,* 11, 175, 173.

25. H. Callaway, *Religious Systems of the Amazulu,* 154–55, 5, 142–43. Bryant, *Zulu Medicine and Medicine-Men,* 20, 48. Samuelson, *Zululand,* 142.

26. Bryant, *Zulu People,* 623. Webb and Wright, *James Stuart Archive,* 2:176, 187; 3:86. Grout, *Zulu-land,* 134–35. H. Callaway, *Religious Systems of the Amazulu,* 403.

27. Klopper, "Art of Zulu-Speakers," 133.

28. "History of Camperdown for the Jan van Riebeeck Festival, 1952," MS 65359, Killie Campbell Africana Library, Durban. Slater, "Land, Labour and Capital," 257, 271, 262.

29. According to Bryant, Shaka had introduced this new method of carrying milk in gourds from Mtetwaland. *Zulu People,* 271. Fynn implied that Shaka believed frying in soup fat would allow people to share food more readily because food fried in butter could not be exchanged; all milk products were to be used only by members of the producing household. *Diary,* 145. Grout wrote in the early 1860s that Zulu people cooked in clay pots, while photographs taken in the 1870s reveal mainly metal ones. Grout, 100. Roman Catholics, however, continued to eat the meat from sick beasts. Webb and Wright, *James Stuart Archive,* 4:16.

30. Henry Fynn, "Replies to Queries Transmitted for Report," n.d., Fynn Papers, A 1382, file 11, NAB.

31. H. Callaway, *Religious System of the Amazulu,* 182; Bleek, "Translation of Callaway," 46.

32. See also Wylie, "Changing Face of Hunger."

33. Krige, *Social System,* 67–68; Goody, *Cooking, Cuisine and Class,* 192.

34. Bourquin and Filter, *Paulina Dlamini,* 52–53.

35. Max Weber, "Science as a Vocation," in Gerth and Mills, *From Max Weber,* 139.

36. Ibid.

3. The Politics of Famine

1. Philip, *Researches in South Africa,* 2:141, 84. The Indian analogy was made by a missionary named Gleig whom Philip was quoting as he described the alleged indifference of wealthy, non-Christian Tswana to the suffering of their fellow tribesmen; the Cape crisis occurred in 1824 when "hordes" of hungry Tswana came into the colony looking for bread after their harvest failed, provoking white farmers to ask the Cape government if they were going to be allowed to come and "how they were to be provided for."

2. Hyman Basner speaking in the South African Senate in 1946, quoted in Lewsen, *Voices of Protest,* 27.

3. CMT A. H. Stanford to Undersecretary for Native Affairs, CT, 26 Sept. 1910, CMT 3/540 file 10, KAB; Notes of a meeting with a deputation from Chief Marelane, Umtata, 27 Feb. 1919, 1/LSK 13 file 2/2, KAB.

4. RM, Lusikisiki, 30 July 1925, 1/LSK 2/24/2, KAB; Edgar Brookes, writing in the *Rand Daily Mail* in 1923, quoted in Dubow, *Racial Segregation,* 85.

5. Wylie, *A Little God,* 78.

6. W. G. Mears, SNA (1944–1949), even balked at describing his employees as bureaucrats, because of the respect, confidence, and affection in which, he said, Africans held them as they led them "along the difficult path of advancement toward

the goal of local government." And yet, the General Council of the Transkeian Territories (Bunga) and the fate of its resolutions vividly illustrate the contradictory role of the magistrates; a purely advisory body, the Bunga had more than half its resolutions rejected by ministers or Transkeian magistrates in the early 1940s (Evans, *Bureaucracy and Race,* 166, 186).

7. Dubow, *Racial Segregation,* 115–17.

8. G. R. Searle, quoted in ibid., 94.

9. Harris, "Political Thought and the Welfare State," 116–41.

10. In *Political Economy of Pondoland,* Beinart calculated that the general area of the Transkei experienced droughts of varying intensity every six or seven years, citing the following dates of recorded drought: 1862, 1863, 1877, 1894, 1895, 1901, 1903, 1904, 1911–1912, 1919–1920, and 1926–197.

11. So many people died from the 1918 influenza epidemic, for example, that there was not enough strong local labor left to plow the fields; as a result people were said to have nearly starved during and after the 1919–1920 plowing season.

12. Beinart, *Political Economy of Pondoland,* 71, 173; Robert Callaway, quoted in G. Callaway, *Pioneers in Pondoland,* 141, 149.

13. Qangiso Ndamase, Libode, to CMT, 8 Nov. 1912, CMT 3/902 file 725 (1), KAB.

14. RM, Tabankulu, to CMT, 4 Nov. 1912, CMT 3/902 file 725 (1), KAB.

15. RM Arthur Gladwin, Lusikisiki, 21 Jan. 1914, 1/LSK 6 13/2/6, KAB.

16. RM, Tabankulu, to CMT, 4 Nov. 1912, CMT 3/902 file 725 (1), KAB.

17. CMT Stanford, Umtata, to Headman Qangiso Ndamase, Libode, 20 Nov. 1912, CMT 3/902 file 725 (1), KAB.

18. Dietler, "Driven by Drink," 352–406.

19. RM, Kentani, to CMT, 21 Jan. 1914, CMT 3/902 725 (3), KAB.

20. CMT to SNA, Pretoria, telegram no. 17057, 1912, CMT 3/902 file 725 (1), KAB.

21. Haines, "Transkei Trader," 207, 213.

22. E. Barrett, NAD, to CMT Stanford, 4 Nov. 1912, CMT 3/902 file 725 (1), KAB.

23. Paraphrased by the SNA, Pretoria, to CMT, 4 Nov. 1912, CMT 3/902 file 725 (1), KAB.

24. Pritchard to SNA, Pretoria, telegram, 13 Nov. 1912, CMT 3/902 file 725 (1), KAB.

25. CMT to RM, Umzimkulu, 25 Nov. 1912, CMT 3/902 file 725 (1), KAB.

26. The dearth of mealies had been caused partly by the decision of grain dealers in Alfred Division, Natal, not to send any grain south as long as prices were lower than they wanted; they were trying to get out of agreements they had made earlier with local buyers when the price of grain was lower. CMT Stanford to SNA, 31 Dec. 1912, CMT 3/902 725 (2), KAB.

27. RM, Bizana, to CMT, 3 Dec. 1912, and RM, Idutywa, to CMT, 9 Dec. 1912, CMT 3/902 file 728, KAB.

28. RM Armstrong, Ngqeleni, to CMT, 7 Dec. 1912, CMT 3/902 file 728, KAB.

29. Haines, "Transkei Trader," 202.

30. Councillors Nohi, Jackson Makaula, and Nota, in United Transkeian Territories General Council, Proceedings, 26 Apr. 1917, 79.

31. United Transkeian Territories General Council, Proceedings, 19 Mar. 1914, 39–40.

32. United Transkeian Territories General Council, Proceedings, 25 Mar. 1914, 94; Councillor Ndima, in ibid., 28 Apr. 1920, 62.

33. Mr. Baumann, Bergfontein, Fauresmith, OFS, to CMT, 4 Nov. 1912, CMT 3/902 file 725 (1), KAB.

34. RM, Tabankulu, to CMT, telegram, 16 Nov. 1912, CMT 3/902 file 725 (1), KAB.

35. SNA Edward Dower to CMT, 21 Nov. 1912; CMT Stanford to Casper van der Merwe, Bankfontein, Reitz, OFS, 25 Nov. 1912, CMT 3/902 file 725 (1), KAB. Van der Merwe had proposed advancing Africans their train fare to his farm and then deducting the amount from their wages.

36. CMT speaking in Umtata to deputation from Chief Marelane in connection with the famine conditions in eastern Pondoland, 20 Nov. 1912, CMT 3/902 file 725 (1), KAB.

37. Ibid.

38. Pondoland General Council resolution forwarded to CMT, 14 Apr. 1913, CMT 3/902 file 728, KAB.

39. CMT to SNA, n.d., CMT 3/902 file 728, KAB. SNA Garthorne replied, 1 July 1913, that he agreed.

40. Deputation from Chief Marelane in the CM's office, 13 June 1913, 1/LSK 13 file 2/2, KAB.

41. Notes of a meeting with a deputation from Chief Marelane, Umtata, 27 Feb. 1919, 1/LSK 13 file 2/2, KAB.

42. Food Supply to Zululand Natives, 1911–1913, NTS 98 6011/1911/F179, SAB.

43. Since maize needs between twenty-five and fifty inches of rainfall a year, only the very wettest summer on the flats was likely to give a decent maize harvest. Cole, *South Africa,* 169, 600–611.

44. Acting Sub-Native Commissioner V. Addison, Barberton, to SNA, 10 Apr. 1922, NTS 7845 32/336, SAB.

45. Supt. Norman Burley, Komatipoort Mission, to NC, Barberton, 18 Apr. 1927, NTS 7845 32/336, SAB.

46. Senator G. G. Munnik reminded General Hertzog, minister of native affairs, in a letter dated 14 Feb. 1927, that the 1896 drought was so severe that people had to eat grass and Kruger arranged for shiploads of Australian grain to be sent by wagon from Durban to Pretoria from where they were railed to the affected districts, which must have included the Lebombo flats (GNLB 240 68/16/180, SAB). Kruger's autobiography and biographies make no mention of this gift.

47. NC, Barberton, to SNA, 2 Mar. 1927 and 21 Apr. 1927, NTS 7845 32/336, SAB.

48. SNA (Garthorne), Pretoria, to NC, Barberton, 6 Mar. 1927, NTS 7845 32/336, SAB.

49. NC, Barberton, to NAD (Garthorne), 23 Mar. 1927, NTS 7845 32/336, SAB. Garthorne cabled the SNA who was in Cape Town attending Parliament suggesting

approval. The SNA replied (29 Mar. 1927) that he had no objection but asked Garthorne to "consider the legal aspect."

50. NC, Barberton, to SNA, Pretoria, 25 May 1927, NTS 7845 32/36, SAB. Garthorne wrote to the secretary that the amount was in excess of normal requirements in ordinary years (2 June 1927).

51. Garthorne to Secretary of Agriculture, 18 Jan. 1926, quoted in Dubow, *Racial Segregation,* 120, 206.

52. Lowveld Regional Development Association, *South Eastern Transvaal Lowveld.*

53. Eastern Middelburg Agricultural Farmers' Association to SNA, 18 July 1927, NTS 7845 32/336, SAB.

54. Hyatt, Secretary of the Lowveld Farmers Association, to W. H. Rood, House of Assembly, Cape Town, 6 June 1927; NC, Barberton, to SNA, Cape Town, 7 June 1927; Herbst to Secretary for Finance, 7 June 1927, asking whether Finance would furnish authority to meet "indispensable," modified requirements. Herbst (to NC, Barberton, 15 June 1927) asked Bennett to ascertain the white farmers' labor requirements and justified his lower allocation by saying, "This provision should tide the natives over for at least a month by which time you will have been able to go thoroughly into the whole position with the Agricultural Societies . . . and to submit a further report." NTS 7845 32/336, SAB.

55. H. S. Webb, Hectorspruit, to Prime Minister and Minister for Native Affairs, 4 July 1927; Webb to SNA, 17 July 1927; KAIS to SNA, telegram, 6 July 1927; Webb to Prime Minister and Minister for Native Affairs, 4 July 1927, NTS 7845 32/336, SAB.

56. NC, Barberton, to SNA [Bennett's history of the event], 18 Oct. 1927; SNA to KAIS, and SNA to NC, Barberton, 7 July 1927 (2 different cables), NTS 7845 32/336, SAB.

57. Bennett to SNA, 7 July 1927, NTS 7845 32/336, SAB.

58. Prime Minister J. B. M. Hertzog to W. H. Rood, Nelspruit, 1 Aug. 1927, NTS 7845 32/336, SAB, translated from Afrikaans by Jannie Gagiano.

59. SNA D. L. Smit to Secretary, KAIS, 8 Aug. 1938, NTS 7845 22/336 part 2, SAB.

60. J. M. Latsky, "Nutritional Aspects of Distress Conditions in the Southern Ciskei (May, 1945)," Ballinger Papers (A410), E2.5, Wits.

61. Nutrition Officer Latsky to Secretary for Health, 22 May 1945, NTS 7887 115/336 (9), part 1, SAB; NC Smuts, Alice, to SNA, 21 July 1945, "Drought Conditions: Victoria East District," NTS 7891 131/336 (part 2), SAB; Rodseth to SNA, "Food and Health Conditions in the Ciskei," 12 Mar. 1946, Ballinger Papers, B2.14.9 (file 2), Wits.

62. Ballinger to B. B. Mdledle, 13 Dec. 1943, in Lewsen, *Voices of Protest,* 127–29.

63. Quoted in Evans, *Bureaucracy and Race,* 204.

64. See especially Union of South Africa, Inter-Departmental Committee on the Social, Health and Economic Conditions of Urban Natives (chaired by SNA D. L. Smit), *Report;* and Union of South Africa, Witwatersrand Mine Natives' Wages Commission on the Remuneration and Conditions of Employment of Natives on Witwatersrand Gold Mines, *Report.*

65. Ballinger, *From Union to Apartheid,* 74–75.

66. CNC, King William's Town, to NC, Middledrift, 6 Aug. 1941, NTS 7891 127/336, SAB.

67. One NC in Camperdown, Natal, even said that it was unfair to force men to choose between the mines and starvation. When he decided to give relief work to the able-bodied so that they would not have to leave home to survive, he was "discouraged" by the highest levels of his department. NC, Camperdown, to CNC, Pietermaritzburg, 15 Mar. and 21 June 1945, NTS 7891, 131/336 part 1, SAB.

68. Latsky, "Nutritional Aspects of Distress Conditions," 5.

69. See, for example, NC, Nylstroom, to SNA, 31 Aug. 1942, NTS 7891 130/336, SAB.

70. Union of South Africa, Inter-Departmental Committee on Poor Relief and Charitable Institutions, *Report,* par. 13.

71. Social Security Committee and Social and Economic Planning Council, *Social Security,* par. 129.

72. Rodseth to SNA, Cape Town, 12 Mar. 1946, 12, Ballinger Papers, B2.14.9 (file 2), Wits.

73. SNA W. G. Mears to Provincial Secretary, 24 Aug. 1945, NTS 7887 115/336 (9), SAB.

74. J. Addison, CNC, Ciskei, to SNA, 28 May 1945, and Memorandum from NAD to SNA, 23 Aug. 1945, NTS 7887 115/336 (9), part 1, SAB.

75. National Nutrition Council, *Second Report,* 1947, 13, U.G. 53–1947.

76. B. Taute, Assistant Professional Officer (Dietetics) in the Department of Public Health, *Report,* Ballinger Papers, B2.14.9 (file 1), Wits.

77. Dr. T. W. B. Osborn, "Remedies for Malnutrition," *Leech* 17, no. 1 (Dec. 1946): 27–29. Osborn was senior lecturer in the Department of Physiology at Wits., becoming Labour party M.P. for Benoni in order to try to put the knowledge he had learned from laboratory experiments and nutritional experiments into practical effect; see Tobias, "Medicine in Its Broader Setting," 27.

78. E. Roux, "Hunger Introduces New Foods to Africans," *Guardian,* 20 Dec. 1945, 2. I am grateful to Colin Bundy for this reference.

79. G. D. Alexander (agricultural editor of the *Natal Mercury*) to Ballinger, 15 Feb. 1946, Ballinger Papers, B2.5.39, Wits.

80. J. M. Latsky to Secretary for Health, 22 May 1945, NTS 7887 115/336 (9), part 1, SAB.

81. Ballinger to Mrs. P. Epstein (South African League of Women Voters), 2 Apr. 1946, Ballinger Papers, B2.14.9 (file 2), Wits.

82. Bokwe to Ballinger, 24 Sept. 1945, Ballinger Papers, B2.5.37, Wits.

83. Keiskammahoek Native Survey, Aug. 1950, VDG 179 VN 401/4, SAB.

84. Bokwe to Ballinger, 24 Sept. 1945, and Ballinger to Bokwe, 10 Sept. 1945, Ballinger Papers E2.5, Wits.

85. Latsky, "Nutritional Aspects," and Nutrition Officer to the Secretary for Public Health, Pretoria, 17 July 1945, VWN 2528 SWF 3/1/1, SAB; Latsky to Secretary for Public Health, 17 July 1945, VWN 2528 SWF 3/1/1, SAB; Taute, *Report,* June–July 1945, 8–9.

86. Latsky, "The Role of Proteins in Undernutrition," *Leech*, 17, no. 1 (1946), 12–14.

87. Ballinger to Bokwe, 10 Sept. 1945.

88. Bokwe to Ballinger, 24 Sept. 1945.

89. Bokwe could not remember the name of Latsky's traveling companion. Bokwe to Ballinger, 24 Sept. 1945 and 20 Nov. 1945, Ballinger Papers, B2.5.37, Wits.

90. Bokwe to Ballinger, 20 Nov. 1945 and 13 Dec. 1945, Ballinger Papers, B2.5.37, Wits.

91. Dr. W. J. Cooper, Medical Superintendent of Lovedale Hospital, to NC, Alice, 4 May 1945, quoted in Latsky, "Nutritional Aspects."

92. Bokwe to Ballinger, 20 Nov. 1945.

93. Roux, "Hunger"; African Food Fund, First Annual Statement, 31 Oct. 1946, SAIRR, reel 20, 63.1.4, SML. Papu reported that in Mfiki location there were forty-eight adults who owned among them twenty-eight head of cattle; twenty-two of these people, many of them widows, owned no land. The proportions were similar in the three other locations he named: Ngwaxa, Qanda, and Mxumbu.

94. United Transkeian Territories General Council, Proceedings, 27 Apr. 1944, 50–51.

95. J. J. Yates and Councillor B. Siroqo, in United Transkeian Territories General Council, Proceedings, 23 Apr. 1947, 72.

96. Rodseth to SNA, 12 Mar. 1946, and Revs. K. Craig and W. Kinsey, conversation with Rodseth and Colonel Lever, controller of native settlements, 21 Jan. 1946, at NAD office, Pretoria, Ballinger Papers B2.14.9 (file 2), Wits. The Presbyterian missionaries praised Rodseth's "sympathetic" attitude and the NAD's energetic response.

97. Iliffe, *African Poor*, 123.

4. Scientific Paternalism

1. Gertrude Kark, Report of a Survey Nov. 1944 to June 1946: A Study of a Pocket of Ill Health, Alexandra Health Committee Memoranda, SAIRR AD 843 B74.5, microfilm MISC 1044, reel 24, SML.

2. J. E. Mathewson, Manager, NAD, Benoni, speaking to the SAIRR in 1955, quoted in Evans, *Bureaucracy and Race*, 82.

3. His focus on food set Rowntree's work apart from that of his even more famous contemporary social scientist, Charles Booth. Booth based his study of London's poor more generally on "conditions" and earnings. *Life and Labour of the People in London* (London, 1892). Booth stated that his purpose was "to show the numerical relation which poverty, misery, and depravity bear to regular earnings and comparative comfort, and to describe the general conditions under which each class lives." Quoted in Himmelfarb, *Poverty and Compassion*, 101.

4. Rowntree, *Poverty*, chap. 4 and p. 304.

5. Mollat, *Poor in the Middle Ages*, 295. Geremek argues in *Poverty* that medieval charities grew in tandem with the idea that alms-givers were buying their salvation; the poor were the means by which the rich gained access to the afterlife (chap. 1).

6. Rowntree, *Poverty*, 305.

7. Livi-Bacci, *Population and Nutrition*, 24. Even these new figures are inflated

because, to address all body types, the standard is set at 20 percent above the average requirement. See also Levenstein, *Paradox of Plenty,* 150.

8. Grigg, *Transformation of Agriculture,* 69.

9. Mintz, *Sweetness and Power,* 145.

10. United Kingdom, Parliament, Inter-Departmental Committee on Physical Deterioration, *Report,* 44.

11. The Beveridge Plan was published as a command paper (Cmd 6404) under the title *Social Insurance and Allied Services* in 1942. See also J. Beveridge, *Beveridge and His Plan.*

12. The Social Science Association (1857–1886) existed at the national level, but there were also sociological and statistical associations at the local level until their role was taken over by more expert bodies in the 1880s. Harris, "Political Thought," 116–41.

13. The British commissioners argued against social Darwinism by noting that disease harmed even those who survived (Cd. 2175, 16). Bruce-Bays, "Injurious Effects," 263. Van Heyningen notes that as late as 1910 South African cities were said to be free of European forms of pauperism and actual starvation; all unemployment was seen as temporary, and so no permanent relief measures were needed; few relief agencies in Cape Town were willing to help Africans. Van Heyningen, "Poverty, Self-Help and Community," 128–43.

14. For the first nine years after Union the government left such questions to private charities and missionary bodies. Then, in 1919 it set up institutional structures — local boards of aid — to distribute aid to the destitute. The provincial governments bore responsibility for distributing rations to paupers and, occasionally, rent to the needy. Only in 1940 did the Union government begin to take some of this burden away from the provinces when it set up the Department of Social Welfare to administer the distribution of rations and rent, and even lay down the maximum amount of food the parcels could contain. The general logic behind the parcels was to avoid "pauperization," that is, the creation of a class dependent on state handouts, while "it is a rule in the case of Natives that poor relief must not be allowed to disturb tribal custom which provides for the maintenance of the poor of each community." Union of South Africa, Inter-Departmental Committee on Poor Relief and Charitable Institutions, *Report;* Social Security Committee and Social and Economic Planning Council, *Social Security,* 17.

15. Union of South Africa, Inter-Departmental Committee on Poor Relief and Charitable Institutions, *Report,* par. 13.

16. Memorandum, "Nutrition Conference," [1939?], NTS 7875 115/336 (1), SAB.

17. Evans, *Bureaucracy and Race,* 33, 132, 146; Paton, *Hofmeyr,* 379, 382. The Native Revenue Accounts were set up to prevent township surpluses from being transferred to the city's general account; the 1914 Tuberculosis Commission had noted that Grahamstown, for example, actually derived a profit from its Fingo Village; in 1941, Dr. R. Bokwe and two other African leaders observed that some of Grahamstown's townships still got less than their due in municipal services. Davenport, *Black Grahamstown,* 12.

18. Macmillan had written the first study of white urban poverty in 1915 with reference to Grahamstown, and in 1929 a multivolume research project into the poor

white problem was launched with the financial backing of the Carnegie Corporation of New York. Krige published one of the first studies of African urban diet ("Social and Economic Facts"). She was followed by the medical officer of health in Benoni, Anning ("Nutrition of the People" and "Health Policy").

19. Rheinallt Jones, "Social and Economic Condition of the Urban Native," in Schapera, *Western Civilization,* 177.

20. Atkinson, "Native Budgets," 499–506.

21. Palmer's M.A. thesis quoted in Marks, *Not Either an Experimental Doll,* 4.

22. Atkinson, "Transition from Subsistence," 124, 120.

23. Ibid., 117.

24. Marks, *Not Either an Experimental Doll,* 12.

25. "Native Budgets," 503, 500. Webb wrote in 1903 that the urgent question of the day was the "character of consumption," noting with apparent regret that "[a]t present we leave this vital problem of character of consumption to be solved by the appetites of each individual, even to the extent of permitting them to poison themselves and their children." Quoted in Himmelfarb, *Poverty and Compassion,* 375. These consumer concerns were not limited to the Fabians; Rheinallt Jones called attention to wastage due to uneconomic buying and use, "certainly contributory causes of poverty among the native urban dwellers as among the urban poor white." "Urban Native," 181.

26. Atkinson, "Transition from Subsistence," 123; Atkinson, "Native Budgets," 505, 506.

27. R. Phillips never explained the significance of spending his youth in a mixed-race city. It would seem that he believed his background made him sensitive to the two races' need to understand one another if race relations were to be harmonious.

28. Rich, *White Power and Liberal Conscience,* 12.

29. R. Phillips, *Bantu in the City,* 19, x, 35, 409.

30. Province of Transvaal, Local Government Commission, *Report,* par. 42.

31. R. Phillips, *Bantu in the City,* 409.

32. Ibid., 35, 49.

33. Ibid., xiv.

34. Ibid., x, xxviii.

35. Rich, *White Power and Liberal Conscience,* 12–13.

36. Phillips, *Bantu in the City,* 58, 384.

37. Hellmann, *Rooiyard,* 3.

38. Sachs, *Black Hamlet,* 123; see also 131, 143–44.

39. Hellmann, "Johannesburg Slum Yard," 41; Rheinallt Jones, "Urban Native," 186.

40. Hellmann, *South African Institute of Race Relations,* 11. Ralph Bunche was apparently unimpressed by her earlier attitudes: visiting the Hellmanns in Johannesburg in 1937, one of her four servants called him "massa," and "that gripes me"; and he quoted Hellmann as thinking that Africans were naturally indifferent to punctuality and attendance. Edgar, *An African American in South Africa,* 162, 167–68. See also Hellmann, *Handbook on Race Relations.*

41. Hellmann, *Rooiyard,* 116; Hellmann, "Johannesburg Slum Yard," 49.

42. Dubow, *Racial Segregation,* 285. Hellmann defined her work as following "cul-

ture contact theory" in the same manner as Monica Hunter; followers of Bronislaw Malinowski, they both explained African cultural changes as resulting from interaction with Western culture, and they took a more sanguine view of it than the pessimists who warned of detribalization and degeneration.

43. Batson, "Official Report of the Social Survey Conference, 1942," quoted in Phillips, *University of Cape Town*, 278–79; Batson, "Nature of Poor Relief," 18.

44. Verwoerd, quoted in Evans, *Bureaucracy and Race*, 66.

45. Joslin, "Poverty in the Union," 9; Batson, "Income Levels and Purchasing Habits," 106–20.

46. Phillips, *University of Cape Town*, 279.

47. Three articles by Professor Batson on the Beveridge Report, reprinted from the *Cape Times*, 3–5 Feb. 1943, SAL. I am grateful to Elizabeth van Heyningen for alerting me to Batson's role in Cape Town charities.

48. In 1938, Laidler, the medical officer of health in East London, lamented that he was unable to reproduce the family budgets he had gathered to show that the South African urban environment, not "racial susceptibility," was responsible for the interrelationship of tuberculosis, venereal disease, and malnutrition among the poor. "The Unholy Triad," 664–65.

49. Krige, "The Social Background of Malnutrition and Gastro-Enteritis Cases at King Edward VIII Hospital, Durban," [1952], VDG 181 VN 402/1, SAB; "World Bank Living Standards and Development Survey," *Weekly Mail*, 20–26 Jan. 1995.

50. The same pattern—of people buying more expensive foods when their incomes rise, but eating few vegetables and fruit when they earn little—held true for western European history until the nineteenth and early twentieth centuries. Grigg, "Nutritional Transition," 247–61.

51. Hellmann, "Urban Native Food in Johannesburg," 288.

52. Hellmann, *Rooiyard*, 77.

53. Gibson observed in 1954, "'Meat,' of course, can mean almost anything remotely connected with animal life. Most frequently what we saw by this name was a pathetic, not always clean scrap of meat and bone, with a lump of fat thrown in to make up the weight." *Cost of Living for Africans*, 14.

54. Rogerson, "Feeding the Common People," 56–73.

55. Fox, "Diet in the Urban Locations as Indicated by the Survey," app. 1 in Janisch, *African Income and Expenditure*, 33.

56. Batson, "Improvement in the Socio-Economic Condition," 109.

57. *Incumbe*'s "fortifying" ingredients comprised: whey powder, soya bean flour, wheat flour, maize flour, malted sorghum, sucrose, calcium carbonate, dried brewer's yeast.

58. This profile was drawn from the annual reports of the medical officer of health (A. B. Xuma), records of the Alexandra Health Committee and the Alexandra Clinic, microfilm, SML.

59. Ibid.

60. The bulk of the Alexandra Health Committee revenue came from the sanitary fees, supplemented by license fees paid by butchers, bakers, vehicle owners, peddlers,

boardinghouse keepers, eating house and café or tea room proprietors, sellers of groceries and fruit, millers, milk purveyors and dairymen, and "slaughtermen."

61. SAIRR, *Survey of Race Relations* (1950), 49. Posel, *Making of Apartheid*, 32. Prices had risen throughout South Africa during the war, because labor had been drawn away from food production and food had to be imported at higher prices. Paton, *Hofmeyr*, 389. Union of South Africa, Commission Appointed to Inquire into the Operation of Bus Services for Non-Europeans on the Witwatersrand and in the District of Pretoria and Vereeniging, *Report*, 21.

62. Chairman, AHC, to Provincial Secretary, Pretoria, n.d., AHC Minutes and Reports, 1933–1943, SAIRR (AD 843), Cullen, Wits.; Alexandra Health Committee, "Statement on the Future of Alexandra Township" (pamphlet), Johannesburg, July 1943, 32.

63. Because of the lack of censuses, we cannot quantify the precise size of the influx, but comparing the number of people vaccinated during a 1937 smallpox epidemic (27,000) with the bus commission's estimate of 45,000–50,000 in 1944, the increase seems to have been of the order of 20,000 in seven years. Ruth Cowles, "AHC Report for 1937," ABC 15.4, vol. 44, Houghton Library, Harvard Univ.; Bus Commission Report, 1.

64. Cowles, "Report for AHC 1 June 1935–31 May 1936," ABC 15.4, vol. 44, Houghton Library, Harvard Univ. Because there was no social service center in the township, the center also distributed monthly pauper rations such as milk to the children of unemployed men, and some pensions, on behalf of the NAD, to more than one hundred crippled, poor, and blind people.

65. A. B. Xuma, "The Socio-Economic Aspects of Native Health or Health and Wealth of the South African Natives, a Paper Delivered by Dr. A. B. Xuma at the Annual General Meeting of the Pretoria Joint Council of Europeans and Natives, Pretoria, on Wednesday, June 19th, 1940," 12–13, Ballinger Papers E1.75, Cullen, Wits.; Kark, Report of Survey, 137.

66. Xuma, "Changes Taking Place in Health and Diet of Natives in Urban Areas and Their Effects" (paper presented at New Education Fellowship Conference [African Education Section], Johannesburg, 18 July 1934), Xuma Papers, card 30, SML. Xuma, Medical Officer of Health's [MOH] Report for the Year Ended 30 June 1939, 8–9, AD 843/RJ Na 1.2 file 2, Cullen, Wits.

67. Xuma, "Socio-Economic Aspects," 2, 1940; Xuma, MOH Report 30 June 1933; "Changes in Health and Diet," Xuma Papers.

68. Xuma, Speech to Welcoming Party at Alexandra Township, 9 Dec. 1938, Xuma Papers, fiche 57, SML.

69. Xuma, "Socio-Economic Aspects," 14; Kark, Report of Survey, 125.

70. "Socio-Economic Aspects," 1940.

71. Basner, *Am I an African?*, 157–58.

72. Inside back cover of reprint of *Libertas* article on Alexandra, Aug. 1942, SAIRR, reel 24.

73. G. Hibbert, "Alexandra Township and Its Relation to Johannesburg," Rotary Club address, circa Mar. 1942, SAIRR, B box, 74.4 (file 3), reel 24.

74. Ibid.; "Challenge to Democracy, Rand's Problem Township," *Libertas* 2, no. 9 (Aug. 1942): 16–29.

75. "£1,875,000 Loan Required to Expropriate Alexandra Township," *Rand Daily Mail*, n.d., SAIRR (film misc 1044), reel 15, SML.

76. Alexandra Vigilance and Protection Standholders Committee to H. G. Lawrence, 30 Sept. 1942, SAIRR, B box, 74.4, reel 24, SML.

77. Standholders' Committee to Minister of Native Affairs, 4 Jan. 1935, AD 843/RJ, Na. 1.2 (file 2), Cullen, Wits.

78. Alexandra Vigilance and Protection Standholders Committee, Memorandum, 30 Sept. 1942, SAIRR, B box, 74.4, reel 24, SML.

79. Principals of Alexandra Schools, Deputation to Interview Professor Hoernlé on the Question of Sanitary Charges for the Schools, 6 Feb. 1943, SAIRR, reel 15, SML.

80. Alexandra Standholders' Committee to Minister for Native Affairs, 16 May 1942, quoted in Duncan, "Liberals and Local Administrators," 485.

81. Basner, *Am I an African?*, 173.

82. Alexandra Anti-Expropriation Committee, Memorandum, [Mar. 1943], SAIRR, B box, 74.4 (file 3), reel 24, SML.

83. Ibid., 4.

84. Ibid., 3.

85. SAIRR, B box, 74.4 (file 3), [29 ? 1943], SML.

86. T. Davis Peters, Secretary of Alexandra Anti-Expropriation Fund Committee, to Hoernlé, 26 Apr. 1943, ibid.

87. Hoernlé to Molteno, [Apr. 1943], SAIRR, B box, 74.4 (file 3), [29 ? 1943], SML.

88. Ibid.

89. Hoernlé, "An Open Letter to the Citizens of Johannesburg on the Future of Alexandra Township by the Alexandra Health Committee" (in pamphlet), Johannesburg, 1943, 12.

90. D. L. Smit, Chairman, et al., to Minister of Native Affairs, 30 Jan. 1947, "Irregular Squatting: Alexandra Township," U.G. 15–49 (1946–1947).

91. Evans, *Bureaucracy and Race*, 85; Rich, *White Power and Liberal Conscience*, 72.

92. The African urban population grew by 57.2 percent—from 1,141,642 to 1,794,212—between 1936 and 1946. Posel, *Making of Apartheid*, 24.

5. The Threat of "Race Deterioration"

1. Slack, *Poverty and Policy*, 116. Pick argues that biomedical fears of degeneration began in Britain in the 1850s and 1860s in tandem with discussions of the viability of mass democracy and the fate of the body in the city, but that they intensified in the 1880s when demonstrations and riots coincided with the birth of organized socialism. *Faces of Degeneration*, 189–203.

2. C. F. K. Murray, "Public Health Legislation in South Africa," *SAMJ* 1, no. 2 (1893): 20–22. I am grateful to Molly Sutphen for this reference. Watkins-Pitchford, "Hygiene in South Africa," 74, 73.

3. Bruce-Bays, "Injurious Effects of Civilisation," 263–68; Skotnes, *Miscast*, 17.

4. K. Bremer, M.P. (Graaff Reinet), House of Assembly *Debates,* 9 Aug. 1938, 702.

5. Assistant Health Officer for the Union, Bloemfontein, to the Secretary for Health, Pretoria, 17 Sept. 1920, 3, GNLB 292 file 191/18/103, SAB.

6. Committee of Medical Officers of Mines to the Commissioner of Native Affairs, Transvaal, Report on the Mortality among Natives Employed on the Mines of the Witwatersrand, 6 June 1903, in TLC, *Report* (1904), 557.

7. Cartwright, *Doctors of the Mines,* 143.

8. Fleming, "Nutrition in the Mining Industry," Chamber of Mines Research Organization, Johannesburg. In 1898, G. A. Turner was sent by the Cape Colony government to investigate a scurvy outbreak at Kimberley, which he judged to result from war, drought, and rinderpest, and whose cure was, he believed, green vegetables. Fox, "South Africa Became Interested," 395–96.

9. Fleming's report indicates that the Chamber of Mines began to lobby the government to suspend the import duty on maize in 1912, asked the Department of Agriculture to lower its standards for grading and therefore pricing mealies the following year, and from 1936 unsuccessfully opposed the Maize Industry Control Board for arbitrarily fixing the price of maize. In 1945 the chamber wrote to the minister for agriculture warning that the rising price of food would endanger the mines' working costs, but no price controls were thereafter instituted.

10. TLC, *Report* (1904), 562.

11. Loeser, "Diet of Mine Natives," 154, 157, 159.

12. TLC, *Report* (1904), 558

13. Loeser, "Diet of Mine Natives," 157; unidentified doctor commenting on evidence of Bengani Mxosa, Qumbu, 7 Sept. 1905, MOH 75/255, KAB.

14. Autopsy Report of Pali Wondle, signed by DS Henry Chute, King William's Town, 24 Oct. 1903, MOH 75/255, KAB.

15. MOH 75/255, KAB.

16. Williams, "Food and Feeding," 1.

17. Lagden, Evidence to the TLC, 127.

18. RM John Cleverly, Elliot, Transkei, to Medical Officer, 26 Sept. 1905, MOH 75/255, KAB. The African miners told Cleverly that 10 of the 150 men working at the Glencoe Collieries since October 1904 started to develop the symptoms of scurvy in June 1905.

19. TLC, *Report* (1904), 561–62; Dr. M. M. Klein, article in *South African Medical Record* (1905), quoted in Fox, "South Africa Became Interested," 396.

20. According to Judge Krause's Mining Regulations Commission reporting in 1959(?), the official diet was not necessarily fed or consumed (Fleming Report). Similarly, M. Smith has compared the 1903 diet schedule with the 1904 returns of food actually consumed, and concluded that there was "a vast discrepancy . . . between the mines'" and "the Chamber's recommendations and actual practice on the mines." "Working Paper."

21. Evidence Submitted by the Chamber of Mines to the TLC, 1904, 589. The statement came specifically from the Rand Mines Subsidiary Companies.

22. MacRae, "Scurvy in South Africa," 1838–1840.

23. Hoernlé, "Supplementary Note" (p. 226) to Orenstein, "Dietetics of Natives," 223. Orenstein, "Elementary Hygiene," (1934), 35; M. Smith, "Working in the Grave," 34–35. In the mid- to late 1930s breakfast began to be introduced, and Williams reported in 1938 that 30 to 40 percent of black miners actually ate it.

24. Evidence given in Durban Circuit Court, 19 Feb. 1878, Imperial Blue Book, C. 2220, p. 176.

25. Rev. F. Suter, Evidence to the TLC, 24.

26. Natives Grievances Inquiry, 1913–1914, U.G. 37–14, 16. African grievances had been focused on "loafer tickets," their failure to get paid if they did not drill enough inches.

27. *Rand Daily Mail,* 24 Feb. 1923, quoted in M. Smith, "Working in the Grave," 115. Striking gold mine workers mentioned food as one of their major grievances nine times 1938–1942 and twenty-seven times between 1943 and 1947. Dunbar Moodie, "Moral Economy of the Strike," 24.

28. Loeser, "Diet of Mine Natives," 152.

29. Goldsmith, "Mine Medical Officer Aspect," 30; Williams, "Food and Feeding," 21.

30. Actuary and Labour Adviser, Transvaal Chamber of Mines, Department of Labour and Statistics, to Director of Native Labour, NAD, Johannesburg, 15 Jan. 1921, GNLB 292, file 191/18/103, SAB.

31. M. Smith, "Working Paper," 18.

32. Gorgas and Hendrick, *William Crawford Gorgas,* 276–91.

33. The Gorgas Report, 1914, quoted in Tuberculosis Research Commission, "Tuberculosis in South African Natives," 49. Native Grievances Inquiry, 16. Gorgas was not the first doctor to say this, simply the most influential: Dr. M. M. Blaney had read a paper to the South African Association of Engineers in 1903, criticizing the two pound daily mealie meal ration as excessive; Dr. M. M. Klein of Apex Mine and Rand Collieries had suggested in 1910 that the mealie meal ration be reduced and peas, beans, rice, and fresh vegetables be substituted to avoid the "monotony" that encourages the incidence of scurvy. Fox noted in 1963 that Klein was proud of his ability to lower the cost of mine rations. Fox, "South Africa Became Interested," 396.

34. Jeeves, *Migrant Labour.*

35. The reserve was so crowded and dry that people migrated east to work on white farms to get food to bring home with them. Van Onselen, *Seed Is Mine,* 140.

36. In 1916 people at these diggings spent most of their meager income at the Kaffir Eating House where they bought a plate of mealie meal for a tickey (threepence) with perhaps a tin of fish for relish. A dramatic rise in the cost of living in 1920 led women to raise money by brewing more beer on the diggings; more diamonds were stolen, and strikes and riots met increased police aggression. Ibid., 62, 67.

37. W. Walker, Inspector, NAD, to DNL, 17 Dec. 1920, NTS 6752 48/315, SAB.

38. Assistant Health Officer G. A. Park Ross, Union, to Assistant General Manager, SAR, 27 Feb. 1925; Secretary for Public Health W. A. Murray to DNL, 7 May 1928, NTS 6752 48/315, SAB.

39. Magistrate F. Hutchinson to SNA, Pretoria, 4 Dec. 1926; Statement of Rhodes

Ndandani of Nqamakwe, 18 May 1927, to the NAD, Cape; Officer-in-Charge of Native Affairs, Lüderitz, quoted in Secretary of State for South West Africa to SNA, Pretoria, 2 July 1927, NTS 6752 48/315, KAB.

40. SNA, Pretoria, to CNC, Pietermaritzburg, 10 Mar. 1928, NTS 6752 48/315, SAB.

41. D. M. MacRae, "Bechuanaland Protectorate," 78, 59.

42. Cluver, "Pellagra," 751–54.

43. Turner, "Diet of South African Natives."

44. E. H. Cluver to Secretary for Public Health, Report on Native Rations, 30 Oct. 1928, quoted in M. Smith, "Working in the Grave," 113; Loeser, "Diet of Mine Natives," 163. Loeser did add that people trekking long distances to get to the mines may have endured privations en route rather than at home.

45. "Deaths from Scurvy amongst Native Labourers Employed by Mines and Contractors in [Thirteen] Districts for the Years 1918, 1919 and January to August, 1920," GNLB 292 191/18/103, SAB. This chart reveals that the highest percentage of mine deaths attributable to scurvy occurred in 1918 among recruits from Cape Province (1.52%) and Southern Rhodesia (4.79%), in 1919 from Natal and Zululand (2.41%) and Mozambique (6.84%), and in 1920 from Cape Province (2.05%), Natal and Zululand (1.55%), and Swaziland (3.56%).

46. In 1903 the substance had begun to be chemically analyzed at the Union Health Department's laboratories in Bloemfontein. The Cape Department of Agriculture was circulating in 1906 articles on the nature and composition of "kaffir beers," and in 1908 the director of agriculture asked NAD officials to send him specimens of their ingredients because one authority, Joseph Orpen, believed that death and disease in mines and jails could be avoided if beer were used as the "cheapest possible substitute for a varied vegetable diet." NTS 46 file 519/13/37, SAB.

47. Malan, *In Quest of Health,* 293.

48. Carpenter, *Scurvy and Vitamin C,* 181.

49. Delf, "Studies in Experimental Scurvy." Extracts from this report may be found in GNLB 333, file 152/21/97, SAB.

50. Fox argues that due to Delf's research the ration scale was amended the following year to include germinated beans and peas as well as citrus fruit ("Recent Work on the Vitamins," 13); Orenstein confirms that her findings were given "practical application" in the 1922 ration scale. "Dietetics of Natives," 222. At least half of the three ounces of peas or beans served daily to each man were to be germinated and kept in cooking pots as short a time as possible, while the citrus requirement was phrased far less stringently. If, during the months of July, August, September, and October, an orange or other approved substitute were issued every second day, doctors surmised, the vegetable ration could be reduced to three ounces a day.

51. Malan, *In Quest of Health,* 295; Levenstein, *Revolution at the Table,* chap. 9.

52. Levy and Fox, "Antiscorbutic Value of Foodstuffs," 181–86. After examining eleven specimens of "kaffir beer" from various gold mine compounds on the Rand, they concluded that the "concentration of vitamins is low," and a quart ration would yield as much vitamin C as half an ounce of orange juice. In Fox and Stone, "Antiscorbutic Value of Kaffir Beer," the authors determined by chemical methods that the

antiscorbutic value of a variety of home-brewed "kaffir beers," obtained for them by the NAD, proved also to be low, and so it was the large quantity consumed by rural Africans that was "of definite prophylactic value against scurvy" (14).

53. In 1939, Fox and Dangerfield administered tests to 950 African miners (one group on the usual mine diet, which contained twelve to twenty-five milligrams of ascorbic acid; one consuming an extra forty milligrams of vitamin C in the form of concentrated orange juice). Though their research revealed that people need less vitamin C daily than had been previously supposed, Fox recommended doubling the amount required in mine rations in order to eliminate scurvy. Fox and Dangerfield, "Scurvy and Native Mine Labourers," 287, 304. In 1936, Orenstein had said the amount required depended on how much work a man was called on to do. Orenstein and Gordon, "Notes on Elementary Hygiene," 47. In 1974 an *SAMJ* article stated that no one knows the desirable level of vitamin C intake for optimum health. M. E. Visagie et al., "Vitamin A and C Levels," 2502. Cartwright, *Doctors of the Mines*, 144.

54. In 1971, for example, the medical researcher Lategan expressed the suspicion in the PMMOA that chronic, nonincapacitating scurvy might be associated with the rise of osteoporosis in black miners, but this latter, bone-weakening condition, rather than scurvy, was the focus of concern. "Nutritional Observations." In the research of the 1970s, medical men rarely used the word *scurvy* to describe the subclinical vestiges that were apparent in the delayed healing of miners' wounds and their tendency to become septic. (Visagie, Du Plessis, and Laubsher, "Effect of Vitamin C Supplementation.") The mines were indeed bringing nutritional deficiencies down to subclinical levels, and their success was accompanied by waning investment of time and money in scurvy-related research. According to the official history of the SAIMR, the last major study of vitamin C conducted by the institute focused on the rarity of scurvy in black infants, but this 1956 study "left many questions unanswered and was unfortunately never followed up." (Malan, *In Quest of Health*, 298.) Eleven people managed to die from scurvy in the 1922–1923 mine population of about 178,000 men in service (U.G. 9–24; Read, "Native and the Gold Mines," 400); 220 fell ill from scurvy out of 350,000 miners in 1938–1939 (Fox et al., "Vitamin C Requirements"), but by the early 1970s only six cases of clinical scurvy occurred among a mine population of more than 157,000 black men (Visagie et al., "Vitamin A and C Levels," 2503).

55. Loeser, "Diet of Mine Natives," 163, 152.

56. Union of South Africa, Department of Native Affairs, Departmental Committee Appointed to Enquire into and Report upon Certain Questions Relating to Native Labour in Zululand, the Transkeian Territories and the Ciskei, *Report*. Within eight years, the committee predicted, "the increasing requirements of the gold mines and a possible revival in the base mineral industry and in diamond mining, assuming that mining methods continue as they are, the supply of Native labour will have to be supplemented from other sources [than the Transkeian Territories]" (16).

57. I have found only about seven articles in the *SAMJ* prior to 1929 concerned with malnutrition; they focus on dental caries and the health of schoolchildren. African physiques were seen as superior to those of Europeans because the latter ate too much sugar, machine-ground grain, and "delicacies."

58. Paton and Finley, *Poverty, Nutrition and Growth;* Brock, "Nutritional Science and Practical Dietetics." Levenstein argues in *Revolution at the Table* that American culture in 1920s became newly child-centered and preoccupied with consumption rather than production; for these reasons, nutritionists focused on encouraging children's growth by feeding them more milk, and the malnutrition scares of the 1920s began to disappear (chap. 12).

59. United Kingdom, Parliament, Economic Advisory Council, *Nutrition in the Colonial Empire;* Worboys, "Colonial Malnutrition"; Orr and Gilks, *Studies of Nutrition,* 64. I am grateful to Yusufu Lawi, University of Dar es Salaam, for insights into the shortcomings of this work. See also Brantley, "Kikuyu-Maasai Nutrition," 49–86.

60. The special 1936 issue of *Africa* also contained articles on the food of the Congo, the Tallensi of the Gold Coast, and milk in French West Africa. A. Richards's first book, *Hunger and Work in a Savage Tribe,* was written to provide the Diet Committee of the International Institute of African Languages and Culture with the social and cultural information that its nutritional surveys needed. Kuper, "Audrey Richards, 1899–1984."

61. Porter, *Greatest Benefit to Mankind,* 551–60. In 1912 vitamin deficiency was first identified by Casimir Funk at the Lister Institute in London; in the 1920s most vitamins were isolated, while their synthesis generally took place in the 1930s and 1940s. Sir Albert Howard, *An Agricultural Testament* (London: Oxford Univ. Press, 1940). A British agronomist working since 1910 in Indore, India, Howard argued for the conservation of the soil by the use of compost.

62. Beinart, "Introduction," 148, 161; I. B. Pole-Evans quoted in Dodson, "Environment, Ideology and Politics."

63. Cluver, "Nutritional Problem in South Africa," 85; S. Kark, "Health Service," 198.

64. Murray, *Poor White Problem,* 67, 52.

65. Cited by Cluver, "Nutritional Research," 336.

66. F. W. Fox and Douglas Back, "The Causes of Malnutrition among Europeans in the Rural Areas of South Africa, a Brief Summary of Our Main Findings and Recommendations for Consideration by the Research Committee of the National Nutrition Council," 2 May 1941, 7, NVR 4 file 43, SAB.

67. Leipoldt, *Bushveld Doctor,* 44; Fox and Back, "Causes of Malnutrition," 7, 3.

68. F. W. Fox and Douglas Back, "A Brief Preliminary Report on Our Visit to the Ciskei and the Transkei," 10 Sept. 1937, Chamber of Mines Archives, Johannesburg; Fox and Back, Agricultural and Nutritional Problems, 1, SML. The report was not publicized until 1943 when Hyman Basner asked in parliament that it be released.

69. Fox, "Some Nutritional Problems," 88; Fox and Back, Agricultural and Nutritional Problems, 6; NEC, *Report,* 7.

70. Levenstein, *Revolution at the Table,* 115. The scale used height, weight, eyesight, breathing, muscularity, mental alertness, and rosiness of complexion as the indicators of nutritional well-being. Cluver, "Nutritional Research," 331. Kark and LeRiche, "Nutrition and Health of Bantu Schoolchildren"; Brock and Latsky, "Cape Nutrition Survey," 255–60.

71. Golberg and Thorpe, "Vitamins in South African Foodstuffs," 95.

72. SAIRR, Evidence Submitted to the Commission Considering the Feeding of School Children, AD 1715, 9.1, Wits; Janisch, *African Income and Expenditure*. Batson's reports calculated and recalculated the PDL; published food value tables for sociological use; and recorded population increases (1841–1941) and distribution (1865–1936), the distribution of poverty, occupations, and housing types among Coloured and European households, the incidence of poverty and overcrowding in relation to age, and the occupational stratification of households. Batson explained, "the job of the Survey was to produce the facts and figures. It must be for other people to make use of them"; and so, a conference of Cape Town's citizens formulated nonracial, social welfare resolutions in Feb. 1942 and sent them to the prime minister, who "promised financial assistance to enable the Survey to continue its work." Official Report of the Social Survey Conference, Cape Town, 1942, 80.

73. Sigerist, "University Education" and "A Physician's Impression of South Africa," 25–27. I am grateful to Heinrich von Staden, Yale University, for this reference. Sidney Kark, interview by author.

74. Medical Superintendent, Mt. Coke Hospital, King William's Town, quoted in Fox and Back, Agricultural and Nutritional Problems, 207; Major J. F. Herbst, Major M. G. Apthorp, and Dr. F. C. Wilmot, Report on Assistance to Indigent Native Tuberculotics, 30 May 1938, 5, BC 79 I3, UCT; Packard, *White Plague, Black Labor,* 246; Dormer, Friedlander, and Wiles, "A South African Team Looks at Tuberculosis," 82.

75. Williams, "Food and Feeding," 37, 8.

76. Goldsmith, "Mine Medical Officer Aspect," 28, 33; Williams, "Food and Feeding," 1, 9.

77. Goldsmith, "Mine Medical Officer Aspect," 37.

78. Anning, "Nutrition of the People," 123; Maister, "Social Welfare as Public Problem," 10; Cluver, "Food and Citizenship," 2; Gluckman, "Findings of the National Health Commission," 58.

79. Trowell and Muwazi, "Severe and Prolonged Underfeeding," 110; Carpenter, *Protein and Energy,* 220.

80. Ancel Keys, for example, studied the bodily changes of conscientious objectors at the University of Minnesota while they ate semifasting diets, confirming the existence of protective mechanisms reducing the body's daily energy requirements. Holland during the winter of 1944–1945 and the Warsaw ghetto in 1942 revealed the relatively low incidence of epidemics in a population eating a starvation diet. Prisoner-of-war camps in Germany and Japan revealed only an increase of intestinal infections under similar conditions. Livi-Bacci, *Population and Nutrition,* chap. 3.

81. Brock later wrote that he had had to use subterfuge to get kwashiorkor onto the agenda of the first FAO/WHO Expert Committee at Geneva in 1949; he asked the chairman to allow him to speak about "infantile pellagra" under the agenda item "Pellagra," and the following debate "started a new direction of enquiry." Brock, "Nutritional Science and Practical Dietetics," 657. Joshua Ruxin, Ph.D., The Wellcome Trust for the History of Medicine, personal communication, Boston, 6 Nov. 1996; Carpenter, *Protein and Energy,* 159, 160.

82. H. H. Stott to Dr. Noel Mann, Mar. 1960, personal communication.

83. Brock, "Nutritional Science and Practical Dietetics," 654; Ryle quoted in Porter, *Greatest Benefit to Mankind,* 643–44.

84. Brock and Fox, "Study of Nutritional Factors," 1000–1010; Brock, "Malnutrition in South Africa," 6. In a 1946 article in *The Leech,* Brock had alluded to the need to reorganize the economic system radically but, to my knowledge, he never elaborated on such allusions in print.

85. Carpenter, *Protein and Energy,* 150; Hansen, "John Fleming Brock," 1817.

86. Brock, "Medical Approach," 5.

87. Robertson, Hansen, and Moodie, "Gastro-Enteritis and Malnutrition," 338–44; Hansen, interview by author.

88. Wittmann et al., "Nutritional Status and Infection," 680, 682; Hansen, "Advances in Knowledge," 703; Hansen, "Nutrition and Child Health," 126–34.

89. Robertson, Hansen, and Moodie, "Gastro-Enteritis and Malnutrition," 342; Hansen, interview; Hansen, "John Fleming Brock," 1818.

90. Walker, interview by author; Walker, "Nutrition and Physique," 17; Walker, "Thoughts on Malnutrition," 700.

91. Walker, "Nutrition and Physique," 15.

92. Walker, "Thoughts on Malnutrition," 696; "Biological and Disease Patterns," 1132; and "Nutrition and Physique," 697, 699.

93. Ingrid Glatthaar, Department of Human Nutrition, MEDUNSA, personal communication, Apr. 1993.

94. Carpenter, *Protein and Energy,* 223; O. Sacks, *Island of the Colorblind,* 180.

95. Kuhn, *Structure of Scientific Revolutions.*

6. Missionaries of Science

1. Halley Stott, The Valley Trust Annual Report [VT AR], 1957, 7; DS, Libode, Annual Health Report for Year Ending 30 June 1947, 1/LBE 34 13/2/6 (vol. 1), KAB.

2. Swanson, "Sanitation Syndrome," 387.

3. Beinart, "Transkeian Smallholders and Agrarian Reform," 183.

4. Drewe, "From Holy Cross Hospital, Feb., 1938," 3, and Drewe's History of HCH, n.d., SPG M785; Drewe, Open Letter to the SPG., 5 Aug. 1922, SPG M784; Drewe in Report by Nina Clisby, Nov. 1934, SPG M785, RH. When I first visited Holy Cross in 1989, Drewe's prediction had come true: the hospital was run by Ugandans, Kenyans, and Ghanaians, who spoke even more dismissively of local medical beliefs than Drewe had done half a century earlier.

5. Drewe to Miss Farwell, 21 Mar. 1921, SPG M784, RH.

6. Walter E. Stanford, Annexation of Pondoland (Mar. 1894) 2, A 256, KAB; Drewe, History of HCH; Drewe, "Fifty Years a Missionary Doctor," in 1970–1971 Annual Report, M386, p. 21, RH; G. Callaway, *Pioneers in Pondoland,* 151. Archdeacon Leary had explained to Chief Ndaliso in 1911, "[W]e do not wish to have land on which to locate 'school kaffirs' but just sufficient ground for buildings, lands and access to

water." Leary to RM, Lusikisiki, 20 May 1911; E. Tshongwana, Secretary to the Paramount, to RM, Lusikisiki, 23 Sept. 1911; Jackson Maswakeli Sigcau, Paramount Chief Regent for Eastern Pondoland, The Great Place, Qaukeni, to Chief Magistrate, Umtata, 25 Apr. 1929, CMT 3/1104, file 14/9/8/1, KAB; Tshongwana, secretary to Chief Marelane, speaking to CMT, in a meeting held at Umtata, 27 Feb. 1919, 1/LSK 13 file 2/2, KAB. In this meeting Tshongwana expressed his irritation with the missionaries for wanting to pass laws forbidding beer drinking and polygamy and to grab land forcibly without consulting the chief. The idea of a Xhosa medical mission had originated with the missionaries themselves: Henry Callaway, bishop of St. Johns from 1873 to 1884, was a medical doctor who wanted "a physician of deep religious sensibility for Kaffraria [between the Keiskamma and Kei Rivers]"; and in 1888 his successor, Bransby Key, wrote from Umtata to the SPG in London asking for a medical missionary. G. Callaway, *Pioneers in Pondoland,* 51; Bransby Key to SPG, 3 Apr. 1888, SPG CLR 123, RH.

7. Drewe, selection from his diary published in HCH leaflet #5, Feb. 1965, SPG M785, RH; Malherbe, "Canon Dr. Frank Swinburne Drewe," 19.

8. Malherbe, "Canon Dr. Frank Swinburne Drewe," 9; Tembani, "Extracts from the Work of a [Holy Cross] Hospital Interpreter," 1935, SPG M785, RH; H. S. Matee, the African overseer of the hospital farm, "Witchcraft from the Native Point of View," 1935, SPG M785, RH. Matee argued that people were believed to inherit relationships with the spiritual agents and then sold or transferred their contacts to those wishing to do harm. Drewe, HCH Annual Report for 1922, SPG M386, RH.

9. This definition of witchcraft comes from Matee, "Witchcraft," 1.

10. Hunter, *Reaction to Conquest,* chap. 6. Also, Evidence of M. Leqela, Native Interpreter, Mt. Fletcher sitting of NEC, 31 Oct. 1930, in "Transkei: Health and Welfare," Herbst Papers, UCT. Frank Drewe, Notes for Lantern Lecture, 22 Apr. 1925, SPG M785, RH.

11. Matee, "Witchcraft," 6, 1.

12. W. P. Nicol, DS, Lusikisiki, to Secretary of the Interior, 24 Jan. 1915, 1 LSK 6 13/2/6, KAB.

13. Malherbe, "Canon Dr. Frank Swinburne Drewe," 16, 26. The year of the Kokstad donation is not given.

14. A hospital was established in Bizana by Roman Catholics in the mid-1950s, and St. Elizabeth's, also Catholic, was founded in Lusikisiki in the early 1960s. Drewe, Remarks Made in Cape Town, June 1946, before the Select Committee Considering the Draft Hospital Ordinance, SPG M785, RH. Drewe calculated that the Draft Ordinance would cause Holy Cross to lose 70–80 percent of its maintenance funds and gain only 50 percent.

15. G. Callaway, *Pioneers in Pondoland,* 140. The Witwatersrand Native Labour Association made out the check.

16. Drewe, Address at Medical Meeting, 1937, SPG M785, RH.

17. While he was on leave, the acting superintendent of the hospital wrote to Major Herbst, the SNA, in Pretoria, expressing concern that the new isolation wing might have to close down due to lack of funds. Herbst replied that the depression had caused

a shortfall in African taxes and so the revenues in the Native Development Fund had decreased. May Anderson to Herbst, 11 July 1932; Herbst to Anderson, 19 July 1932, NTS 2868 24/303, SAB.

18. Memorandum on the Report of Dr. R. Smit, Inspector for the Department of Public Health, on his Inspection of HCH, 20 May 1942, 1/LSK 45, KAB.

19. Drewe, Address at Medical Meeting, 1937, SPG M785, RH.

20. Resha, *My Life in the Struggle*, 27.

21. Drewe, Report to the Parishes, 6 May 1920, from The Deanery, Umtata, SPG M784, RH.

22. Drewe on HCH, n.d., SPG M785, RH; Silla, *"People Are Not the Same"*; Lusikisiki Magistrate to Rijno Smit, Medical Inspector, Native Territories, Union Dept. of Public Health, 16 Feb. 1942, 1/LSK 85 13/2/6, KAB.

23. Drewe, Comments on the Evidence Submitted to the National Health Services Commission, n.d., 3, Gluckman Papers, UCT. See Lamla, "Liberated Women," 20–24; Drewe, Evidence to the NEC, Flagstaff, 7 Nov. 1930, in "Transkei: Health and Child Welfare," 51, Cullen, Wits. When he actually ran his tests a year later, he discovered that 16.4 percent of his sample of 100 Pondo miners tested positive and 12 percent of another sample—235 Amampondo living within fifteen miles of the hospital—had tested positive. Spencer Lister, Director, SAIMR, to Drewe, 2 Nov. 1931, Howard Pim Papers, Cullen, Wits. Drewe, "Comments on the Evidence Submitted to the National Health Services Commission on Behalf of the Christian Council of South Africa," 3, 4, Gluckman Papers, UCT.

24. Drewe to Miss Farwell, USPG, 21 Mar. 1921; Drewe, open letter [to SPG], 5 Aug. 1922, SPG M784, RH; Drewe, Evidence to the NEC, 53. Silicosis or fibrosis of the lungs comes from inhaling silicosis dust and may lead to tuberculosis by activating dormant bacilli. Drewe to Howard Pim, Hotel Imperial, Umtata, 25 Apr. 1933, Pim Papers, Cullen, Wits. Drewe, Comments on Evidence Submitted to NHS, 3.

25. Drewe, "Maternity Advice by Doctor in Medical Mission, Ante-Natal Care of Native Mothers," *Imvo Zabantsundu*, 1 Oct. 1938, 10.

26. Dr. Joseph Gillman to National Nutrition Council, 27 Jan., 1944, NVR 14 132, SAB. Drewe did, however, make good nutrition the main theme of his work with lepers.

27. Juliana Drewe Taylor, Dr. Drewe's daughter, to author, 11 Apr. 1989.

28. Drewe, Evidence to the NEC and "From Holy Cross Hospital, February, 1938."

29. Drewe, "From Holy Cross Hospital, February, 1938."

30. NEC Evidence; van der Horst, "Enema and the African Child," 465–66.

31. Klopper, "Art of Zulu-Speakers," 134; Dr. Bleek to his parents, Pietermaritzburg, 24 Feb.-20 Apr. 1856, in *Natal Diaries*, 37; Hunter, *Reaction to Conquest*, 156.

32. Synopsis of Evidence Given by Dr. M. R. Mahlangeni to the Native Economic Commission at Umtata, 14 Nov. 1930, 3380–85; Synopsis of B. S. Ncabene's Evidence to the NEC at Port St. Johns, 10 Nov. 1930, in "Transkei: Health and Child Welfare," 3017–18.

33. Drewe to Deferred Pay Board, 2 Mar. 1940, 1/LSK 80, file 3/11/3, KAB; Drewe, "Report on a Visit to Johannesburg, 17 to 21 April, 1940," 1/LSK 45, KAB. HCH's story

is typical of the fifty mission hospitals serving rural African health by 1950. See, for example, R. L. Paterson, "Rural and Mission Hospitals in Relation to Disease and Health in the Bantu," *Leech* 21, no. 1 (1950): 90–94.

34. Drewe, Comments on Evidence to NHS, 7.

35. Drewe, Memorandum on Report of Dr. R. Smit, Medical Inspector, Native Territories, 20 May 1942, 1/LSK 45, KAB.

36. Drewe, 1948 Report, *South African Outlook,* 1 Feb. 1949, SPG M785, RH.

37. RM D. S. Cooke, Bizana, to CMT, [Sept. 1948?], 1/BIZ 6/27 13/2/3, KAB.

38. DS, Annual Report for the District of Libode for the Year Ending 30 June 1942, 1/LBE 34 13/2/6 (vol. 1), KAB.

39. Tuberculosis and Malnutrition Survey, 1938, 1UTA 13/7/4/1, KAB. The committee was composed of Major J. F. Herbst (chair), Major M. G. Apthorpe, and Dr. F. C. Wilmot, and its rubric was to inquire into the extent of tuberculosis among indigent Africans, the extent to which African schoolchildren were undernourished and suffering from starvation, and what form of assistance should be given.

40. RM, Bizana, to DS, Bizana, Minute, 17 Feb. 1948, on letter from Deputy Chief Health Officer (East London) to Magistrate, Bizana, 6 Feb. 1948, 1/BIZ 6/27 13/2/3, KAB.

41. Testimony of Dr. McGregor cited in Report of Committee Appointed to Inquire into Overstocking in the Transkeian Territories, 26 Aug. 1941, United Transkeian Territories General Council, Proceedings, 35, Cullen, Wits. Ironically, diarrhea caused by inability to digest carbohydrates commonly occurs in people who, lacking one or more intestinal enzymes, are lactose intolerant, that is, they cannot digest milk.

42. Ibid., 33–34.

43. "Blessing and Opening of the Drewe Wing," 23 July 1942; P. H. Peppin, "Why a Farm?," 1945, SPG M785, RH.

44. United Transkeian Territories General Council, Proceedings: Cr. Tsengiwe, 1937, 187; Cr. Sakwe, 1938, 239; Cr. W. W. Dana, 1941, 93; Cr. Ndamase, 1947, 32.

45. Drewe, Comments on Evidence to NHS, 5.

46. James E. Cawthorne, Report, 1 July 1950, USPG, M785, RH; Malherbe, *Canon Dr. Frank Swinburne Drewe,* 27. A drought afflicted Pondoland for the first half of the decade, but from 1956 until 1964 the area sustained a series of reasonable harvests.

47. HCH Report, May 1959; Cawthorne, Report, 21 Apr. 1952, SPG M785, RH.

48. Eileen Hope, Report, 11 Nov. 1950; Dr. Dennis W. Patient, "First Impressions of Holy Cross," Dec. 1960; D. Patient, Report, Oct. 1961; Mrs. Patient, Report, 20 July 1961, SPG M785, RH.

49. Grace Pike, Report up to December 1955; Dr. Bride Dickson, Report, 1 Dec. 1957; Dr. R. A. Spalding, Report, [1958?], SPG M785, RH.

50. Hope, 11 Nov. 1950.

51. Bruce-Bays, "Infant Feeding," 91; Odendaal, "Nutrition in Public Health," 482. Psychiatrists like Sachs, who practiced in Johannesburg in the 1930s, believed that Africans' personalities were shaped by sudden weaning at a late age, which led mature Africans to seek favors and protection constantly; Sachs gave a talk to the Durban Left Club in 1944 arguing that Africans needed mother-craft propaganda to correct the

trauma they had sustained from sudden weaning. (Sachs, *Black Hamlet.*) Report by Hope, 11 Nov. 1950.

52. This hypothesis was suggested to me by Nurse Elizabeth Pooley, Oxford, after I showed her the chart. Her energetic and intelligent engagement with the explanatory problems posed by the graph in 1990 stand in contrast to the medical testimony of all HCH personnel in the 1950s.

53. L. M. Mhlana, interview by author.

54. Peppin, "Why a Farm?"

55. HCH Report for 1953–1954, SPG M785; Wilkins to CMT, 20 Nov. 1953, file 3/11/3, 1/LSK 81, KAB; Dr. Bruce Buchan, interview by author; D. Patient to Overseas Secretary, SPG, 15 Dec. 1962, SPG M785, RH.

56. Nurses' complaints quoted in H. O. Wilbraham, Magistrate, Lusikisiki, Report on Disturbances at HCH, 13 Apr. 1953, CMT 3/1104 file 14/9/8/1, KAB.

57. Jackson Hanxa to NC, NAD, Pretoria, 16 Feb. 1953, CMT 3/1104 file 14/9/8/1, KAB.

58. Sidney Kark's Pholela Health Center became the pilot project in the health center movement that was spawned by the National Health Services Commission in 1944. Its aim was to cure, prevent, and promote health by employing health educators to explain disease, nutrition, sanitation, and venereal disease. During its first ten years it reported that it had managed to reduce cases of gross nutritional failure, prevent epidemics, and bring about a steady decrease in crude mortality and infant mortality rates. S. Kark and Cassel, "Pholela Health Center." See also S. Kark and E. Kark, *Promoting Community Health.*

59. VT AR, 1957, 7.

60. Stott, "Valley Trust Socio-Medical Project," 52.

61. Ibid., quoting the South African Sugar Cane Growers' Association, noted that rural African sugar consumption had increased tenfold between 1953 and 1964 (pp. 119, 54, 49).

62. Stott, "Pilot Health Study," 25, 18, 52.

63. G. W. Gale, Secretary for Health, to SNA, 29 Feb. 1952, VDG 181, VN 402/1, SAB; Stott, Address to Soil Association, London, 11 Sept. 1958, reprinted in *Mother Earth* 10, no. 5 (1959).

64. The book was J. D. Comrie's *Diet in Health and Sickness* (London, 1933).

65. The adjacent Botha's Hill Health Centre, taken over by the Department of Health in 1951, did administer drugs such as penicillin, but to discourage the mushrooming numbers of patients, they were asked from 1955 to pay a shilling a visit. The Botha's Hill Health Centre also had an educational bias. Stott, "Pilot Health Study," 59.

66. VT AR, 1955, 1.

67. The Valley Trust, Brief Summary of Objectives and Functions, n.d.

68. VT AR, 1958, 42; W. T. Webber, House of Assembly, *Debates,* First Session, Third Parliament, 8 Aug. 1966, Hansard.

69. Report on a Brief Visit by J. M. Latsky, Chief Adviser, Dept. of Nutrition, 20 Jan. 1956, VDG 179 VN 401/1, SAB.

70. J. D. Krige, "Valley Trust Research Objectives and Activities," in VT AR, 1957,

23. R. C. Albino, "Thinking in Africans," in VT AR, 1965, 17–18; R. Gilbey, Psychology Department, University of Natal, Pietermaritzburg, "A Psychological Study of the Effects of Kwashiorkor on Children in the Valley of a Thousand Hills," in VT AR, 1961, 19; Wheeler, "Types of Malnutrition," 8.

71. Krige, "Research Objectives and Activities," 32.

72. Vilakazi, *Zulu Transformations,* 2.

73. For examples of these expulsions see the following files in the Natal Archives: 1/CPD 3/1/1 (1905); CNC 189 1812/1914 (1914); CNC 224 1915/1576 (1916); 1/CPD 3/2/2/5 file 2/1/13/1A (1922). Preston-Whyte and Sibisi, "Ethnographic Oddity or Ethnographic Sense?," 308; the authors write that immigrants provided the service of "protect[ing] the boundaries" of the established descent groups.

74. *Times* (London), 19 Oct. 1934, p. 13. These two clans were named Embo and Ngcolosi. Minutes of a Meeting Held at the Maziyana Store, Botha's Hill, 3 Feb. 1939, 1/CPD 3/2/3/2/2, file N2/3/3/2, NAB.

75. Malie, "Nyuswa Crops and Diet," 9.

76. VT AR, 1957, 31; Malie, "Nyuswa Crops and Diet," 27.

77. VT AR, 1955, 7.

78. These files refer to 1941–1946: Inter-Provincial Removal of Natives to Camperdown, NTS 2587 2081/295, SAB; Inter-Provincial Removal of Natives to Pinetown, NTS 2587 2076/295, SAB. E. J. Krige, "Some Aspects of the Impact of the Valley Trust on the Nyuswa and Quadi [sic] of the Valley of a Thousand Hills," VT AR, 1962, 15.

79. Friedman, "Health Profile," 66.

80. Bryant, *Zulu Medicine,* 48; Rodseth to SNA, 12 Mar. 1946, Ballinger Papers, B2.14.9 (file 2), Wits.; VT AR 1975, 8.

7. Denial and Coercion

1. Ashforth, *Politics of Official Discourse.*

2. Scott, *Seeing like a State,* chap. 3.

3. de Swardt, "Agricultural Marketing Problems," 22.

4. The key legislation was the Dairy Industry Control Act 1930, Maize Control Act 1931, Meat Trade Control Act 1932, Maize Marketing Act 1936, and Marketing Act 1937. de Kiewiet, *History of South Africa,* 257–60; Packard, *White Plague, Black Labor,* 116–17.

5. In 1938, South African butter sold for eight pence a pound in London and for one shilling and six or seven pence a pound in South African towns. House of Assembly, *Debates,* 9 Aug. 1938, 728.

6. Richards, "Subsidies, Quotas, Tariffs."

7. House of Assembly, *Debates,* 9 Aug. 1938, 706, 712, 716.

8. Ibid., 721.

9. Ibid., 706, 703, 702.

10. J. M. Tonetti to Margaret Ballinger, 4 June 1946, Ballinger Papers, B2.14.9 (file 3), Wits.

11. "Malnutrition among Natives," *Midland News* (Cradock), 8 Feb. 1938. I owe this reference to Jeffrey Butler.

12. Acting CNC, Natal, to SNA, 26 Mar. 1945, NTS 7891 131/336 (I), SAB.

13. SAIRR, "Production and Sale of Margarine," 19 Dec. 1949, AD 1947, box 16 32.8.1, Wits.

14. Unsigned letter from a trader in de Kol to T. B. Bowker, M.P., 27 Mar. 1946, Ballinger Papers, B2.14.9 (file 2), Wits.

15. Kassier Commission, *Report,* 3; Posel, *Making of Apartheid,* 168.

16. Posel, *Making of Apartheid,* 154. Clarke, De Jongh, and Jokl, "Effect of Mid-Day Meal," 41. The number of private manufacturing plants rose from 13,879 in 1948–1949 to 16,838 in 1957–1958, and the value of their gross output rose from £610,000,000 to £1,503,000,000. Clarke, De Jongh, and Jokl, "Effect of Mid-day Meal"; Memorandum by the Appointed Members of the Commission, Report of the Native Affairs Commission, U.G. 42–1941 (1939–1940), 59.

17. Union of South Africa, Inter-Departmental Committee on the Social, Health and Economic Conditions of Urban Natives, *Report,* 7.

18. Union of South Africa, National Health Services Commission, *Report,* chap. 1; Annual Report of Department of Public Health, 1937, U.G. 49–38, 13; Collie Commission, *Report,* 71.

19. Gluckman, "Findings of the National Health Commission," 58; Paton, *Hofmyer,* 392; Marks and Andersson, "1944 National Health Services Commission," 158.

20. Evans, *Bureaucracy and Race,* 285–86; Social Security Committee and Social and Economic Planning Council, *Social Security,* pars. 105, 108; Report 2: par. 70. The committee members were: Dr. H. J. van Eck, Dr. P. Allen (secretary for public health), Prof. H. R. Burrows, J. D. F. Briggs, G. A. C. Kuschke (secretary for social welfare), W. J. G. Mears (undersecretary for native affairs), Major D. A. Pirie (commissioner of pensions), and I. L. Walker (secretary for labor).

21. Social Security Committee, par. 66; Paton, *Hofmyer,* 379–81.

22. Paton, *Hofmyer,* 381, 439.

23. John Latsky, Department of Public Health, document headed "Strictly Confidential," 31 Oct. 1944, attached to letter from Latsky to Margaret Ballinger, 3 Apr. 1946, Ballinger Papers (A410), B2.14.9 (file 2), Wits.

24. Hellmann, *Handbook on Race Relations,* 389.

25. NNC, press statement, 26 Nov. 1941; and *Cape Times,* 13 Dec. 1941, NVR 14 183, SAB.

26. First Report of the Activities of the NNC, 1944, 4.

27. Ibid., 16.

28. Joseph Gillman, "Report to the Scientific Research Committee of the Nutritional Council for the Need of Supporting the Research on Bantu Diets," 27 Jan. 1944, NVR 14 132, SAB.

29. Posel, *Making of Apartheid,* 47.

30. Verwoerd quoted in Evans, *Bureaucracy and Race,* 68.

31. "Urban Areas—Committee of Enquiry—Location Free Milk Fund," 1 Nov. 1941, Ballinger Papers, A 410 B2.14.10, file 1, Wits.

32. "Native School Feeding Opposed in Parliament," *Imvo Zabantsundu,* 9 Feb. 1946.

33. In the meantime local school boards and committees should contribute a reasonable amount and the state should provide no money to farm schools; the Depart-

ment of Education would include schools in town only at its own discretion; food would be given to no students over fourteen years old. Funding was on a per capita basis and there was no restriction on enrollment. Whyte, "Native School Feeding," 6; Minister of Education, "School Feeding of Native Children," 14 Apr. 1949, 3, SAIRR (AD 1947), box 15, Wits. Union of South Africa, Department of Education, Arts, Science, Commission of Enquiry into School Feeding, *Report,* 39.

34. Hansard, House of Assembly, *Debates,* vol. 68, 1949, 4 May 1949, col. 5109.

35. Ibid., cols. 5074, 5083; Commission of Enquiry into School Feeding, *Report,* 50.

36. Hansard, House of Assembly, *Debates,* vol. 68, 4 May 1949, cols. 5091, 5138, 5137.

37. These cuts were made despite the fact that a 1951 survey of schoolchildren conducted by medical officers revealed the following figures for "extensive" undernourishment: Europeans 3.2 percent, Bantu 24.5 percent, Coloureds 7 percent, Asiatics 42.8 percent (based on an Asian sample size of 7!). That year African schools were receiving £600,000 for school meals, whereas European schools received £871,359, and Asian and Coloured schools together got £503,652. SAIRR, *Survey of Race Relations,* 1951–1952, 67, 73. In 1953 spending declined to £585,000, that is, £30,000 less than the preceding year, but in 1955–1956 it went up to £641,487.

38. SAIRR, *Survey of Race Relations,* 1956–1957, 193.

39. The Department of Nutrition was set up in 1951 to organize research, propaganda, and technical development, rather than to control prices or agricultural production, which remained the responsibility of the Department of Agriculture. For example, the department bore the cost of the pre-mix for Bremer bread supplied to bakers and of advertising the bread itself. SAIRR, *Survey of Race Relations,* 1951–1952, 69. The department also advocated subsidizing foodstuffs with high nutritive value. In 1953 it began an experimental scheme with the Pretoria municipality to sell skimmed milk and buttermilk cheaply in African and subeconomic European areas.

40. SAIRR, *Survey of Race Relations,* 1952–1953, 93; 1955–1956, 214; 1958–1959, 284–85.

41. Ibid., 1959–1960, 246.

42. Ibid., 1961, 263.

43. Dr. F. J. Van Biljon, Managing Director, Rand Cold Storage and Supply Co., Johannesburg, "The Current Situation and Prospects for 1963, in the Primary Products Sector of the Economy (with Special Reference to Agriculture and the Food Industry)," Address to National Management Conference, 1963, 7, SAIRR (AD 1947), 32.3.2.5, Wits.

44. This philosophy was stated by the 1954 Financing of Voluntary Welfare Organizations Committee. SAIRR, *Survey of Race Relations,* 1953–1954, 141–42.

45. Ibid., 1962, 208; 1965, 290. In time, when money became harder to collect from donors, some of Kupugani's regional branches failed and the organization was superseded by one called Imqualife, which sought to ensure that it would cover its costs by making a profit. Martiny, interview by author.

46. SAIRR, *Survey of Race Relations,* 1953–1954, 140.

47. Ibid., 1963, 254.

48. Anthony Barker, Superintendent of Charles Johnson Memorial Hospital, Nqutu, quoted in SAIRR, *Survey of Race Relations,* 1969, 231.

49. J. P. Kotze, "Facts Regarding Malnutrition in South Africa" (pp. 3–10), and B. D. Richardson, "Controversies Surrounding the Anthropometric Evaluation of Malnourished Children" (pp. 18–27), in Griesel, *Malnutrition in Southern Africa*.

50. Hansen to author, 27 July and 15 Aug. 1998.

51. Nigel Purry, Medical News from HCH, 1966, SPG M785, RH.

52. P. G. Vermeulen to Chief Accountant, 27 Oct. 1955, CMT 3/1447 36/9/1, KAB.

53. South African Campaign against Malnutrition by the Head Committee under Chairmanship of S. J. J. de Swardt, secretary for agricultural economics and marketing, *Report*, Oct. 1962, 6, AD 1947, 32.3.2.3, Wits. The legal authority for carrying out betterment was based on section 25 of the Native Administration Act of 1927, which gave the governor-general the power to issue proclamations about soil erosion. Proclamation 199 of 1937, amended by 168 of 1942, provided for the maintenance of soil conservation works, and Proclamation 116 of 1949 for the control and limitation of livestock in the reserves and for the proper usage of the land.

54. Lusikisiki Magistrate, Annual Report, 14 Aug. 1953, KAB CMT 3/1458 38/9/3, KAB.

55. Posel, *Making of Apartheid*, 69.

56. Lusikisiki Magistrate, Annual Report, 21 July 1948, 1/LSK 73 2/16/5, KAB.

57. Chairman, Planning Committee, to CMT, 13 Sept. 1952, CMT 3/1327 24/9/4 part 1, KAB.

58. Daniel Tabalaza to CMT, 12 July 1950; CMT Yates, handwritten note dated 19 July 1950, CMT 3/1327 24/9/4 part 1, KAB.

59. Minutes of a meeting held in the office of the CMT, Umtata, 23 Oct. 1953, CMT 3/1327 24/9/4 part 1, KAB.

60. CMT T. D. Ramsay to J. V. Jensen, Massey-Harris Co., East London, 19 June 1956, CMT 3/1621 file 99F, KAB.

61. Evans, *Bureaucracy and Race*, 240, 242.

62. Tomlinson Commission, *Summary of the Report*, 77; SAIRR, *Survey of Race Relations*, 1955–1956, 142, 151; Union of South Africa, State Information Office, *Sequel to Tomlinson Report*, 18.

63. State Information Office, *Sequel to Tomlinson Report*, 10, 33; Tomlinson Commission, *Summary of the Report*, 117.

64. Hobart Houghton, "Native Reserves," 31; Matthews and M'Timkulu, "Future in the Light"; Marquard, *South Africa's Internal Boundaries*. Matthews and M'Timkulu's attack focused on the political implications of the report. The *Race Relations Journal* published only one other article written by Africans between 1957 and 1960, a report on African farm labor by Matthews and D. D. T. Jabavu.

65. T. F. Coertze, Paper read at Conference of Magistrates and School Inspectors, Umtata, 26–27 Oct. 1954, p. 2, 1/LSK 156 N11/1/2 (vol. 1), KAB.

66. United Transkeian Territories General Council, Proceedings, 30 Apr. 1950, 65; and 25 Apr. 1949, 47.

67. J. O. Cornell (chairman, District Council, Ngcobo), in United Transkeian Territories General Council, Proceedings, 17 Apr. 1951, 83.

68. Director of Food Supplies and Distribution to SNA, 3 Mar. 1952, CMT 3/1636

file 108A, KAB; United Transkeian Territories General Council, Proceedings, 1951, 3; and 17 Apr. 1951, 82–84; Dr. V. M. Malherbe, DS, Flagstaff, 22 Apr. 1959, 1 FSF 6/20 13/2/6, KAB; Bantu Affairs Commissioner, Lusikisiki, to Chief Bantu Affairs Commissioner, Umtata, Annual Report for 1959, 12 July 1960, I/LSK 142, KAB.

69. Crais, "Men, Magic and the Law."

70. The men who belonged to the Intaba movement blamed corruption on Chief Botha Sigcau and his minions. They argued that if his half brother, Nelson, had been made chief in 1938, they would not be suffering in 1960. They had only accepted Botha as paramount because they were a "subject nation."

71. HCH, Inpatient Register, 1958–1960, HCH storeroom. Bruce Buchan, the DS at Lusikisiki at the time, remembers performing fourteen or fifteen postmortems at the site a few days later, but by then some of the bodies had been removed, so we may assume that the actual death toll was higher. (Interview by author.) The missionary then resident at Holy Cross complained to the government on behalf of "the Pondo in the vicinity" that many more men had died than the six admitted by the government; he requested a judicial inquiry. (Rev. F. E. C. Vaughan-Jones to CMT, 25 July 1960, I/LSK 114 file N. 1/9/2, KAB.)

72. Eighth Speaker, Meeting held at Nkunzimbini, 16 June 1960, p. 2, CMT 3/1479 file 42/9, KAB.

73. "Disaffection in Lusikisiki District" [Fenwick Report], 1 June 1960, CMT 3/1479 file 42/9, KAB; Albert Somadlangati, Evidence to van Heerden Commission of Inquiry into the Pondoland Revolt, 1960, 128.

74. Nofitshane Tshumane, referring to shops in his home area, the Vlei, interview by author.

75. Tshumane, interview; Somadlangati, Evidence, 129–30, 144; Elijah Lande, Evidence to Van Heerden Commission, 280.

Epilogue

1. Gilroy, *"No Black in the Union Jack,"* 11–12.

2. Fredrickson, *Black Image*.

3. The phrase was used by the Transvaal Indigency Commission to describe what one class of poor whites (the ignorant and lazy) had "fallen behind." *Report*, 4.

4. Herbst, Apthorp, and Willmot to SNA, "Starving or Under-Nourished Native Children."

5. A. Smith, *Moral Sentiments*, 62.

6. Westcott and Stott, "Extent and Causes of Malnutrition," 963; Thomas, "Social Background of Childhood Nutrition," 551–55.

7. Cedric de Beer, personal communication, Aug. 1986.

8. Dumo Baqwa, Address to the African Studies Center, Boston University, Boston, 23 Feb. 1998.

9. Stubbs, *Steve Biko*, 102.

10. Serote, *Longer Poems*, 26.

11. Ngubane, "Aspects of Clinical Practice," 365; Campbell, *Called to Heal*.

Bibliography

Manuscript Collections and Archives

Cape Archives Depot, Cape Town
    Chief Magistrate of the Transkei. Correspondence.
    Pondoland District Officers' and District Surgeons' Correspondence.
Central Archives Depot, Pretoria
    Department of Nutrition and National Nutrition Council. Files.
    Department of Public Health. Annual Reports.
    Government Native Labour Board. Files.
    Native Affairs Department. Files.
Chamber of Mines Research Organization, Johannesburg
    Fleming, P. W. "A History of Nutrition in the Mining Industry, 1889–1961." [1966?].
        Project 709/65, Research Report 65/66.
Holy Cross Hospital, Pondoland
    Inpatient Register.
Houghton Library, Harvard University, Cambridge, Mass.
    American Board of Commissioners for Foreign Missions. Files on Alexandra Health
        Centre and Ruth Cowles.
Killie Campbell Africana Library, Durban
    Camperdown Agricultural Society. Minute Book.
Natal Archives Depot, Pietermaritzburg
    Camperdown Files.
    Fynn, Henry F. Papers.
    Secretary for Native Affairs and Chief Native Commissioner. Files re Qadi, Nyuswa,
        Ngcolosi, and Mbo.
Rhodes House, Oxford
    Society for the Propagation of the Gospel. Papers.
South African Library, Cape Town
    Bleek, W. H. I., trans. "Translation of the Manuscript Legends and Customs Col-
        lected by Rev. H. Callaway in 1858." (G. 39d.36).
    Imvo Zabantsundu (newspaper).
Sterling Memorial Library, Yale University, New Haven, Conn.
    Fox, F. W., and Douglas Back. A Preliminary Survey of the Agricultural and Nutri-
        tional Problems of the Ciskei and Transkeian Territories with Special Reference

to Their Bearing on the Recruiting of Labourers for the Gold Mining Industry. 1941. Microfilm.

SAIRR Papers. Microfilm.

Xuma, A. B. Papers. Microfilm.

Transkei Archives Depot, Umtata

Agricultural Statistics.

University of Cape Town Library (Manuscripts and Archives), Cape Town

Gluckman, Henry. Papers.

Herbst, J. F. Papers.

Stanford, Walter E. Papers.

University of the Witwatersrand, Cullen Africana Library, Johannesburg

Ballinger, Margaret. Papers.

Native Economic Commission. Report and Evidence.

Pim, James Howard. Papers.

SAIRR Papers.

United Transkeian Territories General Council (Bunga). Proceedings, 1908–1959.

Van Heerden Commission. Report and Evidence.

Valley Trust, Botha's Hill, Natal

Annual Reports. 1955–1985.

Malie, M. "Preliminary Report on Nyuswa Crops and Diet." 1957.

Selected Official Publications

Natal (Colony) Commission Appointed to Inquire into the Past and Present State of the Kafirs in the District of Natal, and to Report on Their Future Government, and to Suggest Such Arrangements as Will Tend to Secure the Peace and Welfare of the District for the Information of His Honor the Lieutenant Governor. *Proceedings.* Pietermaritzburg: Archbell, 1852.

United Kingdom. Parliament. *Further Correspondence Respecting the Affairs of South Africa.* C. 2220. London, 1878–1879.

Transvaal Labour Commission. *Report.* Johannesburg, 1904. (United Kingdom, Parliament, Cd. 1896, 1904.)

United Kingdom. Parliament. Inter-Departmental Committee on Physical Deterioration. *Report.* Cd. 2175, vol. 32. London, 1904.

Transvaal Indigency Commission. *Report.* T.G. 13–'08. Pretoria, 1908.

Union of South Africa. Natives Grievances Inquiry, 1913–1914. *Report.* U.G. 37–1914. 1914.

Province of Transvaal. Local Government Commission (1921). *Report.* T.P. 1–1922. 1922.

Union of South Africa. Department of Public Health. Annual Reports. 1930s–1940s.

———. Native Economic Commission, 1930–1932. *Report.* U.G. 22–1932. 1932.

———. Department of Native Affairs. Departmental Committee Appointed to Enquire into and Report upon Certain Questions Relating to Native Labour in Zululand, the Transkeian Territories and the Ciskei. *Report* [Welsh Report]. 1935.

——. Departmental Committee of Enquiry on National Health Insurance [Collie Commission]. *Report.* U.G. 41–1936. 1936.

——. Inter-Departmental Committee on Poor Relief and Charitable Institutions. *Report.* U.G. 61–1937. 1937.

United Kingdom. Parliament. Economic Advisory Council. *Nutrition in the Colonial Empire.* Cmd. 6050, vol. 10. 1938–1939.

Union of South Africa. House of Assembly. *Debates.* 1938, 1939, 1945, 1946, 1949, 1966.

——. Native Affairs Commission. *Report.* U.G. 42–1941. 1939–1940.

——. Inter-Departmental Committee on the Social, Health and Economic Conditions of Urban Natives. *Report.* 1942.

——. National Health Services Commission. *Report.* U.G. 30–1944. 1942–1944.

——. Witwatersrand Mine Natives' Wages Commission on the Remuneration and Conditions of Employment of Natives on Witwatersrand Gold Mines. *Report.* U.G. 21–1944. 1943.

——. Social Security Committee and Social and Economic Planning Council. *Social Security, Social Service and the National Income.* U.G. 14–1944. 1944.

——. Commission Appointed to Inquire into the Operation of Bus Services for Non-Europeans on the Witwatersrand and in the District of Pretoria and Vereeniging. *Report.* U.G. 31–1944. 1944.

——. Department of Education, Arts, Science. Commission of Enquiry into School Feeding (1949). *Report.* 1951.

——. Commission for the Socio-Economic Development of the Bantu Areas within the Union of South Africa [Tomlinson Commission]. *Summary of the Report.* U.G. 61–1955. 1955.

——. State Information Office. *The Sequel to the Tomlinson Commission Report.* 1957.

Republic of South Africa. Committee of Inquiry into the Marketing Act [Kassier Commission]. *Report.* Dec. 1992.

Selected Interviews by Author

Buchan, Bruce, and Margaret Barlow. Durban, 7 Apr. 1989.

Gear, J. H. S. SAIMR, Johannesburg, 29 Apr. 1993.

Glatthaar, Ingrid. Pretoria, Apr. 1993.

Hansen, John D. L. Johannesburg, 1 May 1993.

Kark, Sidney L., and Emily Kark. Jerusalem, 9 Mar. 1998.

Martiny, Oluf. Johannesburg, 20 Dec. 1988.

Pooley, Elizabeth. Oxford, 1990.

Stott, Halley. Botha's Hill, Natal, Apr. 1989.

ter Haar, Gerrit. Rietvlei, 13 June 1989.

Thomas, G. C. Cape Town, 2 July 1989.
Walker, A. R. P. SAIMR, Johannesburg, 29 Apr. 1993.

Interviews in Pondoland

Cukana, Rose. Lambasi, 5 Mar. 1989.
Feeley, James. Umtata, 16 June 1989.
Fikeni, Gqatshula, and Shusha Fikeni. Mbotyi, 4 Mar. 1989.
Ginyabantu, Momtshoniswa. Hombe, 20 June 1989.
Jack, J. Umtata, 16 June 1989.
Mgoduka, Jameson. Lusikisiki, 7 Mar. 1989.
Mgwili, Majayiya. Ngqouza Hill, 18 June 1989.
Mgwili, Nomatshinka. Ngqouza Hill, 18 June 1989.
Mhlana, Lina Mfolozi. Holy Cross Hospital, 24 Feb. 1989.
Mkovana, Sikutshwana. Ngqouza Hill, 17 June 1989.
Mngqingo, Tshaluti. Hombe, 20 June 1989.
Ndabeni, Mnukwa. Dubana, Feb. 1989.
Ndengese, Nodada. Lambasi, 5 Mar. 1989.
Pikani, Mamtiseli. Lower Ntafufu, 3 Mar. 1989.
Sifo, Vina Manikwe. Lambasi, 4 Mar. 1989.
Sigcau, Hilda Kiyelwa. Holy Cross Hospital, 26 Feb. 1989.
Sokana, Abigail. Lusikisiki, Feb. 1989.
Tshumane, Nofitshane. Taweni location, Lusikisiki, 19 June 1989.
Xabo, Vubeni. Taweni location, Lusikisiki, 18 June 1989.

Interviews in Valley of a Thousand Hills

Hlophe, Esther, and Jackson Hlophe. Qadi, 11 July 1989.
Mpemba, Gasta. Qadi, 11 July 1989.
Ngcobo, Velangezihyo. Qadi, 12 July 1989.
Ntaka, Dubumbuso. Qadi, 11 July 1989.
Nzama, Dick. Qadi, 12 July 1989.
Pewa, Bixa. Nyuswa, July 1989.
Thabete, Florence. Nyuswa, July 1989.

Selected Articles

Anning, C. C. P. "Health Policy in Relation to Nutrition Needs." *Race Relations* 6, no. 1
    (1939): 33–37.
———. "Studies in the Nutrition of the People of Benoni." *SAJMS* 4, no. 4 (1939):
    117–24.

Atkinson, Mabel (Mrs. Palmer). "Notes on Some Native Budgets Collected in Durban." *SAJS* 25 (1928): 499–506.

———. "Some Problems of the Transition from Subsistence to a Money Economy." *SAJS* 27 (1930): 117–25.

Batson, Edward. "The Nature of Poor Relief: Its Principles." In *Report of the Committee Appointed to Study the Scale of Rations Prescribed by the Union Department of Social Welfare.* Cape Town: Cape Coordinating Council of Social Welfare Organizations, 1942.

———. "A Contribution to the Study of the Relative Roles of Income Levels and Purchasing Habits in the Determination of Sub-Standard Food Consumption." *SAJE* 2 (1943): 106–20.

———. "The Improvement in the Socio-Economic Condition of the Coloured People of Cape Town, 1938–51." *Journal for Social Research* 5, no. 2 (1954): 93–112.

Beinart, William. "Soil Erosion, Conservationism and Ideas about Development: A Southern African Exploration, 1900–60." *JSAS* 11, no. 1 (1984): 52–83.

———. "Introduction: The Politics of Colonial Conservation." *JSAS* 15, no. 2 (1989): 143–62.

———. "Transkeian Smallholders and Agrarian Reform." *JCAS* 11, no. 2 (1992): 178–99.

Bonnassie, Pierre. "Consommation d'aliments immondes et cannibalisme de survie dans l'Occident du Haut Moyen Age." *Annales, Economies, Sociétés, Civilisations* 44, no. 5 (1989): 1035–56.

Brantley, Cynthia. "Kikuyu-Maasai Nutrition and Colonial Science: The Orr and Gilks Study in Late 1920s Kenya Revisited." *IJAHS* 30, no. 1 (1997): 49–86.

Brock, John F. "Malnutrition in South Africa." *SAMJ,* 24 July 1943, 1–7.

———. "The Medical Approach to the Problem of Malnutrition," *Leech* 17, no. 1 (1946): 5–6.

———. "Nutritional Science and Practical Dietetics." *SAMJ* 32, no. 36 (28 June 1958): 654–58.

———. "The Evolution of Medical Research in South Africa." *SAMJ* 34, no. 21 (1960): 420–21.

Brock, John F., and F. W. Fox. "The Study of Nutritional Factors Affecting Human Health and Welfare in Africa." *SAMJ* 23 (1949): 1000–1010.

Brock, John F., and John M. Latsky. "The Findings of the Cape Nutrition Survey." *SAMJ* 16 (1942): 255–60.

Bruce-Bays, J. "Infant Feeding." *TMJ,* Nov. 1908, 90–94.

———. "The Injurious Effects of Civilisation upon the Physical Condition of the Native Races of South Africa." *SAJS* 5 (1909): 263–68.

Clarke, Daphne, T. W. De Jongh, and E. Jokl. "Effect of Mid-Day Meal upon the Physical Efficiency of Schoolchildren." *Manpower* 1, no. 2 (1943): 30–41.

Cluver, E. H. "Pellagra among the Maize Eating Natives of the Union of South Africa," *BMJ,* 26 Oct. 1929, 751–54.

———. "The Nutritional Problem in South Africa." *SAMJ* 13, no. 3 (1939): 83–86.

———. "Nutritional Research in the Union of South Africa." *Bulletin of the Health Organization of the League of Nations* 9, extract 5 (1941): 327–41.

———. "Food and Citizenship." *Leech* 17, no. 1 (1946): 2–3.

Crais, Clifton. "Of Men, Magic, and the Law: Popular Justice and the Political Imagination in South Africa." *Journal of Social History* 32, no. 1 (1998): 49–72.

Cunningham, A. B. "Collection of Wild Plant Foods in Tembe Thonga Society: A Guide to Iron Age Gathering Activities?" *Ann. Natal Mus.* 29, no. 2 (1988): 433–46.

Delf, Marion E. "Studies in Experimental Scurvy with Special Reference to the Antiscorbutic Properties of Some South African Foodstuffs." *SAIMR Publication No. 4*, 14 Sept. 1921.

de Swardt, S. J. J. "Agricultural Marketing Problems in the Nineteen Thirties." *SAJE* 51, no. 1 (1983): 1–28.

Dietler, Michael. "Driven by Drink: The Role of Drinking in the Political Economy and the Case of Early Iron Age France." *Journal of Anthropological Archaeology* 9 (1990): 352–406.

Dormer, B. A., J. Friedlander, and F. J. Wiles. "A South African Team Looks at Tuberculosis." *PMMOA* 23, no. 257 (1943): 80–82.

Duncan, David. "Liberals and Local Administration in South Africa: Alfred Hoernlé and the Alexandra Health Committee, 1933–43." *IJAHS* 23, no. 2 (1990): 475–93.

Eberstadt, Nicholas. "Poverty in South Africa." *Optima* 36, no. 1 (1988): 20–33.

Fetter, Bruce. "The Mines of Southern and Central Africa: An Ecological Framework." *Health Transition Review* 2, supplemental issue (1992): 125–35.

Fox, F. W. "A Short Review of Recent Work on the Vitamins." *Journal of the Medical Association of South Africa*, 11 Jan. 1930, 3–15.

———. "Some Nutritional Problems amongst the Bantu in South Africa," *Premeiro congresso medico de Lourenço Marques*, vol. 3 (12 Sept. 1938), 93–114.

———. "The Nutritional Aspect." *PMMOA* 22, no. 233 (Sept. 1941): 23–28.

———. "How South Africa Became Interested in Nutrition." *SAMJ* 37 (1963): 395–98.

Fox, F. W., and L. F. Dangerfield. "Scurvy and the Requirements of Native Mine Labourers for the Antiscorbutic Vitamin: An Experimental Study." *PMMOA* 19 (1940): 267–304.

Fox, F. W., L. F. Dangerfield, S. F. Gottlich, and E. Jokl. "Vitamin C Requirements of Native Mine Labourers: An Experimental Study." *BMJ* 2 (1940): 143–47.

Fox, F. W., and William Stone. "The Antiscorbutic Value of Kaffir Beer." *SAJMS* 3, no. 1 (Jan. 1938): 7–14.

Gluckman, Henry. "The Application of the Findings of the National Health Commission in Planning for the Future of the Problem." *Leech* 17, no. 1 (1946): 57–60.

Golberg, Leon, and J. M. Thorpe. "A Survey of Vitamins in South African Foodstuffs." *SAJMS* 7 (1942): 95–108; 10 (1945): 1– 8, 87–94; 11 (1946): 177–85.

Goldsmith, A. W. "The Mine Medical Officer Aspect." *PMMOA* 22, no. 233 (1941): 30–33.

Grigg, David. "The Nutritional Transition in Western Europe." *Journal of Historical Geography* 21, no. 3 (1995): 247–61.

Haines, E. S. "The Transkei Trader." *SAJE* 1, no. 2 (1933): 201–16.

Hansen, John D. L. "Nutrition and Child Health in South Africa." *Proceedings of the Nutrition Society of Southern Africa* 3 (1962): 126–34.

———. "Advances in the Application of Knowledge of Protein Calorie Malnutrition." *SAMJ* 47, no. 16 (1973): 702–4.

———. "John Fleming Brock." *Journal of Nutrition* 117 (1987): 1815–19.

Harris, Jose. "Political Thought and the Welfare State, 1870–1940: An Intellectual Framework for British Social Policy." *P&P* 135 (May 1992): 116–41.

Hellmann, Ellen. "The Importance of Beer-Brewing in an Urban Native Yard." *Bantu Studies* 8 (1934): 39–60.

———. "Native Life in a Johannesburg Slum Yard." *Africa* 8, no. 1 (1935): 34–61.

———. "Urban Native Food in Johannesburg." *Africa* 9 (1936): 277–90.

Hobart Houghton, D. "The Place of the Native Reserves in South Africa's Changing Economy." In *South Africa's Changing Economy.* Johannesburg: SAIRR, 1955.

Joslin, F. G. "Poverty in the Union: Its Manifestations." In *Poverty and Poor Relief* (Proceedings at a Symposium, 23 Feb. 1943). Cape Town: Cape Coordinating Council of Social Welfare Organizations, report series no. 4, Dec. 1943.

Kark, Sidney L. "A Health Service among the Rural Bantu." *SAMJ* 16, no. 10 (1942): 197–98.

Kark, Sidney L., and John Cassel. "The Pholela Health Center: A Progress Report." *SAMJ* 26 (9 and 16 Feb. 1952): 101–4, 131–36.

Kark, Sidney L., with Harding LeRiche. "The Nutrition and Health of South African Bantu Schoolchildren." *Manpower* 3, no. 2 (1944).

Krige, Eileen Jensen. "Some Social and Economic Facts Revealed in Native Family Budgets." *Race Relations* (Oct.–Nov. 1934): 94–107.

Kuper, Adam. "Audrey Richards, 1899–1984." In *Cambridge Women, Twelve Portraits,* ed. Edward Shils and Carmen Blacker. Cambridge: Cambridge Univ. Press, 1996.

Laidler, P. W. "The Unholy Triad: Tuberculosis, Venereal Disease, Malnutrition." *SAMJ* 12, no. 18 (1938): 658–66.

Lamla, M. "Liberated Women: An Explanation and Exposition of a Local Mpondo Problem." *South African Journal of Ethnology* 8, no. 1 (1985): 20–24.

Lategan, L. R. "Nutritional Observations Made on Bantu Recruits on Engagement with Special Reference to Osteoporosis." *PMMOA* 51, no. 410 (May–Aug. 1971): 105–25.

Levy, L. F., and F. W. Fox. "The Antiscorbutic Value of Some South African Foodstuffs as Measured by Their Indophenol Reducing Power." *SAMJ* 9, no. 6 (1935): 181–86.

Lewis, Jack. "The Rise and Fall of the South African Peasantry: A Critique and Reassessment." *JSAS* 11, no. 1 (1984): 1–24.

Loeser, H. A., "Diet of Mine Natives." *TMJ*, Mar. 1912, 154–59.

MacRae, D. M. "Notes on Scurvy in South Africa, 1902–4," *Lancet,* 27 June 1908, 1838–40.

Maister, M. "Social Welfare as Public Problem from the Housing and Nutrition Aspect." *SAMJ* 14, no. 1 (1940): 7–11.

Marks, Shula, and Neil Andersson. "Industrialization, Rural Health, and the 1944 National Health Services Commission in South Africa." In *The Social Basis of Health and Healing in Africa,* ed. Steven Feierman and John M. Janzen. Berkeley: Univ. of California Press, 1992.

——. "South Africa's Early Experiment in Social Medicine: Its Pioneers and Politics." *American Journal of Public Health* 87, no. 3 (1997): 452–59.

Matthews, Z. K., and D. G. S. M'Timkulu. "The Future in the Light of the Tomlinson Commission Report." *Race Relations Journal* 24, nos. 1–2 (1957): 12–19.

Moodie, Dunbar. "The Moral Economy of the Black Miners' Strike of 1946." *JSAS* 13, no. 1 (1986): 1–35.

Nauright, John, "'The Mecca of Native Scum' and 'A Running Sore of Evil': White Johannesburg and the Alexandra Township Removal Debate. 1935–45," *Kleio* 30 (1998): 64–88.

Ngubane, Harriet. "Aspects of Clinical Practice and Traditional Organization of Indigenous Healers in South Africa." *Social Science and Medicine* 15B (1981): 361–65.

Odendaal, W. A. "Nutrition in Public Health." *SAMJ* 33, no. 23 (1959): 481–85.

Orenstein, A. J. "Notes on Elementary Hygiene, etc. for Compound Officials." Johannesburg: Central Mining–Rand Mines Group, 1934. Reissued, with A. Gordon as coauthor, Johannesburg, 1936.

——. "The Dietetics of Natives Employed on the Witwatersrand Gold Mines." *Africa* 9 (1936): 218–26.

Osborn, T. W. B. "Remedies for Malnutrition, Comparisons with Britain." *Leech* 17, no. 1 (Dec. 1946): 27–29.

Preston-Whyte, Eleanor, and Harriet Sibisi. "Ethnographic Oddity or Ecological Sense? Nyuswa-Zulu Descent Groups and Land Allocation." *African Studies* 34, no. 4 (1975): 283–315.

Read, C. L. "The Union Native and the Witwatersrand Gold Mines." *SAJE* 1 (1933).

Richards, C. S. "Subsidies, Quotas, Tariffs and the Excess Cost of Agriculture in South Africa." *SAJE* 3 (1935): 365–403.

Robertson, Isobel, John D. L. Hansen, and Aileen Moodie. "The Problem of Gastro-Enteritis and Malnutrition in the Non-European Pre-School Child in South Africa." *SAMJ* 34, no. 17 (1960): 338–44.

Rogerson, C. M. "Feeding the Common People of Johannesburg, 1930–62." *Journal of Historical Geography* 12, no. 1 (1986): 56–73.

Roux, E. "Hunger Introduces New Foods to Africans." *Guardian,* 20 Dec. 1945.

Sigerist, Henry. "University Education" and "A Physician's Impression of South Africa." *Bulletin of History of Medicine* 8 (1940): 3–27.

Slack, Paul. "Dearth and Social Policy in Early Modern England." *Social History of Medicine* 5, no. 1 (1992): 1–17.

Slater, H. "Land, Labour and Capital in Natal: The Natal Land and Colonisation Company, 1860–1948." *JAH* 16, no. 2 (1975): 257–83.

Susser, Mervyn. "Recollections of Alexandra and the Kark Movement to 1956." In *Health Activism in Southern Africa: Nurses and Primary Health Care*. New York: Columbia University, Institute of African Studies, 1986.

Swanson, Maynard. "The Sanitation Syndrome: Bubonic Plague and Urban Native Policy in the Cape Colony, 1900–1909." *JAH* 28, no. 3 (1977): 387–410.

Thomas, G. C. "The Social Background of Childhood Nutrition in the Ciskei." *Social Science and Medicine* 15A (1981): 551–55.

Tobias, Phillip V. "Medicine in Its Broader Setting in South Africa." *Leech* 51, no. 2 (1981): 23–27.

Trowell, H. C., and E. M. K. Muwazi. "Severe and Prolonged Underfeeding in African Children (The Kwashiorkor Syndrome of Malignant Malnutrition)." *Archives of Disease in Childhood* 20, no. 103 (1945): 110–16.

Tuberculosis Research Committee. "Tuberculosis in South African Natives with Special Reference to the Disease amongst the Mine Labourers on the Witwatersrand." *Publications of the South African Institute of Medical Research* 5, no. 30 (1932).

Turner, George Albert, "The Diet of the South African Natives in Their Kraals," *TMJ*, Mar. 1909, 183–84; Apr. 1909, 198–207; May 1909, 227–33; June 1909, 269–70.

van der Horst, Ronald. "The Enema and the African Child." *SAMJ* 38, no. 22 (1964): 465–66.

van Heyningen, Elizabeth. "Poverty, Self-Help and Community: The Survival of the Poor in Cape Town, 1880–1910." *SAHJ* 24 (1991): 128–43.

Vilakazi, A. "A Reserve from Within." *African Studies* 10, no. 2 (1957): 93–101.

Visagie, M. E., J. P. Du Plessis, G. Groothof, A. Alberts, and N. F. Laubsher. "Changes in Vitamin A and C Levels in Black Mine-Workers." *SAMJ* 48, no. 70 (11 Dec. 1974): 2502–6.

Visagie, M. E., J. P. Du Plessis, and N. F. Laubsher. "Effect of Vitamin C Supplementation on Black Mineworkers." *SAMJ* 49, no. 22 (1975): 889–92.

Walker, A. R. P. "Some Aspects of the Nutrition and Physique of Bantu Communities." Panel 7: Three Hours around the World—New Possibilities in Nutritional Research. Washington, D.C., Fifth International Congress on Nutrition, 1–7 Sept. 1960.

——. "Biological and Disease Patterns in South African Inter-Racial Populations as Modified by Rise in Privilege." *SAMJ* 46, no. 32 (1972): 1127–34.

——. "Infant Feeding Practices in South Africa: An Appraisal of Their Significance to Health." *SAMJ* 54, no. 20 (1978): 820–22.

——. "Some Thoughts on Malnutrition, Dietary Intervention and Amelioration of High Death Rates in Young South African Blacks." *SAMJ* 57, no. 17 (1980): 696–700.

Watkins-Pitchford, Wilfred. "Hygiene in South Africa." *TMJ*, Oct. 1908: 67–75.

Westcott, G. M., and R. A. P. Stott. "The Extent and Causes of Malnutrition in Children in the Tsolo District of Transkei." *SAMJ* 52, no. 24 (1977): 963–68.

Wheeler, Erica. "Types of Malnutrition." Part 2 of *Nutrition in Practice 1, Basic Nutrition and Malnutrition, an Introduction*. London School of Hygiene and Tropical Medicine, 1985.

Whyte, Quintin. "Native School Feeding, Summary of the Report of the Commission of Enquiry into School Feeding, 1949." SAIRR, 1949.

Williams, L. S. "The Food and Feeding of Mine Native Labourers." *PMMOA* 22, nos. 231–32 (July and Aug. 1941): 1–21.

Wittmann, W., et al. "An Evaluation of the Relationship between Nutritional Status and Infection by Means of a Field Study." *SAMJ* (22 July 1967): 664–82.

Worboys, Michael. "The Discovery of Colonial Malnutrition between the Wars." In *Imperial Medicine and Indigenous Societies,* ed. David Arnold. Manchester: Manchester Univ. Press, 1988.

Wylie, Diana. "The Changing Face of Hunger in Southern African History, 1880–1980." *P&P* 122 (1989): 159–99.

Young, B. S. "The Valley Trust: Experiment in African Development." *Canadian Geographical Journal,* June 1965, 3–10.

Selected Books

Alberti, Ludwig. *Account of the Tribal Life and Customs of the Xhosa in 1807*. Trans. William Fehr. Cape Town: A. A. Balkema, 1968.

Arnold, David. *Colonizing the Body: State Medicine and Epidemic Disease in Nineteenth-Century India*. Berkeley: Univ. of California Press, 1993.

Ashforth, Adam. *The Politics of Official Discourse in Twentieth- Century South Africa*. Oxford: Clarendon Press, 1990.

Ballinger, Margaret. *From Union to Apartheid: A Trek to Isolation*. New York: Praeger, 1969.

Barkan, Elazar. *The Retreat of Scientific Racism: Changing Concepts of Race in Britain and the United States between the World Wars*. Cambridge: Cambridge Univ. Press, 1992.

Basner, Miriam, ed. *Am I an African? The Political Memoirs of Hyman Basner*. Johannesburg: Wits. Press, 1993.

Becker, Marjorie. *Setting the Virgin on Fire: Lázaro Cárdenas, Michoacán Peasants, and the Redemption of the Mexican Revolution*. Berkeley: Univ. of California Press, 1995.

Beinart, William. *The Political Economy of Pondoland 1860–1930*. Cambridge: Cambridge Univ. Press, 1982.

Benson, Mary, ed. *The Sun Will Arise*. London: Defense and Aid, 1981.

Berglund, Axel-Ivar. *Zulu Thought-Patterns and Symbolism*. Bloomington: Indiana Univ. Press, 1989.

Beveridge, Janet. *Beveridge and His Plan*. London: Hodder and Stoughton, 1954.

Bleek, W. H. I. *The Natal Diaries of Dr. W. H. I. Bleek, 1855–1856*. Trans. O. H. Spohr. Cape Town: A. A. Balkema, 1965.

Booth, Charles. *Life and Labour of the People in London*. London, 1892.

Boserup, Ester. *The Conditions of Agricultural Growth: The Economics of Agrarian Change under Population Pressure*. Chicago: Aldine, 1965.

Bourquin, S., ed. and trans., and H. Filter, comp. *Paulina Dlamini, Servant of Two Kings*. Durban: Killie Campbell Africana Library, 1986.

Braudel, Fernand. *Civilization and Capitalism, Fifteenth-Eighteenth Century*. Vol. 1, *The Structures of Everyday Life, the Limits of the Possible*. New York: Harper and Row, 1981.

Brillat-Savarin, Jean Anthelme. *The Physiology of Taste; or, Meditations on Transcendental Gastronomy*. Trans. and annotated by M. F. K. Fisher. San Francisco: North Point, 1986.

Bryant, A. T. *A Description of Native Foodstuffs and Their Preparation*. Pietermaritzburg: Natal Govt., 1907.

———. *Zulu Medicine and Medicine-Men*. Cape Town: Centaur, 1983. Originally published in *Annals of the Natal Museum*, 1909.

———. *The Zulu People as They Were before the White Man Came*. Pietermaritzburg: Shuter and Shooter, 1948.

Bundy, Colin. *The Rise and Fall of the South African Peasantry*. Berkeley: Univ. of California Press, 1979.

Callaway, Rev. Canon Henry, *The Religious System of the Amazulu*. Pietermaritzburg, 1870.

Callaway, Godfrey. *Pioneers in Pondoland*. Alice, South Africa: Lovedale, [1938].

Campbell, Susan Schuster. *Called to Heal: Traditional Healing Meets Modern Medicine in Southern Africa Today*. Halfway House, South Africa: Zebra, 1998.

Camporesi, Piero. *Bread of Dreams: Food and Fantasy in Early Modern Europe*. Chicago: Univ. of Chicago, 1989.

Carnegie Commission. *The Poor White Problem in South Africa*, 5 vols. Stellenbosch, South Africa: Pro Ecclesia, 1932.

Carpenter, Kenneth J. *The History of Scurvy and Vitamin C*. Cambridge: Cambridge Univ. Press, 1988.

———. *Protein and Energy: A Study in Changing Ideas in Nutrition*. Cambridge: Cambridge Univ. Press, 1994.

Cartwright, A. P. *Doctors of the Mines: A Commemorative Volume Published in 1971 to Mark the Fiftieth Anniversary of the Founding of the Mine Medical Officers' Association of South Africa*. Cape Town: Purnell, 1971.

Coetzee, Renata. *Funa, Food from Africa: Roots of Traditional African Food Culture*. Durban: Butterworth, 1982.

Cole, Monica M. *South Africa*. New York: Dutton, 1961.

Comaroff, John L., and Jean Comaroff. *Of Revelation and Revolution*. Vol. 2, *The Dialectics of Modernity on a South African Frontier*. Chicago: Univ. of Chicago Press, 1997.

Cooper, Frederick, and Ann Laura Stoler, eds. *Tensions of Empire: Colonial Cultures in a Bourgeois World*. Berkeley: Univ. of California Press, 1997.

Cranefield, Paul F. *Science and Empire: East Coast Fever in Rhodesia and the Transvaal*. Cambridge: Cambridge Univ. Press, 1991.

Davenport, T. R. H. *Black Grahamstown: The Agony of a Community*. Johannesburg: SAIRR, 1980.

De Beer, Cedric. *The South African Disease: Apartheid Health and Health Services*. Johannesburg: Southern African Research Service, 1984.

de Kiewiet, C. W. *A History of South Africa, Social and Economic*. London: Oxford Univ. Press, 1941.

Dubow, Saul. *Racial Segregation and the Origins of Apartheid in South Africa, 1919–1936*. Oxford: Macmillan in assoc. with St. Antony's College, 1989.

———. *Scientific Racism in Modern South Africa*. Cambridge: Cambridge Univ. Press, 1995.

Dyer, Christopher. *Standards of Living in the Later Middle Ages*. Cambridge: Cambridge Univ. Press, 1989.

Edgar, Robert R., ed. *An African American in South Africa: The Travel Notes of Ralph Bunche, 28 September, 1937–1 January, 1938*. Athens: Ohio Univ. Press, 1992.

Eldredge, Elizabeth A. *A South African Kingdom: The Pursuit of Security in Nineteenth Century Lesotho*. Cambridge: Cambridge Univ. Press, 1993.

Evans, Ivan. *Bureaucracy and Race: Native Administration in South Africa*. Berkeley: Univ. of California Press, 1997.

Farley, John. *Bilharzia: A History of Imperial Tropical Medicine*. Cambridge: Cambridge Univ. Press, 1991.

Forster, Elborg, and Robert Forster, eds. *European Diet from Pre-Industrial to Modern Times*. New York: Harper and Row, 1975.

Forster, Robert, and Orest Ranum, eds. *Food and Drink in History: Selections from the "Annales, Economies, Sociétés, Civilisations,"* Vol. 5. Baltimore: Johns Hopkins Univ. Press, 1979.

Fox, F. W., and M. E. Norwood Young. *Food from the Veld: Edible Wild Plants of Southern Africa*. Craighall, South Africa: Delta, 1982.

Fredrickson, George M. *The Black Image in the White Mind: The Debate on Afro-American Character and Destiny, 1817–1914*. Hanover, N.H.: Wesleyan Univ. Press, 1987.

Freund, Bill. *Insiders and Outsiders: The Indian Working Class of Durban, 1910–1990*. Portsmouth, N.H.: Heinemann, 1995.

Fynn, Henry F. *The Diary of Henry Francis Fynn*. Ed. James Stuart and D. McK. Malcolm. Pietermaritzburg: Shuter and Shooter, 1950.

Gann, Lewis H., and Peter Duignan. *The Burden of Empire: An Appraisal of Western Colonialism in Africa South of the Sahara*. New York: Praeger, 1967.

Gelfand, Michael. *Livingstone the Doctor, His Life and Travels: A Study in Medical History*. Oxford: Blackwell, 1957.

Geremek, Bronislaw. *Poverty: A History*. Oxford: Blackwell, 1994.

Gerth, H. H., and C. Wright Mills, trans., eds. *From Max Weber: Essays in Sociology*. New York: Oxford Univ. Press, 1946.

Gibson, Olive. *The Cost of Living for Africans: The Results of an Enquiry into the Cost of Living for Africans in the Locations and African Townships in Johannesburg and Alexandra*. Johannesburg: SAIRR, 1954.

Gilroy, Paul. *"There Ain't No Black in the Union Jack": The Cultural Politics of "Race" and Nation*. London: Hutchinson, 1987.

Goody, Jack. *Cooking, Cuisine and Class: A Study in Comparative Sociology*. Cambridge: Cambridge Univ. Press, 1982.

Gorgas, Marie D., and Burton J. Hendrick. *William Crawford Gorgas: His Life and Work*. New York: Doubleday, 1924.

Griesel, R. D., ed. *Malnutrition in Southern Africa*. Pretoria: Unisa, 1980.

Grigg, David. *The Dynamics of Agricultural Change: The Historical Experience*. London: Hutchinson, 1982.

———. *The Transformation of Agriculture in the West*. Oxford: Blackwell, 1992.

Grout, Lewis. *Zulu-land; or, Life among the Zulu-Kafirs of Natal and Zulu-land, South Africa*. Philadelphia, 1864.

Hammond-Tooke, W. D., ed., *The Bantu-Speaking Peoples of Southern Africa*. 2d ed. London: Routledge, 1974.

Harries, Patrick. *Work, Culture and Identity: Migrant Laborers in Mozambique and South Africa, c. 1860–1910*. Portsmouth, N.H.: Heinemann, 1994.

Headrick, Daniel R. *The Tools of Empire, Technology and European Imperialism in the Nineteenth Century*. New York: Oxford Univ. Press, 1981.

Hellmann, Ellen. *Rooiyard: A Sociological Survey of an Urban Native Slum Yard*. Cape Town: Oxford Univ. Press for Rhodes- Livingstone Institute, 1948.

———. *The South African Institute of Race Relations 1929–1979: A Short History*. Johannesburg: SAIRR, 1979.

———, ed. *Handbook on Race Relations in South Africa*. Cape Town: Oxford Univ. Press for SAIRR, 1949.

Himmelfarb, Gertrude. *The Idea of Poverty: England in the Early Industrial Age*. New York: Vintage, 1985.

———. *Poverty and Compassion: The Moral Imagination of the Late Victorians*. New York: Vintage, 1992.

Hunter, Monica. *Reaction to Conquest: Effects of Contact with Europeans on the Pondo of South Africa*. 2d ed. London: Oxford Univ. Press for International African Institute, 1961.

Iliffe, John. *The African Poor: A History*. Cambridge: Cambridge Univ. Press, 1987.

Isaacs, Nathaniel. *Travels and Adventures in Eastern Africa*. Vol. 1. Ed. Louis Herrmann. Cape Town: van Riebeeck Society, 1936.

James, William. *The Varieties of Religious Experience: A Study in Human Nature.* New York: Viking, 1982.

Janisch, Miriam. *A Survey of African Income and Expenditure in 987 Families in Johannesburg.* Johannesburg, 1941.

Jeeves, Alan H. *Migrant Labour in South Africa's Mining Economy: The Struggle for the Gold Mines' Labour Supply, 1890–1920.* Kingston, Ont.: McGill-Queen's Univ. Press, 1985.

Kark, Sidney L., and Emily Kark. *Promoting Community Health, from Pholela to Jerusalem.* Johannesburg: Wits. Press, 1999.

Kark, Sidney L., and Guy W. Steuart, eds. *A Practice of Social Medicine: A South African Team's Experiences in Different African Communities.* Edinburgh: E. & S. Livingstone, 1962.

Krige, Eileen Jensen. *The Social System of the Zulus.* 2d ed. Pietermaritzburg: Shuter and Shooter, 1950.

Kuhn, Thomas S. *The Structure of Scientific Revolutions,* 2d ed. Chicago: Univ. of Chicago Press, 1970.

Laslett, Peter. *The World We Have Lost.* 2d. ed. London: Methuen, 1979.

Leipoldt, C. Louis. *Bushveld Doctor.* 1937. Cape Town: Human and Rousseau, 1980.

Levenstein, Harvey A. *Revolution at the Table: The Transformation of the American Diet.* New York: Oxford, 1988.

———. *Paradox of Plenty: A Social History of Eating in Modern America.* New York: Oxford, 1993.

Levine, Donald. *Wax and Gold: Tradition and Innovation in Ethiopian Culture.* Chicago: Univ. of Chicago Press, 1965.

Lewsen, Phyllis, ed. *Voices of Protest: From Segregation to Apartheid, 1938–48.* Craighall, South Africa: Ad. Donker, 1988.

Livi-Bacci, Massimo. *Population and Nutrition: An Essay on European Demographic History.* Cambridge: Cambridge Univ. Press, 1991.

Lowveld Regional Development Association. *The South Eastern Transvaal Lowveld: A Survey of the Resources and Development of the Southern Lowveld Region of the Eastern Transvaal.* 1954.

Mackenzie, John. *Austral Africa, Losing It or Ruling It, Being Incidents and Experiences in Bechuanaland, Cape Colony and England.* 2 vols. London, 1887.

MacLean, Colonel John, comp. *A Compendium of Kafir Laws and Customs, Including Genealogical Tables of Kafir Chiefs and Various Tribal Census Returns.* 1866. London: Frank Cass, 1968.

Macmillan, W. M. *The South African Agrarian Problem and Its Historical Development.* Johannesburg: Central News Agency, 1919.

Malan, Marais. *In Quest of Health: The South African Institute for Medical Research, 1912–73.* Johannesburg: Lowry, 1988.

Malherbe, Margaret. *Canon Dr. Frank Swinburne Drewe.* Privately published, 1983.

Marks, Shula, ed. *Not Either an Experimental Doll: The Separate Worlds of Three South*

African Women. Durban: Killie Campbell Africana Library; Pietermaritzburg: Univ. of Natal Press, 1987.

Marks, Shula, and Anthony Atmore, eds. *Economy and Society in Pre-Industrial South Africa*. London: Longman, 1980.

Marquard, Leo. *South Africa's Internal Boundaries*. Johannesburg: SAIRR, 1958.

McKeown, Thomas. *The Modern Rise of Population*. New York: Academic, 1976.

McManners, John. *Death and the Enlightenment: Changing Attitudes to Death among Christians and Unbelievers in Eighteenth Century France*. Oxford: Clarendon, 1981.

McNeill, Geraldine, and Erica Wheeler. *Basic Nutrition and Malnutrition: An Introduction, Nutrition in Practice 1*. London: London School of Hygiene and Tropical Medicine, Dept. of Human Nutrition, 1985.

Mintz, Sidney W. *Sweetness and Power: The Place of Sugar in Modern History*. New York: Viking, 1985.

Miracle, Marvin P. *Maize in Tropical Africa*. Madison: Univ. of Wisconsin Press, 1966.

Mollat, Michel. *The Poor in the Middle Ages: An Essay in Social History*. New Haven, Conn.: Yale Univ. Press, 1986.

Montanari, Massimo. *The Culture of Food*. Oxford: Blackwell, 1994.

Moore, Henrietta L., and Megan Vaughan. *Cutting Down Trees: Gender, Nutrition, and Agricultural Change in the Northern Province of Zambia, 1890–1990*. Portsmouth, N.H.: Heinemann, 1994.

Murray, W. A. *Health Factors in the Poor White Problem*. Vol. 4, *The Poor White Problem in South Africa. Report of the Carnegie Commission*. Stellenbosch, South Africa: Pro Ecclesia, 1932.

Nyembezi, C. L. Sibusiso. *Zulu Proverbs*. Pietermaritzburg: Shuter and Shooter, 1963.

Orr, John Boyd, and John L. Gilks. *Studies of Nutrition: The Physique and Health of Two African Tribes*. London: Medical Research Council, Privy Council, special report series no. 155, 1931.

Pacey, Arnold, and Philip Payne, ed. *Agricultural Development and Nutrition*. London: Hutchinson, 1985.

Packard, Randall M. *White Plague, Black Labor: Tuberculosis and the Political Economy of Health and Disease in South Africa*. Berkeley: Univ. of California Press, 1989.

Paton, Alan. *Hofmeyr*. London: Oxford Univ. Press, 1964.

Paton, D. N., and L. Finley. *Poverty, Nutrition and Growth: Studies in Child Life in Cities and Rural Districts in Scotland*. Medical Research Council, Great Britain, special report series no. 101, 1926.

Philip, John. *Researches in South Africa; Illustrating the Civil, Moral and Religious Condition of the Native Tribes Including Journals of the Author's Travels in the Interior, together with Detailed Accounts of the Progress of the Christian Missions, Exhibiting the Influence of Christianity in Promoting Civilization*. 2 vols. 1828. New York: Negro Univ. Press, 1969.

Phillips, Howard. *The University of Cape Town, 1918–48, the Formative Years*. Cape Town: UCT Press, 1993.

Phillips, Ray E. *The Bantu in the City: A Study of Cultural Adjustment on the Witwaters-rand.* Alice, South Africa: Lovedale, [1938].

Pick, Daniel. *Faces of Degeneration: A European Disorder c. 1848–c. 1918.* Cambridge: Cambridge Univ. Press, 1989.

Porter, Roy. *The Greatest Benefit to Mankind: A Medical History of Humanity.* New York: Norton, 1998.

Posel, Deborah. *The Making of Apartheid, 1948–1961, Conflict and Compromise.* Oxford: Clarendon, 1991.

Post, John D. *Food Shortage, Climatic Variability, and Epidemic Disease in Preindustrial Europe: The Mortality Peak in the Early 1740s.* Ithaca, N.Y.: Cornell Univ. Press, 1985.

Resha, Maggie. *Mangoana Tsoara Thipa ka Bohaleng, My Life in the Struggle.* Johannesburg: Congress of South African Writers, 1991.

Rich, Paul. *White Power and the Liberal Conscience, Racial Segregation and South African Liberalism.* Johannesburg: Ravan, 1984.

Richards, Audrey. *Hunger and Work in a Savage Tribe: A Functional Study of Nutrition among the Southern Bantu.* London: G. Routledge, 1932.

Rotberg, Robert I., and Theodore K. Rabb, eds. *Hunger and History: The Impact of Changing Food Production and Consumption Patterns on Society.* Cambridge: Cambridge Univ. Press, 1985.

Rousseau, Jean-Jacques. *The Basic Political Writings.* Indianapolis: Hackett, 1987.

Rowntree, B. Seebohm. *Poverty: A Study of Town Life.* London, 1902.

Sachs, Wulf. *Black Hamlet.* Boston: Little, Brown, 1947.

Sacks, Oliver. *The Island of the Colorblind and Cycad Island.* New York: Vintage, 1998.

SAIRR. *A Survey of Race Relations in South Africa.* Johannesburg: SAIRR, 1930–1970 (incorporated into SAIRR Annual Report, 1930–1950).

Samuelson, L. H. *Zululand, Its Traditions, Legends, Customs and Folklore.* Durban: T. W. Griggs, 1974.

Schapera, I. *Native Land Tenure in the Bechuanaland Protectorate.* Alice, South Africa: Lovedale, 1943.

——, ed. *Western Civilization and the Natives of South Africa: Studies in Culture Contact.* London: Routledge, 1934.

Schofield, R., D. Reher, and A. Bideau, eds. *The Decline of Mortality in Europe.* Oxford: Clarendon, 1991.

Scott, James C. *Seeing like a State: How Certain Schemes to Improve the Human Condition Have Failed.* New Haven, Conn.: Yale Univ. Press, 1998.

Sen, Amartya. *Poverty and Famines: An Essay on Entitlement and Deprivation.* Oxford: Clarendon, 1981.

Serote, Mongane Wally. *Longer Poems: Third World Express, Come and Hope with Me.* Cape Town: Mayibuye and David Philip, 1997.

Shammas, Carole. *The Pre-Industrial Consumer in England and America.* Oxford: Clarendon, 1990.

Silla, Eric. *People Are Not the Same: Leprosy and Identity in Twentieth-Century Mali.* Portsmouth, N.H.: Heinemann, 1998.

Skotnes, Pippa, ed. *Miscast, Negotiating the Presence of the Bushmen.* Cape Town: Univ. of Cape Town Press, 1996.

Slack, Paul. *Poverty and Policy in Tudor and Stuart England.* London: Longman, 1988.

Smith, Adam. *The Theory of Moral Sentiments.* Oxford: Oxford Univ. Press, 1976.

Stubbs, Aelred, ed. *Steve Biko: I Write What I Like.* San Francisco: Harper and Row, 1978.

Turshen, Meredeth. *The Political Ecology of Disease in Tanzania.* New Brunswick, N.J.: Rutgers Univ. Press, 1984.

van Heynigen, Elizabeth. *The History of Shawco, 1943–75.* Cape Town: Shawco, 1975.

van Onselen, Charles. *Studies in the Social and Economic History of the Witwatersrand, 1886–1914.* Vol. 1, *New Babylon.* New York: Longman, 1982.

———. *The Seed Is Mine: The Life of Kas Maine, a South African Sharecropper, 1894–1985.* New York: Hill and Wang, 1996.

Vilakazi, Absolom. *Zulu Transformations: A Study of the Dynamics of Social Change.* Pietermaritzburg: Univ. of Natal Press, 1965.

Walter, John, and Roger Schofield, ed. *Famine, Disease and the Social Order in Early Modern Society.* Cambridge: Cambridge Univ. Press, 1989.

Webb, C. de B., and J. B. Wright, eds. *The James Stuart Archive of Recorded Oral Evidence Relating to the History of the Zulu and Neighbouring Peoples.* 4 vols. Pietermaritzburg: Univ. of Natal Press, 1976–1986.

Willich, A. F. M. *Lectures on Diet and Regimen: Being a Systematic Inquiry into the Most Rational Means of Preserving Health and Prolonging Life: Together with Physiological and Chemical Explanations, Calculated Chiefly for the Use of Families, in Order to Banish the Prevailing Abuses and Prejudices of Medicine.* London: 2d ed., 1799.

Wilson, Francis, and Mamphela Ramphele. *Uprooting Poverty: The South African Challenge, a Report for the Second Carnegie Inquiry into Poverty and Development in Southern Africa.* New York: Norton, 1989.

Wilson, Monica, and Leonard Thompson. *The Oxford History of South Africa.* 2 vols. Oxford: Oxford Univ. Press, 1969–1971.

Wrigley, E. A. *Continuity, Chance and Change.* Cambridge: Cambridge Univ. Press, 1988.

Wylie, Diana. *A Little God: The Twilight of Patriarchy in a Southern African Chiefdom.* Hanover, N.H.: Wesleyan Univ. Press, 1990.

Unpublished Sources

Dodson, Belinda. "Environment, Ideology and Politics: Soil Conservation in 1940s South Africa." Paper presented at the Canadian Research Consortium on Southern Africa Conference, Kingston, Ont., May 1998.

Friedman, I. B. "A Health Profile of the Zulu Community in the Valley of a Thousand Hills." Paper submitted in fulfillment of the requirements for part 2 of the membership of the Faculty of Community Medicine of the Royal Colleges of Physicians of the United Kingdom, London, 1983.

Klopper, Sandra. "The Art of Zulu-Speakers in Northern Natal- Zululand. An Investigation of the History of Beadwork, Carving and Dress from Shaka to Inkatha." Ph.D. diss. Wits., 1992.

MacRae, D. M. "The Bechuanaland Protectorate, Its People and Prevalent Diseases: With a Special Consideration of the Effects of Tropical Residence and Food in Relation to Health and Disease." M.D. thesis, Univ. of Glasgow, 1920. Botswana National Archives, Gabarone.

Mushingeh, Andrew. "A History of Disease and Medicine in Botswana, 1820–1945." Ph.D. diss., Cambridge Univ., 1984.

Sheldon, Kathleen. "Pounders of Beans: The Ideology of 'Mozambican Women' and Nation Building." Berkshire Women's History Conference, 1993.

Smith, Matthew. "Working Paper: A Study of the Formation of the Health System on the Witwatersrand Gold Mines, 1901–1930," July 1989.

———. "Working in the Grave": The Development of a Health and Safety System on the Witwatersrand Gold Mines, 1900–39," M.A. thesis, Rhodes Univ., 1993.

Stott, Halley H. "A Pilot Health Study of the Zulu Community of Botha's Hill, Natal, South Africa." Expert Committee on Public Health Administration, World Health Organization, Geneva, 1959.

———. "The Valley Trust Socio-Medical Project for the Promotion of Health in a Less Developed Rural Area." D.M. thesis, Univ. of Edinburgh, 1976.

Index

RECONSIDERATIONS IN
SOUTHERN AFRICAN HISTORY